Ɔ. ȮB.

The Politics
of
U. S. Foreign Policy Making

The Politics
of
U. S. Foreign Policy Making

A Reader

Douglas M. Fox

University of Connecticut

GOODYEAR PUBLISHING COMPANY, INC.
Pacific Palisades, California

© 1971 by
GOODYEAR PUBLISHING COMPANY, INC.
Pacific Palisades, California

Library of Congress Catalog Card Number: 79-141159
ISBN: 0-87620-714-X

Y-714X-5

Current printing (last number):
10 9 8 7 6 5 4 3 2 1

Printed in the United States of America

For my Mother

Contents

Preface

The goal of this volume of readings is to convey a sense of the domestic political arena in which postwar American foreign policy decisions have been made. Except for a brief introductory essay, there are no materials in this book which analyze the nature of world politics in the postwar period. Several excellent collections of writings concerned with the international political arena since 1945 are already available, and can be used in conjunction with this text. This book has as its central concern the topic of foreign policy decision making within the United States. Any such volume must confront the question of the nature of power in American society, and a number of the readings in this work have been carefully chosen to represent the two principal contemporary schools of thought on this subject. Writers of the first, or "pluralistic," school argue that American politics is characterized by a roughly equal distribution of political power among many different groups in the society, guaranteeing access to political decision making for almost all groups. The second, or "elitist," school argues that a relatively small group of like-minded persons, typically composed of top corporate leaders and persons with an upper economic class background, control political decision making in the United States. While some of the authors represented here are neither pluralists nor elitists, almost all of the items in this book relate directly to the question of which groups in American society have power to make which kinds of decisions in the area of foreign policy. That this is a question rather than a body of established fact is made clear by the readings.

Introduction to the Foreign Policy Making Environment

The external environment of foreign policy makers has changed greatly since the end of World War II, as the editor points out in his introductory essay. Whether the domestic foreign policy making process has changed is questionable, however. Richard Neustadt has characterized this situation as "emergencies in policy with politics as usual." Henry A. Kissinger, the author of the second article in this section, would agree with Neustadt's statement. Kissinger, a political scientist who has served as President Nixon's Assistant for National Security Affairs, argues that the nature of administrative structure makes it very difficult for the President to control his own foreign policy bureaucracy. One of Kissinger's chief jobs as the President's Assistant has been to devise a revamped National Security Council which will enable the President to more adequately control this bureaucracy. As of this writing, however, there is no evidence to indicate that the author has been able to overcome the problems sketched in his article. (See Edward A. Kolodziej's article on the subject appearing on page 187 in this volume.)

Theodore J. Lowi argues that different types of power relationships among the actors involved characterize different types of foreign policy decisions. Except for his observations on "crisis" decisions, however, there is no convincing evidence to support Lowi's hypotheses. His propositions, then, must be regarded as provocative and stimulating aids to thought, rather than the definitive statement on the subject.

Warner E. Schilling provides the reader with a summary of those descriptions of the American foreign policy making process which describe this process as one which is slow and characterized by compromise. While it is difficult to take exception to Schilling's thesis, one should note here that Schilling's description of foreign policy making probably describes domestic policy making in the United States equally well.

The Politics
of
U. S. Foreign Policy Making

1

THE FOREIGN POLICY
MAKING ENVIRONMENT

THE NEW WORLD POLITICS OF THE POSTWAR ERA

Until 1945, the United States avoided the continuous and ubiquitous participation in international politics characteristic of nations like Great Britain and France. That this country did so was due to several factors. In the first part of her history she lacked the resources to compete with powers like Great Britain and France, and had the full-time job of settling the west of the nation. In the period after World War I, the leaders of this nation did not feel that full-scale participation by the United States in great power politics was in the national interest. After World War II, however, this nation's leadership felt it necessary for the United States to enter the world political arena on a permanent basis. The previously existing world state system in which several major European powers competed with each other for hegemony had been replaced by a Europe in which the Soviet Union was the predominant actor. The United States was the only nation strong enough to have acted as a counterpoise to the Soviet Union, which was thought by virtue of its communist ideology to have an insatiable desire to expand its borders at the expense of its neighbors. Since technology had destroyed the ability of the Atlantic and Pacific oceans to shield the United States from sudden attack, America's leaders felt directly threatened by the Soviet Union. Further, even without the Soviet Union, it would have been necessary for the United States to play a much more active role in Europe than had ever been the case before, due to the collapse of the European economic system after the Second World War. The viability of the American economy was based upon trade with an economically healthy Europe.

In spite of its new role on the world scene, however, the United States immediately demobilized its armed forces at the end of World War II, trusting for its security in the "umbrella" of the atomic bomb. In the aftermath of the

1

Soviet Union's successful explosion of an atomic bomb (1949) and the North Korean invasion of South Korea (1950), however, the U.S. greatly increased its military commitment. After demobilization and before Korea, some five per cent of the gross national product was spent on the armed forces; since 1950, an average of some ten per cent of the gross national product of this country has been devoted to military expenditures. At the same time, foreign aid declined from $6.5 billion in 1949 to less than $2 billion in 1970, leading Gabriel Almond to argue that the United States has become increasingly dependent upon military solutions of international problems. Whether or not this nation is so dependent, there is no question that it devotes an enormous amount of resources to the implementation of its foreign policies.

What is the nature of the world political arena in which the United States acts today? This arena has undergone a great change since 1945. In the late 1940's, one could argue very forcefully that the world international system was a bi-polar one, that the United States and the Soviet Union headed two rival camps of bitterly opposed antagonists. Since the middle 1950's, however, this situation has changed drastically. The membership of the United Nations has expanded from 50 to 130. The colonial territories of the Western powers have become independent nations, most of whom espouse a neutralist foreign policy, seeking to align themselves with neither the communist nor the capitalist blocs. Nations like India, for example, receive substantial economic aid from both the Soviet Union and the United States. Further, the unity of both the eastern and western camps has greatly declined. The contemporary world scene is characterized less by monolithic capitalist and communist alliances, than by substantial conflicts between allies. In the 1960's, for example, China made clear her independence of the Soviet Union, as did France her independence of the United States. While few analysts would deny that the communist nations, on the one hand, and the capitalist nations, on the other, have more in common with each other than they do with members of the other bloc, one must acknowledge the substantial differences of opinion within each bloc. These differences are reflected in such occurrences as bloody Russian-Chinese border conflicts, or in the termination of most French-American joint military endeavors.

In a decentralized world state system, the possession by the U.S.A. and the U.S.S.R. of nuclear weapons sufficient in number to destroy the population of the world many times over has awesome implications. Today, there is more danger that a nuclear holocaust will result from the Middle East conflict between Arab and Israeli, than it will from the conflict between the East and the West in Vietnam. The Soviet Union and the United States often seem more interested in bringing about a peaceful resolution of the Arab-Israeli conflict than do the combatants. This is the case because the Soviet Union, which supports the Arabs, and the United States, which supports Israel, fear that each may have to eventually confront the other directly if the conflict continues. A cardinal rule of the "cold war" has been that the nuclear superpowers shall not directly confront each other. When such a confrontation did take place during the Cuban missile crisis, the threat of a nuclear conflict was tangible. Whatever the causes of the cold war may have been, the United States and the Soviet Union find themselves in a dilemma today. While each side would like to reduce or eliminate the chances of a nuclear holocaust, each finds it very difficult to trust the other to disarm along with it. At the same time, there are now three other nations besides the Soviet Union and the United States who possess atomic weapons—Great Britain, France, and China—and some ten additional nations who have the capacity to begin manufacturing such weapons tomorrow. The possession of nuclear weapons, however small, by small nations in desperate economic straits, would not increase the stability of the international political system.

It can be argued that the basic division in world politics today is not one between communist and capitalist blocs, but rather one between poor and rich nations. By the living standards of Europe and the United States, most nations in the world are extremely poor. Further, the disparity between the rich and poor nations grows greater daily, as the poor nations are unable to industrialize their agriculturally-based economies in a manner enabling them to keep pace with a greatly expanded population growth made possible by a rise in health standards. As a result, it is likely that there will be more than one major world famine before the end of this century. Some observers of the world scene fear a rapid spread of the militant brand of communism practiced by the Chinese in these poor nations of the underdeveloped world. China, herself basically an under-developed nation, has been able to pull herself up by her bootstraps and become a power in space as well as a nuclear power. This example, and the energetic proselytizing of the Chinese, will supposedly cause the conversion of a great number of underdeveloped nations to the Chinese brand of communism, with a resultant inevitable violent conflict between the exponents of this energetic ideology and the capitalist nations of the world.

Other analysts point out that the Soviet Union was itself a "militant" power during its early history; that is, it unceasingly declared that there could never be any stable, long-term cooperation between communism and capitalism. How-ever, with an increased standard of living, and the acquisition of enough nuclear weapons to destroy the world, the Soviet Union has ceased to speak in such militant tones. Likewise, it is argued that the Chinese will change their policies as they grow in power and prosperity. In this connection, it should be noted that the militant rhetoric of the Chinese is belied by the conservative foreign policy of that nation. Although the United States has been waging a war in Vietnam, close to China's borders, for several years, the Chinese have not intervened directly in this war.

It is in this context that we must consider the current debate on the proper role of the United States in world politics. Until this nation began to commit a very large number of resources to the prosecution of the Vietnamese war, there was almost no dissent among her citizenry from the proposition that the United

States should play an active and aggressive role in world politics, especially in checking the advance of communism. Disenchantment with our Vietnamese policy has led many critics to argue that we must reduce the size of our military establishment, and cease our role as the "world's policeman." Rather, we should supposedly be more concerned with exploring ways in which we can cooperate with the poorer nations of the world, whether they be communist or non-communist. A number of these critics argue that our policy is motivated by a fear of losing foreign markets and access to strategically necessary materials, rather than in any desire to protect "democratic" nations from communism, which administration spokesmen have argued is a chief motive of our foreign policy. Other critics have called attention to the host of domestic problems which confront this country, and contend that it is more important to solve problems at home than to contain communism in Vietnam. Poverty and racial strife are seen by many Americans as more important problems than the question of which form of government will prevail in the underdeveloped world, an area which has never known democracy in the Western sense. Opponents of this viewpoint have argued that communist nations have always had as an explicit goal the extinction of the capitalist system, and that to be unconcerned with the spread of communism is to invite one's own demise.

In any case, although the nature of American involvement on the world scene may change in the years ahead, the scope of this involvement is unlikely to decline in any significant manner. In economic and military terms, the United States is the most powerful nation on earth. To expect such a great power to sit back and become a mere spectator of world events is to entertain a vain hope. In a world made tiny by a technological revolution, and interdependent by its economic system, the United States will continue to act. And her actions and decisions will be matters of the utmost consequence—indeed, matters of life and death for the citizens of the United States and of other nations.

SUGGESTIONS FOR FURTHER READING

This short bibliography is intended as a guide to some of the principal works on U.S. foreign policy making in the postwar period. The number of selections under a given topic does not represent the judgment that this topic is more or less important than the other subject areas listed here, but is rather a rough reflection of the availability of valuable literature on the subject.

I. The Foreign Policy Making Process

1. Graham T. Allison, "Conceptual Models in the Cuban Missile Crisis," *American Political Science Review* 63, September 1969, pp. 689-718. Analyses the utility of three widely accepted models of the policy making process as applied to one decision.
2. Joseph H. deRivera, *The Psychological Dimension of Foreign Policy.* Columbus, Ohio: Charles E. Merrill Publishing Company, 1968. Demonstrates how psychological factors interact with political and historical facts to produce foreign policy.

3. Joseph Frankel, *The Making of Foreign Policy: An Analysis of Decision Making.* New York: Oxford University Press, 1963. A model of foreign policy making.
4. Roger Hilsman, "Congressional-Executive Relations in the Foreign Policy Consensus," *American Political Science Review* 52, September 1958, pp. 725-44.
5. Roger Hilsman, "The Foreign-Policy Consensus: An Interim Research Report," *Journal of Conflict Resolution* 3, 1959, pp. 361-82.
6. Roger Hilsman, *To Move a Nation.* Garden City, N.Y.: Doubleday and Company, 1967. Chapters 1, 35, and 36 in this book and the two articles by this author listed immediately above constitute a key contribution to the study of foreign policy making in the United States.
7. Elting E. Morison, ed., *The American Style.* New York: Harper and Brothers, 1958. The essays in this book by George F. Kennan and W.W. Rostow set forth the basic ideas of these two important writers concerning the foreign policy making environment of the United States.
8. Richard C. Snyder, H.W. Bruck, and Burton Sapin, *Foreign Policy Decision Making.* Glencoe, Ill.: The Free Press, 1962. A schema for investigating foreign policy making.

II. American Society and Foreign Policy

A. PUBLIC OPINION

1. Gabriel Almond, *The American People and Foreign Policy.* New York: Harcourt, Brace and Company, 1950. The "classic" work on the subject.
2. Richard A. Brody, *et al.,* "Vietnam, The Urban Crisis and the 1968 Presidential Election: A Preliminary Analysis," paper presented at the 1969 meeting of the American Sociological Association. Research indicating that the Vietnam war issue was not a major factor in the outcome of the 1968 Presidential election.
3. William R. Caspary, "The Mood Theory: A Study of Public Opinion and Foreign Policy," *American Political Science Review* 64, June 1970. Argues that Almond's contention that American public opinion is characterized by vague and volatile "moods" is incorrect.
4. Bernard C. Cohen, "The Military Policy Public," *Public Opinion Quarterly* 30, Summer 1966, pp. 200-211. That portion of the public which follows military affairs is much smaller than the portion which is aware of foreign policy events in general.
5. Alfred E. Hero, *The Southerner and World Affairs.* Baton Rouge: Louisiana State University Press, 1965. An exhaustive examination of the attitudes of residents of one region of the United States towards world affairs.
6. Richard F. Hamilton, "A Research Note on Mass Support for Tough Military Initiatives," *American Sociological Review* 33, June 1968, pp. 439-45. Contests Almond's assertion that the American public is unlikely to support an aggressive foreign policy.
7. Frank L. Klingberg, "The Historical Alternation of Moods in American Foreign Policy," *World Politics* 4, 1952. This fascinating article argues that U.S. foreign policy has varied between "introvert" and "extrovert" moods, and implies that the United States might begin to withdraw again from world affairs at the end of the 1960's. Given the current controversy over the proper role of the United States in the world, this essay merits careful reading.

8. James N. Rosenau, *Public Opinion and Foreign Policy*. New York: Random House, 1961. After Almond, the best book in the area.

B. *THE COMMUNICATIONS MEDIA*

1. William O. Chittick, *State Department, Press, and Pressure Groups*. New York: John Wiley and Sons, 1970. The only "behavioral" work on the foreign policy press, based largely on 156 interviews with the actors mentioned in the title. For a more complete notice, see the editor's review of this book in the May, 1971, issue of *The Journal of Politics*.
2. James Reston, *The Artillery of the Press*. New York: Harper and Row, 1967. Reflections of a leading journalist on the proper relationship between government and the press.
3. Eugene J. Rosi, "Elite Political Communication: Five Washington Columnists on Nuclear Weapons Testing, 1954-1958," *Social Research* 34, Winter 1967, pp. 703-727. Examines the assumptions of leading Washington columnists concerning world politics.

C. *INTEREST GROUPS AND ELITES*

1. Robert Gilpin, *American Scientists and Nuclear Weapons Policy*. Princeton, N.J.: Princeton University Press, 1962. Probes the role of atomic scientists in determining atomic weapons policy.
2. Irving Kristol, "American Intellectuals and Foreign Policy," *Foreign Affairs* 45, 1965, pp. 594-609. Argues that those American intellectuals who criticize our foreign policy offer irrelevant criticism because they do not understand the nature of foreign policy.
3. C. Wright Mills, *The Power Elite*. New York: Oxford University Press, 1956. An "elitist" classic.
4. Ronald Radosh, *American Labor and Foreign Policy*. New York: Random House, 1969. Argues that organized labor in this country has always backed administration foreign policy in return for concessions on the domestic front.
5. Arnold Rose, *The Power Structure*. New York: Oxford University Press, 1967. A "pluralist" response to Mills.
6. Eugene B. Skolnikoff, *Science, Technology and American Foreign Policy*. Cambridge, Mass.: M.I.T. Press, 1967. A detailed examination of scientists and science agencies in the federal government relevant to foreign policy.
7. Bruce L. R. Smith, *The RAND Corporation*. Cambridge, Mass.: Harvard University Press, 1966. Excellent case study of the most famous "think tank," a new phenomenon on the American scene.

III. Federal Government and Foreign Policy.

A. *CONGRESS*

1. Holbert N. Carroll, *The House of Representatives in Foreign Affairs*. Boston: Little, Brown, 1965. A comprehensive treatment of the activity, and relative inconsequence, of the House in foreign affairs.
2. Cecil V. Crabb, *Bipartisan Foreign Policy*. Chicago: Row, Peterson, 1957. The problems involved in getting political parties, the two houses of Congress, and the President to pull together in foreign policy making.
3. David Howard Davis, "The Price of Power: the Appropriations Process for Seventeen Foreign Affairs Agencies," *Public Policy* 18, Spring 1970, pp. 355-82. Examines the differential treatment of foreign policy agency budget requests at the hands of Congress.

4. David N. Farnsworth, *The Senate Committee on Foreign Relations*. Urbana: University of Illinois Press, 1961. Although dated, a valuable treatment of the leading Congressional foreign policy committee.
5. Harold Green and Albert Rosenthal, *Government of the Atom*. New York: Atherton Press, 1963. An excellent analysis of a Congressional "giant," the Joint Committee on Atomic Energy.
6. Charles O. Lerche, Jr., *The Uncertain South*. Chicago: Quadrangle Books, 1964. Examines the changing attitudes of Southern congressmen on foreign affairs in the postwar period.
7. Edward A. Kolodziej, *The Uncommon Defense and Congress*. Columbus: Ohio State University Press, 1966. A lengthy examination of the role of Congress in postwar military policy making.
8. H. Bradford Westerfield, *Foreign Policy and Party Politics*. New Haven, Conn.: Yale University Press, 1955. Probes the nature of bipartisan foreign policy and the problems involved in it for the period 1941-1950.

B. THE PRESIDENCY

1. Keith C. Clark and Laurence J. Legere, eds., *The President and the Management of National Security*. New York: Frederick A. Praeger, 1969. An examination of the administrative machinery used by recent presidents to manage foreign policy making.
2. Thomas E. Cronin and Sanford D. Greenberg, eds., *The Presidential Advisory System*. New York: Harper and Row, 1969. A fine collection of articles dealing with the means by which the president receives information relevant to policy making.
3. Stanley L. Falk, "The National Security Council under Truman, Eisenhower, and Kennedy," *Political Science Quarterly* 79, September, 1964, pp. 403-434. The NSC is what the President makes it.
4. Paul Y. Hammond, "The National Security Council as a Device for Interdepartmental Coordination: An Interpretation and Appraisal," *American Political Science Review* 54, December 1968, pp. 909-910. Conflicting goals pose a dilemma for presidential control of foreign policy machinery.
5. Senator Henry M. Jackson, ed. *The National Security Council*. New York: Frederick A. Praeger, 1965. Selected testimony and reports of the Jackson subcommittee on national security, which conducted an exhaustive investigation into national security machinery in the late 1950's and early 1960's.
6. Mark Kesselman, "Presidential Leadership in Congress on Foreign Policy," *Midwest Journal of Political Science* 5, August 1961, pp. 284-89.
7. Mark Kesselman, "Presidential Leadership in Congress on Foreign Policy: A Replication of a Hypothesis," *Midwest Journal of Political Science* 9, November 1965, pp. 401-406. These studies of the Eisenhower and Kennedy administrations indicate that presidents are able to change to some extent the foreign policy voting behavior of members of Congress from their own party.
8. Louis W. Koenig, *The Chief Executive*. New York: Harcourt Brace and World, 1964. Chapters 9, 10, 13 and 14 of this leading work on the presidency are of special relevance to the student of foreign affairs.
9. Alex B. Lacy, Jr., "The White House Staff Bureaucracy," *TRANS-action* 6, January 1969, pp. 50-56. Probes the background of White House staff members, and the method of operation of the staff under recent presidents.

10. Richard E. Neustadt, *Presidential Power*. New York: Wiley, 1960. An outstanding discussion of limitations on the President's power.

C. THE MILITARY ESTABLISHMENT

1. Omer L. Carey, ed., *The Military Industrial Complex and United States Foreign Policy*. Pullman: Washington State University Press, 1969. This fine collection contains five essays, written from different points of view, on the "military-industrial" complex.
2. Paul Y. Hammond, *Organizing for Defense: the American Military Establishment in the 20th Century*. Princeton, N.J.: Princeton University Press, 1961. The best study of the evolution of the U.S. military establishment in the twentieth century.
3. Paul Y. Hammond, "A Functional Analysis of Defense Department Decision Making in the McNamara Administration," *American Political Science Review* 62, March 1968, pp. 57-69. Explains McNamara's mastery of the Defense Department in terms of basic functions fulfilled by component parts of the Department.
4. Samuel P. Huntington, *The Common Defense*. New York: Columbia University Press, 1961. The leading study of military policy making in the period 1945-1960.
5. Samuel P. Huntington, *The Soldier and the State*. Cambridge, Mass.: Harvard University Press, 1957. A brilliant examination of the place of the professional military officer in American society from the very beginning.
6. Morris Janowitz, *The Professional Soldier*. Glencoe, Illinois: The Free Press, 1960. The leading work we have on the military bureaucracy and its members.
7. John C. Ries, *The Management of Defense*. Baltimore: The Johns Hopkins Press, 1964. A detailed examination of the evolution of the Defense Department in the postwar period.
8. Bruce M. Russett, *What Price Vigilance?* New Haven, Conn.: Yale University Press, 1970. This exploratory effort is the first serious attempt by a leading social scientist to apply the techniques of modern social science in analyzing whether there is a military-industrial complex.
9. Herbert I. Schiller and Joseph D. Phillips, eds., *Super-State: Readings in the Military-Industrial Complex*. Urbana: University of Illinois Press, 1970. A comprehensive collection of the available materials on this poorly explored subject.

D. THE STATE DEPARTMENT

1. Dean Acheson, *Present at the Creation*. New York: W.W. Norton Co., 1969. The superbly written memoirs of the man who was Secretary of State from 1949-1953.
2. W. W. Blancke, *The Foreign Service of the United States*. New York: Praeger, 1969. An introductory examination of the role of the Foreign Service today.
3. Zbigniew Brzezinski, "Purpose and Planning in Foreign Policy," *The Public Interest*, Number 14, Winter 1969. Critical analysis of State Department planning by an academic who served on the Department's Policy Planning Staff.
4. Robert Elder, *The Policy Machine*. Syracuse, N.Y.: Syracuse University Press, 1960. Although dated in some respects, this is a valuable examination of the administrative structure of the State Department.

5. James L. McCamy, *Conduct of the New Diplomacy*. New York: Harper and Row, 1964. Probes the evolving role of the State Department and provides data on Foreign Service officers.
6. Charlton Ogburn, Jr., "The Flow of Policy-Making in the Department of State," in *The Formulation and Administration of the United States Foreign Policy*. H. Field Haviland, ed., Washington: The Brookings Institution, 1960. This examination of the communications flow within the State Department is a classic, as shown by the fact that it has been included in a countless number of anthologies since its first appearance.
7. Smith Simpson, *Anatomy of the State Department*. Boston: Beacon Press, 1967. This polemic by a former Foreign Service officer is one of the best in a fascinating and voluminous body of protest literature written by alumni of the State Department.

E. THE INTELLIGENCE AGENCIES

1. Roger Hilsman, *To Move a Nation*. Garden City, New York: Doubleday and Company, 1967. Part III, "President Kennedy and the CIA," pp. 63-88. Is a discussion both of the role of the CIA and the problems its control poses for a democratic society.
2. Young Hum Kim, ed., *The CIA: Problems of Secrecy in a Democracy*. Lexington, Mass.: D.C. Heath and Company, 1968. This representative collection of readings provides a number of different perspectives on the role of the CIA.
3. Harry Howe Ransom, *Central Intelligence and National Security*. Cambridge, Mass.: Harvard University Press, 1958. This book remains a leading work on the subject.
4. Sol Stern, "NSA and the CIA," *Ramparts*, March 1967, pp. 29-37. This critical account details the role of the CIA in subsidizing the National Student Association.
5. H. Bradford Westerfield, *The Instruments of America's Foreign Policy*. New York: Thomas Y. Crowell, 1963. Chapters 21 and 22 of this work examine the role of the CIA from the viewpoint of a writer who is convinced of the necessity of the covert intervention of the U.S.A. into the politics of other nations.

IV. Case Studies

1. Elie Abel, *The Missile Crisis*. Philadelphia: J.B. Lippincott, 1966. A good journalistic study of the 1962 Cuban missile crisis.
2. Raymond A. Bauer, *et al.*, *American Business and Public Policy: The Politics of Foreign Trade*. New York: Atherton Press, 1963. An excellent study of the evolution of America's foreign trade policy.
3. Townsend Hoopes, *The Limits of Intervention*. New York: David McKay, 1969. An examination of the Johnson administration's 1968 decision to de-escalate the Vietnamese war, written by the then Undersecretary of the Air Force.
4. Glenn E. Paige, *The Korean Decision*. New York: The Free Press, 1968. An outstanding analysis of this nation's decision to intervene in the 1950 Korean conflict, written by a social scientist who had access to the major actors in the decision in gathering the data for this report.
5. James N. Rosenau, *National Leadership and Foreign Policy*. Princeton, N.J.: Princeton University Press, 1963. An analysis of the 1958 attempt of the

Eisenhower administration to rally national support for its foreign aid program.

6. Warner E. Schilling, *et al., Politics, Strategy, and Defense Budgets.* New York: Columbia University Press, 1962. Three excellent case studies of military policy making. Schilling's analysis of the making of the military budget for 1950 is superb.
7. Harold Stein, *American Civil-Military Decisions.* University of Alabama: University of Alabama Press, 1963. This large volume is a fine collection of studies of military policy making.

Domestic Structure
and
Foreign Policy

HENRY A. KISSINGER

In the contemporary period, the very nature of the governmental structure introduces an element of rigidity which operates more or less independently of the convictions of statesmen or the ideology which they represent. Issues are too complex and relevant facts too manifold to be dealt with on the basis of personal intuition. An institutionalization of decision-making is an inevitable by-product of the risks of international affairs in the nuclear age. Moreover, almost every modern state is dedicated to some theory of "planning"—the attempt to structure the future by understanding and, if necessary, manipulating the environment. Planning involves a quest for predictability and, above all, for "objectivity." There is a deliberate effort to reduce the relevant elements of a problem to a standard of average performance. The vast bureaucratic mechanisms that emerge develop a momentum and a vested interest of their own. As they grow more complex, their internal standards of operation are not necessarily commensurable with those of other countries or even with other bureaucratic structures in the same country. There is a trend toward autarky. A paradoxical consequence may be that increased control over the domestic environment is purchased at the price of loss of flexibility in international affairs.

The purpose of bureaucracy is to devise a standard operating procedure which can cope effectively with most problems. A bureaucracy is efficient if the matters which it handles routinely are, in fact, the most frequent and if its procedures are relevant to their solution. If those criteria are met, the energies of the top leadership are freed to deal creatively with the unexpected occurrence or with the need for innovation. Bureaucracy becomes an obstacle when what it defines as routine does not address the most significant range of issues or when its prescribed mode of action proves irrelevant to the problem.

When this occurs, the bureaucracy absorbs the energies of top executives in reconciling what is expected with what happens; the analysis of where one is

From *Daedelus*, Vol. 95, Spring 1966, pp. 506-518. Reprinted by permission of Daedelus © 1966.

overwhelms the consideration of where one should be going. Serving the machine becomes a more absorbing occupation than defining its purpose. Success consists in moving the administrative machine to the point of decision, leaving relatively little energy for analyzing the merit of this decision. The quest for "objectivity"—while desirable theoretically—involves the danger that means and ends are confused, that an average standard of performance is exalted as the only valid one. Attention tends to be diverted from the act of choice—which is the ultimate test of statesmanship—to the accumulation of facts. Decisions can be avoided until a crisis brooks no further delay, until the events themselves have removed the element of ambiguity. But at that point the scope for constructive action is at a minimum. Certainty is purchased at the cost of creativity.

Something like this seems to be characteristic of modern bureaucratic states whatever their ideology. In societies with a pragmatic tradition, such as the United States, there develops a greater concern with an analysis of where one is than where one is going. What passes for planning is frequently the projection of the familiar into the future. In societies based on ideology, doctrine is institutionalized and exegesis takes the place of innovation. Creativity must make so many concessions to orthodoxy that it may exhaust itself in doctrinal adaptations. In short, the accumulation of knowledge of the bureaucracy and the impersonality of its method of arriving at decisions can be achieved at a high price. Decision-making can grow so complex that the process of producing a bureaucratic consensus may overshadow the purpose of the effort.

While all thoughtful administrators would grant in the abstract that these dangers exist, they find it difficult to act on their knowledge. Lip service is paid to planning; indeed planning staffs proliferate. However, they suffer from two debilities. The "operating" elements may not take the planning effort seriously. Plans become esoteric exercises which are accepted largely because they imply no practical consequence. They are a sop to administrative theory. At the same time, since planning staffs have a high incentive to try to be "useful," there is a bias against novel conceptions which are difficult to adapt to an administrative mold. It is one thing to assign an individual or a group the task of looking ahead; this is a far cry from providing an environment which encourages an understanding for deeper historical, sociological, and economic trends. The need to provide a memorandum may outweigh the imperatives of creative thought. The quest for objectivity creates a temptation to see in the future an updated version of the present. Yet true innovation is bound to run counter to prevailing standards. The dilemma of modern bureaucracy is that while every creative act is lonely, not every lonely act is creative. Formal criteria are little help in solving this problem because the unique cannot be expressed "objectively."

The rigidity in the policies of the technologically advanced societies is in no small part due to the complexity of decision-making. Crucial problems may—and frequently do—go unrecognized for a long time. But once the decision-making apparatus has disgorged a policy, it becomes very difficult to change it. The alternative to the status quo is the prospect of repeating the whole anguishing process of arriving at decisions. This explains to some extent the curious phenomenon that decisions taken with enormous doubt and perhaps with a close division become practically sacrosanct once adopted. The whole administrative machinery swings behind their implementation as if activity could still all doubts.

Moreover, the reputation, indeed the political survival, of most leaders depends on their ability to realize their goals, however these may have been arrived at. Whether these goals are desirable is relatively less crucial. The time span by which administrative success is measured is considerably shorter than that by which historical achievement is determined. In heavily bureaucratized societies all pressures emphasize the first of these accomplishments.

Then, too, the staffs on which modern executives come to depend develop a momentum of their own. What starts out as an aid to decision-makers often turns into a practically autonomous organization whose internal problems structure and sometimes compound the issues which it was originally designed to solve. The decision-maker will always be aware of the morale of his staff. Though he has the authority, he cannot overrule it too frequently without impairing its efficiency; and he may, in any event, lack the knowledge to do so. Placating the staff then becomes a major preoccupation of the executive. A form of administrative democracy results, in which a decision often reflects an attainable consensus rather than substantive conviction (or at least the two imperceptibly merge). The internal requirements of the bureaucracy may come to predominate over the purposes which it was intended to serve. This is probably even more true in highly institutionalized Communist states—such as the U.S.S.R.—than in the United States.

When the administrative machine grows very elaborate, the various levels of the decision-making process are separated by chasms which are obscured from the outside world by the complexity of the apparatus. Research often becomes a means to buy time and to assuage consciences. Studying a problem can turn into an escape from coming to grips with it. In the process, the gap between the technical competence of research staffs and what hard-pressed political leaders are capable of absorbing widens constantly. This heightens the insecurity of the executive and may thus compound cither rigidity or arbitrariness or both. In many fields—strategy being a prime example—decision-makers may find it difficult to give as many hours to a problem as the expert has had years to study it. The ultimate decision often depends less on knowledge than on the ability to brief the top administrator—to present the facts in such a way that they can be absorbed rapidly. The effectiveness of briefing, however, puts a premium on theatrical qualities. Not everything that sounds plausible is correct, and many things which are correct may not sound plausible when they are first presented; and a second hearing is rare. The stage aspect of briefing may leave the decision-maker with a gnawing feeling of having been taken—even, and perhaps especially, when he does not know quite how.

Sophistication may thus encourage paralysis or a crude popularization which defeats its own purpose. The excessively theoretical approach of many research staffs overlooks the problem of the strain of decision-making in times of crisis. What is relevant for policy depends not only on academic truth but also on what can be implemented under stress. The technical staffs are frequently operating in a framework of theoretical standards while in fact their usefulness depends on essentially psychological criteria. To be politically meaningful, their proposals must involve answers to the following types of questions: Does the executive understand the proposal? Does he believe in it? Does he accept it as a guide to action or as an excuse for doing nothing? But if these kinds of concerns are given too much weight, the requirements of salesmanship will defeat substance.

The pragmatism of executives thus clashes with the theoretical bent of research or planning staffs. Executives as a rule take cognizance of a problem only when it emerges as an administrative issue. They thus unwittingly encourage bureaucratic contests as the only means of generating decisions. Or the various elements of the bureaucracy make a series of nonagression pacts with each other and thus reduce the decision-maker to a benevolent constitutional monarch. As the special role of the executive increasingly becomes to choose between proposals generated administratively, decision-makers turn into arbiters rather than leaders. Whether they wait until a problem emerges as an administrative issue or until a crisis has demonstrated the irrelevance of the standard operating procedure, the modern decision-makers often find themselves the prisoners of their advisers.

Faced with an administrative machine which is both elaborate and fragmented, the executive is forced into essentially lateral means of control. Many of his public pronouncements, though ostensibly directed to outsiders, perform a perhaps more important role in laying down guidelines for the bureaucracy. The chief significance of a foreign policy speech by the President may thus be that it settles an internal debate in Washington (a public statement is more useful for this purpose than an administrative memorandum because it is harder to reverse). At the same time, the bureaucracy's awareness of this method of control tempts it to shortcut its debates by using pronouncements by the decision-makers as charters for special purposes. The executive thus finds himself confronted by proposals for public declarations which may be innocuous in themselves—and whose bureaucratic significance may be anything but obvious— but which can be used by some agency or department to launch a study or program which will restrict his freedom of decision later on.

All of this drives the executive in the direction of extrabureaucratic means of decision. The practice of relying on special emissaries or personal envoys is an example; their status outside the bureaucracy frees them from some of its restraints. International agreements are sometimes possible only by ignoring safeguards against capricious action. It is a paradoxical aspect of modern bureaucracies that their quest for objectivity and calculability often leads to impasses which can be overcome only by essentially arbitrary decisions.

Such a mode of operation would involve a great risk of stagnation even in "normal" times. It becomes especially dangerous in a revolutionary period. For then, the problems which are most obtrusive may be least relevant. The issues which are most significant may not be suitable for administrative formulation and even when formulated may not lend themselves to bureaucratic consensus. When the issue is how to transform the existing framework, routine can become an additional obstacle to both comprehension and action.

This problem, serious enough *within* each society, is magnified in the conduct of international affairs. While the formal machinery of decision-making in developed countries shows many similarities, the criteria which influence decisions vary enormously. With each administrative machine increasingly absorbed in its own internal problems, diplomacy loses its flexibility. Leaders are extremely aware of the problems of placating their own bureaucracy; they cannot depart too far from its prescriptions without raising serious morale problems. Decisions are reached so painfully that the very anguish of decision-making acts as a brake on the give-and-take of traditional diplomacy.

This is true even *within* alliances. Meaningful consultation with other nations becomes very difficult when the internal process of decision-making already has some of the characteristics of compacts between quasi-sovereign entities. There is an increasing reluctance to hazard a hard-won domestic consensus in an international forum.

What is true within alliances—that is, among nations which have at least some common objectives—becomes even more acute in relations between antagonistic states or blocs. The gap created when two large bureaucracies generate goals largely in isolation from each other and on the basis of not necessarily commensurable criteria is magnified considerably by an ideological schism. The degree of ideological fervor is not decisive; the problem would exist even if the original ideological commitment had declined on either or both sides. The criteria for bureaucratic decision-making may continue to be influenced by ideology even after its élan has dissipated. Bureaucratic structures generate their own momentum which may more than counterbalance the loss of earlier fanaticism. In the early stages of a revolutionary movement, ideology is crucial and the accident of personalities can be decisive. The Reign of Terror in France was ended by the elimination of a single man, Robespierre. The Bolshevik revolution could hardly have taken place had Lenin not been on the famous train which crossed Germany into Russia. But once a revolution becomes institutional-ized, the administrative structures which it has spawned develop their own vested interests. Ideology may grow less significant in creating commitment; it becomes pervasive in supplying criteria of administrative choice. Ideologies prevail by being taken for granted. Orthodoxy substitutes for conviction and produces its own form of rigidity.

In such circumstances, a meaningful dialogue across ideological dividing lines becomes extraordinarily difficult. The more elaborate the administrative structure, the less relevant an individual's view becomes—indeed one of the purposes of bureaucracy is to liberate decision-making from the accident of personalities. Thus while personal convictions may be modified, it requires a really monumental effort to alter bureaucratic commitments. And if change occurs, the bureaucracy prefers to move at its own pace and not be excessively influenced by statements or pressures of foreigners. For all these reasons, diplomacy tends to become rigid or to turn into an abstract bargaining process based on largely formal criteria such as "splitting the difference." Either course is self-defeating: the former because it negates the very purpose of diplomacy; the latter because it subordinates purpose to technique and because it may encourage intransigence. Indeed, the incentive for intransigence increases if it is known that the difference will generally be split.

Ideological differences are compounded because major parts of the world are only in the first stages of administrative evolution. Where the technologically advanced countries suffer from the inertia of overadministration, the developing areas often lack even the rudiments of effective bureaucracy. Where the advanced countries may drown in "facts," the emerging nations are frequently without the most elementary knowledge needed for forming a meaningful judgment or for implementing it once it has been taken. Where large bureaucracies operate in alternating spurts of rigidity and catastrophic (in relation to the bureaucracy) upheaval, the new states tend to make decisions on the basis of almost random pressures. The excessive institutionalization of one and the inadequate structure of the other inhibit international stability.

THE NATURE OF LEADERSHIP

Whatever one's view about the degree to which choices in international affairs are "objectively" determined, the decisions are made by individuals who will be above all conscious of the seeming multiplicity of options. Their understanding of the nature of their choice depends on many factors, including their experience during their rise to eminence.

The mediating, conciliatory style of British policy in the nineteenth century reflected, in part, the qualities encouraged during careers in Parliament and the values of a cohesive leadership group connected by ties of family and common education. The hysterical cast of the policy of Imperial Germany was given impetus by a domestic structure in which political parties were deprived of responsibility while ministers were obliged to balance a monarch by divine right against a Parliament composed of representatives without any prospect of ever holding office. Consensus could be achieved most easily through fits of national passion which in turn disquieted all of Germany's neighbors. Germany's foreign policy grew unstable because its domestic structure did little to discourage capricious improvisations; it may even have put a premium on them.

The collapse of the essentially aristocratic conception of foreign policy of the nineteenth century has made the career experiences of leaders even more crucial. An aristocracy—if it lives up to its values—will reject the arbitrariness of absolutist rule; and it will base itself on a notion of quality which discourages the temptations of demagoguery inherent in plebiscitarian democracy. Where position is felt to be a birthright, generosity is possible (though not guaranteed); flexibility is not inhibited by a commitment to perpetual success. Where a leader's estimate of himself is not completely dependent on his standing in an administrative structure, measures can be judged in terms of a conception of the future rather than of an almost compulsive desire to avoid even a temporary setback. When statesmen belonged to a community transcending national boundaries, there tended to be consensus on the criteria of what constituted a reasonable proposal. This did not prevent conflicts, but it did define their nature and encourage dialogue. The bane of aristocratic foreign policy was the risk of frivolousness, of a self-confidence unrelated to knowledge, and of too much emphasis on intuition.

In any event, ours is the age of the expert or the charismatic leader. The expert has his constituency—those who have a vested interest in commonly held opinions; elaborating and defining its consensus at a high level has, after all, made him an expert. Since the expert is often the product of the administrative dilemmas described earlier, he is usually in a poor position to transcend them. The charismatic leader, on the other hand, needs a perpetual revolution to maintain his position. Neither the expert nor the charismatic leader operates in an environment which puts a premium on long-range conceptions or on generosity or on subordinating the leader's ego to purposes which transcend his own career.

Leadership groups are formed by at least three factors: their experiences during their rise to eminence; the structure in which they must operate; the values of their society. (In the section excerpted here, the author discusses one type of leadership. In the original work, he discusses ideological and revolutionary-charismatic types as well.)

Bureaucratic-Pragmatic Leadership

The main example of this type of leadership is the American élite—though the leadership groups of other Western countries increasingly approximate the American pattern. Shaped by a society without fundamental social schisms (at least until the race problem became visible) and the product of an environment in which most recognized problems have proved soluble, its approach to policy is *ad hoc*, pragmatic, and somewhat mechanical.

Because pragmatism is based on the conviction that the context of events produces a solution, there is a tendency to await developments. The belief is prevalent that every problem will yield if attacked with sufficient energy. It is inconceivable, therefore, that delay might result in irretrievable disaster; at worst it is thought to require a redoubled effort later on. Problems are segmented into constitutent elements, each of which is dealt with by experts in the special difficulty it involves. There is little emphasis or concern for their inter-relationship. Technical issues enjoy more careful attention, and receive more sophisticated treatment, than political ones. Though the importance of intangibles is affirmed in theory, it is difficult to obtain a consensus on which factors are significant and even harder to find a meaningful mode for dealing with them. Things are done because one knows how to do them and not because one ought to do them. The criteria for dealing with trends which are conjectural are less well developed than those for immediate crises. Pragmatism, at least in its generally accepted form, is more concerned with method than with judgment; or rather it seeks to reduce judgment to methodology and value to knowledge.

This is reinforced by the special qualities of the professions—law and business—which furnish the core of the leadership groups in America. Lawyers—at least in the Anglo-Saxon tradition—prefer to deal with actual rather than hypothetical cases; they have little confidence in the possibility of stating a future issue abstractly. But planning by its very nature is hypothetical. Its success depends precisely on the ability to transcend the existing framework. Lawyers may be prepared to undertake this task; but they will do well in it only to the extent that they are able to overcome the special qualities encouraged by their profession. What comes naturally to lawyers in the Anglo-Saxon tradition is the sophisticated analysis of a series of *ad hoc* issues which emerge as problems through adversary proceedings. In so far as lawyers draw on the experience which forms them, they have a bias toward awaiting developments and toward operating within the definition of the problem as formulated by its chief spokesmen.

This has several consequences. It compounds the already powerful tendencies within American society to identify foreign policy with the solution of immediate issues. It produces great refinement of issues as they arise, but it also encourages the administrative dilemmas described earlier. Issues are dealt with only as the pressure of events imposes the need for resolving them Then, each of the contending factions within the bureaucracy has a maximum incentive to state its case in its most extreme form because the ultimate outcome depends, to a considerable extent, on a bargaining process. The premium placed on advocacy turns decision-making into a series of adjustments among special interests—a process more suited to domestic than to foreign policy. This procedure neglects the long range because the future has no administrative constituency and is, therefore, without representation in the adversary proceedings. Problems tend to be slighted until some agency or department is made responsible for them. When this occurs—usually when a difficulty has already grown acute—the relevant department becomes an all-out spokesman for its particular area of responsibility. The outcome usually depends more on the pressures or the persuasiveness of the contending advocates than on a concept of over-all purpose. While these tendencies exist to some extent in all bureaucracies they are particularly pronounced in the American system of government.

This explains in part the peculiar alternation of rigidity and spasms of flexibility in American diplomacy. On a given issue—be it the Berlin crisis or disarmament or the war in Vietnam—there generally exists a great reluctance to develop a negotiating position or a statement of objectives except in the most general terms. This stems from a desire not to prejudge the process of negotiations and above all to retain flexibility in the face of unforeseeable events. But when an approaching conference or some other pressures make the development of a position imperative and some office or individual is assigned the specific task, a sudden change occurs. Both personal and bureaucratic success are then identified with bringing the particular assignment to a conclusion. Where so much stock is placed in negotiating skill, a failure of a conference may be viewed as a reflection on the ability of the negotiator rather than on the objective difficulty of the subject. Confidence in the bargaining process causes American negotiators to be extremely sensitive to the tactical requirements of the conference table—sometimes at the expense of longer-term considerations. In internal discussions, American negotiators—generally irrespective of their previous commitments—often become advocates for the maximum range of concessions; their legal background tempts them to act as mediators between Washington and the country with which they are negotiating.

The attitudes of the business élite reinforce the convictions of the legal profession. The American business executive rises through a process of selection which rewards the ability to manipulate the known—in itself a conciliatory procedure. The special skill of the executive is thought to consist in coordinating well-defined functions rather than in challenging them. The procedure is relatively effective in the business world, where the executive can often substitute decisiveness, long experience, and a wide range of personal acquaintance for reflectiveness. In international affairs, however—especially in a revolutionary situation—the strong will which is one of our business executives' notable traits may produce essentially arbitrary choices. Or unfamiliarity with the subject matter may have the opposite effect of turning the executive into a spokesman for his technical staffs. In either case, the business executive is even more dependent than the lawyer on the bureaucracy's formulation of the issue. The business élite is even less able or willing than the lawyer to recognize that the formulation of an issue, not the technical remedy, is usually the central problem.

All this gives American policy its particular cast. Problems are dealt with as they arise. Agreement on what constitutes a problem generally depends on an emerging crisis which settles the previously inconclusive disputes about priorities. When a problem is recognized, it is dealt with by a mobilization of all resources to overcome the immediate symptoms. This often involves the risk of slighting longer-term issues which may not yet have assumed crisis proportions and of overwhelming, perhaps even undermining, the structure of the area concerned by a flood of American technical experts proposing remedies on an American scale. Administrative decisions emerge from a compromise of conflicting pressures in which accidents of personality or persuasiveness play a crucial role. The compromise often reflects the maxim that "if two parties disagree the truth is usually somewhere in between." But the pedantic application of such truisms causes the various contenders to exaggerate their positions for bargaining purposes or to construct fictitious extremes to make their position appear moderate. In either case, internal bargaining predominates over substance.

The *ad hoc* tendency of our decision-makers and the reliance on adversary proceeding cause issues to be stated in black-and-white terms. This suppresses a feeling for nuance and makes it difficult to recognize the relationship between seemingly discrete events. Even with the perspective of a decade there is little consensus about the relationship between the actions culminating in the Suez fiasco and the French decision to enter the nuclear field; or about the inconsistency between the neutralization of Laos and the step-up of the military effort in Vietnam.

The same quality also produces a relatively low valuation of historical factors. Nations are treated as similar phenomena, and those states presenting similar immediate problems are treated similarly. Since many of our policy-makers first address themselves to an issue when it emerges as their area of responsibility, their approach to it is often highly anecdotal. Great weight is given to what people say and relatively little to the significance of these affirmations in terms of domestic structure or historical background. Agreement may be taken at face value and seen as reflecting more consensus than actually exists. Opposition tends to produce moral outrage which often assumes the form of personal animosity—the attitude of some American policy-makers toward President de Gaulle is a good example.

The legal background of our policy-makers produces a bias in favor of constitutional solutions. The issue of supra-nationalism or confederalism in Europe has been discussed largely in terms of the right of countries to make independent decisions. Much less weight has been given to the realities which would limit the application of a majority vote against a major country whatever the legal arrangements. (The fight over the application of Article 19 of the United Nations Charter was based on the same attitude.) Similarly, legal terms such as "integration" and "assignment" sometimes become ends in themselves and thus obscure the operational reality to which they refer. In short, the American leadership groups show high competence in dealing with technical issues, and much less virtuosity in mastering a historical process. And the policies of other Western countries exhibit variations of the American pattern. A lesser pragmatism in continental Europe is counterbalanced by a smaller ability to play a world-role.

*   *   *

Making Democracy Safe
for the World:
National Politics
and Foreign Policy

THEODORE J. LOWI

There are at least three modern schools of thought on the structure and functioning of American politics. All three are supported by a considerable body of doctrine. All three are grounded legitimately early in political history. All three are illustrable in a considerable range of contemporary cases and events. Each involves quite distinctive moral consequences. Each represents itself to be the American political system.[1]

One school, what we shall call Theory 1, begins with the fragmentation of society and economy and concludes that the polity is no different. The popular basis of sovereignty builds the fragmentation into the polity, leading to both constitutional and informal decentralization. Walter Lippmann, the modern prophet of this school, sees in this a "devolution of power" down into the constituencies and a derangement of relations among institutions.[2] E. E. Schattschneider's work offers much empirical support as well as further theoretical justification. Political relationships are seen largely in terms of logrolling, the pork barrel, and so on. These are inescapable in a world of extreme particularism. They are the inevitable means of building up consensus for decisions at the national level.[3] In his later work, Schattschneider began to view party as the essential means for saving the system from devolution. But that is only a more or less realistic solution to the problem, not a fact about this system. Decentralization characterizes the politics of this system; the basis of relationships among the participants in this system is logrolling. The outcome may often manifest itself in a fairly stable centralized "power structure"; but this a congeries rather than an elite, a leadership based on conspiracy more than consensus.

The second of the schools, or Theory 2 is more self-consciously a school. It has a name, *pluralism*, and it has for some years been the prevailing ideology among American political scientists. It begins upon the same factual base as the first system—fragmentation, or social pluralism. But to the pluralist, the system is not fragmented and decentralizing. It is fragmented and self-correcting. It represents classical economics applied to the political system. Bargaining among directly conflicting interests is the basic pattern of politics, and the "power structure" is dynamic as well as rational. Logrolling is not basic but is merely one occasionally used strategy, usually employed among interests on the same "side" of the conflict in order to extend and intensify the conflict. A coherent system as well as a public interest are produced out of the fragments. But there is no center of the system, no elite, no meaningful order below the order of the system itself. The system is "multicentered." There may be an elite for each center, but it is not stable and legitimate as an elite. The reality, instead, is an interaction among leaders. The political process is one of bargaining among like or comparable interests. The "power structure" is the coalitions that are the outcome of the bargaining, and public policy is the mere ratification.

The third major school of thought, Theory 3, recognizes the fragmentation as a societal fact but treats it as largely irrelevant to the political system. All the activity in the fragmented society simply helps ensure the legitimacy of the elite. This approach has never been popular among political scientists but is very much alive as the prevailing ideology among American sociologists. To some, the political elite is derived from a socioeconomic class whose members hold all the "command posts" and make all the "key decisions." To others, perhaps the more sophisticated, the elite is comprised of the holders of the command posts whose members ultimately constitute a class. In either (or any other) case, power is centralized and power relations are highly stable. They are based on consensus. Thus, agreement on the most important issues can often be reached with ease, without publicity, and yet highly legitimately because conflict tends to be managed by regular, hierarchical means ("through channels"), and the ultimate settlement of conflict can take place by relatively informal means among like-minded gentlemen, without debates and votes.

It is not necessary to go at length into each school of thought as a theory.[4] It is only necessary first to point to the existence of the multitude of inconsistencies among them and then to decide how to operate as an analyst in face of those inconsistencies.

One way to deal with the extraordinary degree of inconsistency among the prevailing schools of thought is to abandon all three. But that is all too likely to involve rejection of an extremely valuable feature common to them all, and that is their focus on real institutions and real decisions in the real political system.[5] Another way is to embrace them all and then to try to find the limits of the applicability of each. This I have done and, as I have argued elsewhere,[6] each theory turns out to be an extremely rich (and truthful) source of logically related, empirically grounded propositions. In short, once each puts an end to its claim to universality and contents itself with being a theory for only a subsystem, it approaches the standards of scientific theory. The empirical support associated with each as a subsystem becomes stronger rather than weaker.

In sum, therefore, the American system is not all of a piece but is composed of several fundamental subsystems. Internally, these have developed around the most fundamental functions of the state. When public policy is facing the *redistribution* of resources, the system is elitist in very much the theoretical and empirical terms laid down by Mills and others. When public policy is facing the *regulation* of resources, the system is pluralist in all of the specific issues fought out and decisions made. A system very much like the one Lippmann disdainfully describes develops around public policy that deals in the *distribution* of resources.[7] Since each of these three types of public policy is a function of the state, and therefore an ongoing process, it is not inconceivable that each becomes a subsystem with a distinctive political structure, process, and morality. This is also perfectly consistent with our present notions about differentiation in modern politics. After all, this is a form around the basic functions of the state; and it is highly adaptive: (1) On the occasional issues (redistribution) that can trigger revolutions and class warfare, the political structure is highly centralized, and the participants are the holders of the most highly legitimate and highly prized statuses in society. The prevailing political relationship is, thus, one of hierarchy or management. (2) On the more frequent occasions when directly coercive restrictions (regulation) must be placed on alternative uses of resources, there is a subsystem that is decentralized and open usually resulting in the application of general rules or precedents to conduct. Here the prevailing political relationship is one of bargaining. (3) On by far the most frequent occasions, when existing public domain must be "divvied up," decisions can be made quite amorally (without application of a general rule). However, the result is highly co-optative and stabilizing without need of consensus.[8]

In this chapter it is assumed that the "domestic political system" is of the tripartite nature described above. There is much ground for controversy about the assumption that three functions of the state or areas of policy—distribution, regulation, and redistribution—are the essential determinants of the three subsystems. But that need not deter us here. The important point is that there is ample evidence for the existence of the three subsystems and that each would clearly have consequences for American foreign policy if it were also the dominant power pattern in foreign policy making.

The question is, then, what sort of a power pattern can be found in foreign policy? Is it elitistic, pluralistic, or massified? What kind of a subsystem is it? This is a proper enough academic subject. But it is also merely a more academic way of asking (or perhaps answering) two more immediately significant questions: (1) To what extent do domestic political factors influence the making of foreign policy? Put another way, to what extent does our politics change as the interests of the whole country are involved? (2) More normatively, to what extent do our own institutions facilitate or hinder the most rational use of the country's resources toward realization of its vital interests?

In one way or another, each of the papers in this volume has something to offer on these questions, but in all such cases the dimension involved is that of the relation of the formal leadership to the mass, or mass public opinion, in one form or another. Assessments differ on the amount, direction, and virtue of the influence exercised, but the assessments are no less those of elite-mass relations. Thus there remains untreated the other dimensions: By this I mean *the actual relations among the formal leaders and among the institutions of foreign policy making that create the formal leadership positions.* Only by inspecting relations among the formal leaders and the governmental units they control can we hope to settle the questions posed above. Ultimately, this would reconcile the various points of view toward the relationships between the foreign policy leaders as elite and the informal forces of groups and mass opinions. A reconciliation would be found by discovering the conditions under which one or another power pattern prevails. These conditions will be found in (1) events, (2) institutions, (3) policies, and (4) types of policies.

Before proceeding to the inquiry into the events, institutions, and policies that explain our foreign policy establishment, it might be useful to state in a few brief propositions the terms of discourse. These propositions may also serve to summarize and conclude this introductory section:

1. A modern, highly differentiated state generates conflict that cannot altogether be taken care of by mere elite management but must necessarily involve, under varying circumstances, a great deal of bargaining and logrolling.
2. These three fundamental political relations—hierarchy or management, bargaining, and logrolling—form the basis for three distinct subsystems within the American political system.
3. These three types of political relations are indexes to the pattern of power in any political institution or unit of government.
4. Evidence for these relations can be found in the ordinary workings of the institutions and units, and the workings of these units can be found in the nature and impact of their outputs. That is to say, the statute (or other policy expression) properly understood is a valid source of data on institutions and processes; therefore, we can know about the political system through the policy outputs of its units without need of "inside dope."

EVENTS AND ELITES

Events shape foreign policy making in any number of ways. Events in Asia intensify or relax our diplomatic, military, and economic activity there. Certain events intensify economic over military or military over diplomatic activities. And so on. But the most important aspect of the event in the operation of our foreign policy establishment is the time dimension. Is the event a crisis or is it not? Does the event allow time for consideration of alternative policies or time only for a conditioned reflex? Are we on the brink of violence, civil or military, or are the events taking place at some point away from the brink where responses rather than reflexes, preventives rather than cures, may be appropriate?

In regard to events or situations of the first type, crises, the foreign policy record of the United States has been outstanding.[9] Postwar examples of United States behavior in crises include Greek-Turkish aid, the Berlin airlift, response to the Korean invasion, the 1956 Arab-Israeli intervention, the Cuban missile crisis. Due to our relatively poor record in most noncrisis situations, our adversaries consistently underestimate our capacity to react in time to crises.

Crisis situations are special conditions underlying special operations of the foreign policy establishment. The aforementioned crisis decisions involved less bargaining than discussion preceding consensus. Only command-post positions were involved; the public and its institutions were far removed; the decisions made by the elite were highly legitimate; public and semipublic responses were largely ceremonial and affirmative. In sum, there was hardly any politics at all.

Each of these decisions in crisis seems, therefore, to portray the foreign policy establishment much in the image offered by Mills as the whole truth about the United States: "Within the higher circles of the power elite, factions do exist. But more powerful than these divisions are the internal discipline and the community of interests that bind the power elite together . . ."[10] But on further inspection, Mills did not go far enough. As is well known, Mills defined his power elite as all the holders of the top "institutional positions" in the military, in the executive branch of national government and in industry. In crisis decisions, inspection shows that actually the participants have always consti-tuted an elite *even smaller than the elite identified by Mills*. Even when the crisis offers a small grace period, such as was true for instance of Dienbienphu in 1954 and aid to Greece and Turkey in 1947, rarely has more than a small portion of the standard power elite been involved in the making of the decision, and it was a very special segment.

These facts suggest the more accurate proposition that *crisis decisions in foreign policy are made by an elite of formal, official office-holders*. Rarely is there time to go further. Apparently rarely also is there need to go further, except immediately after the decision through ceremonies of affirmation and perhaps long after the decision, through criticism and "electoral punishment." Thus, a corollary to this obvious, albeit often overlooked, first proposition is that the people who make decisions in times of crisis are largely those who were elected and appointed to make such decisions. That is to say, *in foreign affairs crises our government has operated pretty much as it was supposed to operate*. There is a normative corollary as well: Since our record of response to crisis is good, then the men in official positions have been acting and are able to act rationally.

So far, then, all we have established is that foreign policy making is influenced by events and that critical events produce a distinctive type of process and leadership. But this statement is clearly true of only one type of situation—crisis—and not necessarily of all foreign policy decisions. It would be a serious mistake to assume that all important foreign policy decisions occur at moments of crisis just as it would be a mistake to assume that the existence of a crisis is irrelevant to the pattern of politics in foreign policy.

*   *   *

POLICIES: OVERSELL, NOT OVERKILL

The institutions of foreign policy formulation and coordination created after World War II were essentially policies, as well as being instruments for making policies. . . . Analysis of some of these policies and the continuities in the manner of their formulation will provide further evidence and more useful indexes for our final assessment of the politics of foreign policy. Put in the most concrete, operational terms, the question here is: What are the policy consequences of the "separation of powers" prevailing among the units of foreign policy formulation? The policy consequences will be viewed primarily from their most fundamental perspective—the presidency.

Somehow a President must try to make a ministry out of what is at best a coalition. Any man who can engineer his own nomination in one of our national conventions and then hold together his winning cadre for election victories in a large number of states, has an impressive array of political skills. The requirement of possession and use of such skills is a reflection of the dispersed, coalitional character of political power in America. The presence of such behavior in the formulation of foreign policy ought then to offer an additional set of dependable indexes for the patterns of power in this particular issue-area.

Presidential behavior since World War II can be summarized as "oversell": the President has been forced to (1) oversell the crisis and (2) oversell the remedy. These are the continuities in the formulation of foreign policy. In reverse order, each of the types of oversell will be analyzed and illustrated.

*   *   *

The current situation in Vietnam is an . . . instance of this point. It has been just one more crisis made out of the decentralized system. The outbreak of fighting in Vietnam itself was not of our making; the crisis was. It was sold by American policy-makers and image-makers as a case of unambiguous aggression and as a case of the need for unambiguous victory. It may be a case of both of these things, but to sell it on the front pages as that sort of a package left diplomats almost no options. Add the Rusk Doctrine of the total involvement of our credibility throughout the world, the rigidity becomes almost complete for the United States and also for its allies, whose choice now seems only to be whether to be or not be an official ally. Under popular pressure, magnified by congressmen who rightly feel they have not been properly treated in the matter, the extremities of oversell are exceeded over and over again. Finally, in order to justify everything else, the Ky regime itself is oversold for its strength and legitimacy. We spread it on so thick, topping it off with Presidential bearhug, that the regime itself came perilously close to a fall and may still bring itself and our shaky justification down with it.

When experiments must be sold as sure things and limited sure things must be sold as cure-alls, frustration and failure are inevitable. An experiment can be partially successful; but after oversell partial success can only be defined as failure. Failure leads to distrust and frustration, which lead to more oversell and to further verbal excesses, as superlatives become ordinary through use. Since international politics is special in the amount of risk involved, these responses become especially intense. All of which leads to the worst possible abuse of oversell, the rhetoric of victory. While it has been resisted, with exceptions, up to now, the rhetoric of victory is constantly on the verge of gaining ascendancy. It is the last stage before the end of politics.

Overselling the Threat

The second type of oversell is essentially the attempt to create the moral equivalent of war. It is the conversion of cues into incidents, incidents into challenges, and challenges into crises for the purpose of imposing temporary and artificial cohesion upon the members of the foreign policy establishment. It is the escalation of meanings. When peace is in peril, all Presidents have found it necessary to create that sense of self-restraint, self-sacrifice, and devotion to higher causes that seems to come about so naturally in war. For modern Presidents, this tactic has become necessary, compelling, and regular whether there is a true crisis or not.

Typically, a Britisher provided us with our most important concepts. In the vocabulary of oversell no doctrines have been as important as "cold war" and "iron curtain." (Also typically, the British proceeded to take it all less seriously than we.) There were, of course, varying amounts of truth underlying both terms. Perhaps there is a total but unseen war. Perhaps there has been a communist devil who will "get you if you don't watch out." But the analytic value of the terms was lost to their hortatory value: We can get some cohesion in a power elite if we can only attribute to our enemies a singleness of purpose and a perfection of rational means to achieve it. These two themes proved to fill basic psychological and political needs in our system, and they have been used to help oversell crises ever since.

"Containment," first seized upon to help provide a package for Greek-Turkish aid, was also found to be generally valuable. Thus it became a significant American contribution to the more pervasive themes of cold war and iron curtain. It helped show that all local wars, guerilla actions, *coups d'état*, and other types of upheaval were interrelated and cumulative.

Along with these pervasive themes are the more specialized, *ad hoc* emotions whipped up for campaigns on more specific issues. President Eisenhower had an important oversell mechanism in McCarthyism. Functionally, McCarthyism was the internal equivalent of containment, and it helped bring the twenty-year Democratic, tea-sipping, and Soviet-friendly State Department into line as well as to silence much independent opposition. Late in his Administration, Eisenhower found overselling of foreign crises increasingly valuable as his personal prestige declined. Dulles became famous for such talk as the "brink of war" and "massive retaliation." The latter was particularly good because it helped oversell the positive value of atomic over conventional arms, and at the same time helped create the sense of the seriousness and the immediacy of the threat that made retaliation necessary. Dulles opposed containment as "negative, futile and immoral" and implied its replacement with rhetoric that (especially for Europe) verged on preventive war. But he continued to sell all outbreaks the world over as interrelated and cumulative. Finally there was the use of Sputnik for a variety of issues in the arms race during the "Sputnik age."

Much of the activity in Kennedy's short span was of the same nature. In fact, Kennedy spent more of his earlier months on creating a moral equivalent of war than on just about anything else. The "ask not" passage of his inaugural address was a suitable transition from missile gaps to something more substantial (and truthful). The idea of man-on-the-moon-by-1970 had all sorts of value besides the increasing of space appropriations. The Bay of Pigs, once survived, became an excellent means for creating a sense of unity, then some real unity, on a host of defense-related items. (It is hard to forget the Kennedy-MacArthur, Kennedy-Hoover, Kennedy-Truman, and so forth, unity pictures.)

Again it should be emphasized that any critism expressed or implied is subsidiary to the essential point, which is how these themes are reflective of the system and fulfill needs in the system. Overselling the nature of the crisis is not as specific and selective as the techniques of overselling the cures. This is why themes have been stressed. But it is no less a reflection of the conflictive system. Facing real political stress, and committed to real goals about which there is usually a great deal of consensus, the President is impelled into domestic strategies that may give him the means of realizing the goals without having to mortgage so much as to make the means eventually fashioned (the partial decision) useless to him. There is always hope, as we must judge from his actions, that he can reverse the aphorism, "He who mobilizes the elite mobilizes the public." What has become important to the President is the possibility that "He who mobilizes the public mobilizes the elite."

Turning again to pathology, overselling the crisis is dangerous precisely because it is so nonspecific. Even if it may provide the proper setting for putting the important policy across, it can create expectations of war that can falsely affect business, alienate the attentive publics and allies, or, more gravely, reduce the President's own flexibility at a later point when he would like the crisis to "be over." He might, in other words, wish it on at will, but he cannot so easily wish it off (e.g., McCarthyism). Given the regular use of oversell despite such obvious dangers, the need for oversell must be enormous.

All the more significant is the fact that the tactic seems to be so unsuccessful. While this cannot be proven conclusively, it is possible to observe that all the other forms of political interaction continue unabated. The President continues to manufacture an occasional crisis out of a minor challenge, but he still gets partial decisions. He must still mortgage large parts of trade control as an instrument of politics in order to get any trade act at all. He must still expect to be forced into an occasional war, be forced to fight it one-handed, and then be expected to win an unambiguous victory. In diplomacy, the only thing worse than unambiguous defeat is unambiguous victory. That is the Scylla and Charybdis of presidential power in survival politics.

CONCLUSIONS

Regardless of ideology or context, conflict tends to decentralize power. Decentralization is a function of continuous conflict. In answer to the iron law of oligarchy, there is an equally ferrous law of democracy. They are merely converse expressions of the same law, each being a statement for its appropriate extent and degree of conflict. . . .

There is conflict in foreign policy politics. Separated agencies, each with constitutional or legal rights to independent identity, access, and participation, guarantee the continuity of conflict. The President's efforts to propagandize all his colleagues and his publics through the risky tactics of oversell attest to the extent of conflict and consequently to the broad base of participation and relatively extreme decentralization of power in the foreign policy establishment. We have seen the process largely through the instruments so fashioned and the actions so taken. The process of conflict-and-conflict-resolution in some form was the only explanation for most cases, because rational men could never have arrived at these instruments or actions through reason and consensus. In most cases it is difficult to conceive of instruments or actions more poorly designed for the rational pursuit of any rationally defined (self-interested) goals. Democracy is, of course, unsafe for the world so long as democracy is not set up for consistently rational action, because the enemy can too easily miscalculate. And instruments and actions cannot be rational or consistent so long as they are arrived at as simply the outcome of a meandering process. However, the prospect of rationality is less important here than the system that has made its prospect so dim. What remains to be done, therefore, is to make more explicit and theoretically relevant my basic arguments about the system.

. . . It seems that *the only instances in which the makers of foreign policy were truly separated and insulated from broad publics and worked truly in unison, even if not always in harmony, were crisis.* Here it is easy to cite reasons, among which are anxiety and insufficient time. But can we do better than isolate merely this one important subsystem of foreign policy behavior? What about other subsystems? It would be possible to let the matter rest here, with the sufficiently weighty and far from unanimously accepted contention that in all other situations, foreign policy is "pluralistic." This would imply two things, both fairly close to the truth: (1) that inside the "elite" there is much organized bloc actions, not unlike domestic patterns of pluralism; and (2) that American foreign policy is subject to domestic political forces to a degree unknown to other modern democratic or nondemocratic states. But I think it is possible to take another step beyond this position toward a more elaborate notion of foreign policy as an "issue-area" or "arena." This is to identify the type of policy involved.

From the cases above, and one or two others cited below, it is possible to identify two distinct subsystems within the general field of noncrisis foreign policy-making. To summarize, this gives us three predictable subsystems of foreign policy-making, although they are not identical to the three domestic ones earlier described. The first is the elitist subsystem (although involving a much smaller elite than the "power elite") that prevails (a) in crisis and (b) in any noncrisis situations in which in the short run no internal resources are involved at all. Recognition of a country with no immediate United States commitments beyond mere recognition might prove such an example; however, it is difficult to imagine many noncrisis situations of any great importance where no internal resources are involved. Thus it follows that there is little eliteness in noncrisis foreign policy politics.

The key factor, once internal resources are involved, is not how much involvement there is (which would push us toward *post hoc* and truistic propositions), but what kind of involvement. This means classifying foreign policies in terms of their impact upon the United States. Thus, subsystem 2 is a logrolling pattern. The logrolling pattern is decentralized and nonconflictive just as the elitist pattern is centralized and nonconflictive. This subsystem gives the appearance of being elitist only because it is nonconflictive. This subsystem is similar to the domestic pattern I have called distributive politics, and for the same reason: It develops around policies that can be disaggregated into a multitude of isolated, small units. Subsystem 3 is decentralized and conflictive— in a word, pluralistic. When foreign policies depend for their success upon direct and relatively coercive regulation of internal resources, it is impossible to avoid conflict. It is also impossible to disaggregate the issues into their many negotiable parts. Such situations are the most decentralized and the outcomes are most unpredictable. Foreign policy considerations are least insulated from domestic forces.[11]

Now let us look at three different noncrisis situations to see how much is to be gained from the imposition of distributive and regulatory categories upon them. The test is whether political relations among participants could have been predicted from knowledge of whether the foreign policy was distributive or regulatory in its involvement with internal resources.

The Tariff

The best example of the relation between technique and process, and therefore the best introduction to the theoretical value of the approach is the tariff. It is a good example because it has undergone a redefinition from a distributive to a regulatory type of policy in recent times and thus provides an experimental situation. The traditional tariff was a classic case of distributive techniques. The scope of tariff coverage could be expanded indefinitely and the schedules could be broken up into smaller and smaller items almost infinitely. The inevitable conflicts among participants could be accommodated without ever requiring face-to-face conflict by simply giving to each a portion of what he wanted. Even potential combatants could find a basis for cooperation: logrolling. Eventually, someone has to pay the piper; but this moral equation could be balanced easily by the simple process of displacement onto the world system and onto the future.

The politics of the traditional tariff, so clearly captured by Schattschneider, was neither pluralistic nor power elitist. There was an elite, but it was not based upon an upper class or the command posts, but was specifically a congressional committee (House Ways and Means). Relations among participants were highly stable around the committee, but it was a stability among uncommon interests rather than one of consensus. There can hardly be said to have been a "group process" at all; nor does there appear to have been any executive control whatsoever.

Beginning with 1934, and increasing after World War II, tariff underwent very significant changes in the manner of its use as the United States emerged as a regular world participant. Even before the outbreak of war, the United States had entered into agreements affecting over 1,000 major tariff items. Reciprocal trade renewal in 1945 established 1945 rates as a new standard below which the President could reduce rates by still another 50 per cent. Under the most favored nation clause, the tariff had obviously become a means whereby we could affect world trade and also bargain for nontrade concessions *if we were willing to bargain with our own rates*. Thus it was only a matter of time before tariff became the reverse of its earlier form. Earlier it was a means of manipulating international affairs for domestic purposes. Now it had become a means of regulating the domestic economy of international purposes.

Without arguing cause and effect, it is possible to observe significant political changes in the tariff during the same period. The field shifts from committee to Congress in classic interplay with the executive. The "group process" emerges. Larger and larger categories of commodities (rather than single items) become involved, until they are formally incorporated into the Trade Expansion Act of 1962 and the Tariff Classification Act, passed earlier in 1962. The entire story becomes a great deal more public.

Aid, Not Trade

I have already made a great deal of the proposition that an important aspect of the Marshall Plan was whether or not it was to be a set of powers granted to the State Department. I conceived of this largely as an issue over whether the State Department or any other department would be granted powers that amounted to the regulation of our economy for international purposes. The politics of ECA appeared to be one of consensus; but it was neither consensual nor elitist except in superficial appearance. Once ECA was set up independently, it became simply a new segment of public domain available for distribution. The politics of aid could be predicted, because aid looks pretty much like the politics of the traditional tariff, of water resources, or of agriculture subsidy.

ECA did not actually engage directly in the purchase of supplies (making the imposition of regulatory disciplines an all the more remote threat). Procurement was left to recipient countries buying almost completely through regular private trade channels. Each application for a commodity—by a government, a firm, or an individual—was reviewed by ECA, which in turn issued a "procurement authorization" to a cooperating bank guaranteeing reimbursement once the purchase from the American firm was made. When ECA decided a loan was more appropriate, it was authorized to turn over the funds to the Export-Import Bank, which was to administer the loan according to the terms set down by the ECA administrator (Section 111 (c)(2)). However, the difference between loans and grants has been politically unimportant because (1) in most cases the recipient had to put up the equivalent of the grant in local (counterpart) funds; (2) there were many strings tied to grants and many types of loans were very "soft"; and (3) ultimately the individual American supplier faced a customer with cash no matter what the customer had to do about the cash later on.

A formal reading of the Act and official interpretations reveals the meaning of ECA as a bundle of techniques. In the short run, essentially no governmental regulations at all were imposed upon the resources of the United States. There was an expansion of domain that attracted the support of industrial and financial interests facing postwar recession. The prospect of sales to totally trustworthy (U.S. guaranteed) foreign accounts is bound to have had a major impact on how businessmen related to each other and to Congress and the executive. It is not necessary to know what each man's motives were to know that his political relations with all others having Marshall Plan interests in common were quite different from what these relations would have been if, for instance, the Act had involved such lend-lease techniques as direct presidential and Army-Navy procurement decisions, "set-asides" for particularly desirable commodities, or discretion in the use of ECA goods as items in bargaining and diplomacy with Marshall Plan countries. As a consequence, and as predictable, the politics of Marshall Plan was quiet, appearing to be almost without conflict.

Far more than the published accounts say explicitly, the process centered in Congress, particularly in the Senate Foreign Relations Committee. Bipartisanship was a harness designed strictly for Chairman Vandenberg, but he was as often the driver as the driven.

There is some experimental value in a brief look at the more recent history of "foreign aid." The dollar gap was closed during the early 1950s, and not too long afterwards the opposite problem emerged, which became the gold flow. As a strategy, foreign aid remained more or less the same, but its national politics undoubtedly changed. Insofar as aid is responsible for an unfavorable balance of trade and a gold outflow, it is responsible to that extent for direct contraction of the domestic economy (actually by a multiplier of as much as five times that amount). This has a fiscal impact on the domestic economy that requires adjustment among many individual firms. This impact, in turn, has brought about an interconnection of aid decisions that hitherto were taken up one at a time and in isolation. For example, President Eisenhower's directive of November 16, 1960, to reduce to "the lowest possible figure" the amount of commodities purchased abroad with ICA funds required (1) a contraction that in turn required (2) ICA to make hard choices among claims that triggered (3) competition among claims. No longer could the aid program enjoy being merely a set of expanded opportunities.

The political changes associated with these changes in the relation of foreign aid to the domestic economy are consistent with the theory. Increasingly in the late 1950s, reaching a climax in 1964; conflict began to develop around almost all aspects of foreign aid. This contrasts to the tendency of most American policies to become part of the consensus after being around for a long time. Probably for the first time in American history an "independent commission" lost its statutory independence and became incorporated in a department–in this case the dreaded Department of State. In Congress, aid became conflictive rather than consensual. Control of aid moved dramatically away from committee; the floor came to have real functional value. The President had to return, after over a decade, to the public, in hopes of mobilizing the elite. Otto Passman has been more a reflection than a leader.

Thus, the politics of foreign aid changed because foreign aid as a policy changed. Many leaders no doubt began to oppose foreign aid in the late 1950s because of dissatisfaction with the experience of foreign aid programs abroad. But that would be sufficient explanation only for revival of aid *as an issue*. The concern here is not to explain why, when, and what people become dissatisfied. It is, rather, to explain why certain kinds of political relationships develop and to speculate on the consequences of each, once the question is raised. In the case of aid, the first decade was distributive policy, and the political patterns developed accordingly. More recently, for many reasons, aid programs are related to our own resources in a much more regulative way, and the politics of aid has begun to be quite different from before.

Arms and Armaments

Unification had worked during World War II because there was a war and because resources could be treated as though they were unlimited. After 1945, there was neither war nor unlimited resources. Setting hard budgetary ceilings in the pre-Korean period intensified interservice rivalries beyond all reason. The ceilings made clear that there was a pie that had to be sliced three ways. This made relations among the services a zero-sum game; and the absence of war removed most restraints on how to respond to it. On the other hand, the size and scope of the decisions each service had to make in the postwar period meant that it would be impossible for President or Budget Bureau or Congress to break up the issues into small, negotiable units. The most spectacular battle among the services, the so-called B-36 controversy, was so large a procurement item that it basically involved a decision on "a theory of war." Thus, conflict could be displaced neither through expansion of available resources nor through further and further disaggregation of the existing resources. All decisions were elevated to a degree of inclusiveness as great as could be achieved by compromise and coalition—i.e., the level of the Service and whole sectors of the economy dependent on that Service. Decisions, therefore, tended to be so inclusive and also so conflictive that some kind of doctrine (a "theory of war") was almost a requisite. Like domestic regulatory decisions, the politics of tight budgets or of contraction, or of major changes in roles and missions, takes place among large, organized sectors and bureaucracies in a classic interplay with Congress. Conflict and compromise, not logrolling and not elite consensus, describe the process that inevitably expands beyond the original parties (e.g., Air Force vs. Navy). To emphasize the point, the politics of disarmament cannot be the same as its opposite, an arms race. Ironically, the latter is politically much more peaceful.

The politics inside each military service is typically one of dramatic contrasts to that between and among the services. Here, to carry out its policies once the big decisions requiring doctrine have been made, each service operates as a distributive arena. Contracts can break up the total budget into units of almost any size and can accommodate to the conflicts among industrial and local claimants, just as the Corps of Engineers and the Public Health Service can. Whatever the substance at issue, this kind of activity is basically co-optative. The politics of intraservice activity is consequently quieter, more elitist (to the level of the service), more stable, centered less in Congress and more in congressional committee. External relations are truly of an agency-clientele nature. The distributive politics of *intra-service* activity, of course, is significant in itself but doubly so because it in turn supports and provides the resources for the regulatory politics of *interservice* struggle.

A major problem in the study of politics, especially the politics of foreign policy, is that of escaping the uniqueness of events. The ultimate data are policy decisions, and their great relevance is also their greatest shortcoming. Faced with policy-making cases, theory becomes a set of afterthoughts tagged on to untheoretical chronicles, unless we develop conventions for answering the ultimate question: Of what class of cases is this case?

There may be several useful directions away from the unique event toward theory, several bases of classification. The classification formulated here for noncrisis foreign policy is derived from an understanding of that limited number of means by which men can use government to control other men and their environment. Properly categorized, these techniques of control are the functions of the state. Therefore it is not too much to expect that political relationships among political participants will be determined in large part by what technique of control they have in common. In domestic affairs, two men may appear to have "agriculture policy" or "education policy" in common. But that only describes and predicts their political interests. Their political relations will be determined and structured according to whether agriculture, for example, is to be manipulated by subsidies, by licensing, by marketing controls, or by credit; or, concerning education, whether by loans, grants, tax rebates, building programs, or "aggregate demand." Such an analysis does not attempt to tell all about either agriculture or education. Its purpose is to reveal the essential political ingredient of the issue: How is the object to be controlled? This is simply an attempt to characterize policies for purposes of analysis just as we often take ideologies, interest groups, or roles as the relevant aspect of broader and larger phenomena.

In foreign affairs such an effort seems equally useful. An approach to noncrisis foreign policy politics through the techniques of internal control does not tell all about any decision or development. But it does tend to clarify one vital dimension of foreign policy and helps avoid the confusion of trying to deal with several dimensions at once. Such an approach emphasizes the domestic sources, strengths, and limitations of foreign policy. It may be even more useful in establishing stronger continuities, academically speaking, between foreign and domestic theories of politics. The effort here resolved itself into three subsystems or arenas of power in domestic politics and two subsystems in noncrisis foreign politics, because only three categories of control techniques (functions of the state) could be identified. Congressional and executive roles, relations between Congress and its committees and between committees and interest groups, degree and type of group involvement, degree and type of public and mass involvement—all these seem to vary according to conditions created by the type of technique involved.

However, the principle of analysis—classifying the techniques of control and predicting political relations for each technique—is more important than my particular realization of it. The superior realization of the principle of analysis will arise not out of more elaborate cases or technically superior data but rather out of a superior understanding of the functions of the state as the source of politics.

NOTES

[1] For a full, critical treatment, see my "American Business, Public Policy, Case Studies and Political Theory," *World Politics* 16, (July 1964), pp. 677-715, and the essays of Dahl and others cited there.

[2] Walter Lippmann, *The Public Philosophy* (Boston: Little, Brown and Company, 1955).

[3] E. E. Schattschneider, *Politics, Pressures and the Tariff* (New York: Prentice-Hall, 1935).

[4] Some of this can be found in Lowi, *op. cit.*, and in the excellent criticisms representatives of each school cast upon the others.

[5] The "transactional" approach offered by Raymond A. Bauer and associates in *American Business and Public Policy* (New York: Atherton Press, 1963), 460, does not recommend anything but rejection of Theory II, the "pressure-group model" as they call it. But more than that is implied, as with other communications approaches, such as Milbrath's in *The Washington Lobbyist* (Chicago: Rand McNally, 1963). Likewise for most who use the so-called decision-making approach, where single organizations are taken as systems. Cf. R. C. Snyder, *et al., Foreign Policy Decision-Making* (New York: The Free Press, 1962), pp. 86ff.

[6] Lowi, *op. cit.*, especially pp. 686ff., and also *Arenas of Power*, a book in progress.

[7] See my article cited above for a more detailed distinction between distribution and redistribution. Suffice it here to say this: In the long run, all governmental decisions either redistribute or threaten to redistribute resources. But in the short run some decisions can be made involving resources already on hand, e.g., public land, franchises, tariff privileges. In this case, the participants obviously bear a quite distinctive relation to one another.

[8] The distinction between bargaining and logrolling is a conventional one that is simply taken more seriously here than usual. Bargaining refers to relations among men bearing common or tangential interests in which each expects to give in somewhere in the expectation of net gain. A logrolling relation is not one born of tangential interest in which direct conflict and compromise are expected, but, on the contrary, is a relation among men who have absolutely nothing in common.

[9] I make such judgments frequently throughout the essay. In all instances the judgment is grounded in these assumptions: (1) that the United States has vital and legitimate interests abroad; (2) that the United States is acting rationally when it pursues these interests; and (3) that rational foreign policy is good foreign policy and irrational foreign policy is bad foreign policy. Since I will so often be critical of our establishment, my description of its attributes and patterns should be called a pathology rather than a physiology. However, this is more an issue of language than of science.

[10] C. Wright Mills, *The Power Elite* (New York: Oxford University Press, 1956), p. 283.

[11] In light of the earlier discussion, it is interesting to note the absence of a foreign policy variant of redistribution. This might be due to my incomplete coverage rather than to a datum about the system. Devaluation might be an example of a redistributive use of resources in foreign policy.

The American
Foreign Policy Making Process

WARNER E. SCHILLING

The key components of the foreign policy process, following closely the terminology and concepts of Gabriel Almond, can be broadly described as follows: an elite structure characterized by a large number of autonomous and competing groups; and a mass structure characterized by a small, informed stratum, attentive to elite discussion and conflict, and a much larger base normally ignorant of and indifferent to policy and policy-making.

The condition responsible for the competitive character of the elite structure is obvious; members of the policy elite normally differ and differ significantly about both the ends and the means of foreign policy. The autonomy of the elite structure is the result of the fact that power is both widely dispersed among the participants in the policy process and drawn from a variety of sources independent one from the other. The group character of elite politics reflects both of these circumstances. The diffusion of power means that various members of the policy elite must group together on the basis of some amalgam of interest if they are to have any prospect of seeing their individual preferences compete successfully against the goals and programs advanced by others. The absence of a single locus of power or a base from which it can be monopolized also means that policy, once formulated, must continue to depend upon the voluntary coordination of elite groups if it is to be effective.

It is this dependence of the elites, one upon the other, for both the formulation and the conduct of policy, and the absence of any single chain of command whereby their cooperation can be assured, that Roger Hilsman has highlighted with his description of the policy process as one of "conflict and consensus-building." For the would-be policy advocate must do more than contend with the opponents of his program; he must develop support for it throughout the relevant parts of the elite structure and, on occasion, the mass structure as well. If, by means of persuasion and judicious accommodation to

From "The Politics of National Defense: Fiscal 1950," in Warner E. Schilling, Paul Y. Hamond, and Glenn H. Snyder, *Strategy, Politics, and National Defense Budgets*, Columbia University Press, 1962, pp. 19-27. Reprinted by permission.

the interests of others, he is able to bring the weight of opinion to his cause, the resulting agreement will probably insure the adoption of his policy and its effective implementation. Failing such support, or lacking the political skills and prestige prerequisite for an opportunity to secure it, or confronted from the beginning by a wide and politically unassailable consensus to the contrary, the realistic policy advocate will turn his political energies to more promising issues. For however wise his idea and cogent his argument or extensive his personal influence, his will remain a voice in the policy wilderness.

The characteristics of elite structure and elite relations just outlined are general to all policy-making situations, although the number, size, and kind of elite groups necessary for the formulation and conduct of policy—and, therefore, the kind of consensus required—will, of course, vary greatly with the issues and circumstances involved. The policy process is by no means confined to the structure of government, and the policy elite includes a very large number of people who are not government officials. However, since the issues and circumstances with which this study will later be concerned involve mainly government elites and government structure, it will be useful to continue the development of the above concepts primarily in this context.

It is, to begin with, important to note that there are two basic causes for policy conflict among government elites and that these lead to two different kinds of groupings among them. Many of these conflicts simply reflect the diversity of opinion Americans are likely to hold, in the absence of sanctions to the contrary, regarding the state of the world and what America should do in it. The groups that coalesce in support of one or another of these views appear, for the most part, to cut across formal institutional and organizational lines (Congress, Executive, State, Defense).

In contrast, some policy conflicts are "institutionally grounded." These are differences that result from the peculiar responsibilities (with respect either to values or to skills) of various government institutions and organizations. Not sharing the same responsibilities (or, put the other way, not charged with the representation of the same values or skills), government organizations will necessarily bring divergent interests and approaches to common problems. When conflicts of this order occur, the lines of battle are more likely to conform to the boundaries of the organizations involved. These are also the more enduring of the two kinds of group conflict. Specific ideas about what to do in the world will change, and with them the ad hoc groupings that once espoused them. But divergent responsibilities are built into the structure of government. The allocation of responsibility may be changed, but the effect is usually to shift the location of battle rather than to bring it to an end.

Conflicts caused by divergent institutional interests and approaches are an integral part of the policy-making process. They are especially evident, as will be seen, in the budgeting process as it takes place among the "quasi-sovereign powers"—the departments, bureaus, and agencies—that make up the Executive branch of the government. The general character of conflict between such "powers" is in many respects comparable to the diplomatic struggle among contending nations. Each endeavors to isolate the other, to secure "allies" for itself, and to gain the favorable opinion of "neutrals"—activities of great importance given the dispersion of power among elite groups. Discussions between the contending parties are negotiatory rather than analytical in character. The object is to persuade the opponent that his position is unreasonable (either by arguments designed to show that it will not really serve his interest or by appeals to other interests alleged to be both common and more important), or, failing that, to search for grounds on which a satisfactory settlement can be made. This may take the form of a direct compromise on the issue concerned (where the incentive to accommodate stems from the desire to avoid the costs of even a winning fight) or of a bargain reached by bringing into negotiation another issue in dispute and thereby permitting each (provided they evaluate the two issued disproportionately) to give up something of less value than that which it receives. In inter-institutional as in international relations, however, not all negotiations terminate in settlements, and the course of conflict is therefore marked by the postponement of disputes and by truces as well as treaties.

There is, of course, a very important difference between the conflicts of nations and those of government organizations: the coercive options available to the latter do not include the infliction of death. As a result, although the elements of conflict and accommodation are present in both relationships, the basic orientation of the two is quite different. The diplomacy of nations is ever oriented to the prospect of war, and conflict is marked by a high propensity to arm and prepare for the worst. The negotiations of government elites, in contrast, are oriented to the prospect of agreement, and conflict is marked by a high propensity to search for a way of resolving it. In sum, the general pattern of these quasi-sovereign relations is marked by two dominant characteristics. Conflict most certainly is one. The other is the "strain toward agreement," the need to build a consensus that includes, as it were, one's enemies as well as one's friends.

The imperative to strive for agreement, to reach some sort of accommodation is a logical derivative of the condition noted earlier: the autonomy of the elite structure. Power is diffused among Executive organizations no less than among other elite groups. The dispersion of power means that the contending groups will need the support of each other, as well as that of allies and neutrals, in order to translate their goals into policy—if not today on this issue, then tomorrow on some other. The opportunities to compel this support are minimal. It must be given, and it is unlikely for long to be given for nothing. The major motive for accommodation is necessity; there are simply not very many occasions when the policy elites can afford the luxury of letting their conflicts terminate in "war." A secondary motive, but one not to be overlooked, is desire. Competing elites not only need to accommodate, they want to. They do have interests in common, and one is the desire not to see the nation without any policy at all on an issue of consequence. To be sure, there will be occasions when "no" policy seems preferable to "wrong" policy, but there will be others when what seems to be a pressing necessity for action will produce some scratch formula for accommodation that the parties would otherwise have dismissed as neither rational nor expedient.

The policy elites are drawn together, then, by the same conditions that permit them to fall apart: the fact that they are many in number and the fact that power is widely diffused among them. For those interested in the parallel with international relations, it should be noted that the same two conditions (many states, none of which has a hegemony of power) are responsible for the "strain toward equilibrium"—the effort to maintain the balance of power—in the conflict among nations. Equilibrium is thus the functional analogue of agreement. Here, too, dependence provides the motive, so long as the diversity of interests pursued by the nations making up the system makes plausible the expectation that today's ally may be tomorrow's enemy, and vice versa.

The existence of this "strain toward agreement" does not mean, of course, that the policy process puts Humpty Dumpty back together again There are conflicts, and they do persist. Accommodation does not always have the effect of resolution. The life expectancy of "treaties" among Executive agencies is probably no greater than it is for those made in international relations, and many accommodations are mere makeshifts made for the moment. Indeed, as Samuel Huntington has pointed out, in some instances the necessary minimum of voluntary coordination is secured only by an agreement to postpone the occasion for disagreement, that is, by postponing decision. In this case the strain toward agreement produces the facade, not the substance, of agreement. The conflict is put off, but so too is the policy problem at issue and the opportunity to reach a consensus as to what to do about it.

This last point is a proper introduction to the question of the relationship between the characteristics of the policy-making process and the form of the policy produced by that process. American foreign policy is, in fact, subject to a variety of symptoms as a result of the way in which it is made. The symptoms that make up this "policy syndrome" derive, in one way or another, from the autonomous and competing character of the policy elites and the resultant necessity for voluntary coordination among them.

Most of the consequences of such an elite structure have been well marked by Almond. There is, to begin with, the clear possibility that the policy elites may produce "no policy at all." Their conflict can result in pure stalemate. Equally obvious are the possibilities for "compromised policy," where alternatives may be so watered by accommodation that the direction of choice is hardly evident; "unstable policy," where changes in the ad hoc groupings of elites point policy first in one and then in another direction; and "contradictory policy," where the quasi-sovereign power and responsibility of government institutions and organizations permit them independently to follow different policies.

Additional symptoms derive from the need to achieve a consensus for the support of policy, especially if the consensus has to be a wide one. Here there is the possibility of "paper policy," the case where policy has been duly and officially promulgated, but the support necessary for effective implementation by all concerned is simply nonexistent. Where policy problems happen to be new or technical in nature, those members of the elite perceptive and informed enough to recognize them may find it difficult if not impossible to secure this recognition from others, much less build a consensus for action. The result is what they at least would characterize as "blind policy "

Other symptoms mark the style of the policy process itself. It is "slow." Competition and consensus-building cannot take place overnight, and the delay between the recognition of a problem and the development of a policy for it may sometimes take longer than the exigencies of the situation seem to warrant or, in fact, permit. The policy process also has a tendency to be "leaderless." The diffusion of power and responsibility places the initiative everywhere with the result that it is sometimes exercised nowhere; the elites assume a "radar approach" to policy-making, each watching and waiting upon the other. The absence of a single source for coordination may also permit the process of accommodation to produce such a composite of everyone's interests that the rationale of the final result will not be apparent to anyone. A third stylistic symptom is the tendency of the policy process to be "indecisive." As previously noted, the desire to avert conflict may easily take the form of avoiding choice.

Finally, as William Fox has observed, the policy process exercises a "gyroscopic" effect on policy. Policies once set in motion tend to go on and on, without much regard, at times, for changes in the circumstances that first occasioned them. In part this is related to the need for agreement; the best way to maintain a consensus is not to disturb it. It also reflects the fact that the time and energy of the policy elites are limited. Most policy problems are very difficult; so, too, is the process of reaching an agreement on what to do about them. The combination of the two difficulties can easily lead the policy elites, once they have thought and fought their way through to an operational consensus, to adopt an attitude of leaving well enough alone. And so they do until some drastic change occurs in their environment which sharply and dramatically challenges the wisdom and feasibility of the previous course of action. The policy consequence is "outmoded policy," and the stylistic consequence is "crisis-oriented" diplomacy.

The tendency of policy change to wait on crises is reinforced whenever the required consensus necessitates the participation of the general public. Being, as noted, normally ignorant of and indifferent to policy events, the masses can be spurred to action (that is, to part with their blood, treasure, or votes) only when the elites confront them with what seem to be the gravest of problems. But once aroused, since the public's response is emotional rather than intellectual in content, its participation may produce such policy symptoms as "over-reaction" (more apprehension or belligerence than the elites may find appropriate) and "short-reaction" (where the public sense of crisis disappears before the problem is actually resolved).

2

AMERICAN SOCIETY
AND
FOREIGN POLICY

Important actors in foreign policy making are not to be found only within the federal government. The selections in this section describe the role played by nongovernmental groups in the policy formation process.

Kenneth Waltz describes the impact of public opinion, especially as it manifests itself in elections, upon policy making, and concludes that elite and mass opinion have been in substantial agreement. Like other writers on the subject, Waltz argues that the stance of the President is a key factor in determining the direction of public opinion on foreign policy.

This volume contains two selections relating to the role of the press in foreign policy formulation, but none on the role of the electronic media. This is not because we believe that the electronic media, especially television, are unimportant compared to the press, but rather because no worthwhile studies have been done on the political impact of these "newcomers." Douglass Cater, a Washington reporter and former staff assistant to President Johnson, details the ways in which the foreign policy reporter tries to break the administration's monopoly of information relating to foreign policy. Bernard C. Cohen probes the norms of the foreign policy reporter, and analyzes the way in which these norms determine the reporter's coverage of a foreign policy news event.

In a second article, Cohen argues that interest groups have much less impact on foreign policy making than they do on domestic policy making. It should be noted, however, that Cohen's data base is relatively small, so that the last word is not yet in on the subject.

G. William Domhoff contends that postwar American foreign policy making has been dominated by an economic elite. While no rebuttal of Domhoff's piece has yet appeared, it should be noted that his position is controversial. Paul

Hammond, for example, in his *Organizing for Defense*, argues that Eberstadt was not nearly so important a figure in the passage of the National Security Act as Domhoff's argument would have us believe. In the next article, Gabriel Kolko provides data on the socio-economic background of top government officials in foreign policy agencies and contends that the use of such data, in isolation, misleads those who wish to understand the nature of foreign policy decision making.

An unparalleled phenomenon in the postwar period has been the rise to power of the expert. Whether he be physical scientist or specialist in some other area of human knowledge, the expert now occupies key posts throughout the American government. A run-down of university professors who recently occupied key foreign policy making posts in the United States would include Henry A. Kissinger, Zbigniew Brzezinski, Walt W. Rostow, and Roger Hilsman. In his essay, Chadwick F. Alger contends that these "external bureaucrats" make for a more "pluralistic" policy making process. A similar case has been made by Bruce L. R. Smith in his study of the RAND Corporation. In an article excerpted here, Phillip Green, however, argues that Smith's analysis is misleading, in that "think tanks" like RAND do not question the basic premises of U.S. foreign policy.

Opinion and Crisis
in American Foreign Policy

KENNETH N. WALTZ

ELECTORAL PUNISHMENT AND INTERNATIONAL CRISES

Democracies have often been thought defective not only in their ability to sustain costly military establishments in time of peace but also in their ability to move with speed and finesse in response to the shifting currents of international affairs. May one not say of the years since World War II that the close concern of the American people with problems of foreign policy has made it difficult for their government to conduct an international policy of feint and maneuver? Is it not likely that the more people care about foreign policy the more closely their opinions will limit the government? Such an effect has not been noticeable, partly because the concern of the public has outpaced its knowledge.

An international event ordinarily does not disturb the nation unless it has first obsessed the government. In the face of such an event, the people rally behind their chief executive, as one would expect them to do in any cohesive country. William Gladstone long ago commented in a letter to the Duke of Argyll that if the justification for the continuation of the Crimean War by England was that the people approved of the war and supported it, then such justification could be given for any war that England ever waged within eighteen months of its commencement. A comparable statement, adjusted for the speed with which events are now publicly registered, can be made of America's reaction to crises. Franklin Roosevelt's popularity fluctuated in accordance with the recurrence of crises in Europe. The outbreak of fighting in Korea gave a lift to President Truman's low standing with the public. In June of 1950, immediately before the attack, 37 percent of those polled approved of the way Truman was doing his job, while 45 percent did not. In July of 1950, the corresponding figures were 46 percent and 37 percent. The invasion of Egypt by Britain and France, coming late in the American electoral campaign of 1956, apparently added a little to Eisenhower's wide margin of victory. A year and a half later, in April of 1958,

From Kenneth Waltz, *Foreign Policy and Democratic Politics,* pp. 274-75, 286-97.

47

the deepening of an economic recession, following upon Russia's lofting her first Sputnik, drove Eisenhower's popularity down to 49 percent, which for him was a low point. The following summer, a *contretemps* in Lebanon, which led the President to send American troops, boosted him to his 1958 high of 58 percent. The Cuban missile crisis of October, 1962, worked similar wonders for Kennedy. In April of that year, 77 percent had approved of the way he was handling "his job as President." A gradual decline then set in, to 73 percent in May following April's crisis in steel, to 71 percent in June following a slump in the stock market, to 67 percent in September after federal troops were sent to Mississippi, and to 61 percent before the confrontation with Russia in October. In December, however, 74 percent expressed themselves as satisfied with the President's performance in office.

The first effect of an international crisis is to increase the President's popular standing. One may wonder if this is so only when the response of the President is firm or when he otherwise gives the impression of being able to deal with the situation effectively and without inconvenience to the public. It is in fact not necessary to add such qualifications to the statement that so far as the public is concerned the President in a moment of crisis has the widest freedom of action. President Kennedy, facing threats to Berlin, sent additional troops to Europe and in the summer of 1961 called up 150,000 reservists, an act usually thought to be politically dangerous. The political costs, on balance, were nil. Several months earlier, the United States had unofficially sponsored an invasion of Cuba at the Bay of Pigs. In the wake of the ill-fated attempt, President Kennedy's popular standing reached its highest point ever, 83 percent, as compared with an average of 70 percent during his thirty-four months in office.

*   *   *

GOVERNMENTAL FREEDOM OF ACTION

The chances that a President will be unable to carry out a controversial policy are slight, nor is it at all likely that he will be dissuaded from pursuing a difficult and possibly unpopular line of policy by the fear that he and his party will thereby be electorally punished. Parties and Presidents must care about losing a little of their popularity on one issue or another if democratic government is to be responsive to the wishes and worries of the people. At the same time, in politics as in all human affairs, there are situations in which one is damned if he does and damned if he does not. No man and no party can govern without accepting this truth. If the United States disengages in Southeast Asia and North Vietnam sweeps to the tip of the Camau peninsula, the President in power and the party that he leads will be found to be at fault. But they will also be found at fault if the scale of American involvement is increased in order to hold what remains of the peninsula or to regain lost ground. In the most difficult matters, and international crises are certainly among them, there is no single policy whose widespread popularity would survive the test of action. If the world is a mess and the United States must act in it, then Presidents will often be in a position of deciding which of several unpopular policies they will follow. They will have no chance to pick a policy that will lose them no votes at all. If timidity and quiescence were truly and clearly more popular than boldness and action, then one would rightly worry that democratic countries would always fall prey to the aggressive thrusts of others. If belligerence were always more admired, then one would live teetering on the brink of nuclear war. If either condition prevailed, Presidents would always experience pressure to act in one way whether or not it was appropriate to the situation at hand.

Brzezinski and Huntington suggested that a President steadily losing public support may find himself boxed in, as to a considerable extent Truman did. After months of costly and inconclusive fighting, withdrawal would have been humiliating, and to threaten the use of unlimited means in order to achieve a limited end, as Eisenhower and Dulles did later, would have failed of acceptance at home and lacked credibility abroad. The box, however, was not built by "mass demands for quick victories and simple solutions." ... [N] o such demands were made. Nevertheless, as the war dragged on, impatience grew, and the country lost confidence in the competence of the government. [Some writers] thereupon concluded that the constraints of political competition severely limit America's contrivance and conduct of policy. Since World War II, foreign policy has usually been the most prominent of issues, but its electoral effect has nevertheless been diluted by juxtaposition with other problems and policies when voters made their decisions. One who bases his vote in part on performance in office must also ask himself how the competing candidate and party are likely to do. Numerous surveys have indicated that both parties are looked upon as competent to manage foreign policy. Furthermore, most people continue to vote in the present as they have voted in the past, whether or not the policies and programs of their preferred party have pleased them. When such countervailing factors are borne in mind, the fear that electoral punishment will dramatically affect foreign policy loses most of its force. International affairs have gone badly while Presidents of both parties were in power. Neither party has suffered any very deep political damage as a result.

The competition of two parties for the people's favor is sometimes said to lead both of them to espouse policies and programs that they know to be bad. In contrast, George M. Trevelyan, giving the Romanes Lecture in the Sheldonian Theatre at Oxford forty years ago, strongly argued that the principal virtue of a two-party system is that where one party is weak, the other may be strong; where one party has failed, the other may succeed. "No one party," he asserted, "can cover all the ground." The party that reacted correctly to the French Revolutionary and Napoleonic Wars could scarcely have approached the questions of Parliamentary reform with a proper attitude, "so powerful in the political mind is the instinct to associate ideas not logically connected with one another." If Fox and Grey in the 1790's had joined Pitt in opposition to the

Jacobins, Trevelyan averred, there would have been no Whig reform bill in 1830. In much the same way, it may well have appeared that the Democratic Administration, having begun the Korean War, was unable to end it either by military victory or diplomatic settlement. It is strange then that the Republican victory of 1952 has so often been described, in relation to the problem of limited war, as an indication of democracy's weakness rather than as a demonstration of its strength. "Weakness" would be an apt term only where the demise of the administration meant the loss of its policy, even though conditions had not changed sufficiently to make a policy of different intent appropriate to the national situation. "Weakness" would also apply if the political system provided no routine way of discarding a leader or ruling group when its policy, once popular, had taken on a sickly hue and when the people had lost confidence in the integrity and competence of the administration's leading members. Democracies permit a change of persons and parties to be easily and gracefully made. Because they do, policies that remain necessary though they have become unpopular can often more easily be continued. The situation found in a monarchy only upon the death of a king is the recurring condition of a democratic state. In the relation of crown prince to king, it was frequently thought by the people that the son would be saner and sounder and generally more pleasing than his father. In democratic countries, such a situation may be repeated every four or five years. It can then be said, and usually is by members of the opposition party, that the government has done everything wrong and that they, if elected, will do much the same things and, of course, do them much better.

One difficulty with Trevelyan's statement would seem to be this: it might just as plausibly be said that the constructive policies of one party may be lost later when a party of contradictory tendencies gains office or that the weakness and confusion of one party will be reinforced by the uncertainty and stupidity of the other. The mutual reinforcement of the virtues of parties for the benefit of the state depends upon their policy positions being sensible and upon their being separated only by a harmonious third rather than by an entire octave or some dissonant interval. When such is the situation of parties, their alternation can be the glory of democracy. The election of 1952 is a case in point. The Republicans stood for a policy of liberation, which was the administration's aspiration in North Korea and which was, in reference to Poland, the promise of any politician who happened to be speaking in Buffalo, Hamtramck, or Chicago. The responsible leaders of both parties and the vast majority of people in general wished to stand firm against the Soviet Union and Communist China, to set somebody free if that would not be too dangerous, and to avoid fighting and dying if that were at all possible. The Republican Party won the election on a platform that was different from the Democratic platform mainly in tone and in emphasis.

The American government had apparently decided before the event that it would not meet force with force in Korea. But it did. Numerous statements by Eisenhower, Dulles, and others indicated that in Indochina in the spring of 1954 the United States would fight or somehow retaliate if the Communists contined to drive forward. But this time, it did not do so. In neither case can it be said that fear of the people's opinion or of domestic political consequences noticeably affected the final decision. Nor had weariness with the war in Korea persuaded the public that giving way in other parts of the world would be preferable to fighting. Asked in May and September of 1953 and again in April of 1954 whether the American air force should be used if necessary to prevent the Communists from taking over all of Indochina, from 52 to 60 percent agreed that it should. In all three polls, a larger percentage still, that is from 59 to 65 percent, favored sending American troops, with always about a third of the sample opposed to either alternative. For the next decade, as economic and military commitments grew, American policies in Indochina were viewed with a mixture of mild disinterest, mature skepticism, and judicial calm, with never an inclination to force the government's hand. Following the naval incidents of Tonkin Bay early in August of 1964, President Johnson proposed and the Congress overwhelmingly accepted a resolution that practically gave the President a free hand in Southeast Asia (Public Law 88-408). In February of 1965, the American bombing of North Vietnam began. In March of that year, 27,000 American troops were serving in Vietnam; in June, 54,000; in September, 128,500; by May of 1966, more than 250,000. Against the background of these events and in the presence of continued political unrest in South Vietnam, Americans, in their answers to pollsters, revealed themselves as being reluctantly willing to fight, amenable to settlement, anxious to negotiate, and, though obviously wary, worried, and confused, willing to give the President wide latitude.

Such a pattern of opinion persisted, even as the scale of American involvement increased and the toll of American lives rose. In the late spring of 1964, for example, of the 74 percent who then knew of the fighting in Vietnam, 53 percent opposed and 28 percent favored "the United States getting out of the Viet Nam war completely." At the same time, 46 percent favored trying for some such "compromise agreement with Communist China" as "making all Viet Nam neutral," with 29 percent against doing so. In January of 1965, the respondents of the Gallup Poll affirmed by a margin of four to one their belief that the Vietcong were defeating the South Vietnamese, and by a margin of two to one their opinion that the latter would not be able to form a stable government. Still, by a margin of almost two to one they subscribed to the statement that the United States was right to have become militarily involved. At the same time, 81 percent expressed themselves in favor of President Johnson's calling an international conference with Chinese and Southeast Asian leaders to see if a peace agreement could be arranged, while only 11 percent dissented. In February and March of 1966, a group of behavioral scientists, most of them located at Stanford University, sponsored a survey to find what the deeper attitudes were. Though the questioning, conducted by the National Opinion Research Center, was more detailed, the attitudes uncovered were much the same as those previously reported. For example, 52 percent would favor "a new government in which the Vietcong took some part," 36 percent would not. Offered three choices, 49 percent said they would continue to do in Vietnam as their government was then doing, 23 percent would prefer to fight a major war, and 19 percent would simply withdraw. Some 60 percent would fight a major war if the only alternative to it were withdrawal of American troops. At the same time, 88 percent favored "negotiations with the Vietcong if they were willing to negotiate," while 8 percent opposed them. In general, President Johnson's actions in Vietnam were endorsed by 61 percent and disapproved of by 29 percent, while 10 percent expressed no opinion.

What thoughts lay behind the answers? Did the public perhaps entertain such notions as these—that delaying actions at low cost are worth mounting, that it is well to demonstrate that nothing is free for the taking, but that, all things considered, the time to leave had arrived if leaving could be gracefully arranged? While it is too much to attribute such intricacy, clarity, and precision of thought to the public mind, the state of the people's opinion permitted the President to fashion such an interpretation of America's position should he have wished to. It could not at any rate be said that public opinion constituted a pressing limit upon Presidential action, nor did the warning of the Korean experience lead the government to avoid military involvement. As difficulties in Vietnam multiply, criticism of the government will grow. Indeed, by the spring of 1966, disenchantment had begun to set in. In fairly steady progression, those approving of the way "Mr. Johnson is handling his job as President" declined from 69 percent of those asked in July of 1965 to 66 percent in early November and to 58 percent in March of 1966. If the public standing and moral authority of the administration should gravely weaken, it will be time for a change, whether or not blame has been justly accorded. Obviously President Johnson has been keenly aware of the domestic political risks he was running. To have changed policies because of electoral fears for the future would not have been honorable. Examination of public opinion in periods of crisis has led us to the conclusion that it would not have been practical either. In their foreign policies, governments of all types have sometimes been fainthearted. One need not fear that pusillanimity is especially encouraged by the pressures of public opinion as it operates in the American democracy.

The fears born of the military and electoral struggles of the Korean era have faded. In the 1950's, it was fashionable to affirm that the American democracy would not sustain distant and indecisive military engagements firmly or long enough. In the 1960's it has become more common to suppose that the

American government is impervious to criticism and given too free a hand even during protracted periods of crisis. Both worries are important; each has in its day been exaggerated. Two dangers threaten especially. With multiplication internationally of the arenas of major contention, it will become more difficult to remember that American security interests require military engagement only where the adversary is of such strength that he is or may become a threat to the nation. Beyond that, though the margin of power that America enjoys over any other contender may be a source of comfort to her citizens, it may also worry the observer. Powerful nations have often abused their power to the detriment of themselves and of others. More than has been the case with any modern state, the restraint of the American nation must now be self-imposed. A nation as powerful as America may become impatient with the defensive pose it has struck and long maintained. Senator J. William Fulbright has detected in American foreign policy "signs of that fatal presumption, that overextension of power and mission, which brought ruin to ancient Athens, to Napoleonic France and to Nazi Germany." He has warned his country not to become "what it is not now and never has been, a seeker after unlimited power and empire." Is Senator Fulbright premature in his pessimism and unduly alarmed by the experience of war in Vietnam?

In the case of Vietnam, spokesmen for the administration have asserted the vital importance of showing that insurgencies are costly, damaging, and doomed to defeat; they have argued that China must be contained for a time as the Soviet Union was earlier. One may wonder if the assertion and the argument do not rest on an overestimation of Chinese capability, a failure to appreciate the penchant for independence of the Indochinese whatever the political orientation of their governments, and an overlooking of the possibility that any increase in Chinese strength would be more of a worry to the Soviet Union than to the United States. The questions involved are, however, difficult ones on which no light can be shed by demonstrations and little by public debates. Nonetheless, with international restraints pressing less closely, internal correctives become all the more important. The American government is well supplied with them. To critics such as Senators Mike Mansfield, J. William Fulbright, and Robert Kennedy, the administration pays the closest heed; for institutionally and politically their positions are strong. Fulbright's eloquent warnings are not misplaced. It is because of him and other powerful critics that the dangers of hubris are lessened.

One of the valuable qualities of the American political system is the persistence of effective criticism. Opposition to the President's foreign policy has most often since the war centered in the House of Representatives; on questions of foreign aid, for example, it lodged in the Appropriations Committee. In contrast, the Foreign Relations Committee, strong enough to influence the whole Senate, soon converted its members, even those once isolationist, to support of the country's new policies. That was the pattern until recently. In his first years of office, President Johnson showed an unusual ability to keep issues closed, to prevent arguments from occurring in publicly conspicuous places. From February of 1965 onward, from the time when American military forces were first committed to battle in Southeast Asia, however, Senator Fulbright reluctantly permitted his Committee to begin to oppose the President's policies—in Vietnam, with regard to China generally, and on matters of foreign aid. The function of opposing, like the task of providing leadership, sometimes migrates from one political institution to another.

CONCLUSION

There is no end to one's worries. One who is not busily worried about a possible absence of support for waging limited wars is liable instead to fear that the United States is politically prevented from acquiescing in defeat on those occasions when losing would be the least unhappy of all the unhappy choices. The American reaction to the Chinese Revolution after World War II supposedly illustrates one type of recurrent difficulty: an unwillingness to acquiesce in "necessary" defeats. Unwilling (and sometimes wisely so) to expend the manpower and materiel that a drive for victory would require, the government is also reluctant to say simply that the goal is not worth its price. One may then fear that the American people will be overly eager to fight, ever unwilling to compromise, and thus be able to press a government to rashly adventurous actions. Denis Brogan created a phrase that caught on when he attributed the McCarthyite hysteria of the early 1950's to America's "illusion of omnipotence," understandable in view of her history but unforgivable as the attitude of a country that stood as the leader of the "free world." Internal political criticism first focused on the "loss" of China, grew with Representative Nixon's dramatization of the charges against Alger Hiss, became still more widespread when McCarthy made his flamboyant charges in February of 1950 that there were 205 or 57 or whatever number of Communists in the State Department, and reached a crescendo in the years of the Korean struggle. The frenzied frustration and self-indulgent hysteria of the McCarthy-Korea years could be interpreted charitably as a momentary reaction, a relapse after the vigorous and wholly unaccustomed activities in international policies that the Truman Doctrine, the Marshall Plan, and the formation of NATO represented. They could also be seen as the awkward and erratic responses of a parvenu who did not know how to behave in the international arena. Finally, of course, they could be and sometimes were taken as demonstrations of the proposition that her political institutions and national character make America unfit for a leader's role in the world.

Are the American people hopelessly naïve and in their naïveté a danger to the world? Is America given to vacillation between the poles of international commitment and national withdrawal? Is the American political system incurable without institutional surgery? Taking America's policy toward China as a difficult last example will enable us to suggest answers to these questions and at the same time make summary comments on the present chapter.

Though opinion on the sensitive subject of China has often been contradictory, it has neither been rashly belligerent nor naïve about the causes of American difficulties. Early in 1954, for example, the Gallup Poll asked: "What, in your opinion, are the main reasons that China went Communist?" Seventy-three percent of those polled thought the reasons were to be found in the ignorance of the Chinese masses, the skill of the Communists, and the corruption of the Nationalist regime; 10 percent blamed American policy and traitorous action; 17 percent gave miscellaneous replies; and 23 percent did not know. Though multiple responses to the single question cloud the finding, it is nevertheless some evidence of maturity of political outlook that only 10 percent of the replies ascribed to American officials responsibility for events in China. Asked in April of 1955 whether we should "be friendly to Red China and try to win her away from Russia," or should "treat her as an enemy," 47 percent preferred the first alternative and 40 percent, the second. At the same time, 78 percent opposed China's admission to the United Nations and 65 percent were against trading with her. More recently, 53 percent of those who realize that China's government is Communist opposed her admission to the United Nations (31 percent were in favor); but 75 percent of the same sample would stay in the United Nations "if Communist China gets in," and only 5 percent would thereupon leave. While distaste for the Chinese Communist regime is deep and persistent, 62 percent oppose and only 10 percent favor "helping Nationalists to attack Communists."

If the American people in general are more sophisticated than is sometimes supposed, are they not still in their inclinations dangerously unsteady? Paul Ramsey has recently written that "perhaps because of the Calvinism gone to seed in the atmosphere, and the lack of any doctrine of the Two Realms in which a human destiny is played out, the American people are ill prepared for the self-discipline necessary for the limitation of warfare." His conclusion may once have been true, though not necessarily for the reasons he suggests. William C. Foster, a man of both business and political affairs, seems to have thought so. "We must," he once urged, "attempt to get away from the strange dichotomy with which we have traditionally viewed force, refusing to consider it except as a last resort, then approaching it in a crusading manner with a 'punish the bandit' view which has been prevalent in our recent conflicts." While the religious beliefs of the general public have not changed noticeably since the Cold War began, America's notions of the place of force in foreign policy have evolved as her expectations of an easy international life have dwindled. Samuel Lubell, who is not the most scientific of pollsters but who may be the most perceptive, has drawn a sharp distinction between the typical American reaction of 1952 and of 1962. He reports that in 1952 he found people saying, "I'm against this idea that we can go on trading hills in Korea indefinitely." In other words, they implied, it may be well to strike at the enemy with all the power at our command. Early in 1962, in contrast, he reported the prevalent fear as being that "if we throw a nuclear bomb at them we'll get it back in this country." With the feeling that "all-out war" has become "unthinkable," acceptance of the likelihood of small wars has grown, and so has the willingness to fight them. "It's just a little country," Lubell found some people saying, "but if we let the Reds walk off with it we will be lowered in the eyes of the world."

Ever since 1948, 80 percent or more of Americans polled have replied affirmatively to such questions about Berlin as this one: "Should we stay in Berlin even if doing so means war with Russia?" Should the audacity of the reply cause one to fear that the President may order shots to be fired so that by doing what the people seem to want he will look more like a leader? Or should one think of such responses as indicating a reluctant willingness to fight in situations of tremendous risk if the government should decide that other policies would be riskier still?

For several reasons, it is the latter question that merits an affirmative answer. (1) In an era of Cold War, the American people have not, despite what is frequently said, demanded either victory or withdrawal, though occasionally articulate minorities and a few highly placed public officials have done so. (2) Reluctance to retreat and willingness to fight in order to avoid having to do so are more the product of the international condition of bipolarity than of internally generated political pressures. People *and* Presidents, the public at large *and* the dominant elites have united in their belief that the United States must stand firm in the face of aggression abroad. (3) One must ask what it means to "stand firm." The actions and words of the President, more than of anyone else, will define for the public this difficult term. To put it crudely: defeats will be described as unimportant and compromises, as triumphs, if it is at all possible to do so. The Cuban confrontation in October of 1962 was said to be an American victory over Krushchev—he removed the Russian missiles. But Castro remained in power and a number of the Soviet Union's technicians remained in the country. Krushchev was able to retreat, which is said to demonstrate that dictators enjoy freedom from internal constraint. But the United States, it should also be noted, was able to settle for something less than the achievement of ends that had earlier been widely proclaimed.

*   *   *

The people react to what the President does, and some of them at least form an opinion of how well he does it. If a President says that we need not fight, as Eisenhower in effect did when the French were besieged at Dienbienphu, no spontaneous rush to the colors is likely. Willingness to fight should not be identified with eagerness to do so. Reluctance to give way should not be confused with a stubborn unwillingness to compromise. It would seem from the record that the mass of the American people have learned to live with danger, to tolerate ambiguity, to accept setbacks, and to understand that victory is sometimes impossible or that it can be gained only at a price the wise would refrain from paying.

The Unending Fight
Against Secrecy

DOUGLAS CATER, JR.

The battle over uncontrolled slippage of government secrets into print has been waged repeatedly in recent years. A junior official in the Department of Defense expressed the sense of frustration felt by some dealing in military secrecy: "At each day's end, I, along with many other officials of the Department of Defense, carefully lock my classified working papers in a safe that is in turn doublechecked by a colleague and triplechecked by a night security guard. More than once, I have come home to find the same kind of information I had just locked away detailed in my evening newspaper or a magazine."

Both of the postwar Presidents have joined in the complaint. President Truman once claimed that "ninety-five per cent of our secret information has been published by newspapers and slick magazines," and argued that newsmen should withhold some information even when it has been made available to them by authorized government sources. President Eisenhower, in 1955, told a press conference, "For some two years and three months I have been plagued by inexplicable undiscovered leaks in this Government." He said that "technical military secrets" of value to Russia had been made public. Secretary of Defense Charles E. Wilson estimated that this country was giving away military secrets to the Soviets that would be worth hundreds of millions of dollars if we could learn the same type from them.

*   *   *

A . . . contemporary horror story concerns an American engineer, untrained in intelligence methods, who decided to learn what he could about the U.S. guided missile program while waiting for government security clearance. By diligent reading in his public library, he compiled a forty-five-page report giving information on our arsenal of missiles—name, model designation, manufacturer, guidance system, method of propulsion, length, diameter, range, and altitudes. The report was so accurate that it was promptly classified.

*   *   *

For the Washington reporter there is a note of unreality about much of the outcry over security and secrecy. He feels that it fails to get at the heart of the matter—the method and the motivation for the leakage of secret information to the press. Comparatively little of the traffic is in classified documents. The stuff of the news is not composed of such documentation. The Alsop brothers, who have disclosed more than their share of secrets over the years, claim that neither one has read a classified document since 1947. "Furthermore, if anyone now made us a present of a classified document," they have testified, "we should reject it as firmly as we should reject a pot of poison."

How does the press acquire its secrets? The techniques of the "scoop" in this field are varied. First of all, the astute reporter learns a good deal by intuition. He reflects quietly on the processes that must be going on within the government in response to a given situation. . . .

The reporter follows his hunches, picks up a piece of the story here, another piece there. He plays one source off against another. Soon the pattern of a story—not necessarily the complete story—begins to emerge.

*   *   *

Part of the technique comes from a reporter's sense of timing—the calculation of the exact moment when pressure applied at a precise point in the government will yield results. The late Anthony Leviero, of the *New York Times*, revealed extraordinary talents in this. His exclusive story giving details of the Truman-MacArthur conference on Wake Island in 1951 was a case in point. Leviero has left a first-person description of how he got this story:

> It is not possible to tell all details of how the Wake Island story was obtained. It has to be done with some gobbledegook as to sources. On a rented television set on April 19, we watched and listened in the bureau office as MacArthur spoke before Congress. It soon became obvious that the speech would have a terrific impact and when it was over I said to Luther Huston that the country seemed to have forgotten that Truman and MacArthur had met at Wake and were supposed to have agreed on almost everything.
>
> I said I thought I ought to go after the Wake Island conference report. Huston told me to go ahead. (This disposes of the stories about a "plant," although I or any other Washington correspondent would gladly accept a planted authentic document.)
>
> I put in a call to source No. 1; he was out. Source No. 2 was in a conference, and that was also the story on source No. 3. I left a message in each instance and then it was a matter of waiting. The numbers have no

significance as to the importance of the sources; they merely indicate the order in which they were called . . .

All afternoon I monitored my telephone and if I went to the men's room I told the switchboard girl that if anybody called to keep him on the wire until I returned. No. 3 called back first, after 7 P.M. I put the proposition to him that perhaps now was the time to tell the story of the Wake conference. I said I would have to see the whole story and promised to use discretion in covering up my method of obtaining it.

No. 3 promised to see what he could do, as he had to go to higher authority. About an hour later No. 1 called. I told him the proposition I had made to No. 3 and asked his support if he saw fit. At 11 P.M., while still in the office doing a Sunday story, No. 3 called and I told him what I had told No. 1.

When I arrived at the office at 11 A.M. next morning I found an urgent message to call home. Having just moved into a house, I could only think that the boiler had exploded, or the roof caved in. But Mrs. Leviero said that No. 3 had called to say that I should call No. 2.

No. 2 told me to come to such-and-such place at noon. I filled two fountain pens and went. He put the source material before me in its original authenticated form. I horrified him by asking if I could use a typewriter. So I used the pens, using up one and part of the other in two hours of feverish scribbling. I had lunch and returned to the office, my arm still numb with writer's cramp.

A final word on the claims of discomfited rivals that this was an Administration "plant." Without conceding the story came from the White House, I can say that never in more than three years of covering the place did a member of the President's staff offer me a story. But I often scored by asking at the right time. I believe that at least a dozen reporters for rival newspapers, if they had figured out the prevailing mood of administration sources that day and made the right approach, could have had the story.

But the reporter's intuition and sense of timing are only one side of the business of transmitting the secrets of government. Leviero would never have got his story if a government official had not decided to provide him the information. What causes the leak? [William S. White] has written, "The leak or exclusive story is rarely an example of a reporter's persistence and skill. More often it is simply an evidence of the harassed necessity of some official to put a situation before the public with a spurious sense of drama in order to gain attention for it." On occasion, of course, human frailties—vanity, desire for vengeance or recognition—have led an official to disclose secrets that he ought not to have. But the primary cause for the almost constant revelation of behind-the-scenes episodes of government is the power struggle that goes on within the government itself or among the governments doing business in Washington.

*   *   *

The realistic analysis of the situation reveals just how futile the absolutist position . . . really is. Our system of government itself operates to nullify the "seamless web" of security. . . . Much as [some] might wish to make it so, the National Security Council does not constitute a single orderly channel through which the high policies of government must flow before decisions are made. Important decisions are constantly being made all along the line. Frequently policies depend for their life or death on the publicity that can insure the public support and the funds from Congress to make them operable. Conversely, vital policies can be killed without trial or verdict by the National Security Council simply because of failures of publicity.

This is the way our government works and will likely continue to work even in a time of national peril. The misguided official who attempts to clamp an iron-handed control on the flow of information is doomed to frustration. Congress, far from tightening the laws on secrecy, has been more disposed to investigate and expose excessive security imposed by the Executive departments.

*   *   *

A DISQUISITION ON LEAKING

In Washington it is always embarrassing when the lid blows off a story that was meant to be strictly "not for attribution." Like the small-town gambler who gets word from the police department that the heat is on, the reporter knows that for some unpredictable time there are going to be slim pickings in the vicinity. His job of reporting the news behind the news is going to be made a great deal more difficult.

For the government official, it is no less embarrassing. Not only have policies got caught and perhaps irredeemably mangled in the machinery of publicity; the official himself has been exposed in a practice which officialdom can never, never admit goes on. In all the literature of government, there is not one word on the technique of what has been variously called the "leak," or "cloaked news."

*   *   *

. . . Cloaked news has become an institutional practice in the conduct of modern government in Washington, part of the regular intercourse between government and the press. During periods of high tension when formal channels of communication such as the President's and the Secretary of State's press conferences are cut off, it often becomes the major means by which important news is transmitted. In the words of one newspaperman describing the time of the Middle East crisis in 1956, "During the most critical period in recent months, at a time when any word out of Washington was considered of international significance, what had developed, it appeared, was government by leak."

The leak in the form of selected news privately passed to a favored correspondent has an ancient history in Washington. . . .

But it was not until the Second World War that the background briefing became a systematic practice. Two of the highest military officers, General George C. Marshall and Admiral Ernest J. King, instituted it by confiding to selected journalists some of the most delicate secrets of a nation at war.

*   *   *

After the war, the practice of the background briefing expanded and flourished. Its main practitioners continued to be the veteran reporters from wartime Washington, but before long others were horning into the field. Some of the younger journalists went into competition by forming small quasi-social groups of their own for the purpose of dining and grilling the high and the mighty. Inclusion in the more intimate background sessions came to have prestige value in the journalists' caste system. Even the Press Association man, who earlier refused to consider a story without a solid quotable source, began to participate. Only such journalistic lone wolves as Drew Pearson and the Alsop brothers looked with disdain at these goings-on, preferring to gather their secrets by their own private contacts.

The ritual of these briefings is fairly uniform. On a specified evening, a dozen or so correspondents gather in one of the private dining rooms in the Metropolitan Club, or in a nearby downtown hotel. They are joined by the guest of honor, usually a high government official. It is not always clear who initiated the meeting. Usually, the official has graciously "responded" to a standing invitation to meet with the reporters. He may or may not wish to admit that he has something to disclose. Drinks are served and all sit down to dinner. Until this is completed, the conversation follows an aimless pattern. No one likes to appear eager. Then chairs are pushed back, the presiding correspondent raps on his glass, reminds his colleagues of the rules, and the session begins. Usually the official makes no formal remarks. He opens himself directly to questions from the correspondents. If he knows his business, he can always manage to steer things in the direction he wishes to move. Frequently, he does not openly admit that he is outlining a new government program or a drastic new approach to policy. He is merely "talking over" with the reporters some of the problems that confront him. He relies on them to have sense enough to grasp his meaning without having it spelled out for them. This studied casualness, at times, can breed misunderstanding and produce woeful consequences. The session sometimes goes on until quite late. Afterward, the chairman reminds everyone of the rules and each goes his separate way.

As the background briefings grew more frequent, the rules of the game also began to multiply and become more complex. Partly because the matters discussed at the conferences were not so delicate as during wartime, partly because the newsmen chafed at information purely for self-edification, there was an inevitable trend toward relaxing the strictures against publication. Now conferences may range from "deep" background to a variety of lighter hues, depending on the secretiveness of the informant. In the main, the so-called Lindley Rule, first developed by Ernest K. Lindley of *Newsweek*, governs the proceedings. It requires, as has been noted, what amounts to compulsory plagiarism. The journalist may use what he has learned, but strictly on his own authority. Sometimes there are variations permitting him to quote "informed circles" or "a high government spokesman."

Usually there is at least one day's moratorium on the news coming out of such background briefings. If the news is especially hot, it may be arranged that nothing will be printed until the informant gets out of town, so that he can establish a convenient alibi. But nothing is hard and fast about the arrangements. Misunderstandings are frequent, increasing in direct ratio to the importance of the news.

The postwar uses of the background session have been varied. It has been a means of alerting the press to the gravity of a situation being overlooked in the news. Dean Acheson, while still Undersecretary of State, called in a small group of reporters and gave them the "background" on current Soviet demands against the Turks. It helped focus world attention on a situation of indirect aggression that could have grown much worse if it had not been publicized.

The background conference is also used in the attempt to allay press alarm. A dubious instance of this occurred when George Kennan, Chairman of the Policy Planning Board of the State Department, held one at the time of President Truman's announcement of Russia's atomic explosion. Contrary to the facts, Kennan assured reporters that the timing of the Soviet feat did not come as a surprise to American policy planners. He was deliberately trying to play down the story in an effort to avert hysteria among the American people.

For the official, this use of cloaked news as an indirect instrument of persuasion offers many attractions. John Foster Dulles, a regular practitioner of the art, more than once applied it to secure concessions from an ally. Shortly before the London conferences to negotiate the Japanese treaty, Dulles informed reporters for "background purposes" that the treaty was in a grave crisis. The resulting publicity brought tremendous pressure on the British even before they had sat down at the conference table to make the concessions Dulles wanted. Ironically, the British used the same kind of pressure on Mr. Dulles and his colleagues during the 1953 financial and economic conferences in Washington by leaking to certain reporters the story that only the President's intervention had saved the talks.

Most frequently the leak is symptomatic of rivalry in the higher echelons of the government itself. Harold E. Stassen, once Special Assistant to the President on disarmament questions, would hold a background conference to discuss modifying U. S. proposals for arms control. Promptly Secretary of State Dulles would hold his own background conference to "clarify" the news coming out of the Stassen conference.

Mr. Dulles has had the same behind-the-scenes repudiation of his policies. On December 7, 1956, the Washington *Post and Times-Herald* carried the headline: NEW AID TO EUROPE STUDIED: GOVERNMENT MAY REVISE HUGE GIFTS TO ITS ALLIES. The story emanated from a Metropolitan Club dinner reporters held with the Secretary of State. Two days later, the newspapers carried stories sponsored by an anonymous spokesman in the Treasury Department irritatedly disputing the Dulles proposition. The Treasury Department zealously attempts to plug all leaks that have anything to do with the spending of money.

The leak is traditionally used as a method of promoting a new program prior to its formal unveiling before Congress. In Great Britain, where the Cabinet has a strong obligation to report initially to the House of Commons, such use of the press to launch legislative programs would be unthinkable. In Washington it is habitual. Prior to the announcement of the so-called "Eisenhower Doctrine" for the Middle East, Mr. Dulles engaged in three days of systematic leakage to the reporters on the details. By the third day, when congressional leaders were finally informed of the new proposal, one news dispatch noted that they "were cautious in their reaction . . . but the Administration's plan had been so widely publicized before the leaders reached the White House that . . . they can do little more than adopt the new policy as presented."

The often sorely pressed Washington official sees numerous advantages to this system. It gives him a semi-anonymous voice in the cavernous echo chambers of the nation's capital. The responsible official, by keeping members of the press informed, can engage in preventative action against the thousand and one stories that crop up from nowhere and do damage to sound policy. In addition, it permits greater flexibility in taking policy initiatives. Without risking either his or his department's reputation, the official has a chance to take a measure of public—and more immediately important—congressional opinion. If opinion is hostile, he can always fall back on what has been called "the technique of denying the truth without actually lying."

This technique works as follows: Secretary Dulles, in 1953, held a background conference in which he revealed to reporters that he had been doing some tentative thinking about a Korean boundary settlement along the line of the narrow waist of the peninsula. The stories that emerged provoked criticism on Capitol Hill, particularly from Senate Republican Leader William Knowland. Forthwith, there issued a White House denial, drafted by none other than Dulles himself, which stated that "the Administration has never reached any conclusion that a permanent division of Korea is desirable or feasible or consistent with the decisions of the United Nations."

The pertinent words of course were "conclusion" and "permanent." The White House statement was not, in fact, what it seemed—a clear repudiation of what Mr. Dulles told the reporters and what they wrote, perforce on their own authority, for their papers.

* * *

The responsible reporter and the official alike complain of some of the tendencies in reporting background news. Inevitably, it tends to harden the news and to give it a sound of finality that may not have been intended. Apparently Secretary Dulles was a victim of this when the stories coming out about the possible Korean boundary settlement were written with a flatness that he had not intended. Instead of gently floating a trial balloon, he discovered he had inadvertently launched a jet-propelled new policy. He felt obliged to shoot it down in self-defense.

The fault for this is not exclusively the reporter's. Because he cannot quote a source, he finds it almost impossible to convey in his story the subtle gradations of meaning that good reporting requires. The background briefing provides a field day for any colleague who prefers to present the news in stark, cataclysmic terms.

Inevitably, the case against cloaked news gets down to the fundamental concepts of reporting. What is the reporter's responsibility? Is he an intelligence agent for his paper and via it the American public? Or is he to be made a tool of the government's counterintelligence operations? Arthur M. Schlesinger, Jr., has posed the alternatives in fairly stark terms: "Washington newspapermen today hardly know whether to believe the Secretary of State, because they do not know if he is speaking to them as reporters or seeking to use them as instruments of psychological warfare . . . What is the responsibility of a newspaperman when he discovers that some rumored development of policy is really only a psychological warfare trick? Should he print the truth at the risk of wrecking the plans of the Secretary of State? Or should he suppress the truth, betray himself, and deceive the American people?"

In this, as in much that concerns reporting in Washington, the absolutist position has little relevancy to the reporter's workaday world. He cannot narrowly demarcate his sphere of operations. He is caught and intimately involved in the ceaseless battle of intelligence versus counterintelligence. He can remove himself from the battlefield only at the risk of negating his role as a reporter.

A more fruitful inquiry may be directed into the conditions that should be imposed on cloaked news as a technique of communication.

* * *

. . . In his eagerness to get at the inside news, even the good reporter frequently loses the keen discrimination he shows in his more open reporting. As William S. White has written, "Often reporters handle a leaked story with a solemn uncriticalness. The documents, or whatever, are ceremoniously produced for the public—which at times must scratch its head in perplexity as to what the devil they are all about. The motivation for the leak usually is not mentioned, although that may be the most significant part of the story."

*　　*　　*

This war of intelligence *versus* counterintelligence is likely to remain one of the perplexing phenomena of the Washington scene. Though limits may be imposed on its excesses, there is no possibility of ever declaring a permanent truce. The conditions that give rise to it are basic to the American system of government and the free condition of American society. For the reporter, few hard and fast rules can be laid down to serve him as a permanent code of conduct. Instead he must be governed in his daily work by sound and subtle judgments. It is one more measure of the creative role he has to play in the political life of Washington.

The Foreign Policy Reporter

BERNARD C. COHEN

The very notion of "the press" has different meanings to different people; it may be interpreted in a general way as including all of the media of mass communication, or it may be defined more specifically as the printed media. We have adopted the latter course here; this study is based very largely on the newspaper press. . . .

Newspapers as such are not the major subject of study here, however, but rather the people working for them who are responsible for gathering and interpreting foreign policy news in the United States. Given the small number of foreign policy specialists in the American press, there is no important sampling problem involved. Most of the newspapers in this country have no foreign affairs reporters on their staffs; they draw their foreign affairs news from the wire services or from the sources offered by a few of the newspapers with extensive foreign affairs coverage, like the *New York Times*. This is true even of those newspapers that maintain one- or two-man bureaus in Washington, because the job of such a bureau is to cover the full range of public policy as it is presumed to affect the readers of the paper in question; the chances for specialization in any one substantive area like foreign affairs are minimal. The number of American newspapers that maintain staff specialists in the foreign policy field, and that are known for their foreign affairs coverage, is very small indeed—less than two dozen.[1] About six men cover the State Department for each of the major American news agencies. The problem, then, was not so much how to sample these specialists as how to see as many as possible. Seventy interviews were held, with 62 different people, in two series of interviews; these were mostly with newspaper and news agency correspondents and editors, but there was also a scattering of radio, television, and news magazine reporters on the lists, as well as a few correspondents who had only a tangential responsibility for

Selections from Bernard C. Cohen, *The Press and Foreign Policy* (copyright © 1963 by Princeton University Press; Princeton Paperback, 1965). Reprinted by permission of Princeton University Press.

foreign policy. The first of these sets of interviews was undertaken in 1953-1954. . . . The second series was undertaken . . . between 1958 and 1960. . . .

The world of the foreign policy maker is more difficult to investigate than the world of the foreign affairs reporter, both because of problems of access and because there are so many more people involved. Our efforts here were to see as many people with obvious interests and official responsibilities in the foreign policy field as was possible in the time available. Over 150 interviews were held with persons in staff or policy positions throughout the Executive branch, and in the Congress, and also with former holders of these positions. These interviews, too, were conducted in two series, the first in 1953-1954, . . . and the second . . . in 1960. . . .

It is . . . in the description of the political environment and the suggestion of the policy alternatives that give the best promise of managing that environment, that we shall find the press playing such an important role in current thinking about foreign policy. This "map-making" function of the press is very easy to overlook, because the newspaper is so much a part of our everyday life, like the morning cup of coffee with which it is intimately associated. It is overlooked also because of a general tendency to regard the news as objective or factual and hence to think of the possible impact of the press largely in terms of editorial persuasions. . . .

This is to say, then, that the press is significantly more than a purveyor of information and opinion. It may not be successful much of the time in telling people what to think, but it is stunningly successful in telling its readers what to think *about*.

*   *   *

THE REPORTER AND HIS WORK

The web of interaction that connects the press, the policy maker, and the external environment is very closely woven; one has to cut into it somewhere, and we have chosen to begin by focusing on the press and on the way it gathers and produces foreign policy news. As a first step, we shall look at the foreign affairs reporter himself, being especially interested in how he views the processes of democratic foreign policy-making, and in the way he conceives the function of the press in those processes. We do this because it seems useful to preface our inquiry into what the foreign affairs correspondents *actually* do in the course of their work, with a statement of what they *believe* they are doing, or should be doing. Reporters in this field are keenly aware that there is a social significance to their work, even if they have a difficult time defining it precisely; their image of appropriate behavior may thus be taken as a guide—equally imprecise—to what they try to do in their daily reporting stint.

What is the reporter like who specializes in foreign affairs coverage? If the old image of the reporter as a heavy-drinking, hard-bitten cynic, interested only in sensational scoops, still persists in some realms, it has no place here. The foreign affairs specialist among Washington correspondents is a cosmopolitan among cosmopolitans, a man in gray flannel who ranks very high in the hierarchy of reporters. A close observer of the Washington press corps concludes that State Department reporters, along with Congressional reporters, are "the head groups among the Washington press."

The typical reporter is a college-educated man; though "college" sometimes means a school of journalism, courses in the social science curriculum are nevertheless common in his background. The significance of a college education to reporters in this field is apparent from the sensitivity on the matter of the few who did not attend college. This educational pattern is also found among Washington correspondents as a whole, as well as among American correspondents abroad. A study in the early 1960's reports that about 93 per cent of the Washington correspondents attended college and 81 per cent have college degrees; about 31 per cent did graduate work and nearly 20 per cent earned graduate degrees.[2] In the mid-1950's, a study of foreign correspondents reporting for American media in Western Europe revealed that 73 per cent of the Americans in this corps of correspondents had Bachelor's degrees, "slightly less" than 10 per cent had Master's degrees, and 2 per cent had Ph.D. degrees. Seventeen per cent had done graduate-level work while they were employed as correspondents. "A majority of today's foreign correspondents concentrated their college studies in the fields of political science, economics, history, or international relations. This concentration on the social sciences is even more pronounced in advanced degrees and graduate studies."[3]

The foreign affairs reporter in Washington is also a man of long experience in the field of international affairs. Only a few have been reporting foreign affairs for less than half a dozen years; the mean is closer to 15 or 20 years. And a few of the reporters, including some newcomers, have had governmental experience in the foreign affairs field, which adds to their specialization in the subject matter. In addition, almost all of these reporters have been foreign correspondents at some point in their careers, or have had significant foreign reporting experience while stationed in this country, or have lived or worked abroad extensively before they took up foreign affairs reporting. These patterns of education and career specialization reinforce the common description among these reporters that they are, as a group, intensely interested in the subject matter that they write about, and on the whole well-informed with respect to it. By most accounts, furthermore, the working reporter in the foreign affairs field in Washington is conscious of the potential impact of what he writes, and "he does not want to create any more trouble [in foreign policy] than already exists." Many foreign policy officials who deal directly with the press would define "trouble" differently, reflecting their own potful of difficulties, and thus they might not concur with the phrasing of this particular self-evaulation. Nevertheless, in terms of their manifest behavior, they obviously do trust the foreign affairs reporter to behave with substantial discretion as he moves with great freedom in a politically sensitive area. Even though the reporter and the official may not have the same perspective on the functions of the press in reporting foreign affairs, or agree on the nature of desirable policy, the freedom and the trust suggest the stature of the reporter in the political milieu in which he works. It should go without saying, of course, that there are deviations from this norm, and that individual reporters violate the rules of the game from time to time; but the very fact that "violations" can be observed, and described, and even accounted for reinforces the normative code of behavior for reporters who cover foreign affairs.

The Reporter's Conceptions of His Roles

A reporter of public affairs lives a bifurcated professional existence: he is a reporter of the passing scene, yet he is also a part of that scene, in ways that he does not always understand or accept.[4] This duality is evident in almost every phase of his work. He holds two sets of conceptions of the role that the press plays, or should play, in the foreign policy-making process—one set involving him only as a neutral reporter, providing information that enables others to play a part in the fashioning of policy; and another set that defines his active participation in the policy-making process. The first set of role conceptions relates the reporter chiefly toward the public participants in the process; while the second set relates him toward the official policy-making level. These two types of self-images will no doubt be familiar to most readers, since they are both enshrined in our political and constitutional history respecting the nature of the guarantees of a free press in the nascent American democracy.[5] What is significant here is that these two sets of conceptions are not equally reflected in the formal or overt ideology of the reporter (as distinct from that of the editor or the editorial page). The reporter's formal view of the over-all process of foreign policy-making stresses his role as recorder of the passing scene—as servant to the other participants—to the near-exclusion of his role as an active participant in his own right. As a result, his role as a participant more often than not gets "bootlegged" into the reporter's view of the process, accompanied by many of the disadvantages that attend on surreptitious indulgence. Like illicit liquor, the "bootlegged" role is found everywhere, and most reporters know it is there; but political, social, and ideological conventions make it inappropriate to bring it out into the open, where its properties and its impacts can be explicitly discussed and evaluated.

FORMAL VIEWS OF THE PROCESS. Each reporter has his own interpretation of the American foreign policy process, and he expresses that interpretation in an individual style. Yet there is a pattern that incorporates the views of most reporters. In this pattern, foreign policy originates in the Executive branch of government, somewhere in the White House, the Department of State, or the Department of Defense. From the Executive branch it moves to the press, or is picked up by the press, which has the task of reporting it to the public. After careful deliberation the public makes up its mind on the issues and communicates its preferences to the Congress. The Congress then is in a position to act on the issues, or to react to them by letting the Executive branch know what it thinks. The only significant variation in this pattern excludes the stage of public consideration; in this view the press reports directly to the Congress, which then is in a position to act or react as before. In each of these patterns, the press occupies the strategic center, from which it neutrally transmits the facts about foreign policy from one part of the political system to another.

Some reporters will expressly describe one or the other of these patterns in its entirety; others will describe only a segment, leaving the rest implicit. A few will express alternative conceptions of the process, which incorporate a more active role for the press. Several correspondents, for example, see the flow as moving from the Executive to the press, where there may be a side dialogue with the embassies, and then back to the Executive branch again. But the large majority of correspondents appear to be comfortable with one of the former descriptions of the foreign policy process, finding in it a congenial ideology of the press in American society.

The dominant view of the process, in addition to casting the press as a neutral transmission belt, so to speak, stresses the importance of the Executive branch over the Congress in the making of foreign policy. The Executive is the initiator of policy proposals, and the Congress reacts to them, taking into consideration public feelings as they may have been shaped by press coverage. There is additional evidence that the foreign affairs correspondents assign a special position to the Executive branch in this process. Despite the criticism that is directed toward particular individuals or offices in the State Department, and the general feeling that the State Department is "always pushing angles" or "selling something," these reporters will defend the Executive's position against an increase in the foreign relations power of Congress, like that contemplated in the Bricker Amendment in the mid-1950's, on the grounds that such a move would cripple American foreign policy.[6] Furthermore, despite his professional interest in storming the walls of secrecy that surround the operations of government, virtually every foreign affairs reporter acknowledges at least in an abstract way the need for secrecy in the conduct of international diplomacy and of national security matters. He is likely to point out that there are some important judgments to be made by the reporter about the relative priorities of secrecy as against the public's "need to know"; yet the Executive's right to conduct some of its operations in private, and to let the press and thus the rest of the political system in "after the event," is freely granted, both in principle and in practice.

*   *   *

The *modus operandi* of the foreign affairs reporter, the understandings and customary procedures that define how he gets the news, have a noticeable impact on the shape and content of the daily segment of reality that is served with breakfast and again at dinner in this country.

For one thing, the prevailing conceptions of news tend to attract and to focus the dispersed policy attentions of various foreign policy audiences at any particular time on some particular issues, alternatives, and even on modes of policy thinking, at the expense of others. When the correspondents themselves flock to the "big story," they are helping to create and maintain a hierarchy of importance that finally reaches the reader via the make-up of his newspaper. Where space is limited and the make-up of a paper communicates judgments about the relative importance of developments, the pursuit of the big story unavoidably muffles other phenomena; rich news items get richer, while poor ones, with less prominence or even no space at all, get forgotten. Furthermore, the fact that the big story is almost by definition a continuing one—anywhere from a few days to a number of months, as in the cases of Berlin and the Congo in 1958 and 1959—helps to secure its position at the forefront of attention for an extended period, again at the expense, at least temporarily, of things that are simmering in the foreign policy pot.

Whether this focusing of attention is to be regarded as desirable or undesirable, as positive or negative in its effects, depends on many things—on the particular choices of news in a particular context, on the particular foreign policy theories in the eye of the beholder, even on the foreign policy interests and activities of the beholder, and on the particular audience he has in mind. One could argue, for example, that heavy concentration on a few news items is undesirable precisely because it pushes other items out of the readers' sight and thus creates a "distorted" environment of articulate interest and opinion to which the policy official is obliged to respond. Or one can make a case that focusing the attention of the attentive public onto a few policy issues is better than not focusing it—that patterns of press behavior that structure public thinking and hence give some form and content to the elusive dialogue between government and governed are to be preferred to patterns (if one can imagine them) that impose little or no order on a very large range of possibilities. In particular circumstances, too, one can argue for or against the concentration of newspaper space on some items rather than on others, depending on the interests, preferences, and causal relationships that percolate in the mind of the critic. The point being made here is not that the narrowing of attention is inherently or necessarily undesirable, but rather that it is a reality, and that it has variable consequences that need to be spelled out and studied in detail before their significance can be assessed.

These attitudes and procedures of the press not only focus attention on selected parts of reality, but they do this in disconnected and unrelated ways, which perhaps raises more serious problems as far as foreign policy-making is concerned. Correspondents hover around the major foreign policy story like moths around the brightest light; and, like moths, they drift away when the light fades or is surpassed by another. A discerning official with many years of foreign policy experience in Washington observed that reporters "don't bother you unless there is something urgent going on." To follow the "big story" is to "stick with the news that comes to the top," and the outcome of this practice is a moving picture of the world that skips from crisis to crisis, each one in a different locale, with a different cast, a different script, and so on. This coverage might be charted not as a series of discrete jagged peaks and valleys but rather as a sequence of overlapping arcs, each one representing the rise and decline of press coverage of a particular story; as one story begins to wane, the arc of the next crisis begins to rise, and the lines cross. (It becomes a peak-and-valley chart, however, in the hands of those editors who print only the news at the top of each arc.) This pattern is partly due, also, to criteria of selection that emphasize the attractions of conflict and controversy; the correspondents are not only drawn to the "big story," but their predilection is to make the arenas of conflict and controversy the subject of these big stories. But quite apart from the particular news values in any particular conflict—quite apart even from the substantive content of the big stories—the very process of focusing attention on one problem area after another, seriatim, makes for discontinuities in the points of information that comprise one's picture of the foreign policy world. It is like a very slow radar scanner, or one that does not keep scanning the same area; the information it yields comes in so slowly and in such unrelated segments that a sense of the whole cannot be gleaned. Walter Lippmann used another analogy: "It is like the beam of a search light that moves restlessly about, bringing one episode and then another out of darkness into vision."[7] For those many people who depend substantially on the mass media for their basic and continuing picture of the international environment of foreign policy, even a careful reading of foreign policy news may convey an image of an endless succession of problems having little systematic relationship to each other or to some corpus of American values and American political choices. As Lippmann correctly noted, "Men cannot do the work of the world by this light alone."[8] But even though there may be other lights playing on foreign policy problems, this beam is one of the most powerful in the battery, and it impinges on foreign policy-making in ways that we shall have further occasion to explore.

The reporter feels a pressure to write about the biggest news, but he is equally compelled to say something different about it than others have said. "I try to pick a story that I can add some new things to." "What they were saying on Tuesday didn't advance things any, and all I could do was hash over old stuff, not adding anything, so I didn't write." The reaction story commends itself to the correspondent precisely because it allows him to add something new to the big story. But political reactions to political events do more than just "advance the story." They are themselves part of the interplay of politics and by leading or urging others to react publicly, or just by putting different points of view or fragments of ideas in juxtaposition perhaps for the first time, reporters are contributing new ingredients to the foreign policy stew, which in turn become the frame of reference for other reporters the following day. This process might be likened to a duel that is pressed on a pair of reluctant gallants by their eager seconds. It is commonly said that the press overstates the disagreements and understates the accommodations in international relations, by virtue of its special attraction to controversy. But quite apart from the news values involved in controversy as against agreement, the procedure of prying reactions out of officials in order to add something to the news itself adds to the impression that contention is the mainstay of all international political life.

The persistence of a big foreign policy story "at the top of the news" for some days at a time, embellished and extended by the reactions and the reactions-to-reactions of other policy makers, imposes on the uncertainties and approximations of these foreign policy actors an ordering of importance with respect to particular issues, and a necessity to respond to them, that may differ significantly from the priorities as they earlier presented themselves to the policy makers. Again, this process may be either negative or positive in its impact, depending on the same kinds of considerations that were discussed above; and here, too, the consequences merit further exploration.

Finally, the steady obeisance to what is incontrovertibly the news results in the pages of the press being filled with observable events that have already happened—that is, with the "past." By its own canons, the press does an unsystematic, haphazard job of stimulating or structuring discussion of ideas or possibilities in advance of issues, crises, or events. Diligent exploration of the political universe is regarded as part of the general background that the press provides; but it provides it generally either *after* the event, in the train of public interest, or when "things are dull" and the reporter is thereby free to use the story he has been working on but which is not in the news. But, as we noted earlier, this latter kind of exploration explicitly covers terrain that no one else is covering, so that the task of stimulating political foresight is performed in response to no uniform or explicit theory about what kinds of foresight may be either necessary or useful to particular individuals or groups.

It is relevant at this point to recall that democratic ideology argues the need for a free press on the grounds that the people have to be informed with respect to the decisions they will be called upon to make—a doctrine that the philosophers of the press have adopted as the preamble to their own constitution. The fact is, however, that the press itself violates this norm as a matter of course when it stresses what *has* happened at the expense of what *might* happen under varying contingencies, and when it discusses the future in haphazard, unsystematic ways.[9] Whatever else one may wish to say about how people make up their minds on foreign policy issues, it is still clear that more or less rational calculation in this area requires information about future possibilities as well as past certainties; it is also obvious that responsible political participation requires foreknowledge of the patterns and procedures of political choice. The press fails to provide these kinds of knowledge with the abundance or regularity that would make its contribution meaningful.[10] A few foreign affairs analysts in the press are aware of this problem, but they are a small minority and they too are caught up in the daily whirl of the press. Even James Reston, who has often expressed the responsibility of the press to break into the policy-making process before issues are already decided, is of two minds about the practical possibilities of doing this successfully for the average newspaper reader. On the one hand, as we have already seen, he has argued the need for more aggressive reporting during the drafting stages, making possible a timely debate on the policy issues involved. But he is also motivated by his belief that "A distracted people, busy with the fierce competitions of modern life, must be addressed while they are paying attention, which is usually at the moment of some great national or international event."[11] The discrepancy between these competing "truths," and also between the prevailing norms and prevailing practices, will compel us at a later point to reconsider our body of empirical and normative theory concerning this aspect of the role of the press in a democratic polity.

The attitudes and modes of procedure among leading foreign affairs correspondents that contribute to these effects are learned early and well—so well, indeed, that it is often said of an able reporter that he has an "instinctive" sense of news. But it should be clear that the attitudes and modes of procedure themselves are *not* instinctive, nor are they inevitable; they are the product of professional and social group norms. The reporter believes, in essence, that there is an independent flow of news that is beyond his reach—a condition of nearly perfect competition wherein he is unable to affect the market in news in any major way by his own individual choices or decisions. So his major effort is to "keep up with the news," or to "stay on top" of it, rather than to try to reshape it by exercising his independent judgment. But it is a curious sense of the order of things that denies the effects of individual decisions by particular correspondents. By denying his freedom to do as he likes in the face of the flow of the news, the reporter displays his sense of a lack of mastery; but he does not alter his individual share of responsibility for the end product. The few foreign affairs reporters and analysts who do follow their own stars stand apart from, and above, the rest of their colleagues, demonstrating not only that it is *possible* to make independent choices about what is worth writing, but that there is a large and important market that values their products. . . .

* * *

THE EYE OF THE BEHOLDER: POLICY MAKERS' VIEWS OF THE PRESS

An inquiry into the role of the press in foreign policy-making that examined only the behavior of the press would be one-sided, for it would miss the range of interactions that complete the circuit between press and policy maker. The "mirror" that the press holds up "by which its readers can see the world"[12] is not fashioned exclusively by the initiatives of the press, nor is it the product solely of the criteria of judgment that mark the news-gathering and editorial processes. Foreign affairs news comes out of an interplay between the correspondents and the men of responsibility whose thoughts and actions are the objects of the correspondents' interest. The figure of the mirror, indeed, is rather inappropriate on a number of accounts; the glass that the press holds up is refractive rather than reflective, and the beams that come out of it strike the policy makers as well as a larger public. The readers, in particular, include both the members of the press itself and those who dwell in the policy-making structure—that is to say, those who manage the prism are also managed by it. And so in our search for an understanding of the significance of the press in the foreign policy process, we must look at the uses to which the press is put by foreign policy officials, and the patterns of thought that shape those uses. The policy maker both contributes to and extracts from the fund, or the flow, of foreign policy news; and both the putting in and the taking out help to define the nature of the press's participation in the process of foreign policy-making.

A Guide to "The Press"

There were, by recent count, 1,761 daily and 546 Sunday newspapers in the United States;[13] obviously these are all part of the ill-defined, amorphous institution known as "the press." Equally apparent, however, is the fact that no one, not even a large extractive industry like the United States government, can assimilate or even be exposed to more than a small part of the institution. In previous chapters, when we referred to the press, we meant the sector of it that produced the bulk of the foreign policy news and analysis; and we were interested particularly in the correspondents who specialized in this subject. What does the foreign policy press look like to the officials in the Executive and Legislative branches of the American government who have foreign policy responsibilities? There are several layers in the foreign policy maker's image of the press.

THE "PRESTIGE PAPERS." It should occasion no great surprise to discover that foreign policy officials recognize that there is a small and specialized foreign affairs press in the United States; and that the single most important newspaper, by general admission, is the *New York Times* should also be a familiar datum. The *Times*, which regards itself as a newspaper of record, a daily contribution to history, is read by virtually everyone in the government who has an interest or a responsibility in foreign affairs. . . .

*   *   *

There can be no question that the *New York Times* is of prime importance; but it has distinguished company on the desks of foreign policy-making officials, very few of whom limit their consumption to one or even two newspapers: the *Washington Post,* the *New York Herald Tribune,* the *Wall Street Journal,* the *Christian Science Monitor,* the *Baltimore Sun,* the *Washington Evening Star.* Collectively these papers, with extensive foreign affairs coverage and in many cases independent sources of news via their own staffs of foreign correspondents and foreign affairs reporters and analysts, form the prestige press in the foreign policy field. Their relative importance varies, obviously, from individual to individual; but one can hardly avoid recognizing the significance, in Washington, of the *Washington Post* and to a slightly lesser extent (perhaps because it is an evening paper) the *Star.* . . .

* * *

To sum up, then, the prestige press is not a unique newspaper that policy makers depend on for their political intelligence; rather, it is a larger network of communication that helps to define for the policy maker the current political universe. Washington survives when, from time to time, the *New York Times* is not published; it may be sorely missed, but there are a half-dozen other papers that collectively fill the gap. (There may even be secret relief when the pressure to read, and respond to, the *New York Times* is temporarily lifted.) The larger network of communication is marginally, not centrally, affected.

* * *

THE NEWS AGENCIES. For most newspapers in the country, as we noted in a prior chapter, the flow of national and international news from the wire service tickers represents the well into which they must dip for their coverage of national and international affairs. Thus wire service coverage may be regarded as a vast, continuous, unedited newspaper—much more extensive in its coverage of foreign affairs than virtually all newspapers in the country, since no paper that relies on this source publishes all the information it produces. Moreover, not only do the wire service teletype machines define the outer limits of foreign affairs coverage for most newspapers and for many policy makers; they also may be regarded as "tomorrow's paper today," or "this afternoon's paper this morning." They give the news a number of hours before it can be obtained from ordinary newspaper sources.

For both of these reasons, the news tickers occupy a prominent place in the foreign policy makers' world. The State Department's News Office maintains Associated Press, United Press International, and Reuters news tickers; the *Agence France-Presse* ticker in the State Department is located, for language reasons, in the Bureau of European Affairs. And there are also several tickers in the suites of the Secretary and Under Secretary. The machines in the News Office are monitored constantly; eight copies come off each ticker, and additional copies are often duplicated in order to distribute the news items to all the relevant areas in the Department. The News Office rates the tickers as very important; "in fast-breaking situations, the tickers beat [State Department] cables by four or five hours—and in some cases by up to twenty-four hours." . . .

* * *

The same general pattern prevails in the Department of Defense also, where the News Division has the AP and the UPI wires. These teletype machines are also monitored steadily, with eight copies being printed and clipped; and "the relevant clippings" are sent to "the interested people" in the Department. And as in the State Department, officials in the Department of Defense acknowledge that they "often see things first on the ticker."

In the Legislative branch the situation is not very different. There are AP and UPI tickers in the lobbies off the Senate and House floors, and they run just as long as anyone is around to read them. Page boys cut the sheets and hang them up, numbered consecutively, where they are read continuously whenever the Houses are in session. A member of one of the foreign affairs committees said, "The tickers are used steadily; this is the first source of information—many hours before we read it in the press."[14]

Considering the attention that men of top political and governmental rank pay to the wire services, one must include these services as part of the larger "prestige press." Each of them has its own staff of correspondents all over the world. Thus, each news agency represents an independent source of news about world affairs, more extensive in coverage and more rapid in impact than the best of the "prestige" newspapers, which maintain their own staffs of correspondents abroad and in Washington. The political importance of wire service news is additionally—though indirectly—heightened by the Washington newspapers, which rely very heavily on the news agencies for their international news.

THE "PRESS" AS PEOPLE. Foreign policy-making officials also see "the press" as the output of particular reporters and columnists whom they respect or whom they believe to be influential in the political community even if they themselves do not think very highly of them. There is very widespread agreement on who these able and influential individuals are: Walter Lippmann, Joseph Alsop, Marquis Childs, James Reston, C. L. Sulzberger, Hanson Baldwin, Chalmers Roberts, and John Hightower are mentioned most frequently. And all of them, it might be noted, appear in the newspapers that make up the foreign policy "prestige press." These men are put in a somewhat special class; their columns or stories are a kind of personal communication rather than the output of an impersonal communication system. One person with experience in both the Executive and Legislative branches remarked, "I look for by-lines as well as subject matter." The following comments are illustrative of the predominant attitudes toward these men as representatives of the press. A Senate staff man: "A man like Reston must be considered as a statesman."[15] From the State Department: "There are too few Lippmanns in the world"; and "You count on your Lippmanns, your Childs, your Restons, etc., your better columnists, to carry the straight story, without attribution." There are, to be sure, less exalted expressions of respect toward these same men, and even some strong dissents from the very attitude expressed here; some people in the State Department, for example, pointed out that Lippmann does not make the correspondent's customary rounds in the Department and remarked that, if he did, he would not make so many "silly statements" in his columns. One went so far as to say, "Generally all columnists are pretty terrible." But on the whole this "inner circle" of foreign affairs reporters and columnists is esteemed for the excellence of its contacts, and for its intelligent, insightful, and responsible use of information delicately and privately given. In a spiral of cause and effect, the doors of high-level policy officials open more easily for them; and when the policy makers evaluate a columnist as responsible and intelligent in their *own* dealings with him, they will more readily respect the rest of his writings as similarly authoritative, intelligent, and responsible.

NOTES

[1]Cf. Theodore E. Kruglak's estimate, in 1955, that only 16 newspapers maintained full-time correspondents in all of Western Europe. (*The Foreign Correspondents: A Study of the Men and Women Reporting for the American Information Media in Western Europe*, Geneva: Librairie E. Droz, 1955, p. 72.)

[2]William L. Rivers, "The Correspondents After Twenty-Five Years," *Columbia Journalism Review* I, No. 1, Spring 1962, p. 6. Cf. also William L. Rivers, "The Washington Correspondents and Government Information."

[3]Kruglak, *op. cit.*, pp. 48-49.

[4]Cf. Douglass Cater, *The Fourth Branch of Government* (Boston: Houghton Mifflin, 1959), p. 7.

[5]Cf. Bernard A. Weisberger, *The American Newspaperman*, (Chicago: University of Chicago Press, 1961).

[6]Cf. also the statements by Alexander F. Jones, editor of the *Syracuse Herald-Journal*, at the 1960 meetings of the American Society of Newspaper Editors: "My interest is in having better reporting and better newspaper stories, particularly so that the President of the United States will have a chance to make his views known." (*Problems of Journalism*, Proceedings of the American Society of Newspaper Editors, 1960, p. 219.)

[7]Walter Lippmann, *Public Opinion*, p. 275.

[8]*Ibid.*

[9]The norm is also violated when reporters adopt commercial criteria of news selection that work on the emotions sooner than the intellect. The kind of news that results from the application of these criteria—conflict, drama, personalities, etc.—skews the cognitive perceptions of the foreign policy world in the direction of simplistic, personalized, and polarized constructions. Their contribution to either the art or the science of policy appraisal is negligible.

[10]Cf., in this connection, Lewis A. Dexter's remarks on political communication to Congressmen: "Congressman Amiable says, commenting on his wide experience in a state legislature and in Congress, 'You always hear from business too late.' And this is true *in general* because businessmen and their representatives respond to the news. . . ." ("What Do Congressmen Hear: The Mail," *Public Opinion Quarterly* XX, No. 1, Spring 1956, p. 26; emphasis in original.)

[11]Quoted in Joseph Kraft, *Esquire*, November 1958, p. 125.

[12]V. O. Key, Jr., *Public Opinion and American Democracy*, p. 390.

[13]Edward W. Barrett and Penn T. Kimball, "The Role of the Press and Communications," in American Assembly, *The United States and Latin America*, p. 96; since there are frequent changes and combinations in the newspaper business, and different definitions of what constitutes a newspaper, any such figures must be regarded as an "order of magnitude" of the present situation rather than a precise accounting.

[14]Cf. Donald Matthews, who remarks that the tickers "are regularly consulted by all the Senators"—an overstatement, no doubt, but it makes the point. (*U.S. Senators and Their World*, 1960, p. 206.)

[15]Cf. Kraft, **op. cit.**,: "On some big matters the State Department informs him (Reston) almost automatically, as it would the representative of a major power."

The Influence
of Non-Governmental Groups
on Foreign Policy Making

BERNARD C. COHEN

Our purpose here is . . . to ask ourselves, "What do we really know about the dimensions of group . . . influence on the formulation and execution of foreign policy?" A candid summary answer would have to be: not very much.

Perhaps the best introduction is a brief critical discussion of the accumulated literature, so we may know the limits of the material we have to work with. . . . For all practical purposes, most of the pre-World War II literature suffers from a comparable obsolescence; one can feel little confidence in the contemporary applicability of whatever generalizations it might yield, since the basic political conditions prevailing in those years have long since been altered in every important respect.

The relevance of analyses of policy formation increases markedly as they come to deal with the post-World War II period, when the "revolution in American foreign policy" was already under way. But it would be very misleading to imply that the literature of the last fifteen years or so is uniformly instructive. In the first place, most of the studies of group interests and public policy deal with foreign policy in the barest fashion—if indeed they treat it at all. . . .

A substantive and thus more serious weakness in this body of literature is that very little of it is the product of empirical research or deals with concrete evidence; instead, most of it rests on or reflects traditional opinion and interpretation—academic as well as public—in assigning weights to various types of organized groups. As a result, a "legend" of pressure group potency in foreign policy appears to be accepted and passed on without evidence to new generations of students and researchers. For example, . . . Robert A. Dahl writes:

The strength of pressure groups in the determination of legislative policy is no less evident in foreign than in domestic affairs. . . . The arena in which foreign policy is fought out is noisy with the jangle of pressure groups. . . .

Bernard C. Cohen, *The Influence of Non-Governmental Groups on Foreign Policy Making*, pp. 1-19. Reprinted by Permission of World Peace Foundation © 1959.

Nor is it merely the old-fashioned and perennial pressures of economic interest groups that are important today.[1]

But the data that would be required to sustain interpretations of this kind have never been part of the literature.

An even greater substantive failing in the literature of pressure groups and foreign policy, however, is the repeated discussion of the interests, intentions, or actions of specific pressure groups in lieu of any specific discussion about, or investigation into, their *actual* effects. Policy effectiveness may thus be suggested merely by the circumstance that an author chose to discuss the policy interests of a particular group. This approach to the subject is particularly misleading because the interest groups themselves seem generally willing to foster the belief that their opinions or actions have in fact had some important effect on policy. . . .

The available literature, in other words, does not seem to promise very much in the way of pertinent findings. But, in extenuation, it should be emphasized that there are some persistent analytical or conceptual difficulties that tend to hinder the accumulation of directly relevant evidence. The very question being asked is deceptively simple: what nongovernmental groups or individuals have major effects on the making and execution of foreign policy?

In the first place, it is not always easy to make an operational distinction between "groups" and a more widely defined "public." Some of the more important foreign policy interest groups in our recent past have been *ad hoc* "Committees". (e.g., "Citizens Committee for the Marshall Plan," "Committee on the Present Danger") organized on a wide public base generally for the pursuit of limited objectives, and striving to achieve a genuinely mass rather than a highly specialized character. The more successful this type of organization is in stimulating a broad support for policy, the harder it becomes to distinguish the organization from the larger stream of public opinion. A good example is the pre-World War II Committee to Defend America by Aiding the Allies: The Committee was so large and its affiliations so widespread that it became a kind of focal point for the many millions of Americans who favored a policy of assistance to Britain and France. . . . To increase the utility of whatever conclusions we may be able to draw about the influence on policy of nongovernmental individuals and groups (as against a study of the influence of public opinion in the large), we shall try to maintain here the distinction between the discernible and traceable impact on policy of a discrete group or organization, and the diffuse, generalized influence on political decision-making of a large segment of the body politic. The latter is important, to be sure, but it does not fall within the purview of this paper.

Secondly, it is not always easy to draw a clear and useful line of demarcation between foreign policy and domestic policy. . . . Our foreign relations today are constantly affecting or being affected by issues of "domestic" policy-desegregation, for example, with its important political and psychological repercussions in the non-white world; or reciprocal trade legislation, which has so many domestic economic implications, and which is even handled by the House Ways and Means Committee and the Senate Finance Committee rather than by the foreign policy committees in the Congress; or the so-called "crisis in American education": clearly the provision of first-rate intellectual skills in adequate amounts is of prime importance to the United States in its long run political competition with the Soviet Union, but, apart from a relatively modest education bill at the national level, the subject is chiefly a matter for debate among educators, school boards, and parent-teachers' associations, rather than among policy-makers concerned with long range security planning.

To try to draw new and fine distinctions between foreign and domestic policy to suit our present purposes would be ineffectual and unrewarding. The best we can hope to do in this short compass is to rely on common usage, which now includes under foreign policy most aspects of U.S. economic, political and even social and cultural policy (e.g., participation in international expositions) which directly involve us with one or more other countries.

In the third place, it is exceedingly difficult to define what we mean by "major influence" or "major effects" in such a way that one cannot only recognize those effects, but also know how to organize a search for them. Most groups which are concerned with problems of foreign affairs have set themselves the task of influencing public opinion rather than policy in the first instance; by changing the political climate or by creating an articulate public opinion, they hope eventually to exert an influence upon policy makers. In these cases, however, it is virtually impossible to trace major policy influence. So many different factors are involved in the making and execution of foreign policy that a roundabout effort of this kind merges into a larger political process, losing the crucial aspects of its identity. This is no doubt true even of group efforts on a very large scale, such as those preceding World War II. The following observation by Donald C. Blaisdell . . . illustrates this problem:

> Domestic groups outside the government are also operative [in the making of foreign policy], but with what effect it is hard to say. In 1940, in the exchange of British bases for American destroyers, for example, the weight to be attached to the America First Committee, which opposed the deal, and the Committee to Defend America by Aiding the Allies, which advocated it, is not known. Both were active in creating 'public' opinion, both had access to the White House, both were able to generate considerable newspaper support for their respective points of view. Yet, simply because the deal was made, it would be less than accurate to assert that the latter was more influential as a pressure group than the former, given the many other factors which are known to have operated. . . .[2]

Furthermore, the distinction between mere "support" of a policy by an interest group and the exertion of a major influence on policy by the group may disappear in certain cases where a large number of major national organizations are united in support of a given foreign policy. This might be true, for example, where evidence of such support was more than sufficient to counterbalance the force of special interests being exerted on policy makers in more intimate fashion. In this sense, perhaps, one might even define "effects" not as influencing policy in a specific direction to conform to the desires of an interest group, but rather as encouraging (or discouraging) policy makers in proceeding along self-chosen lines. But this is not an operational definition for our present purposes, since all groups can thus be said to have major effects on policy so long as they come out in support of a policy which is also supported by many other groups.

A similar difficulty is encountered in the fact that interest groups may have important effects on foreign policy even when they remain silent. In some cases the silence of major interest groups that are ordinarily quick to take a policy stand may be construed as acquiescence in the course of policy being pursued by the government.[3] Or words may not be required to make clear the feelings of a group: its position on a particular area of policy may be so well known and so important to the policy makers that they are constrained to take it into account in their first formulations of policy. This is one of the hardest kinds of influence for the casual or remote observer to discern; yet it is a type of influence with which we are, or ought to be, interested. . . .

In view of all the complications, perhaps the most meaningful definition of "effects" is one which differentiates direct from indirect effects, no matter what the manner of political expression. This will allow us to concentrate our attention on the evidence of direct, purposeful, immediate influence of interest groups on policy makers and their policy products, without becoming involved in the much more elusive problem of trying to weigh or measure the indirect effects on policy of group participation in the larger political processes of opinion formation.

By way of conclusion here, it is important to keep in mind that the evidence in respect of the effectiveness of particular groups or kinds of groups is rather slight and insubstantial; it consists more often of interpretations or impressions about the processes involved than of objective and systematic observations of political events and relationships. Yet enough is available to enable us to make some tentative generalizations about group influence. And as a starter we might observe, despite frequent assumptions to the contrary, that interest groups seem to have considerably less effect on foreign policy than they do in the domestic realm. . . .

EFFECTIVE GROUPS AND INDIVIDUALS

Turning first to the question of which groups have important direct effects on foreign policy, there is very widespread agreement that the most influential interest groups in the foreign policy field, as in the domestic arena, are economic interest groups—business organizations, trade associations, and the like. Some observers include labor organizations in this category of economic interest groups, while others would rank them a very close second. . . .

What are the particular business and trade groups which are influential on foreign policy subjects? It is impossible to give an adequate answer to this question. Trade associations alone number well into the thousands in the United States, and the task of observing and comparing their activities—not to speak of the activities of related business groups—is enough to discourage even the most ambitious analyst. Certain things can be said, however, even though they cannot claim to be any more than partial answers. The shipping lobby, for instance, must be rated as very effective in those areas of foreign policy which involve ocean transport: witness the success of the maritime unions and the National Federation of American Shipping in gaining and subsequently maintaining the legislative requirement that one-half of the cargoes financed by American aid be shipped to other countries in American vessels. . . .

Another effective interest group is the West Coast fishing industry, whose interest in the matter of tuna imports alone has repeatedly affected our relations with Japan and Peru; the influence of this well-organized industry on the negotiation of a fisheries settlement with Japan after World War II is set forth in Bernard C. Cohen, *The Political Process and Foreign Policy*. There are other instances where business groups seem to have put their effective mark upon international policy, which are, regrettably, mentioned only in passing in this literature. For example, Dayton McKean . . . calls the United States Beet Sugar Association the leading pressure group in the sugar bloc. "The sugar interests strove for years to obtain independence for the Philippines. The Costigan Act and the Sugar Act of 1947 are other examples of their victories. . . ."[4]

Admittedly, this is inadequate evidence to sustain the proposition that business and trade associations are the most influential groups with respect to foreign policy—or rather, with respect to foreign economic policy which seems to be the aspect of foreign policy most susceptible to the pressures of nongovernmental groups. . . . But inconclusive though it is, the evidence at least provides us with a relatively unambiguous hypothesis that could be tested if sufficient resources were ever to be put into the effort to uncover and describe a wider range of instances of group influence. We will explore later some of the reasons that may lie behind the influence of business groups, when we come to discuss why other groups are ineffective; but we may perhaps anticipate that discussion to the extent of noting here the apparent existence among government officials, not of a pro-business bias, but rather of a pro-business orientation—an assumption, in other words, that these policy matters are properly within the sphere of interest and competence of businessmen. . . .[5]

Next to business groups, there seems to be most agreement that ethnic or minority groups are particularly influential in matters of foreign policy. Dahl writes: "Some minority groups—historically the most important, perhaps being the Irish, the Italians, the Poles, the Germans, and among the religious groups,

the Catholics–influence American foreign policy out of all proportion to the
size of the group. . . ." Then he adds, "The rising concern of the Jewish minority
with the fate of the Jews in Palestine and in European displaced persons' camps
is only the latest of a long series of similar actions by other ethnic or religious
groups."[6] The weight of the opinion of others seems to be that this latest in the
series represents the most important contemporary element in ethnic interest in
or influence on American foreign policy. . . .

Other than the above groups, however, there are discouragingly few generalizations that one can make about group influence on foreign policy. To be sure,
one can find many occasions where specific groups seem to have exerted a
specific influence on the course of foreign policy, but these cases seem to be
time- and situation-bound instances of influence, too discrete to permit one to
draw any generalizations about the past, present, or future political behavior of
these groups. . . .

On a different level from . . . anecdotal accounts of individual accomplishment
in the policy making realm, one finds highly generalized descriptions of
"individual influentials" which, although not operationally useful, are sufficiently suggestive of research possibilities to warrant brief mention. In a recent
article based on an analysis of 39 persons of "above-average influence" (selected
according to criteria that would probably not satisfy all tastes) living in a suburb
of Chicago, Kenneth P. Adler and Davis Bobrow have drawn a portrait of the
"non-governmental influential in foreign affairs." They found, for example, that
the "influential" (as distinguished from the merely "interested") is highly
educated, wealthy, Protestant, Anglo-Saxon, and in a professional-technical or
managerial occupation. His influence is often based on high standing in the legal
profession or high executive position in industry, banking, or commerce. Foreign
travel is nearly universal among these suburban influentials, who are linked to
Chicago, to other metropolitan areas, and to Washington by both business
connections and personal friendships.[7] No claim is made, of course, that the
community involved in this study is typical, or that the 39 persons are
representative of persons with contemporary influence on foreign policy. It may
even be that Adler and Bobrow have described only *one type* of foreign policy
influential and that there are many other types to be found in other
environments. In any case, the problem of personal or individual influence on
foreign policy is a fertile field for future explorations.

Up to this point we have asked the question, "What groups and individuals
have important direct effects on foreign policy?" Now we shall explore the
nature of those effects, and the policy circumstances in which they become
evident. Many of the specific effects that have been achieved by identifiable
groups have been mentioned in passing in the prior discussion; it might be useful
here, perhaps, to try to draw some very tentative and low level generalizations
from this all-too-incomplete evidence.

While interest groups follow the whole range of American foreign policy, taking positions and expressing opinions on all aspects of it, the area of direct and significant influence seems to be mostly the protection or advancement of those particular interests which are the *raison d'etre* of the interest groups. This pursuit of essentially private rather than public interest—whether or not it is in the guise of public interest—takes place through whatever policy means are at hand, or which have already been initiated or activated by the government itself. For example, international economic policy may be affected by the pursuit of private gain through tariff provisions or aid legislation; both economic interests and ethnic or minority interests can be achieved by trying to affect relations with particular countries or areas; or effects may be had by the processes of delaying or causing the rejection of whatever kinds of legislation the policy makers have seen fit to introduce.

It is less easy to generalize about the circumstances under which interest groups may have an influence upon policy. But the evidence available here suggests that particular groups are perhaps most effective on an individual basis when the policy issue in which they are interested is, for whatever reason, not in the public eye. There may be general public disinterest in a policy matter for a variety of reasons: it may deal, for example, with only a very narrow subject matter or with technical rather than political issues, or it may suffer the accident of having to compete for dramatic interest with more spectacular and compelling issues of domestic or perhaps even foreign policy. Whatever the reason, however, it would appear that when the "attentive public" is very small, it is much easier for specific interest groups to establish their position as the representatives of the only sectors of the public that are vitally concerned about the policy in hand. But these same circumstances can sometimes be exploited for quite opposite purposes: When there seems to be very little public interest in a policy issue, as in the case of the naval appropriations for Guam in 1939, an organization like the National Council for the Prevention of War can be effective by drawing press and public attention to the problems involved thus delaying formal action on the matter and ultimately securing a reconsideration.

* * *

On how broad a range of issues does a given group exert an important direct influence? The written record permits a more confident answer to this question In general, the span of influence of specific groups seems to be limited to the area of their special policy interest; this limitation seems to hold even though an organization may take an articulate public position on the entire range of foreign policy issues. As Bertram Gross put it:

Strategic positions [occupied by nongovernmental organizations] , however, are only a source of generalized power. The American Medical Association can swing considerable weight to the subject of Government health policies, but its closest friends in Government would not give it much attention on foreign policy.[8]

In the same way, the commodity groups have no effect on foreign policy beyond whatever arrangements they are able to make respecting the treatment of their particular commodities in international trade or a foreign aid program. Ethnic groups have no influence on policy with respect to areas of the world other than those to which they have a direct connection. Trade unions have little influence outside of matters involving international labor. Religious influence on foreign policy seems to be limited to sectarian interests. Perhaps the only major exception to this point is to be found among the general business groups. While their influence may be regarded as highest when it comes to matters of international economic policy, in our contemporary society the businessman is frequently called upon for his advice and administrative experience in a wider range of foreign policy matters. But this exception aside, the general point here is interesting and important: it suggests that an easily identifiable division of labor—more accurately, a division of influence—exists, which is imposed by policy makers themselves whenever there might be temptations to violate it by interest groups.

Finally, what can one say about the ways in which influential groups approach the political process and use it effectively? There are, obviously, a host of political avenues that may be traversed in the effort to exert policy influence. Partly because of the interests of scholars and partly because of the ease of access to the legislative process, the available material on this subject informs us most of all on the avenue to effectiveness through gaining the support of one or more members of Congress. . . .

Existing research tells us considerably less about the operations of foreign policy interest groups within the Executive branch than about attempts to influence Congress. The successful efforts of the West Coast fishing industry to place a responsible spokesman for the industry in an administrative position very close to the policy level in the State Department[9] so that it could better influence the development of policy and negotiations on a fisheries settlement with Japan, are suggestive of a mode of political influence in the foreign policy field that may take place somewhat oftener than it is written about. At lower levels in the administrative hierarchy, we know that trade unions, trade associations, and other special interest groups are often used as advisors in foreign missions, or as advisors and delegates to international conferences on specialized subjects. Finally, a less common path of political influence runs through the political parties. This is uncommon because few interest groups can mobilize any important electoral power in the pursuit of specific foreign policy objectives. V. O. Key, Jr. writes of interest groups in general in this same sense:

A plausible tentative conclusion may be that one must look, in the main, to factors other than their power to punish at the polls to explain the influence of pressure groups. They gain power in some instances merely from having representatives on hand to present their case to the legislature. In others their influence is founded on the simple fact that the legislator tends to go along with whatever interests are powerful in his district. . . . In still others the legislators' convictions may happen to coincide with the interest of particular groups.[10]

But once in a while electoral power can be brought to bear in an apparently successful way, especially when the interest groups involved are organizationally and/or numerically important elements in politically strategic constituencies. This has been true of the West Coast fishing industry on certain international fishing questions, as we shall see in a moment, and of most Jewish groups on the issue of Israel: "Jewish pressure, during the electoral campaign of 1948 in favor of American support of the new state of Israel, influenced both parties to adopt 'Zionist' planks in their party platforms."[11]

Obviously, then, one can find groups working through all the major points of access to the governmental process of foreign policy making: the Congress, the Executive and bureaucracy, and the political parties. Does it make any difference whether an organization chooses to work through one rather than another of these points? The answer is not clear-cut. Even with a poor record of cases on which to found our conclusions, it is readily apparent that there is no single point of access to influence in the process. They all work, and they all seem to work equally well or effectively. But we have to ask whether any particular group can function equally effectively anywhere in the process. I am inclined to believe that the answer is no; there seem to be regularities in the way groups approach the different elements in the process, making and utilizing contacts,[12] and the conditions that determine what sets of relationships are effective are worth exploring in much greater detail than has been done heretofore. For example, the West Coast fishing industry, all phases of which were organized into the Pacific Fisheries Conference, was effective in shaping the North Pacific Fisheries Convention by working at the start through their Congressmen. From this initial point of access all manner of influence flowed, including participation in policy formulation in the State Department. But all this was possible because the businesses and trade and labor associations which were represented in the Pacific Fisheries Conference were very important elements in the constituencies of a territorially compact group of Representatives and Senators who by virtue of geography and history were generally conceded a leading political interest in any settlement with Japan.[13] Had the fishing industry tried to work on the State Department directly, without the intercession of important members of Congress, its accomplishment would no doubt have been far less. But the course of action taken so effectively by the fishing groups is not open to all groups, since it is obviously dependent upon a particular arrangement or constellation of organizations, issues, and political positions.

Another dimension of the influence process that is worth further attention is what might be called the "ideological connection" between the would-be influential and the policy makers. It seems to be the case that policy makers are not often persuaded to act (or not act) in favor of persons or groups with whom they are in basic ideological or political conflict. Put more positively, there generally appears to be a close affinity between the policy maker and the individual or group whose position he is persuaded to support. . . .

INEFFECTIVE GROUPS

In some respects the question of what groups are ineffective in shaping the form or substance of foreign policy is the other side of the coin we have just examined. But it is scarcely an adequate answer to say that all groups which have not been identified as effective are ineffective. By "ineffective" here is meant the exertion of a negligible amount of *direct* influence on policy; yet this should not be taken to mean that groups in this category have no influence of any kind on American policy. They might well have some indirect influence, for example, when they cluster in support of or in opposition to a broad course of policy.

No doubt most major interest groups in the United States think of themselves as influential with respect to public policy, including foreign policy, it would be natural for them to do so, and the public records of most associations indicate that they are quick to suggest, if not to claim, policy influence. Yet there is more evidence in the contemporary literature on the ineffectiveness of nongovernmental groups in the field of foreign policy than there are signs of direct and positive influence. The evidence pointing to a lack of influence is sometimes explicit and sometimes implicit; we will be dealing with both varieties here.

The important point to make at the start is that, just as no one group is uniformly influential, at one time or another all groups that seek to influence foreign policy encounter the kind of failure that is evidence of political ineffectiveness. This is true even of business and commodity groups and trade associations, which we noted above were perhaps the most influential of all. In the case of the Japanese peace treaty, for example, business organizations were treated with cordiality and respect, but it is very doubtful whether they got on the whole any more satisfaction of their policy interests than Mr. Dulles was prepared in any case to give them.[14] Similarly, Administration bills to renew the Reciprocal Trade Agreements Act have gone through Congress relatively untouched year after year, despite the earnest efforts of commodity groups to influence it in their favor. . . .

But if all kinds of organizations are ineffective at one time or another, it still seems to be the case that some groups lack influence (in the direct sense, again) on foreign policy matters most of the time. This seems to be especially true of the large national organizations commonly placed in the categories of civic, professional, fraternal, women's, ideological, and even religious groups. . . .

In a book entitled *The American Legion and American Foreign Policy,*[15] Roscoe Baker has written a noncritical description of the Legion's position on virtually every matter relating to foreign policy in which the Legion has ever been interested. But the author carefully refrains from claiming influence for the Legion; and the net effect of reference after reference to the enactment of legislation which had been opposed by the Legion is the firm impression that the Legion was in fact without much influence on matters of foreign policy. . . .

What can we say about the conditions that make for political ineffectiveness among interest groups? How do these groups differ from others that have a record of major influence on foreign policy? Many different reasons can be adduced to explain the failure of organizations to exert an influence on foreign policy; some of these reasons are institutional, others are situational. But in this as in other respects, it is hard to feel very confident that one has put one's finger on characteristics either of organization or of behavior that permanently or inflexibly distinguish the ineffective groups from the influential ones. As an example of the contradictory evidence that marks this aspect of the subject, Lewis A. Dexter . . . quotes a Congressman as saying that in general, Congress hears from business groups too late: these organizations respond to the news, they write to protest a bill reported out of committee, but by then it is difficult to amend it.[16] But in the case of the Japanese peace settlement . . . it was some of the business groups which were most alert to the treaty's impingement on their own interests and which moved both on Congress and on the Executive at an early stage, whereas the other more general interest organizations intervened much later, in response to news about the development of the issue.

By understanding some of the reasons for the general effectiveness of business groups, one can detect reasons why it may be much harder for other kinds of groups to influence the making of foreign policy. For one thing, there is the suggestion that a group can have little influence on policy unless its interest in the policy problem is recognized as legitimate by policy makers. This is no doubt one of the major factors that works to restrict the span of influence over policy of particular groups and thus to create the "division of influence" we took notice of earlier. . . .

But there are other factors at work here, even in the context of a recognized legitimacy of interest in policy. Thus Bonilla writes that labor groups as well as business groups have a legitimate interest in the tariff, "but whereas *in no single case* did any of the legislators complain about pressures from industry, there were a number of remarks [made during interviews] describing the ineptness, boorishness, or lack of organization evident in labor pressure groups. . . ." The implication here is not, fundamentally, an anti-labor attitude. Rather it seems to be a general, perhaps even a cultural, sympathy with business—a predisposition to regard its interests as legitimate; this is what Bonilla elsewhere . . . calls a "congruence of opinion and sentiment." It is in terms of such congruence that Bonilla distinguishes the psychological and subjective dimensions of pressure; it helps explain the fact (sometimes puzzling to reformers) that demands from businessmen generated little resentment among legislators (even when they ran counter to the views of the Congressman concerned), while appeals from groups like the League of Women Voters provoked animosity in almost every case. . . .[17]

Admittedly, it is difficult to distinguish between the legitimacy of business interest in economic policy and a general sentiment or bias in favor of the "practical businessman," particularly when most of the evidence to support such propositions is drawn from cases involving economic policy. Yet the notion that the businessman represents better than anyone else the kind of feet-on-the-ground practicality of which foreign policy is made is a recurring one. In his monograph for TNEC, Blaisdell wrote,

> While important on occasion, the staying power, resources, and plausibility of program of these peace groups are hardly in the same class as those of the business groups with an economic stake in shipping policy. The peace groups by and large are considered either radical or unrealistic; the business groups, on the other hand, are generally regarded as "sound."[18]

In the case of the Japanese peace treaty, the patent unreality of the policy proposals advanced by the religious, pacifist, and ideological groups made them useless to the policy makers, and so they were dismissed more or less perfunctorily.[19]

One can find other evidence suggesting a not uncommon predilection for the businessman's approach to foreign policy among American officials, many of whom have had business experience themselves. For instance, The Forrestal Diaries ... contains numerous references to Forrestal's belief that the businessman was the really indispensable element if the United States was going to stand up successfully to the Soviet Union. On March 3, 1947, for example, Forrestal wrote about a luncheon with Treasury Secretary Snyder, at which they had discussed the rapidly maturing problem of assistance for Greece and Turkey:

> Talked to him about my beliefs that if we are going to have a run for our side in the competition between the Soviet system and our own, we shall have to harness all the talent and brains in this country just as we had to do during the war. I said I felt very strongly that the world could only be brought back to order by a restoration of commerce, trade and business, and that would have to be done by businessmen.[20]

Senator Vandenberg had somewhat the same notions with respect to the Marshall Plan. Writing to Undersecretary Lovett, "he suggested as a practical matter the desirability of obtaining 'four or five top-level business executives of the country' as 'aggressive witnesses' once the Committee hearings started on the Marshall Plan. This was to be essentially a 'business' program."[21]

Another difference between business and nonbusiness groups which may affect their capacity to influence foreign policy is the degree of specificity of the interest which they represent. Kensuke Yanagiya, in . . . *The Renewal of ERP: A Case Study* . . . found some support both in the State Department and among interest groups for the following views of a State Department official who tried to explain why special-interest groups had more influence on policy than large, national, general-interest organizations. "There are a number of reasons for this: 1) their recommendations are specific, in contrast to the necessarily general ideas of large groups; 2) they are far more interested and zealous; 3) counter-pressures usually do not exist either within or without their own group."[22]

But there are still other reasons why interest groups may be ineffective in matters of foreign policy. One of these reasons must be the consonance of the policy being advocated by a group with the prevailing political temper of the times. No matter how reasonable a policy might once have been, if it is no longer regarded as reasonable or feasible because of the general tenor of developing opinion, the impact of its advocacy is likely to be small. An excellent illustration of this is provided by the America First Committee, which tried in the months before Pearl Harbor to reassert the validity of a foreign policy of utter neutrality and isolation but which failed so completely that it was "not even able to defeat any major administration 'short-of-war' proposal actually put to the test in Congress."[23]

Another reason why groups may lack a direct influence on policy may be found in the temporary existence of an approximate balance of opposing interests. By way of example, in an unpublished interview a former State Department official has described the problem of the recognition of the new Bolivian government after the 1952 coup as "a case where business pressure, usually very influential and articulate, cancelled itself out." Finally, another— and by no means unimportant—reason for the inability of groups to make much headway on foreign policy may be the conclusion of policy makers that the special treatment which they seek may be far too costly in terms of the public good. "The vain struggle of individuals and business enterprises to have private claims recognized in the [Japanese] peace treaty is evidence of the Department's firm interpretation of the greater good in this matter, even when the justice of the individual claims was beyond question."[24] Holbert Carroll similarly argues that the House Committee on Foreign Affairs resisted the particular pleas of all organized pressures with respect to the European Recovery Program, because to the Committee, as to the State Department, "the foreign policy objectives hold the highest priority."[25]

NOTES

[1] Robert A. Dahl, *Congress and Foreign Policy* (New York: Harcourt, Brace and Company, 1950), pp. 52-53.

[2] Donald C. Blaisdell, *American Democracy Under Pressure* (New York: Ronald Press, 1957), pp. 168-69.

[3]See Bernard C. Cohen, *The Political Process and Foreign Policy: The Making of the Japanese Peace Settlement.* (Princeton, N.J.: Princeton University Press, 1957).

[4]Dayton D. McKean, *Party and Pressure Politics* (Boston: Houghton Mifflin, 1949), p. 456.

[5]As an illustration, see the tenor of interviews with Congressmen on the subject of reciprocal trade, as summarized by Frank Bonilla, "When is Petition 'Pressure'?" *Public Opinion Quarterly* 20, Spring 1956.

[6]Dahl, *op. cit.*, pp. 55-56.

[7]"Interest and Influence in Foreign Affairs," *Public Opinion Quarterly* 20, Spring 1956, pp. 92-93.

[8]*The Legislative Struggle.* (New York: McGraw-Hill, 1953). p. 147.

[9]See Cohen, *op. cit.*, Chapter 12.

[10]V. O. Key, Jr., *Politics, Parties and Pressure Groups* (New York: Thomas Y. Crowell, 1947), p. 134.

[11]Gabriel Almond, *The American People and Foreign Policy* (New York: Harcourt, Brace and Company, 1950), pp. 186-87.

[12]See e.g., Cohen, *op. cit.*, especially Chapter 5.

[13]*Ibid.*, Chapter 12.

[14]*Ibid.*, pp. 217-18.

[15]New York: Bookman Associates, 1954.

[16]"What Do Congressmen Hear: The Mail," *Public Opinion Quarterly* 20, Spring 1956, pp. 26-27.

[17]Bonilla, *op. cit.*, pp. 39-46.

[18]Donald C. Blaisdell, *Economic Power and Political Pressures.* (Temporary National Economic Committee, Monograph No. 26, [Washington, D.C., U.S. Government Printing Office, 1941]), p. 166.

[19]Cohen, *op. cit.*, pp. 219-20.

[20]Walter Millis, editor, *The Forrestal Diaries* (New York: 1951), pp. 247-48.

[21]Arthur H. Vandenberg, Jr., editor, *The Private Papers of Senator Vandenberg* (Boston: 1952), p. 383.

[22]Public Affairs 520-D, Woodrow Wilson School of Public and National Affairs, Princeton University, 1952, p. 37. See also Cohen, *op. cit.*, Chapter 5, for other differences in the behavior of special interest groups which might account for whatever differences in influence exist between them and other interest groups.

[23]Wayne S. Cole, *American First: The Battle Against Intervention, 1940-1941.* (Madison: University of Wisconsin Press, 1953), p. vii.

[24]Cohen, *op. cit.*, p. 218.

[25]Holbert Carroll, *The House of Representatives and Foreign Affairs* (Pittsburgh, Penn.: University of Pittsburgh Press, 1958), p. 127.

Who Made
American Foreign Policy,
1945 — 1963?

G. WILLIAM DOMHOFF

In this essay we will attempt to demonstrate that American foreign policy during the postwar era was initiated, planned, and carried out by the richest, most powerful, and most international-minded owners and managers of major corporations and financial institutions. None of the factors that are often of importance on domestic issues—Congress, labor, public opinion—had anything but an occasional and minor effect on foreign policy. If there is one "issue-area" that is truly and solely the domain of a power elite grounded in an American upper class of corporate rich, it is foreign policy.

In preparation for an empirical demonstration of these assertions, it is necessary to provide a general framework. In *Who Rules America?* I presented the evidence for the existence in the United States of a social upper class of rich businessmen and their descendants.[1] This social class of business aristocrats, which is nationwide in its scope, gradually came into existence in the last part of the nineteenth century. Based upon fabulous corporate wealth, it is knit together by exclusive private schools, Ivy League colleges, expensive summer resorts, sedate gentlemen's clubs, and a variety of other social institutions too numerous to mention here. From the point of view of research on the control of foreign policy, the most important outcome of this investigation of the social upper class was a set of criteria for identifying its members. The most useful of these were a listing in any edition of the *Social Register* except for that of Washington, D.C. (which automatically lists important government figures regardless of social background); attendance at the most prestigious of the private schools (e.g., St. Paul's, Choate, Groton, Middlesex); and membership in the most elite of the city clubs for men (e.g., the California Club of Los Angeles, the Pacific Union of San Francisco, the Knickerbocker of New York, the Somerset of Boston, the Rittenhouse of Philadelphia). Using these criteria, along with four minor ones that were less useful, it was possible to show that members of this privileged class control major businesses, large charitable foundations, and

From *Corporations and The Cold War*, edited by David Horowitz, pp. 24-48, 64-67. Reprinted by permission of Monthly Review Press. Copyright © 1969 by the Bertrand Russell Peace Foundation.

leading opinion-forming associations. For example, to present one small part of the evidence, 62 percent of all directors of the largest fifteen banks were members of the upper class, as were 54 percent of the outside directors of the top twenty industrial corporations and 53 percent of all directors of the leading fifteen transportation companies.[2] In the case of charitable foundations, twelve of the thirteen with assets over $100 million in the early 1960's were controlled by this same small group.[3] It is not possible to repeat all of the evidence, but suffice it to say that there were several thousand men, a great many of whom were members of the social upper class, who interlocked and overlapped in most of the major non-governmental institutions of American society.

This group of interlocking overlappers make up what C. Wright Mills called the "power elite."[4] We have borrowed this term from Mills, but redefined it in such a way as to make it more suitable for an analysis based upon socioeconomic classes. Whereas Mills defined the power elite as those who hold command posts in the major institutions of American society, we define the power elite as active, working members of the upper class and high-level employees in institutions controlled by members of the upper class. Thus, for example, the presidents of U.S. Steel and the Rockefeller Foundation are members of the power elite whether they are members of the upper class or not because both of those institutions are controlled by members of that small social group. While this conception of the power elite is formally different from Mills' definition, it leads empirically to identifying the same persons he did as a power elite. Again to take only a quick example, the military, which is one arm of Mills' power elite, is controlled by the corporate rich through their control of the Department of Defense and through non-governmental army, navy, and air force associations which are financed and directed by corporate executives and their companies.*[5]

Building on the aforementioned criteria of upper-class membership and redefinition of the power elite, *Who Rules America?* presented evidence which suggests that the power elite control the most important agencies and departments of the federal government. In particular, the departments most concerned with foreign policy—State, Defense, Treasury—were outposts of the power elite, invariably run by representatives of the biggest and most internationally oriented corporations.[7] However, the book did not go into detail on foreign policy or any other issue-area because the primary goal of that book was to show which institutions, as opposed to issues, are dominated by the power elite. While the issue-area of foreign policy is basically controlled by State, Defense, Treasury, and certain private associations noted in *Who Rules America?*, it is possible and worthwhile to go into greater detail on it. There are two reasons for such an undertaking.

*"Corporate rich," "corporate elite," and "power elite" are roughly synonymous terms. The corporate rich or corporate elite are the core of the power elite which is the operating arm of the social upper class. In turn, this social upper class can be called a "governing class" or "ruling class." It also should be added that the oft-heard phrase "establishment" has about the same meaning as "power elite."[6]

First, if it is true, as many would now argue, that foreign policy issues determine the framework within which all types of policy-making take place, and if the power elite tend to dominate this issue-area, then it follows that the power elite rule America, even if they do not involve themselves or fight for their optimum outcome on every domestic, state, and local issue. Mills put the case very well: "If it is too much to say that, for many of the elite, domestic politics have become important mainly as ways of retaining power at home in order to exert abroad the power of the national establishment, surely it is true that domestic decisions in virtually all areas of life are increasingly justified by, if not made with, close reference to the dangers and opportunities abroad "[8] Second, such a study is able to answer in considerable detail the charge that those claiming control by the corporate rich do not show the specific mechanisms by which this supposed control is accomplished. In the case of foreign policy, at least, we have found such a determination very straightforward.

To begin at the beginning, foreign-policy-making takes place within an "environment" or setting: the international community of nations, American public opinion, the mass media, political interest groups, agencies of the Executive branch, and committees of the Congress. However, as we hope to show, the effect of some of these is rarely felt and is often used as an excuse or rationalization (e.g., public opinion), while others are usually by-passed (e.g., Congress). Furthermore, it is possible to be much more concrete in spelling out the immediate context within which decision-makers function In general, the most important institutions in foreign policy decision-making are large corporations, closely related charitable foundations, two or three discussion and research associations financed by these corporations and foundations, the National Security Council of the federal government, and special committees appointed by the President. To be sure, this is only the most important core, for there are several other private and university-affiliated research and opinion-molding organizations, not to mention several other agencies of the federal government.

THE COUNCIL OF FOREIGN RELATIONS

To give empirical flesh to all these generalizations, there is no better starting point than the Council on Foreign Relations (CFR). It is the key "middle term," so to speak, between the large corporations on the one hand and the federal government on the other. By studying its connections in both directions, we will be able to establish the first link in the specific mechanisms by which the corporate rich formulate and transfer their wishes into government policy. While it would be hard to underestimate the importance of this organization in understanding the overall framework for American foreign policy, we do not want to overemphasize it, and we will see that there are other links between big business and big government.

The Council of Foreign Relations is a non-partisan research and discussion group dedicated to informing citizens about world affairs and creating an interest in international relations. Despite its reputed prominence and the fact that it was founded in 1921, most information on it comes from its own publications: a fifteen-year history, a twenty-five-year history, and annual reports. One of the few who has written on it, Washington journalist Joseph Kraft, noted in 1958 that it was mentioned only five times in *Time* magazine, in the period 1953-1958.[9] We can go one step further and say that there has never been any research paper on it in any scholarly journal indexed in the *Social Science and Humanities Index*. While this is surprising, there are several ways to establish CFR's importance. They include testimony by journalists and scholars, the acknowledged pre-eminence of its journal (*Foreign Affairs*), the nature of its financial backing, the composition of its leadership and membership, and the presence of its members in federal government positions.

To begin with expert testimony, Kraft called CFR a "school for statesmen" which "comes close to being an organ of what C. Wright Mills has called the Power Elite—a group of men, similar in interest and outlook, shaping events from invulnerable positions behind the scenes."[10] Douglass Cater, a journalist who served on the staff of President Lyndon B. Johnson, has noted that "a diligent scholar would do well to delve into the role of the purely unofficial Council on Foreign Relations in the care and breeding of an incipient American Establishment."[11] The *New York Times* called it "a testing ground for new ideas, with enough political and financial power to bring the ideas to the attention of the policy-makers in Washington."[12] Political scientist Lester Milbrath noted that "the Council on Foreign Relations, while not financed by government, works so closely with it that it is difficult to distinguish Council actions stimulated by government from autonomous actions."[13]

Empirically speaking, such "reputational" evidence is the least important of our ammunition. Far more important is CFR's financing and leadership. Aside from membership dues, dividends from invested gifts and bequests, and profits from the sale of *Foreign Affairs,* the most important sources of income are leading corporations and major foundations. In 1957-1958, for example, Chase Manhattan, Continental Can, Ford Motor, Bankers Trust, Cities Service, Gulf, Otis Elevator, General Motors Overseas Operations, Brown Brothers, Harriman, and International General Electric were paying from $1,000 to $10,000 per year for the "corporation service," depending upon the size of the company and its interest in international affairs.* More generally. in 1960-1961, eighty-four large corporations and financial institutions contributed 12 percent ($112,200) of CFR's total income. As to the foundations, the major contributors over the years have been the Rockefeller Foundation and the Carnegie Corporation, with the Ford Foundation joining in with a large grant in the 1950's. According to

---

*The benefits of subscribing to this corporation service are as follows: free consultation with all members of the CFR staff, subscriptions to *Foreign Affairs* for leading officers of the corporation, the use of the council's excellent library (which is second to none in its field), and the right to nominate one "promising young executive" to participate in seminars which the council conducts each fall and spring for the benefit of the corporations.[14]

Kraft, a $2.5 million grant in the early 1950's from the Ford, Rockefeller, and Carnegie foundations made the council "the most important single private agency conducting research in foreign affairs."[15] In 1960-1961, foundation money accounted for 25 percent of CFR income.

The foundations which support CFR are in turn directed by men from Bechtel Construction, Chase Manhattan, Cummins Engine, Corning Glass, Kimberly-Clark, Monsanto Chemical, and dozens of other corporations. And, to complete the circle, most foundation directors are members of CFR. In the early 1960's, Dan Smoot found that 12 of 20 Rockefeller Foundation trustees, 10 of 15 Ford Foundation trustees, and 10 of 14 Carnegie Corporation trustees were members of CFR.[16] Nor is this interlocking recent: in 1922, for example, CFR honorary president Elihu Root was president of the Carnegie Corporation while John W. Davis, the corporation lawyer who ran for President on the Democratic ticket in 1924, was a trustee of both the Carnegie Corporation and CFR.

A consideration of the leadership and membership of CFR are equally conclusive in establishing its relationship to the power elite. Its founders included two lawyers and two Wall Street bankers.[17] The single permanent official at its outset, Hamilton Fish Armstrong, and the first editor of *Foreign Affairs*, Archibald Coolidge, were both from well-known upper-class families. Nor has anything changed since the early 1920's, with 14 of the 22 recent or current directors as of the early 1960's being listed in the *Social Register*. Among the most prominent of the recent directors highly visible in the corporate elite are Frank Altschul, Elliott V. Bell, Thomas K. Finletter (one-time Secretary of the Air Force), Devereux C. Josephs, John J. McCloy, David Rockefeller, and Adlai E. Stevenson.

The CFR limits itself to 700 New York area residents and 700 non-New York residents (no women or foreigners are allowed to join). As of the mid-sixties, 46 percent of the resident members and 49 percent of the non-resident members were listed in the *Social Register*.[18] The council's only other formal associates are the Committees on Foreign Relations that have been formed in about thirty cities across the country. These committees come together at dinners and other occasions to hear speakers (mostly supplied by CFR) and exchange ideas. The committee program has been financed since 1938 by the Carnegie Corporation.[19] We were able to locate information on 509 committee members from 29 cities ranging in size and importance from Philadelphia, Detroit, and Atlanta to Albuquerque, Boise, and Little Rock. A significant minority (41 percent) were corporate executives and bankers. Twenty-one percent were lawyers, almost half of whom (44 percent) were also corporate directors. Thus, a small majority (51 percent) were directly involved in business enterprises. Another significant group consisted of educators (22 percent), most of whom were college presidents, political scientists, economists, and deans. Seven percent of those studied were editors or publishers, while the remainder were small numbers of government officials, politicians, church leaders, physicians, accountants, and museum directors.*

Turning to the all-important question of government involvement, the presence of CFR members in government has been attested to by Kraft, Cater, Smoot, CFR histories, and the *New York Times,* but the point is made most authoritatively by John J. McCloy—Wall Street lawyer, former chairman of Chase Manhattan, trustee of the Ford Foundation, director of CFR, and a government appointee in a variety of roles since the early 1940's: "Whenever we needed a man," said McCloy in explaining the presence of CFR members in the modern defense establishment that fought World War II, "we thumbed through the roll of Council members and put through a call to New York."[20] According to Kraft, "When John McCloy went to Bonn as U.S. High Commissioner, he took with him a staff composed almost exclusively of men who had interested themselves in German affairs at the Council."[21] CFR members were also prominent in the U.S. delegation to the founding of the United Nations, and several dozen have held high posts in postwar administrations. One *Annual Report* noted the following in an obituary notice:

> Mr. Dulles was a member of the Council almost from the start. He wrote an article on "The Allied Debts" for the first issue of *Foreign Affairs* and six more articles thereafter, including two while Secretary of State. He participated in numerous study and discussion groups over the years and spoke often at Council afternoon meetings and dinners, twice as Secretary of State.[22]

Now that we have located CFR in sociological space as an institution of the corporate rich, we are in a position to see what it does and how effective it is in shaping foreign policy. As to what CFR does, in addition to serving as a talent pool and training ground for government service, it is a tax-exempt, non-partisan organization which sponsors education, discussion, and research on all aspects of foreign affairs. As part of its educational effort, it brings before its exclusive membership leading scholars and government officials from all nations to make off-the-record speeches and to answer questions from members. And, as Kraft notes, this not only "educates" the members, but it gives them a chance to "size up" important leaders with whom they will have to deal.**[23] Also under the heading of education, CFR publishes *Foreign Affairs,* by far the most important journal in its field, and three annual surveys—*Political Handbook of the World, The United States in World Affairs,* and *Documents on American Foreign Relations.*

Despite the importance of speeches and publications, we think the most important aspect of the CFR program is its special discussion and study groups,

*My thanks to Sue Brenn, an undergraduate research assistant, for gathering the information on CFR committee members for the early 1960's.
**A perusal of any CFR annual report will show that a foreign official visiting in New York who is anyone at all will be speaking or meeting with the council.

Who Made American Foreign Policy, 1945-1963?

which bring together about twenty-five businessmen, government officials, military men, and scholars for detailed discussions of specific topics in the area of foreign affairs. Discussion groups explore problems in a general way, trying to define issues and alternatives, and often lead to a study group. Study groups revolve around the work of a council research fellow (financed by Carnegie, Ford, and Rockefeller) or a staff member. This group leader usually presents monthly papers which are discussed and criticized by the rest of the group. The goal of such study groups is a detailed statement of the problem by the scholar leading the discussion. In 1957-1958, for example, the council published six books which grew out of study groups. Perhaps the most famous of these was written by Henry Kissinger, then a bright young Harvard product who was asked by CFR to head a study group. His *Nuclear Weapons and Foreign Policy* was "a best-seller which has been closely read in the highest Administration circles and foreign offices abroad."[24] As for his study group, it included "two former chairmen of the Atomic Energy Commission, A Nobel Prize winner in physics, two former civilian secretaries in the Defense Department, and representatives just below the highest level from the State Department, the Central Intelligence Agency, and the three armed services."[25] When economist Percy Bidwell of the CFR staff led a discussion of foreign tariffs, an issue which will be discussed later in this paper, the study group included ten corporate representatives, ten economists, two communications experts from MIT's Center for International Studies, a minor Defense Department official, and a foreign service officer.[26]

It is within these discussion and study groups, where privacy is the rule so that members are encouraged to speak freely, that members of the power elite study and plan how best to attain American objectives in world affairs. It is here that they discuss alternatives and hash out differences, far from the limelight of official government and mass media. As the *New York Times* says of these "unpublicized luncheons" and "closed seminars": "Except for its annual public Elihu Root Lectures, the Council's talks and seminars are strictly off the record. An indiscretion can be grounds for termination or suspension of membership. . . ."*[27] Such discussions also help to reduce the effect of political changes. In Kraft's words: ". . . the Council plays a special part in helping to bridge the gap between the two parties, affording unofficially a measure of continuity when the guard changes in Washington."[28]

Given the privacy of its discussions (it is quite open about everything else), can we know the relationship between CFR and government policy? Can we go beyond the fact that CFR conducts research and discussions and that its

---

*Critics of a power elite theory often call it "conspiratorial," which is the academic equivalent of ending a discussion by yelling Communist. It is difficult to lay this charge to rest once and for all because these critics really mean something much broader than the dictionary definition of conspiracy. All right, then, if "conspiracy" means that these men are aware of their interests, know each other personally, meet together privately and off the record, and try to hammer out a consensus of how to anticipate or react to events and issues, then there is some conspiring that goes on in CFR, not to mention in the Committee for Economic Development, the Business Council, the National Security Council, and the Central Intelligence Agency.

members hold responsible positions in the federal government? It is not only secrecy which makes this question hard to answer; there is also the problem that CFR as an organization does not take a partisan stand. To answer such a question satisfactorily would require a large number of studies of various decisions and their outcomes, including an understanding of who initiated, supported, and opposed various proposals.[29] In lieu of such studies, which are almost impossible under even the best of circumstances, several suggestive examples will have to suffice, along with the general testimony of Kraft ("It has been the seat of some basic government decisions, has set the context for many more") and the *New York Times* ("Discussion groups, scholarly papers, and studies sponsored by the Council laid the groundwork for the Marshall Plan for European recovery, set American policy guidelines for the North Atlantic Treaty Organization, and currently are evolving a long-range analysis of American attitudes toward China").[30] More concretely, Kraft claims that CFR action was responsible for putting Greenland out of bounds for the Nazis, for shaping the United Nations charter, and for softening the American position on German postwar reparations, among others. One of the most impressive pieces of evidence is that four CFR planning groups set up in 1939 with aid from the Rockefeller Foundation, were taken (along with most of their personnel) into the State Department in 1942 "as the nub of its Advisory Committee on Post-war Planning Problems,"[31] And it was supposedly a special CFR briefing session in early 1947 that convinced Undersecretary of State Robert Lovett of Brown Brothers, Harriman that "it would be our principal task at State to awaken the nation to the dangers of Communist aggression."[32]

In summarizing CFR and its role, despite the fact that it is an organization "most Americans have never heard of"[33] we think we have clearly established by a variety of means that it is a key connection between the federal government and the owners and managers of the country's largest corporations. If it is not all-embracing in its importance, it is certainly a considerable understatement to speak of CFR members and members of similar power elite associations, as one scholar does, as "external bureaucrats" who supply the government with information, perspectives, and manpower.[34] In our view, what knowledge we have of CFR suggests that through it the corporate rich formulate general guidelines for American foreign policy and provide the personnel to carry out this policy. But we also know that the evidence we have presented is not enough for those scholars who prefer to analyze actual decisions. Then too, skeptics can point out that CFR has no "policy" (other than the all-important policy of international involvement as opposed to isolationism, for which it is called "Communist" and "un-American" by older-fashioned, nationalistic critics). Furthermore, skeptics can say that CFR's members have other institution and association affiliations that may be more important in determining their outlook. For all of these reasons, we will let the case for CFR rest at this point, noting the presence of its directors and members only in passing, and instead emphasizing the direct corporate connections of important decision-makers.*

OTHER LINKS

The Council on Foreign Relations is by no means the only middle term between the corporations and the federal government in the issue area of foreign policy. There are many others, perhaps the most important of which are the Committee for Economic Development, the RAND Corporation, and a handful of research institutes affiliated with elite universities. Turning to the first of these, the Committee for Economic Development (CED) is a tax-exempt research organization which is in many ways the counterpart on economic policy to the Council on Foreign Relations. While its concentration on monetary and economic problems makes it more prominent on issues involving Treasury and Commerce, it has on several occasions played a major role in shaping foreign policy.[36] Organized in the early 1940's to prepare for postwar reconversion to a civilian economy, CED's original leaders were financier Jesse Jones, then Secretary of Commerce, and millionaires Paul Hoffman and William Benton. These three men brought together corporation executives and bankers with outstanding economists for weekend study sessions which were intensified versions of the CFR study groups. Out of these sessions have come the guidelines for American economic policy in the postwar era, including some of the provisions of the Employment Act of 1946, the stabilized budget concept, long-range fiscal and monetary policy, and certain aspects of the Marshall Plan. Perhaps the most impressive evidence for CED prominence in foreign policy is that its corporate elite members and hired economists were the men who moved into the government to administer the Marshall Plan. That CED head Paul Hoffman of Studebaker and the Ford Foundation became administrator of the Marshall Plan is only the surface of the iceberg.

The relationship of CED to the corporations really does not need to be established, for membership is expressly limited to businessmen and implicitly to representatives of the biggest and most important corporations in the country. Among its original and most active members have been Ralph Flanders, the Vermont toolmaker and Boston banker; Thomas B. McCabe, head of Scott Paper Company; Clarence Francis of General Foods; Marion B. Folsom of Eastman

---

*It should be noted that Kraft is among the skeptics. Despite all the comments we have quoted from him on the power of CFR, he concludes that "even that cock will not fight" as far as calling CFR part of any power elite. This is because CFR has assumed "semi-official duties only in emergencies," because it "has never accepted government financial support," and because its recommendations "have subsequently all stood test at the polls or in Congress." Furthermore, there are "divergent views" within the council, and such an organization is necessary because issues are too complicated for the ordinary citizen, who is all wrapped up in his private life. Kraft's concluding sentence seems to be a challenge to those who might criticize—he quotes Voltaire asking, "What have you got that's better?"[35]

Kodak; William L. Clayton of Clayton, Anderson; William L. Batt of SKF Industires; Charles E. Wilson of General Electric; Eric A. Johnston of the Brown-Johnston Company; Chester C. Davis of the Federal Reserve Bank of St. Louis; and S. Bayard Colgate of Colgate-Palmolive-Peet. As with CFR, many CED members have become officials in the federal government: 38 of the trustees during CED's first fifteen years held elected or appointed positions.[37] Flanders and Benton became senators, McCabe became head of the Federal Reserve Bank under President Truman, and Folsom, Clayton, William C. Foster, and Wayne C. Taylor held important posts in major departments. As of the early 1960's, 48 of 190 CED trustees were at the same time members of CFR.

Perhaps the best-known of the power elite's large research organizations is the RAND Corporation, a name which is an abbreviation of "Research ANd Development." It has been credited with many technical innovations and operational suggestions.[38] Started after the war with government research contracts and Ford Foundation money to "think" for the air force, RAND has since expanded its staff and facilities to provide this service for the entire federal government. Its 500-man professional staff is well paid and well educated (150 have Ph.D.'s) because RAND was purposely set up as a non governmental agency so that civil service rules and salary scales could be avoided in order to attract the finest talent money could buy. It is governed by a board of trustees which is dominated by representatives of the corporate rich. In 1963 when RAND published a report on its first fifteen years, the board included executives from CBS, Hewlett-Packard, Owens-Corning Fiberglass International, Monsanto Chemical, and New England Electric System, as well as the president of one of the Carnegie foundations, a leading official in the Council on Foreign Relations, the former vice-president of the ·Carnegie Corporation (then president of Cornell), and the presidents of MIT and Rice universities.*[39] Seven of the seventeen trustees were members of CFR and of fifteen former trustees, seven were leading figures in the corporate world (the rest were university administrators or physicists). The most important of these former trustees was H. Rowan Gaither, a West Coast attorney and Ford Foundation trustee who was one of RAND's key organizers. His legacy is seen in two of the 1963 trustees who are not with one of the companies listed above: Frederick Anderson is a partner in the investment firm of Draper, Gaither, and Anderson; Edwin E. Huddleson, Jr., is a partner in the law firm of Cooley, Crowley, Gaither, Godward, Castro, and Huddleson.

In addition to CFR, CED, and RAND there are many other associations and research organizations controlled by members of the power elite. About 300 study centers consult for the Defense Department alone.**[40] But instead of

---

*The president of RAND since its inception, F. R. Collbohm, is a former vice-president of Douglas Aircraft.

**Many of these organizations are discussed in Arthur Herzog's *The War-Peace Establishment,* although not all the organizations noted in his book are outposts of the power elite.

trying to outline any more specific links, we want to turn to a more general, less direct link between the corporate rich and the federal government, the world of academic scholarship. As we have seen in the case of CFR, CED, and RAND, corporate leaders are not adverse to seeking advice from professional researchers, a fact which has led to claims that "experts" control the country. Without emphasizing the direct power of these scholars, for they are often ignored and seldom have decision-making roles, we can add that the power elite pay for their training and encourage them by monetary inducements to study certain questions rather than others. This is accomplished, first, by the general framework created at major universities through financing and through service on boards of trustees.[42] Second, it is accomplished by foundation grants which encourage research on specific questions. Thus, Rockefeller, Carnegie, and Ford money are responsible in one way or another for almost all American research on non-Western areas.[43] While many of these grants are to universities for scholarships and to individuals for specific research projects, the foundations also provide money for institutes affiliated with universities. For example, Ford and Carnegie money finance a Russian Research Center at Harvard, Rockefeller money finances a Russian Research Center at Columbia. Consider the situation on the specific topic of military affairs:

> Between 1950 and 1960, Harvard, Princeton, Columbia, Chicago, Pennsylvania, MIT, and Johns Hopkins all opened special institutes for the study of defense problems. . . . Ford ($213,800 for Harvard's Defense Studies Center) and Carnegie ($141,000 for Chicago's Center for the Study of American Foreign Policy and Military Policy) rained down funds. Books by the dozen (fifteen in nine years from Princeton alone) rolled out.[44]

The interrelationship of corporate-controlled foundations, think factories, and university research institutes can be demonstrated by studying the prefaces to leading books in the field of foreign affairs. For example, Gabriel A. Almond of the very prominent Princeton Center of International Studies (publisher of *World Affairs,* which is second only to CFR's *Foreign Affairs* in this field) offers thanks to the Carnegie Corporation for the funds which made possible his study, *The Appeals of Communism.* Carnegie also supplied the funds for *The Civic Culture: Political Attitudes and Democracy in Five Nations,* co-authored by Almond and Sidney Verba. Thomas C. Schelling of the Center for International Affairs at Harvard wrote *The Strategy of Conflict* during a year-long stay at the RAND Corporation, while Herman Kahn did most of the research for *On Thermonuclear War,* published by the Princeton center, while at the RAND Corporation. Lucian Pye's *Aspects of Political Development* was written while at the MIT Center for International Studies, with the help of Carnegie money.

Herzog also testifies to the importance of CFR without discussing it: ". . . a private but highly influential circle that comes close to being the foreign policy establishment of the U.S."[41]

Walt W. Rostow of the MIT center, a leading adviser to Democratic Presidents during the 1960's, wrote his "non-communist manifesto," *Stages of Economic Growth,* during a "reflective year" grant provided by the Carnegie Corporation.* Harry Eckstein edited *Internal War* for the Princeton center with the help of Carnegie funds; an earlier version of Eckstein's own contribution to that book, "On the Etiology of Internal Wars," was published in *Social Science and National Security,* a book which had government circulation only.†

Up to this point we have approached our question from one direction only. That is, we started with various non-governmental institutions known to be involved in foreign affairs and showed through studies of their financing, membership, and leadership that they are controlled by the corporate rich. We then presented evidence as to the importance of these arms of the power elite in determining government policy. As impressive as the evidence from this approach is, it is not sufficient in and of itself. It is also necessary to start from the other direction, the important institutions and agencies within the government that are concerned with foreign policy, and work back to their ties with the corporate elite. It is to this task that we turn in this section. Our goal is to complete the framework within which specific foreign policy events must be analyzed. As with non-government institutions, there are too many government units to analyze them all in any detail. Fortunately, as on the non-government side, there are some that are more important than others. These include the State Department and the Defense Department, and one that stands above all others, the National Security Council (NSC), which was created in 1947 as the top policy-making unit of the federal government.

THE NATIONAL SECURITY COUNCIL

The NSC was developed by the corporate rich, after much debate among the armed services and their various protagonists in Congress, on the basis of

---

*It is now known that this center received CIA funds as well as foundation grants during the 1950's. Its director, Max Millikan, who was also head of the World Peace Foundation during the 1950's, had served as an assistant director of the CIA in Washington.[45]

†According to one source, it is "standard procedure at MIT and elsewhere" to publish two versions, "one classified for circulation within the intelligence community, the other 'sanitized' for public consumption."[46] While we do not believe for a minute that the power elite tell these scholars what to say, it should be clear that members of the power elite see no reason to discontinue their support of such efforts. The whole thing has been explained by political scientist David Easton: "A deeper social reason for the failure of political science to transcend its limitations . . . lies in the proximity of political research to social forces that determine social policy. . . . Entrenched power groups in society, those who have a firm hold on a particular pattern of distribution of social goods, material and spiritual, have a special reason to look askance at this probing into the nature and source of their social positions and activities. They are prone to stimulate research of a kind that does not inquire into the fundamentals of the existing arrangement of things."[47] Or, as noted in a preliminary report of an American Political Science Association committee on professional standards, ". . . problems arise not so much because a scholar is told by his sponsors what to write but rather because a scholar may, wittingly or unwittingly, condition his manuscript to the assumed or divined values of his financial sponsors."[48]

experience in attempting to coordinate departments and military units during World War II. It is strictly an advisory group, headed by the President and now including as statutory members the Vice-President, the Secretary of State, the Secretary of Defense, and the director of the Office of Civil and Defense Mobilization. However, "the President can also ask other key aides to take part in Council deliberations."[49] As statutory advisers it has the director of the Central Intelligence Agency and the chairman of the Joint Chiefs of Staff. The machinery of the NSC is very flexible and has been used in different ways by different Presidents. President Eisenhower, for example, enlarged and formalized the NSC, giving it many powers traditionally thought of as belonging to departments. President Kennedy dismantled much of this machinery, cut its size to a minimum, met with it less frequently, and gave more responsibility for carrying out NSC decisions to the departments. However different Presidents may use it, the NSC is a key foreign policy organ of the U.S. government.*

Before studying the personnel of the NSC, it is instructive to summarize briefly a detailed case study on how the National Security Act was formulated.[50] Such an account demonstrates the importance of specially appointed "outsiders" in shaping government policy. In this case, the key outsider was investment banker Ferdinand Eberstadt, a former partner in the finance house of Dillon, Read who had gone on to start his own investment house. Eberstadt was asked to come up with a plan to satisfy all sides in the argument over how to reorganize the national defense establishment. The appointment came from the Secretary of the Navy, James Forrestal, a former president of Dillon, Read and a good friend of Eberstadt's. Eberstadt in turn talked informally with other financiers, including Bernard Baruch, developing the report which was the basis for the agreement which finally led to the National Security Act.[51] The final form of the act was determined by a compromise between the differences of Forrestal and Secretary of War Robert Patterson, a Wall Street lawyer who had gone into government service early in the 1940's as a special assistant to Secretary of War Henry L. Stimson. Along with military leaders Lauris Norstad, Forrest Sherman, and Arthur Radford, the important figures in bringing about the compromise between Forrestal and Patterson were three very prominent members of the corporate elite, Robert Lovett, John J. McCloy, and Stuart Symington.**[52]

---

*For details on the NSC and its use by various Presidents, see the testimony by members of the power elite and scholars in *The National Security Council: Jackson Subcommittee Papers on Policy-Making at the Presidential Level* (New York: Frederick Praeger, 1965).

**The National Security Act provided for the coordination of the entire defense establishment. In addition to the National Security Council, it also established the Secretary of Defense, the Central Intelligence Agency, and the National Security Resources Board (now reorganized as the Office of Civil and Defense Mobilization). It was a weak act which left the Secretary of Defense in a very tenuous position. Later amendments strengthened his control over the three services (and removed their heads from the NSC) and gave him a larger staff. The amendments also strengthened the control of the Joint Chiefs of Staff over operational military units. With these and other slight modifications, the National Security

Who are the men who sit on the National Security Council? We partially answered this question in *Who Rules America?* by showing that the heads of State, Defense, and Treasury during the postwar years have almost without exception been members of the power elite. (Although not a statutory member, the Secretary of the Treasury has been asked by all three administrations under consideration to sit on the NSC.) For example, Robert Lovett of Brown Brothers, Harriman served as Secretary of Defense, as did Charles Erwin Wilson of General Motors, Neil McElroy of Proctor and Gamble, Artemus Gates of Morgan Guaranty Trust, and Robert McNamara of Ford Motor. Treasurers have included John Snyder of the First National Bank of St. Louis, George Humphrey of Hanna Mining, Robert Anderson of the W. T. Waggoner oil estate and the Federal Reserve Bank of Dallas, and Douglas Dillon of Dillon Read; heads of State included John Foster Dulles of Sullivan and Cromwell, Dean Rusk of the Rockefeller Foundation, Dean Acheson of Covington and Burling, General George C. Marshall, and Boston aristocrat Christian Herter. We can now be more specific by looking at the composition of the NSC when it was studied by journalists during the Truman, Eisenhower, and Kennedy administrations.

When John Fischer of *Harper's Magazine* wrote of "Mr. Truman's Politburo" as "the most powerful and least publicized of all government agencies," it included, in addition to Acheson, Marshall, and Snyder, the following corporate rich: Averell Harriman of Brown Brothers, Harriman, Charles Edward Wilson of General Electric, and Stuart Symington of Emerson Electric.[53] The secretary of the NSC was a big businessman from St. Louis, Sidney Souers. His assistant was James Lay, a former employee of utilities companies whom Souers had met during World War II. Others present for NSC meetings were Alben Barkley, Vice-President, General Walter Bedell Smith, director of the CIA, and General Omar Bradley, chairman of the Joint Chiefs of Staff.*

When *U.S. News and World Report* ran a story in 1956 on "How Ike Makes the Big Decisions,"[55] the following were regularly a part of the NSC, in addition to Dulles, Humphrey, and Charles Erwin Wilson:

Richard Nixon, Vice-President, who was selected and financed for a political career by top corporate executives in Southern California.[56]

Arthur S. Flemming, a lawyer who was formerly president of Ohio Wesleyan University.

Percival Brundage, a partner in Price, Waterhouse & Company.

Allan Dulles, a former partner in the large corporate law firm of Sullivan and Cromwell.

Act and the National Security Council remain at the heart of the U.S. system for foreign and defense policy.

*If Fischer is right, the NSC was especially important under Truman: "Mr. Truman has delegated his authority in foreign affairs to the uttermost limit that the Constitution permits. From the day he took office, he apparently recognized his own shortcomings in this field, and he has leaned heavily—sometimes almost pathetically—on the judgment of his 'experts.' "[54]

Lewis Strauss, investment banker and personal financial advisor to the Rockefellers.

William H. Jackson, a lawyer who managed the investment firm of John Hay Whitney, as well as sitting on the board of Great Northern Paper and Bankers Trust.

Dillon Anderson, a Houston corporation lawyer who was the President's Special Assistant for National Security Affairs.[57]

Harold Stassen, former governor of Minnesota and former president of the University of Pennsylvania.

Admiral Arthur W. Radford, chairman of the Joint Chiefs of Staff.

Managing the NSC for President Kennedy was aristocrat McGeorge Bundy who played a leading role in foreign affairs throughout the 1960's until he left government service to become president of the Ford Foundation. His staff included Walt Rostow of the MIT Center for International Studies, Harvard economist Carl Kaysen, Michael Forrestal (son of the former president of Dillon, Read), and Robert Komer (a government official). The following were members of the NSC Executive Committee which met regularly over a period of two weeks to determine American reaction during the Cuban missile crisis of 1962:[58]

Lyndon Johnson, Vice-President, representative of Texas oil interests.[59]

Dean Rusk, formerly president of the Rockefeller Foundation.

Robert McNamara, formerly president of Ford Motors.

Robert F. Kennedy, a multimillionaire from Boston.

Douglas Dillon, a former president of Dillon, Read.

Roswell Gilpatric, a corporation lawyer from New York.

McGeorge Bundy, a Boston aristocrat who was formerly a dean at Harvard.

Adlai Stevenson, a corporation lawyer from Chicago.

John McCone, a multimillionaire industrialist from Los Angeles.

Dean Acheson, a corporation lawyer and former Secretary of State.

Robert Lovett, an investment banker with Brown Brothers, Harriman.

General Maxwell Taylor, a Presidential adviser at the time, and former chairman of the Mexican Light and Power Company, Ltd.

Major General Marshall S. Carter, Deputy Director of the CIA.

George Ball, a Washington corporation lawyer, later to become a partner in Lehman Brothers.

Edwin M. Martin, a State Department official specializing in Latin America.

Llewellyn Thompson, a foreign service officer.

Theodore C. Sorensen, Presidential speechwriter and adviser.

SPECIAL GOVERNMENT COMMITTEES

It is important to look at one other "institution" of the federal government which is essential in understanding how the corporate rich are involved in foreign policy. These are the special commissions, "blue ribbon" citizen committees, and "task forces" appointed by the President to make recommendations on specific problems:

> Despite the extensive government apparatus for policy-making on problems of national security, the American President in the postwar period has, from time to time, appointed groups of private citizens to investigate particular problems and report to the National Security Council. Some of these groups have performed their task without the public's ever becoming aware of their existence; others have in one way or another come to public attention. Among the latter are those which have become known under the names of their chairman: Finletter, Gray, Paley, Sarnoff, Gaither, Draper, Boechenstein, and Killian.[60]

These committees are almost without exception headed by members of the corporate rich and staffed by the employees and scholars of the foundations, associations, and institutes outlined in previous sections. For example, among the eight committee heads mentioned in the previous quotation, seven are corporate executives and the eighth is the chairman of MIT. All are affiliated with the Council on Foreign Relations, three with the Committee for Economic Development. We believe it is by means of these committees that the policy recommendations of the power elite's non-government groups are given official sanction: they become the "reports" of the specially appointed committees. The circuit between corporations (and their foundations and associations) and the government is thus completed.

Two such committees, the Gaither Committee and the Clay Committee, have been studied in detail by social scientists. The Gaither Committee was appointed in the late 1950's by President Eisenhower to reconsider American military preparedness. H. Rowan Gaither, its head, is the aforementioned attorney and Ford Foundation official who was instrumental in organizing the RAND Corporation. Other members of the corporate elite on the eleven man committee were Robert C. Sprague, William C. Foster, and William Webster (also a trustee of RAND). Two other prominent members were James A. Perkins, a vice-president of the Carnegie Corporation at the time, and scientist Jerome Weisner, who became a "wealthy man" as one of the owners of the Rockefeller-financed ITEK Corporation.[61] Other members were James Baxter, a college president; Robert Calkins, an economist who had been a CED consultant before becoming head of The Brookings Institution (yet another research organization founded, financed, and directed by the corporate rich); John Corson, research director for the Cooperative League of America; Robert C. Prim, a mathematician who directed research for Bell Telephone; and Hector Skifter, a radio engineer who was a consultant for the Department of Defense. Six of the eleven are members of CFR.

Much of the detail work of the Gaither Committee was assigned to a technical staff drawn from the military and from various non-government institutes, including RAND and the Institute for Defense Analysis. The committee also had an advisory panel of corporate and military leaders. The final report, highly critical of the emphasis on nuclear weapons and the de-emphasis of conventional ground forces, was discussed at a special meeting of the NSC on November 7, 1957. Over forty people attended, including financiers Robert Lovett and John J. McCloy, who predicted that the business community would support the President if he requested increased spending for defense.[62] President Eisenhower was hesitant, but it is interesting that the Kennedy Administration adopted an approach much like that advocated by the Gaither Report. Among President Kennedy's appointees who had been on the Gaither Committee or its advisory panel were arms control chief Foster, disarmament negotiator McCloy, and science adviser Weisner.*

Equally impressive was the composition and effect of the Clay Committee, selected by President Kennedy to reconsider U.S. foreign aid policy. In addition to Lucius Clay, a retired army general who sat on the boards of a half-dozen major corporations, the committee consisted of financier Robert Anderson, financier Robert Lovett, banker Eugene Black, corporation lawyer Herman Phleger, corporate leader L.F. McCollum, college president Clifford Hardin, economist Edward S. Mason (a member of CFR, a consultant to CED), physician Howard A. Rusk (no relation to Dean Rusk), and labor leader George Meany. All but Lovett, Rusk, and Meany are in CFR. With Meany dissenting, the committee suggested large cuts and other changes in foreign aid. Although the cuts were apparently more than President Kennedy expected, "In an aid message to the Congress President Kennedy deferentially referred to the Clay Report seven times, setting forth in detail how the new aid program was based on the application of standards 'affirmed by the Clay Committee.' "[66]

NOTES

[1] G. William Domhoff, *Who Rules America?* (Englewood Cliffs, N.J.: Prentice Hall, 1967).

[2] *Ibid.*, pp. 53-55.

[3] *Ibid.*, p. 65.

[4] C. Wright Mills, *The Power Elite* (New York: Oxford University Press, 1956); for a discussion of the "interlocking overlappers" see Richard Rovere's review of *The Power Elite*

---

*The military stance of the 1960's may also derive from the report of a special Rockefeller-financed panel on international security of the late 1950's, said to be very similar to the still-secret Gaither Report.[63] In any case, there were four people who participated in the Gaither Committee work who also helped with the Rockefeller report.[64] More generally, the first three of six Rockefeller-financed panels (*Prospect for America*) were directly concerned with foreign affairs. Members of those three panels who became part of the Kennedy Administration were A.A. Berle, Jr., Chester Bowles, Harlan Cleveland, Roswell Gilpatric, and Dean Rusk.[65]

under that title, as reprinted in his *The American Establishment* (New York: Harcourt, Brace & World, 1962).

[5] Domhoff, *Who Rules America?*, Chap. 5.

[6] *Ibid.*, p. 8, quoting E. Digby Baltzell's *The Protestant Establishment* (New York: Random House, 1964), p. 8.

[7] *Ibid.*, Chap. 4, and later in this essay.

[8] Mills, *The Power Elite*, p. 186.

[9] Joseph Kraft, "School for Statesmen," *Harper's Magazine*, July 1958, p. 64.

[10] *Ibid.*, pp. 64, 68.

[11] Douglass Cater, *Power in Washington* (New York: Random House, 1964), p. 247.

[12] *New York Times*, May 15, 1966, "Experts on Policy Looking to Youth," section one, p. 34.

[13] Lester Milbrath, "Interest Groups and Foreign Policy," in James N. Rosenau, ed., *Domestic Sources of Foreign Policy* (New York: The Free Press, 1967), p. 247.

[14] *Annual Report of the Council on Foreign Relations*, 1957-1958.

[15] Kraft, "School for Statesmen," p. 68.

[16] Dan Smoot, *The Invisible Government* (Dallas, 1962), pp. 168-171.

[17] Kraft, "School for Statesmen," p. 65.

[18] John F. Whitney, Jr., "The Council on Foreign Relations, Inc.," January 1968, a paper for Professor Hoyt B. Ballard's graduate seminar in government at Texas A & I University.

[19] Smoot, *The Invisible Government*, p. 21.

[20] Quoted in Kraft, "School for Statesmen," p. 67.

[21] *Ibid.*, p. 68.

[22] *Annual Report of the Council on Foreign Relations*, 1958-1959, p. 4.

[23] Kraft, "School for Statesmen," p. 66.

[24] *Ibid.*

[25] *Ibid.*

[26] Percy W. Bidwell, *What the Tariff Means to American Industries*, published for the Council on Foreign Relations by Harpers Bros. (New York, 1956).

[27] *New York Times*, May 15, 1966, p. 34.

[28] Kraft, "School for Statesmen," p. 68.

[29] Robert A. Dahl, *Who Governs?* (New Haven, Conn.: Yale University Press, 1961), pp. 66, 331.

[30] Kraft, "School for Statesmen," p. 64; *New York Times*, May 15, 1966, section one, p. 34.

[31] Kraft, "School for Statesmen," p. 67. Much of Kraft's information on CFR involvement in specific issues is drawn from CFR's self-published twenty-five-year history. It contains further details and information on other issues as well. See *The Council on Foreign Relations, A Record of Twenty-five Years* (New York, 1947).

[32] Quoted in Kraft, "School for Statesmen," p. 68.

[33] *Ibid.*, p. 64.

[34] Chadwick F. Alger, "The External Bureaucracy in United States Foreign Affairs," *Administration Science Quarterly*, June 1962.

[35] Kraft, "School for Statesmen," p. 68.

[36] Karl Schriftgeisser, *Business Comes of Age* (New York: Harper & Row, 1960); and David Eakins, "The Development of Corporate Liberal Policy Research, 1885-1965," (Ph.D. dissertation, University of Wisconsin, 1966).

[37] Schriftgeisser, *Business Comes of Age,* pp. 25, 62, 162.

[38] Joseph Kraft, "RAND: Arsenal for Ideas," *Profiles in Power* (New York: New American Library, 1966); Saul Friedman, "The RAND Corporation and Our Policy Makers," *The Atlantic Monthly*, September 1963.

[39] RAND Corporation, *The First Fifteen Years* (Santa Monica, California, 1963).

[40] Arthur Herzog, *The War-Peace Establishment* (New York: Harper & Row, 1965), p. 54.

[41] *Ibid.*, p. 36.

[42] Domhoff, *Who Rules America?*, pp. 77-79.

[43] George M. Beckmann, "The Role of the Foundations," *The Annals of the American Academy of Political and Social Science,* November 1964.

[44] Joseph Kraft, "The Military Schoolmen," in *Profiles in Power*, p. 52.

[45] David Wise and Thomas B. Ross, *The Invisible Government* (New York: Random House, 1964), p. 243.

[46] *Ibid.*

[47] David Easton, *The Political System* (New York: Alfred A. Knopf, 1953), pp. 50-51.

[48] Robert J. Samuelson, "Political Science: CIA, Ethics Stir Otherwise Placid Convention," *Science*, September 22, 1967, p. 1415.

[49] Henry M. Jackson, ed., *The National Security Council: Jackson Subcommittee Papers on Policy-Making at the Presidential Level* (New York: Frederick Praeger, 1965), p. 31.

[50] Demetrios Caraley, *The Politics of Military Unification* (New York: Columbia University Press, 1966).

[51] Margaret Coit, *Mr. Baruch* (Boston: Houghton Mifflin, 1957), p. 623.

[52] Caraley, *The Politics of Military Unification*, pp. 149-51.

[53] John Fischer, "Mr. Truman's Politburo," *Harper's Magazine,* June 1951, p. 29.

[54] *Ibid.*, p. 31.

[55] *U.S. News and World Report,* April 20, 1956.

[56] Ernest Brashear, "Who Is Richard Nixon?" *The New Republic,* September 1 and September 8, 1952.

[57] For details on Dillon Anderson and his role, see "Dillon Anderson of Texas: The Keeper of the Nation's Secrets," *Newsweek*, February 13, 1956.

[58] Wise and Ross, *The Invisible Government*, p. 293; Arthur M. Schlesinger, *A Thousand Days* (Boston: Houghton Mifflin, 1965), p. 802.

[59] Robert Sherrill, "Johnson and the Oil Men," *Ramparts*, January 1967; David Welsh, "LBJ's Favorite Construction Co.," *Ramparts*, December 1967.

[60] Morton H. Halperin, "The Gaither Committee and the Policy Process," *World Politics*, April 1961, p. 360.

[61] For details on ITEK and other such ventures, see "Rocky Ride on Route 128," *Forbes*, September 1, 1965; for details on Weisner and his connection with ITEK, see Lester Tanzer, *The Kennedy Circle* (New York: David McKay, 1961).

[62] Halperin, "The Gaither Committee and the Policy Process," p. 368.

[63] *Ibid.*, p. 382.

[64] Samuel P. Huntington, *The Common Defense* (New York: Columbia University Press, 1961), p. 456.

[65] The Rockefeller Panel Report, *Prospect for America* (New York: Doubleday & Co., 1961), pp. 8, 94, 160.

[66] Usha Mahajani, "Kennedy and the Strategy of Aid: The Clay Report and After," *Western Political Quarterly* 18, 1965, p. 657.

The Class Background
of Foreign Policy Makers

GABRIEL KOLKO

Sociologists such as C. Wright Mills, and often journalists as well, have made too much of . . . social origins, for while interesting and important there is no proof such connections are decisive. Twenty-six percent of the highest federal executives come from working class and farmer origins, and an increasingly larger percentage from the non-Ivy League schools, and there is no evidence whatsoever to prove that social and educational origins determine policies of state. That elite orgins and connections accelerated personal advancement is now sufficiently self-evident not to warrant excessive attention, much less to make these standards the key criterion for explaining the sources and purposes of American power. In brief, the basic objectives, function, and exercise of American power, and not simply its formal structure and identity, are paramount in defining its final social role and significance. Without denigrating the important contribution of Mills, which was brilliant but inconsistent, such an approach fails to come to grips with the dynamics of American power in its historical setting.

A class structure and predatory rule can exist within the context of high social mobility and democratic criteria for rulership, perhaps all the better so because it co-opts the elites and experts of the potential opposition and totally integrates talent into the existing society. The major value in essentially static structural studies of key decision-makers is to illustrate the larger power context in which administrators made decisions, but not to root the nature of those decisions in the backgrounds or individual personalities of an elite. In brief, correlation may not be causation in the power structure, and should high status, rich men ever seek to make decisions dysfunctional to the more permanent interests of dominant power interests, even more powerful leaders would immediately purge them from decision-making roles. The point is that while such men are unlikely to

From *The Roots of American Foreign Policy*, pp. 14-26, 140-142. Copyright © 1969 by Gabriel Kolko. Reprinted by permission of Beacon Press.

make socially dysfunctional decisions so is anyone else who rises to the top of a structure with predetermined rules and functions. To measure power that is latent as well as active, it is often easier to study the decision-makers themselves. The other approach, and by far the more difficult, is to define objective and impersonal interests and roles for the larger classes and sectors of American society, their relationship to each other and to the world, and the manner in which they have exercised their relative power.... I investigated the career cycles and origins of the key American foreign policy decision-makers from 1944 through 1960, excluding the Presidents. My major premise was that even if I could show that such men neither began nor ended in business, there were still many other and more valid ways of gauging the nature of foreign policy. We examined the State, Defense or War, Treasury and Commerce Departments, plus certain relevant executive level agencies indicated in the "Note on Methods," and considered only those with the highest ranks.[1] The study included 234 individuals with all their positions in government during 1944-60, comprising the lesser posts if an individual attained the highest executive level. As a total, these key leaders held 678 posts and nearly all of them were high level and policy-making in nature.

The net result of this study, however imperfect, revealed that foreign policy decision-makers are in reality a highly mobile sector of the American corporate structure, a group of men who frequently assume and define high level policy tasks in government, rather than routinely administer it, and then return to business. Their firms and connections are large enough to afford them the time to straighten out or formulate government policy while maintaining their vital ties with giant corporate law, banking, or industry. The conclusion is that a small number of men fill the large majority of key foreign policy posts. Their many diverse posts make this group a kind of committee government entrusted to handle numerous and varied national security and international functions at the policy level. Even if not initially connected with the corporate sector, career government officials relate in some tangible manner with the private worlds predominantly of big law, big finance, and big business.

Of the 234 officials examined, 35.8 percent, or eighty-four individuals, held 63.4 percent of the posts.... Thirty men from law, banking, and investment firms accounted for 22 percent of all the posts which we studied, and another fifty-seven from this background held an additional 14.1 percent—or a total of 36.1 percent of the key posts. Certain key firms predominated among this group: members of Sullivan & Cromwell, or Carter, Ledyard & Milburn, and Coudert Brothers, in that order among law firms, held twenty-nine posts, with other giant corporate-oriented law firms accounting for most of the remainder. Dillon, Read & Co., with four men, and the Detroit Bank, with only Joseph M. Dodge, accounted for eighteen and ten posts, respectively, and two men from Brown Brothers, Harriman held twelve posts—or forty posts for three firms. It was in the nature of their diverse functions as lawyers and financiers for many corporate industrial and investment firms, as Mills correctly perceived, that these men preeminently represented the less parochial interests of all giant corporations, and were best able to wear many hats and play numerous roles, frequently and interchangeably as each corporate or government problem—or both—required. Nothing reveals this dual function more convincingly than their career cycles. Despite the fact that Sullivan & Cromwell and Dillon, Read men tended to go into the State Department, or lawyers from Cahill, Gordon, Zachry & Riendel to the Navy Department, general patterns of distribution by economic interests—save for bankers in the governmental banking structure—are not discernible. And with one possible exception, all the men from banking, investment, and law who held four or more posts were connected with the very largest and most powerful firms in these fields.

In the aggregate, men who came from big business, investment, and law held 59.6 percent of the posts, with only forty-five of them filling 32.4 percent of all posts. . . .[2] The very top foreign policy decision-makers were therefore intimately connected with dominant business circles and their law firms. And whether exercised or not, scarcely concealed levels of economic power exist beneath or behind the government, and indeed high mobility in various key posts reinforces such interlockings. This continuous reality has not altered with successive administrations, as the state has called upon Fair Dealers and modern Republicans alike to serve as experts in running a going operation which they are asked to administer efficiently within certain common definitions of its objectives. Whether Democrats, such as James Forrestal of Dillon, Read, or Republicans, such as John Foster Dulles of Sullivan & Cromwell, the continuous contact and advice they have received from their colleagues in the world of finance, law, and business have always colored their focus. The operative assumption of such men, as Forrestal once put it, is that "What I have been trying to preach down here is that in this whole world picture the Government alone can't do the job; it's got to work through business. . . . that means that we'll need to, for specific jobs, be able to tap certain people. . . ." It is this process of "tapping" for high level policy tasks that has accounted for high mobility and the concentration of posts in few hands.

Perhaps of even greater interest is the special nature of the government career officials and their relationship to business during their extended professional lives. These sixty men, 25.6 percent of the total, held 31.7 percent of the posts considered, in part because, being full-timers, they were available for a greater number of tasks. But for many of these men government became a stepping stone toward business careers, and we can only speculate on how this possible aspiration influenced their functional policies on economic and other questions while they were in government. "The lure of industry was such that I couldn't pass it up," a former career officer and head of the C.I.A. for fourteen months, Admiral William F. Raborn, Jr., confessed in discussing why he had taken his government post in the first place. "I went there with the thought I could go when I wanted to." Over half these men, perhaps enticed in the same manner, later took up nongovernmental posts, though a significant fraction returned to government for special tasks. Conversely, however, any government employee thwarting the interests of American businesses, as expressed in foreign and national security affairs, risks losing possible future posts, even if he goes to foundations or university administrations. Most of these new private positions were in law firms and industry. But certain of those key career officials who never left for business or new careers the State Department had selected under its pre-1924 or conventional rules, where independent wealth and social connections were always helpful. The fact that John M. Cabot, Assistant Secretary of State and a Boston Cabot, also held the largest number of posts among the twenty-six full-time career officials we examined is not inconsequential. It is within this career group that the conventional elite social background predominates.

For the most part, the technical and policy nature of foreign policy and military security issues has necessitated the selection of men with requisite business backgrounds. The choice of William L. Clayton, rags-to-riches head of the largest world cotton export firm, to deal with Unites States foreign economic policy between 1944-47 was rational and both a cause and reflection of policy. What is most instructive was that Woodrow Wilson and Cordell Hull, President and Secretary of State (1933-44), a professor and small town politician, formulated the essential foreign economic policy, and it is here that we must see the larger ideological and consensual definition of foreign policy as ultimately transcending the decision-maker recruitment process.

BUSINESS AS THE FOUNT

The organizational rungs of governmental power take many other businessmen into the lower hierarchies of administration in much the same manner as their seniors function at the very highest levels. These lower tiers of operation are too extensive to measure in their entirety here, but it is sufficient to point to several readily documented expressions. Such lines of contact are perfectly logical, given the objectives of American policy abroad, and given the fact that Washington generally assigns the management of the Government's relationship to various problems to the businessmen or their representatives with business connections or backgrounds in the various areas. And it is both convenient and more than logical that key federal executives recruit former associates for critical problem-solving posts for which they have responsibility. There is no conflict of interest because the welfare of government and business is, in the largest sense, identical.

This will mean that key law firm executives with major corporate connections will draw on former clients, whom they may again soon represent at the termination of their governmental service; it will simplify the task of the business representatives in Washington—about two-thirds of the top two hundred manufacturing firms maintain them on a full-time basis—who may wish assistance with marketing, legislative, or legal matters. The Government will invariably choose advisers to international raw materials and commodity meetings from the consuming industries, and will select key government executives concerned with specific issues—such as oil—from the interested industry. The existence of businessmen and their lawyers in government, in short, gives the lobbyists and those not in government something to do—successfully—insofar as it is to their interest. These men interact in different roles and at various times, for today's assistant secretary may be tomorrow's senior partner or corporate president. However much such men may have competing specific economic objectives, conflicts that may indeed at times neutralize their mutual goals, what is essentially common among such elites, whether or not they are cooperative, makes them a class with joint functions and assumptions and larger economic objectives that carry with it the power to rule. This is not to say such well placed officials with industry backgrounds are the only source of government policy, but that they exist and, more important, given the larger aims of government it is entirely rational to select personnel in this fashion. From this viewpoint the nature of the bureaucracy is essentially an outcome rather than a cause of policy.

Examples of interlocking government-business leadership are numerous even below the highest decision-making echelons. In the Department of the Interior, to cite one instance, the large majority of key personnel in the Office of Oil and Gas or the Petroleum Administration for Defense in the decade after 1946 came from the industry, often just on loan for fixed periods of time. These bodies, which are largely a continuation of wartime boards, have permitted the regulation of the petroleum industry via governmental agencies, free from the threat of antitrust prosecution and for the welfare of the industry. Pleased with the arrangement, the industry has supplied many of the key administrators and consultants the government needs on a no-compensation basis.

No less typical is the Business and Defensive Services Administration of the Department of Commerce (BDSA), created in the fall of 1953. Composed of 184 industry groups during the period 1953-55, the BDSA committees dealt with a vast number of goods and the problems of their industry, recommending action to the government that was the basis of profitable action and regulation of various economic sectors. These ranged from the division of government purchases among industry members to the review of proposed Export-Import Bank and World Bank loans for the construction of competing industries abroad. In effect, BDSA committees have served themselves via the government in a classic fashion, the precedents for which range back to the early nineteenth century. In this regard they are no different in genesis and function from the federal regulatory movement initiated in 1887.

At every level of the administration of the American state, domestically and internationally, business serves as the fount of critical assumptions or goals and strategically placed personnel. But that this leadership in foreign and military affairs, as integrated in the unified hands of men who are both political and economic leaders, comes from the most powerful class interests is a reflection as well as the cause of the nature and objectives of American power at home and abroad. It is the expression of the universality of the ideology *and* the interests and material power of the physical resources of the ruling class of American capitalism, the latter being sufficient should consensus break down. The pervasiveness of this ideological power in American society and its measurable influence on mass culture, public values, and political opinions is the most visible reality of modern American life to the contemporary social analyst. It means that one can only assess the other institutional structures . . . in relation to the predominance of the economic ruling class which is the final arbiter and beneficiary of the existing structure of American society and politics at home and of United States power in the world.

NOTES

[1] Note on Methods. We examined four Cabinet-level Departments for the period 1944-60: the State, War and Defense, Treasury, and Commerce Departments, their Secretaries, Under and Assistant Secretaries, and Special Assistants to the Secretaries. We included this last-named post because these officials are traditionally the links between the Cabinet members and major problems. In addition, we examined positions designated "Deputy" or "Special" Secretary, Under or Assistant Secretary.

Also surveyed were the Army, Air Force, and Navy Departments, which have similar organizational structures. The other agencies, however, are organized along different lines, and it was possible only to estimate the equivalents of Cabinet posts. Only a random selection of the highest officers is included in the case of the White House staff, the military governments of Germany and Japan, and the E.C.A.-M.S.A.-I.C.A. foreign aid organizations, while the aid organizations incorporate a number of lower level officials. Moreover, the category of "Miscellaneous Government Departments" includes *all* the key individuals' Government posts—in the agencies indicated or others—that do not otherwise qualify for study. The net effect of this technique is to minimize slightly the percentage of posts individuals with law or business backgrounds held. In brief, these data are conservative estimates of the extent of private control of public office.

The data on career backgrounds and history may be found in various issues of *Moody's Industrials, Moody's Manual of Investments, Poor's Register of Directors and Executives, Who's Who, Who Was Who, Martindale-Hubble Legal Directory, Congressional Directory,* and the *New York Times.*

[2] My preceding data were collected in 1966, and in September 1967 the Brookings Institution published *Men Who Govern*, by David T. Stanley, Dean E. Mann, and Jameson W. Doig. The Brookings volume is far superior to any hitherto published study and is unmarred by debilitating ideological biases masked as methodology. It covers 1,041 individuals who held 1,567 key executive appointments from March 1933 to April 1965. These included persons who attained posts—nearly one-third the total—too low to be included in my sample, another one-quarter were Kennedy-Johnson appointees, and somewhat less than this figure served prior to 1944. The authors included all Cabinet-level positions, while I included only four Cabinet agencies. My sample, therefore, covers a more select group of leaders over a shorter time span.

The authors of the Brookings study show that 39 percent of their 1,041 leaders received a private preparatory education, with 60 percent, 46 percent, and 44 percent for the State, Treasury, and Defense Departments, respectively. Nineteen percent attended Yale, Harvard, or Princeton. Twenty-four percent of *all* appointees were principally businessmen before appointment, this figure reaching 40 percent for the Cabinet Secretaries, 56 percent for Military Secretaries, and 42 percent for Under Secretaries. Twenty-six percent of all appointees were lawyers, though the Brookings study does not explore the size or nature of their firms. Sixty-three percent of all Cabinet Secretaries, 86 percent of the Military Secretaries, 66 percent of all Under Secretaries, and 50 percent of all Assistant Secretaries were either businessmen or lawyers prior to political appointment, generally corroborating my findings for a more selective sample.

Including ranks lower than those I considered, the Brookings study revealed that 16 percent of their State Department sample, 1933-65, were principally businessmen before their appointments, and this figure grew to 39 percent in Defense, 57 percent in Commerce and 60 percent in the Navy Department. While businessmen and lawyers accounted for 60 percent of the Eisenhower appointees, the Johnson Administration had the lowest, at 40 percent. President Johnson also appointed more men with master's and doctoral degrees than any of his predecessors, which only tends to prove my contention that the origins of individuals are less responsible for the continuity of the policies of the nation than most critics have cared to admit.

Manufacturing provided 44 percent of the persons designated as businessmen, finance 23 percent, and other forms of capital the remainder. Defense contractors provided 12 percent of the executives considered in the defense-related agencies, reaching a peak of one-fifth under Kennedy. If one removes retirements, deaths, and other statistical imbalances, nearly half the State Department executives had subsequent business and private professional careers, mainly in law, this percentage reaching over three-quarters for most of the other agencies included in my sample.

The External Bureaucracy
in United States
Foreign Affairs

CHADWICK F. ALGER

. . . [M]embers of the social environment may play dual roles, performing both as bureaucrats and as private citizens.

It is with this . . . group of persons that this paper is concerned. We will refer to these persons as "external bureaucrats." Although the external bureaucracy is not a bureaucracy in terms of interrelationships among the external bureaucrats, for they are hired as individuals or in small groups, the term "bureaucrat" is appropriate, because they become a part of the governmental bureaucracy. The adjective "external" indicates that these bureaucrats are not as integrated into the bureaucracy as "internal" bureaucrats. Their outside experiences, affiliations, and loyalties are stronger than those of the full-time bureaucrats. This characteristic distinguishes them from "internal" bureaucrats and also makes them useful to the bureaucracy. For some of these persons the extent of their governmental involvement makes it difficult to classify them as either private citizens or governmental officials. A study of public advisory groups says of an Ohio paper manufacturer: "Mr. [George H.] Mead had served on so many public boards that it was sometimes not clear whether he was inside or outside the government." Some persons playing these dual roles may be well-known figures, such as Eric Johnston, Henry Wriston, and James Killian, but many are less well known, and their governmental participation receives little notice.

* * *

NATURE OF EXPLORATORY INVESTIGATION

This discussion is based on an exploratory study of the external bureaucracy of civilian foreign affairs agencies in the United States. This included the State Department, the foreign information and foreign economic aid agencies, parts of the White House staff, and the Central Intelligence Agency, where information was available. The exploratory study focused on the years 1953 through 1956

From *Administrative Science Quarterly* 7, June 1962, pp. 52-54, 57-60, 75-78. Reprinted by permission of Administrative Science Quarterly and the author.

and was based upon data drawn from congressional files that contained executive responses to congressional questionnaires, congressional reports and hearings, memoirs and biographies of participants, and interviews of some sixty external bureaucrats and governmental officials who had worked with them.

The external bureaucrats of the civilian foreign affairs agencies can be classified in four main categories: individual consultants, public advisory committees, nongovernmental members of delegations to international conferences, and those furnishing a variety of contract services, including research, instruction, evaluations of governmental operations, and the conduct of operations (primarily domestic assistance in the exchange of persons programs, and overseas participation in technical assistance programs). The categories overlap and are intended only to give a general idea of the scope of the activities of external bureaucrats.

SOME FOCI OF INTEREST IN EXTERNAL BUREAUCRACY

For some political analysts the pay-off question on the participation of external bureaucrats in government is: "What is their influence on policy decisions?" The manner in which this question has been asked indicates that specific instances of external bureaucrats having had critical impact in the making of significant decisions were expected. Interesting as this question is, answering it alone may not reveal the full significance of the activities of external bureaucrats. We are asking instead a broader question, which seeks to determine what kinds of effects an external bureaucracy has upon the bureaucracy and upon its social environment. An example may highlight the usefulness of the broader question. Private citizens that fall within our category of external bureaucrats are appointed each year to the United States delegation to the United Nations General Assembly. Asking the narrow question of the influence of our UN delegates might lead one to conclude that their participation is of little significance. Asking the broader question, however, we might find that they communicate information to influential groups and thereby affect the scope of choice perceived by governmental policy makers in future decisions related to the UN. They may also connect the bureaucracy to a previously unconnected communications network, which may provide data altering future decisions. Their influence is no less significant for being indirect and subtle.

* * *

BASIC FUNCTIONS OF EXTERNAL BUREAUCRATS

. . . Statements by external bureaucrats and bureaucrats in interviews and from other materials collected indicate that the functions of external bureaucrats are varied. Four categories seem adequate, however, to summarize the functions of external bureaucrats. First, there is transfer of *information* by the external bureaucrats from the environment to the bureaucracy and vice versa. Second, there is a similar two-directional flow of *perspectives* about relationships between elements of information and about the significance of particular items of information. This arises essentially from the fact that bureaucrats and private citizens view data from different backgrounds and interests. Third, external bureaucrats provide *manpower* to the bureaucracy, helping it at peak periods and supplying skills that are not available to the bureaucracy on a permanent, full-time basis. Fourth, because of their known private affiliations the external bureaucrats convey to observers of the political process an *image of nongovernmental participation* in the bureaucracy. This may help the public, or segments of the public, to identify with a bureaucratic group or allow greater confidence in its activities. It is also true that private citizens who become external bureaucrats carry an image of governmental participation into their nongovernmental relationships that enables them to speak with greater authority on public issues.

From one vantage point, these functions can be seen as brakes on the development of some of the characteristics that make organizations an identifiable social phenomenon. When too fully developed, these characteristics seem to interfere with the ability of an organization to adapt to its environment. March and Simon, summing up in a single quality the distinctive characteristics of organizations, point to *specificity*.[1] They write:

> The high specificity of structure and coordination within organizations—as contrasted with the diffuse and variable relations *among* organizations and among unorganized individuals—marks off the individual organization as a sociological unit comparable in significance to the individual organism in biology.[2]

They cite specificity of both exposure to information and perception of it as well as specificity of roles as two important characteristics of organizations. The functions of external bureaucrats appear to erode this specificity.

In considering *information*, March and Simon claim that organizations provide their members with "selective exposure to environmental stimuli. The division of labor in the organization affects the information that various members receive."[3] The external bureaucrat, however, is connected to an information network outside the bureaucracy, which provides him with more varied information.

As to *perspectives*, March and Simon call attention to the effect of the "filtering action of the frame of reference," defining this as those parts of past stimuli that are evoked in current behavior.[4] The frame of reference of a member of an organization is structured in a particular way as a result of his organizational experiences and tends to be similar to the frame of reference of other members of the organization.[5] Some bureaucrats become extremely sensitive to limitations of their perspective and call in external bureaucrats to supply different perspectives.

On the specificity of organizational roles March and Simon write that roles in organizations

tend to be highly elaborated, relatively stable, and defined to a considerable extent in explicit and even written terms. Not only is the role defined for the individual who occupies it, but it is known in considerable detail to others in the organization who have occasion to deal with him. Hence, the environment of other persons that surrounds each member of an organization tends to become a highly stable and predictable one.[6]

The use of external bureaucrats to provide temporary *manpower* and to convey an *image of nongovernmental participation* tends to have effects contrary to some of these characteristics of organizational roles. In both cases the roles of external bureaucrats often are a vague mixture of governmental and nongovernmental components. It is our hypothesis that when the environment of a bureaucrat includes external bureaucrats it tends to become less stable and less predictable.

Any of the four functions of external bureaucrats may be a goal of the participant, whether internal or external bureaucrat. A bureaucrat, for example, may want additional manpower to enable him to get a job done on schedule. He might also want to convey bureaucratic perspectives to the external bureaucrat. The external bureaucrat may share these goals with the bureaucrat, or his goals may be different. He too may be interested in supplying manpower and obtaining bureaucratic perspectives. In addition, he may be interested in getting information for his own purposes. This may not conflict with the goals of the bureaucrat. However, the differences between the goals of the bureaucrats and the external bureaucrats may bring unwanted effects for one or both of the parties, which would represent the costs of the interaction. The goals of both parties may all be made explicit or at least understood by the participants, but they may not be, with unanticipated costs resulting from goals of the other party not being known.

It is hypothesized that in each case there are consequences of the interaction in each of the four functions, whether these consequences are sought by participants or not. Even though a particular public image of the interaction is not desired, for example, it will be conveyed at least to a portion of the public. The participants may be aware of the unsought effects or be ignorant of them; they may be pleased with them or consider them costs; and they may predict unsought effects or be surprised by them.

SUMMARY OF PROPOSITIONS[7]
AND CONCLUSION

This paper has attempted to develop a scheme for analyzing the behavior of all external bureaucrats and to generate propositions that may be applicable to the behavior of all external bureaucrats whether affiliated with private or public bureaucracies. The position has been developed that the behavior of external bureaucrats has aspects of significance beyond the expert knowledge they bring to an organization, the conflict between their bureaucratic and nonbureaucratic roles, and the concern that their employment represents a departure from democratic norms. Their behavior can be fruitfully analyzed in the context of the total range of relationships between bureaucracy and its social environment.

PROPOSITION 1. The number of external bureaucrats attached to a bureaucracy and the purposes for which they are used are in some measure determined by the full range of relationships between a bureaucracy and its social environment.

In an attempt to probe the significance of the behavior of external bureaucrats for the relationship between the two social worlds which they serve, several propositions were borrowed from literature on other kinds of multiple affiliations.

PROPOSITION 2. External bureaucrats lessen the cleavage in society along the bureaucratic-nonbureaucratic axis.

PROPOSITION 3. External bureaucrats serve as restraints on the activities of both the bureaucracy and outside groups with which external bureaucrats are affiliated.

PROPOSITION 4. External bureaucrats contribute to the stability and continued existence of bureaucratic activities with which they are associated.

From a survey of the literature on organizations it appeared that external bureaucrats may have the kinds of effects indicated in the propositions above partially by preventing extreme development of the characteristics of organizations.

PROPOSITION 5. External bureaucrats serve as brakes on the extreme development of some of the characteristics (e.g., selective exposure to environmental stimuli and specificity of organizational roles) that make organizations an identifiable social phenomenon.

PROPOSITION 6. By inhibiting the extreme development of characteristics that identify the bureaucracy as an organization the external bureaucracy aids the bureaucracy to adapt to its environment.

PROPOSITION 7. When the environment of other persons that surrounds each member of an organization includes external bureaucrats, this environment tends to become less stable and less predictable.

The analysis then attempted to discover how external bureaucrats facilitate the kinds of relationships between bureaucracies and their social environments suggested in the preceding propositions. Four variables were selected: information, perspectives, manpower, and image of nongovernmental participation. Propositions applicable to all of these functions deal primarily with the goals of internal and external bureaucrats and the perception of the activities of the external bureaucracy.

PROPOSITION 8. External bureaucrats may not have the same goals for their activity as the internal bureaucrats have.

PROPOSITION 9. Whenever external bureaucrats are employed, each of the four functions of external bureaucrats are operable, both on the bureaucracy and on its social environment, whether or not these effects are sought by participants.

PROPOSITION 10. Announced purposes for the employment of external bureaucrats are not necessarily the actual purposes.

PROPOSITION 11. External bureaucrats who are experts in one area may be accepted by the public as experts in areas for which they do not have qualifications.

The following propositions were suggested on information:

PROPOSITION 12. The external bureaucrat connects internal bureaucrats with another information network that provides the bureaucrats with more varied information.

PROPOSITION 13. External bureaucrats communicate information to influential groups and thereby affect the scope of choice perceived by policy makers in future decisions.

The following propositions were suggested on image of nongovernmental-governmental participation:

PROPOSITION 14. By conveying an image of nongovernmental participation in bureaucratic activities, external bureaucrats help the public in general and segments of the public to identify with a bureaucratic unit and to have greater confidence in its activities and policies.

PROPOSITION 15. Some foreign governments accept criticism and advice more willingly from foreign persons they perceive as private citizens than from foreign persons they perceive as governmental officials.

PROPOSITION 16. External bureaucrats may convey an image of governmental participation which permits them to speak with greater authority on public issues.

The concluding section of the analysis illustrated some ways in which external bureaucrats are involved in relations between organizations. The relationships discussed were not only between bureaucratic units and private organizations but also between units of the bureaucracy and between two or more private organizations.

PROPOSITION 17. When external bureaucrats are involved in relationships between bureaucratic units and between private groups they affect relationships between the bureaucracy and its social environment.

PROPOSITION 18. Interaction among representatives of private groups who are members of the external bureaucracy helps them to coordinate the activities of their groups and to reach agreement on problems on which their groups are in conflict.

PROPOSITION 19. External bureaucrats obtain knowledge about governmental programs that enables them to arrange private activities so as not to conflict with governmental programs and not to duplicate these programs.

PROPOSITION 20. When governments are unable to make crucial decisions, external bureaucrats are sometimes called in to make them.

PROPOSITION 21. External bureaucrats serve governmental needs by stimulating private persons or groups to perform tasks that tradition or limited resources will not permit the government to undertake for itself.

The scope of these twenty-one propositions suggests that external bureaucrats may play significant roles in interorganizational relations. The external bureaucracy appears to be an adaptive mechanism in societies which have large organizations playing important roles, helping to integrate these organizations into the total society. The efforts of lobbyists, information in the press, letters and other pleas from the public, and the like do not seem to be adequate links between governmental bureaucracy and its social environment. More information about the twenty-one propositions might enable external bureaucrats to be used with more predictable results and also might show how their activities can be structured to avoid conflict with values about how governments should operate.

NOTES

[1] James G. March and Herbert A. Simon, *Organizations* (New York: 1958), pp. 2, 3.

[2] *Ibid.*, p. 4.

[3] *Ibid.*, p. 153.

[4] *Ibid.*

[5] Robert K. Merton uses the term "perspective" also in his "Role of the Intellectual in Bureaucracy," in *Social Theory and Social Structure* (Glencoe, Ill.: The Free Press, 1957), pp. 214-19.

[6] March and Simon, *op. cit.*, p. 4.

[7] The numbering of propositions has been changed from the original sequence to avoid confusion.

Science, Government, and the Case of RAND: A Singular Pluralism

PHILLIP GREEN

At one level, Bruce Smith's *The RAND Corporation* is simply an intensive treatment of a new American form of enterprise, academia, and government action—the nonprofit research or advisory corporation, which Don K. Price has accurately described as "federalism by contract." At this level, Smith's work is excellent and of particular interest both to the student of public administration and to the public administrator himself. The broad question Smith asks is why RAND has been so successful—that is, why it has prospered according to its own outlook and has satisfied its sponsors according to theirs—in contrast to comparable but different types of research or advisory organization. The answer appears to be that RAND has succeeded so well because, both in its foundation and in its continuing operations, it "has been able to avoid a completely dependent status vis-à-vis the Air Force," its original and still primary sponsor. How RAND has managed this and what the most noteworthy particular aspects of its independence have been are the subsidiary questions to which Smith devotes the bulk of his study.

The answers he gives are both informative and instructive; several are worth mentioning here. For example, the fact that RAND came into existence independently and *then* established its relationship with the Air Force has given it its own raison d'être, its own primary tradition with which to generate high morale, loyalty, and a sense of self. Its location in California, away from "the hectic pace of Washington," has given RAND a freedom from the wearing demands of "crash projects," "task orders," and the like, demands that have seriously limited the intellectual independence of such comparable organizations as Analytic Services, Inc., and the Institute for Defense Analyses (pp. 74-76). Again, this freedom was furthered by the initial agreement of its founders that RAND be "neither conceived nor staffed . . . as an organization to provide quick answers for current problems." An example of RAND's determination to avoid

From *World Politics,* Volume XX, No. 2 (Copyright © 1968 by Princeton University Press.) pp. 301-326. Reprinted by permission of Princeton University Press.

this fate is seen in the history of the System Development Corporation, a "spin-off" of RAND which grew out of a personnel training project that RAND management recognized as being inconsistent with the desire to avoid doing routine work for the Air Force.

In addition, RAND's internal organization has also contributed greatly to its success, according to Smith. The aspects of that organization which he particularly notes are decentralization, which prevails to a high degree both between and within departments; emphasis on interdisciplinary work; broad support for "pure"—i.e., undirected—research; and maintenance of RAND control even over projects initiated from outside. Each of these organizational characteristics, like the aspects of RAND's history noted in the previous paragraph, has had something to do with RAND's ability to produce systematic, long-range, "creative" research rather than to engage in mere short-range tinkering with other people's ideas. Of course RAND has also had organizational problems and difficulties, which Smith does not slight; but in general his conclusion seems compelling: "The independent RAND 'atmosphere' in general seems more conducive for the emergence of truly creative ideas in policy research than the working atmosphere of the advisory unit closely tied to the sponsoring agency" (p. 107). At the level at which we have so far conducted this discussion—a level at which no embarrassing questions are asked about words like "creative" or "success"—comparisons between RAND's methods and other methods that have been developed to help science give service to government are helpful. This is so even though Smith seems to say that RAND's success in maintaining its independence has been largely the result of historical accident, for once we know what caused an accident, we can sometimes arrange similar "accidents" for the future, if we so desire.

. . .[H]ow do we go about relating such a study as this one to our knowledge of the political system of which RAND is a minuscule yet important part?

. . .[W]hat Smith has done is to take what I have called the "grab bag" approach to the larger subject of science, government, and democratic politics. He has not, to be sure, come up empty-handed. Rather, as is indicated by the following remarks, he has come up with what is presently the most conventional and approved approach to American politics—the notion that there is some kind of pluralist political order in American democracy which checks particular institutions that might otherwise contribute to an imbalance of political power:

> . . . The pluralism of the advisory system, in which RAND is only one institution among many with access to persons in authority, helps assure that no one group will monopolize the attention of policy makers (p. 315).

> As developments in science and technology increasingly affect other areas of public policy, there can only be a growing need for the kind of advisory service that RAND has provided various defense clients. In general, it would seem highly desirable for similar advisory capabilities to be built up by nondefense agencies. . . . The way to assure that important alternatives are

not neglected in the processes of policy formation is to develop the broadest possible advisory base (p. 317).

Used properly, the advisory institution like RAND can contribute to sensible policy decisions and can help to maintain the dynamism of America's pluralist governing system.

In the net, the device of the RAND-type advisory corporation seems to reflect both the strengths and weaknesses of American pluralism. The presence of a number of advisory institutions like RAND helps to assure decision makers of a broad base of scientific advice and to guard against the dangers of a closed system with a narrow technocracy cut off from the healthy effect of outside criticism. There is very little danger that anything like a monolithic statism or a vast bureaucracy on Weberian lines will emerge, given a system which decentralizes expertise and influence throughout many different institutions in society. The real dangers of this sytem may not be what is commonly supposed. The chief danger may well be that familiar problem of American politics: keeping organizational pluralism within some sort of bounds so that a framework for coherent, unified, and sustained national policies can be maintained (p. 321).

What I shall try to show in the remainder of this dicussion is that every one of these remarks about RAND is at best highly questionable and is indeed sustained not by any evidence that Smith offers—the contrary is the case, in fact—but rather by a kind of simple act of faith in "the system.". . .

[W]hat effect has RAND had on the process of national security policy-making in this country and on the nature of influence in that policy-making process?

The essential point that emerges immediately when we ask this question is that although RAND is far from ideologically monolithic in the broad field of national security policy anaysis, by Smith's own evidence it has been unquestioningly oriented toward the general *perspectives*, if not always the concrete policies, of the foreign policy elite (giving that phrase as wide a coverage as one wishes). And this orientation has had some profound consequences for American "pluralism."

To see this more clearly, let us consider the now famous overseas air bases study of Albert Wohlstetter and his colleagues, which Smith proposes, in his chapter "RAND in Operation: A Case Study," as an example par excellence of the RAND "systems analysis" method at work. This study, Smith tells us, "pointed toward the shattering conclusion that in the last half of the 1950's the Strategic Air Command, the world's most powerful striking force, faced the danger of obliteration from enemy surprise attack under the then-programmed strategic basing system" (p. 208). "The then-programmed system of advanced overseas operating bases . . . would, in consequence [of its vulnerability] , have the least destruction potential of enemy targets of any of the systems. . . . The cornerstone of U.S. policy at the time—deterrence of aggression through the nuclear striking power of the Strategic Air Command and destruction of enemy industrial targets if deterrence failed—was thus seen to be jeopardized by the projected basing system. Indeed, the whole concept of deterrence as it was then conceived seemed in need of revision" (pp. 213-14). Smith adds that after Malenkov's announcement that the USSR had detonated a hydrogen bomb "Wohlstetter and his colleagues capitalized on this announcement in the late summer briefings to dramatize the dangers of an enemy first-strike against vulnerable overseas bases" (p. 225). And in summary he concludes, "Several previous studies had dealt generally with the problem of vulnerability, but none had drawn explicit attention to the need for developing a deterrent force capable of surviving an initial enemy atomic assault and still inflicting unacceptable damage on the enemy" (p. 232).

These passages, I think, adumbrate an uncritical conception of the role of scientists in government, which in turn clearly rests on Smith's uncritical conception of his subject matter itself. (In an earlier chapter Smith throws a decade of sometimes vicious interservice rivalry into the discard with the remark that "RAND's recruitment had benefited in the past from the broad Air Force mission which was almost equivalent to the whole of the nation's defense effort.") Thus he appears to have no interest in the validity of the many assumptions with which the passages just quoted are strewn or in the actual policy outcome itself and the continuing debate about deterrence strategies. On the contrary, his argument is that what is important about RAND's studies is not their outcomes but the process that produced them—that is, RAND's methodological innovations in the field of systems analysis and operations research. But it is not enough to say naively that a new method is "a contribution"; surely we want to know *to whom and to what purposes* it contributes. Such a question Smith never asks, apparently in the belief that the methods I have mentioned are "value-neutral" and have no particular purposes built into them. And this is too bad, for as I have argued elsewhere, RAND's systems analyses have in practice been far from value-neutral, except in the sardonic sense that the systems approach applied to significant questions of public policy will betray, indiscriminately, the biases of whoever is doing the study. Even RAND has not yet discovered a way to make interdisciplinary teams of social scientists see the world with any eyes but their own, and when the most valued objects in the human universe are at stake—life, liberty, happiness—those eyes rarely see with complete dispassion. Therefore we must surely ask if the bias with which RAND workers have seen the world has been a systematic one. If it has been, then the new methods of analysis may very well have had a systematic effect on RAND's work, and thus, since RAND has been an important actor in the political system, on the distribution of influence in government.

With this question now in mind, let us take a more careful look at the RAND overseas bases study. That study rested on two familiar propositions: that vulnerability equals provocation to an "enemy" and that the Soviet Union and the U.S. are (or were) engaged in an undeclared war, with Western Europe as one of the stakes to be defended at all costs. The first proposition purports to stand on a solid evidential base, but is in fact usually asserted, or rather deduced, as a logical corollary of the second. As for that latter proposition, it is simply the root assumption behind the "official" American position in the cold war. Where this assumption came from is a matter for the historian; for our purposes what is most important about it is how all-pervasive it can be, and has been, as a "given" in scholarly analysis.

For example, in a footnote on page 108, Smith recites a long list of RAND-supported projects in the field of Soviet studies. Of those with which I am familiar, none puts that basic assumption to any kind of test. Most of them are indeed meritorious pieces of research—but wholly within the framework of the cold-war perspective. Thus we see that RAND's work strengthens the policy-makers' intuitions about the "enemy," which become in turn the grounding for other RAND work—such as the bases study—in the field of military strategy. This is a familiar pattern of affairs and not necessarily one without value in a policy context; but it also has its dangers.

To take but one instance, several of the works on the Soviet Union listed by Smith—especially those of Leites, Mead, and Selznick—treat Soviet political (and thus, by implication, diplomatic) behavior as taking place within an attitudinal framework marked by extremes of hostility and ideological rigidity. (Like many other Soviet studies in this nation, RAND's seem to have undergone a "thaw" in recent years.) Such studies obviously provided intellectual strengthening for American fears in the cold war; yet in the context of that conflict they are sadly deficient. After all, RAND has never undertaken similar studies of the psychology of its own employers, namely, the U.S. Air Force and important American elected and appointed officials. What might Nathan Leites have made of General LeMay, who has recommended that we should bomb the North Vietnamese "back to the Stone Age"? When asked about the contribution RAND makes to the power of such men, a high RAND official replied that " 'LeMay has the same kind of human qualities that the average man has, just like a teacher or a doctor.' " No doubt he has; and no doubt so do those Russians who engage in "The Ritual of Liquidation," who formulated "The Operational Code of the Politburo," who created "The Organizational Weapon." I am not suggesting that RAND should necessarily undertake analyses of its employers (though if its various analytic techniques are really as sophisticated as they are supposed to be, such work might be helpful). The absence of such studies on our side does not demonstrate that we may be in the hands of paranoid ideologues or that the Soviet "missile gap" is the real danger to world peace; it only demonstrates the peculiar nature of RAND's vaunted intellectual "independence."

Realistically, rather than multiply information bearing on the attitudes and "operational codes" of world leaders—or even on their strategic theories, about which we owe almost everything we know on the Soviet side to RAND—we might do better to concentrate more on their actual behavior in world politics and on some hard thinking about what that behavior may signify. Can the meaning of the cold war to the USSR be deduced by quotation-mongering from Lenin, Stalin, Khrushchev, and Sokolovski, from attitude studies, and so on? Or should we not primarily ask what the USSR and the U.S. have actually *done* to create and carry on the cold war? I think that this is obviously the case—and it then becomes important to note further that RAND, to my knowledge (and Smith gives no examples to the contrary), has produced no important contributions to the ongoing study of the cold war itself.

Thus, although RAND has been intellectually independent to the extent of strenuously questioning its employers' concrete policies, it has *not* been "independent" to the extent of questioning either the nature of the jobs they are performing or their basic values—a point that we can see only if, unlike Smith, we pay attention to the substance of what our subjects do, as well as to how they do it. This point having once been seen, it follows that the "success" of RAND's work in the area I have been discussing does not demonstrate how fortunate American society is in its intellectual pluralism. Rather, RAND's "success" shows how flexible part of our military bureaucracy is, in that it is capable of actually buying the most sophisticated weapons sysems available; and this is a far different matter.

Of course, it is not self-evident that this criticism—that the relationship of particular scientists and government agencies is made more problematical by such a sharing of values and perspectives between the two—is at all noteworthy. With regard to RAND, for example, we can think of several reasons why what has been said here need not be taken as a criticism of even a minor aspect of the American political system. (Some of these reasons are mentioned by Smith; none is discussed at length. Thus a reviewer is left in the position of setting up straw men rather than dealing with real arguments.) These are, first, that RAND has produced work of a more genuinely critical nature than is suggested by my remarks and has had an opportunity that might otherwise have been lacking to convey its critique to policy-makers; second, that RAND researchers have contributed to the nation purely technical advances with which no one could possibly quarrel, from "fail-safe" procedures to new modes of mathematical analysis to new uses for titanium and beryllium; third, that on the subject of military policy vis-á-vis the USSR both RAND and its employers merely reflect the will and the preferences of the American people themselves; and finally, that in any event RAND is in fact only one among plural *and* pluralistic sources of influence employing social scientists and generating usable research in the U.S. These points deserve consideration, for together they cast some additional light on the theory and practice of "democratic pluralism."

The first statement is certainly true. It is no secret, for instance, that some present RAND personnel disagree with American policy toward China and have produced work that can be read as calling into question certain basic American values in this area, rather than mere policy preferences. At the same time, it is impossible to believe that those agencies that fund RAND's work—especially the

Air Force—will continue to support research that does not give them any payoff and is not likely to do so in the future. In a society that values the "free" intellect (at least rhetorically), a sophisticated employer will tolerate, even welcome, large amounts of eccentricity and deviation; that is merely a subsidiary cost to be charged against the overall gains. Smith himself testifies to how great the Air Force has found these gains to be, as in the overseas bases study; RAND has surely paid its way to support a few critics of China policy.

In fact, it is paying its way now, since it has under way several projects supportive of the military effort in Vietnam, one of which is designed to help the Air Force find out how it "might use tactical air support more effectively in combat against the Vietcong." In any event, however, it is not the integrity or the subjective freedom of RAND that is under discussion, but rather the policy process into which RAND fits. That process is one in which government agencies (by now, it should be noted, not the Air Force alone as far as RAND is concerned) are the chief source of funds for a research organization that is supposed, among other things, to provide information affecting agency policies: payment for value received. And the really important question is whether this special relationship should be viewed as adding an increment of strength or an increment of weakness to the pluralist tendencies in the political system.

The answer is not difficult to find. A clue to it can be found in Smith's remark that, in attempting to "sell" the results of the bases study, "Wohlstetter gave 92 briefings (most of them during the period from March [1953] to the end of October)" to the Air Force. One need only ask how many scientists *not* in a special relationship with a government agency get a chance to lobby for the adoption of their proposals *ninety-two times* in a period of less than a year? And with the cachet of being professionally intimate with high officials in that agency? And known, additionally, to have asked no embarrassing questions about that agency's primary mission itself: the deterrence of a supposedly expectable Communist attack on Western Europe or the U.S. itself?

Generally speaking, in any political system the kind of access to decision-making responsibility that RAND obtained in this case depends on the possession of relevant resources. In essence, by supporting RAND the government through the Air Force paid for the recruitment of a new member to the political elite in the area of national security policy-making. But that is only one aspect of what actually happened, for money is only one resource for access. The most relevant resource for access to national strategy councils has always been agreement on fundamentals. This agreement indeed helps define what is meant by "expertise," which then refers to the possession not only of relevant skills but also of acceptable attitudes. In this instance there was a positive payoff for both parties to the transaction because and only because of the compatibility of their attitudes, chief of which was a desire, not to put too fine a point on it, to provide military security as perceived within the intellectual confines of the cold-war perspective. I think it is fair to doubt that any other fundamental attitude would have been acceptable to the Air Force; and even now, were RAND to become known as a prominent lobbyist *against* the administration's Asian policy, as it was *for* deterrence policy, it would surely lose its favored position. Be that as it may, my proposition is certainly not put to the test by the mere fact of RAND's being hospitable to diverse viewpoints. Research embarrassing to the client can, after all, be ignored (as, there is every evidence, work emanating from RAND which is critical of our China policy is being ignored). On the other hand, research deemed helpful by the client has a special chance to be influential—a chance not vouchsafed the work of an ordinary American social scientist, who thus is deprived of equal access to his government. If this form of inequality were distributed randomly, the result would perhaps offend only the most dogmatic of populists or anti-intellectuals. But it is not distributed randomly; it is distributed *by the Air Force*—and even the most sanguine portrayals of the American political system do not mention the military sector as a strength of pluralism, whatever other virtues it may have.

Similar considerations apply to the argument that RAND is only one of many, or at least of several, similar organizations in a plural society, some public, some semipublic, some private. Once again the statement is true but irrelevant. To speak of a meaningful pluralism in this connection we would have to believe, first, that independent research groups with no built-in bias toward the military have as effective an access to government as does RAND, and second, that the agencies they have access to—say the Arms Control and Disarmament Agency— are themselves nearly as influential *and* well-financed as the Air Force. Neither of those propositions is credible.

Furthermore, it should be noted that RAND's access to important loci of power in government is even more special than the story of Wohlstetter's briefings reveals. Smith's account on occasion seems less a history of RAND than a case study on interlocking directorates for an antitrust textbook. The RAND board of trustees in 1965 (p. 185, n. 29) reads like a burlesque of Mills' notions of the "power elite," not merely in who is included—great universities and scientific research centers, public utilities and the monopolistic mass media, big oil, defense industry—but in who is excluded—labor unions or federations, the small liberal arts colleges, public power and rural electrification associations, independent small business or media operators, independent organizations of scientists and scholars. The categories of representation on the board are themselves a study in the new elite: Industrial Trustees, Academic and Scientific Trustees, and "Public Interest" Trustees (whose identity, at least on the 1965 board, is hard to discover). This pattern holds true for all of RAND's history, moreover, from its founding under the auspices of the Douglas Aircraft Company to its later financing by the great foundations. Smith's innocent remark that the "original decision to fill the Board with men of high standing has paid off handsomely for RAND over the years" is certainly true—and is also certainly destructive of any naive ideas about the "pluralism" of the research community, since "men of high standing" are not available to just *any* group of scientists or scholars.

In the end, the only analogy we can find for RAND's operations is Robert Engler's description of "the permeability of oil." Like the oil industry giants (who are themselves incidentally represented at RAND), RAND is everywhere, maintaining "informal contacts" with congressmen and congressional committee staffs, serving on "advisory committees, boards, and consultant groups," of the government, and in general having "a number of friends in high places and a voice in important policy decisions difficult to imagine a decade earlier" (p. 140). And all this political access, in addition, is supported by a tax exemption that, despite Smith's careful defense of it, is quite obviously indefensible except by legalistic appeal to a defective law. Groups such as the Fellowship of Reconciliation and the Sierra Club have been threatened with loss of tax-exempt status for attempting "to influence legislation," and this fact leads Smith to ask whether "carrying on policy-oriented research [is] 'attempting to influence legislation' " (p. 192). He does not answer the question, but since it repays close study by answering itself that does not matter. Plainly, the propaganda activities of, say, the FOR are pitifully thin compared to the intensive lobbying of Wohlstetter and his associates for the bases study or of Herman Kahn and his associates for civil defense. No doubt the law tacitly distinguishes between administrative lobbying and legislative lobbying, but the distinction is maintained not by a realistic assessment of the legislative process in America but by the careful tailoring of most of our lobbying and tax laws to the requirements of big business. The very fact that RAND can cohabit peacefully with a provision that systematically discriminates against political outsiders and systematically favors political insiders is itself the most telling point one can make about RAND's place in our plural political order.

And thus the proposition that RAND contributes an unquestionably positive good to that order becomes itself not entirely credible. The root notion behind all pluralist theory is that somewhere there is a countervailing power for every source of independent power one discovers. If one cannot point to groups or institutions that truly countervail, then pluralism as a descriptive category has become rhetoric rather than analysis. If, keeping this in mind, we return to the criterion suggested earlier for linking case studies of this kind to the macrosystem, we are led to the following conclusion: the RAND Corporation, by making the Air Force a more effective instrument of national policy and by strengthening the Air Force's links with the corporate sector, without making any attempt to help establish *countervailing powers* within or outside of the government, is in fact contributing to the *anti*pluralist tendencies in American politics.

At this point, we clearly must deal with the two remaining arguments suggested above in defense of RAND's value-sharing with government. Some of

RAND's technical and technological innovations, I said, can be seen as having contributed to the *national* security, as its military advice has to *national* strategy; and has there not been a *national* consensus on the cold-war values to which I have been continually referring? If all this is true, surely we do not need to seek the establishment of countervailing powers against the very interest of the whole nation itself; that would be an absurdity. If it is true, then Smith's happy conclusion is correct: everyone has gained and no one has lost by RAND's performance of its special role. Or, as he puts it: "From its position as friendly critic, RAND injected heretical ideas into the Air Force hierarchy which stimulated needed change.... As defense-policy choices become ever more complex, there can only be a growing need for some set of institutions to help serve as a bridge between the realm of 'closed politics' and the larger public.... The advisory corporation like RAND can serve a vital function in tapping the intellectual capabilities of people outside the government for work on public problems and in generally promoting the public understanding necessary for the successful functioning of modern democratic government" (pp. 236, 240).

Unfortunately the viewpoint expressed in the paragraph above is either tautological—"needed change" is change needed by those with the power to make it; the national interest is that interest that national leaders pursue—or else it has a secret meaning discernible only to the mystical nationalist. We can, if comprehensible communication between informed citizens is our aim, often make distinctions between policies aimed at a national interest and those clearly directed to parochial or class interests. But we can do no more than that, except by arbitrary assertion. Where there are competing policies designed to promote "the national interest" we can argue more or less persuasively in favor of our own proposals, but unless our opponents violate the rules of sensible discourse (e.g., engage in self-contradiction, misrepresent the evidence), we cannot establish that ours is *the* policy "actually in" the national interest. That it is eventually chosen by majority rule, or in some cases by a tacit consensus somewhere short of unanimity, would be beside the point, for these are only rules of fairness in decision-making, not criteria of "truth" or "rightfulness."

To return then to our problem, the overseas bases study inspired "needed change" and promoted "public understanding" if and only if the conception of national security forwarded by it happened to be one's own and was in need of greater sophistication. Effectively this means that that study was unquestionably in *the* (one and only) national interest only if there was at the time national *unanimity* on what *the* national interest was.

But of course there was no such unanimity about the national interest, not even at the time of the Korean War. The premises of the cold war itself—that a major nuclear deterrent is (or rather, was) desirable; that the Soviets posed a genuine military threat to Western Europe; that in various corners of the globe an American military presence is necessary to halt Communist expansionism; that, in sum, a struggle for the world has been under way since the end of World

War II—have never been seen as beyond debate in the intellectual community. It is (or was) possible to argue with conviction and intelligence one of the following propositions in response to the overseas bases study: (1) Eventual nuclear disarmament should be the desideratum of American national security policy; the only real military threat to Western Europe was the threat of unintended conflict during a crisis over Berlin or Germany; vulnerable forces would indeed make catastrophe more likely in such a circumstance, but would be, on the other hand, much more adaptable to any proposed disarmament scheme; therefore the risk of accidental war should have been taken at least in the short run, the energies of the government then being devoted not to a build-up of military security but to extrication from the area of potential crisis through some kind of disengagement scheme. (2) Alternatively, the potential destructiveness of accidental war being too great to make such a risk bearable, the rationalization of our nuclear deterrent should have proceeded only to the extent of creating a secure *minimum* deterrent, not (as the RAND study came to signify) as a first step toward the creation of a nuclear force large enough to be an instrument of threats and policy in every cold-war (or hot-war) situation.

If we assume now that by "public understanding" Smith refers to the understanding of those who belong to what Gabriel Almond calls the "attentive public" and that "needed change" refers to change that history has made clear to *all* observers had to be undertaken, then we immediately see that by these standards RAND's contribution to the general welfare has been more questionable and controversial than Smith is willing to allow. Nor is it a blessing under these circumstances that RAND's work has been free from "identification with partisan causes." On the contrary, partisanship in social science may often be constructive, in that it immediately generates its own opposition and qualification, whereas a deep-rooted intellectual bias so broad and so pervasive that it is not even recognized may come to act as a damper on critical thought.

These remarks are not, of course, intended as a complaint about the sponsoring of "controversial" research by government; almost all research would so qualify by the standards implied above. Any government agency will and should do whatever it can (within certain bounds) to defend itself from attack and to improve its performance of its charged duties. What is at stake here are rather the attitude and responsibilities of scientists and scholars themselves: What should they do? What mode of participation in government is it appropriate for them to adopt?

Thus, RAND has chosen not to notice what is questionable in the work it is doing, rather than to ventilate thoroughly all the assumptions that go into its work; that choice in the end has helped narrow the range of options open to policy-makers. Returning to some of the points I made earlier, we see, similarly, that RAND chose to operate under the auspices of the Air Force rather than, say, relevant congressional committees; that choice has affected the distribution of knowledge and know-how between democratically responsible (at least in part) and nonresponsible arms of the national government. RAND has chosen to lobby administratively rather than legislatively for its proposals; that choice has affected the distribution of power over national policy between those same arms of government. RAND has also chosen to do its work and its lobbying privately, rather than to thrash out its assumptions and analyses in the relevant intellectual community before presenting them to the Air Force; that choice has narrowed rather than extended the range of citizen participation in policy-making. And especially, RAND has chosen to do much of its work in a secrecy removed from all critical eyes in that intellectual community (Smith tells us in a footnote on page 158 that in the 1950's about half of RAND studies were classified); that choice has promoted an imbalance in know-how and knowledge between the military and the intellectual community.

In the end, therefore, we must take as ironic Smith's comment that "the military services themselves, in sponsoring organizations like RAND, have greatly strengthened the civilian's role in defense management and policy formation" (p. 25). The price of that strengthening has been, as is often the case, the co-opting by government of a potentially independent group in the community. In 1947 the president of the Rockefeller Foundation remarked as follows (as quoted by Smith): "They [the military] were quite willing to accept civilians on a certain service level in the past. They used to say 'We like to have you around, and if you are awfully smart we will ask you questions and you will answer them as well as you can; but then we will go into another room and shut the door and make our decision.' That, in the past they were quite willing to do. Now, however, they want us in the backroom with them. They want to talk over the really fundamental questions, and they are actually admitting civilians at the planning level. That, I think, is very significant" (p. 35). To be admitted to "the backroom"—that has always been the carrot dangled in front of those whose services the proprietors of that room have wanted to co-opt. Perhaps this trade of independence for participation has been worthwhile from the perspective of a problematical democratic pluralism; perhaps not. In any event, Smith offers no aid toward the answering of that question.

We must also, finally, take as ironic Smith's comment about RAND's "long and arduous struggle" to sell its ideas to the Air Force: "The decision maker does not emerge here in the passive and largely reactive role that Sir Charles Snow portrays in *Science and Government*. Nor is it evident, if the present case is at all typical, that the cardinal decisions are always or even usually made by a 'handful of men.' There is opportunity for laborious dissection of advisory recommendations at various policy levels" (p. 238). Smith's own data show that the bases-study recommendations—and thus the outlines of American nuclear strategy for perhaps decades to come—were adopted through a process in which independent opinion elites and publics and democratically elected representatives had at best a token presence.

Finally, it bears repeating that such criticisms as these are not answered simply by postulating a beneficently working adversary system in social research and political influence. The adversary system in the courts has come under attack on the ground that its operations may hide a gross imbalance of resources between the opposing sides in a legal dispute. The same reasoning applies in the arena of power, and with even more stringency. There is no invisible hand; power is what people make of it, and RAND has helped to strengthen one kind of power in American society. If the host of imitators that have flourished in the wake of RAND's success have had the wherewithal or the opportunity or the will to balance that power, no evidence of their success is forthcoming in *The RAND Corporation*; nor has the essential question even been asked by Smith.

Looking back, then, on our earlier discussion, we can see that although RAND as an organization has had no effect on some of the obstacles to a genuine political pluralism in the United States, in other respects its effect has been considerable. The result of its activities has been to lessen (slightly) democratic control over policy; to aid in the continued parcelling out of public authority on an inequalitarian basis and in the exclusion of a substantial part of the intellectual community from access to the policy process; and in sum to narrow rather than enlarge the foreign policy-making elite, "the major [remaining] area of small-group control."

3

POLICY MAKING
IN THE FEDERAL GOVERNMENT

James A. Robinson leads off this section by presenting a case for the point that Congress is a relatively unimportant actor in the determination of foreign policy. This viewpoint is shared by most authorities on the subject, but is disputed by Ronald C. Moe and Steven C. Teel. Moe and Teel review the literature relating to the position of the President and Congress in the formulation of foreign policy, and conclude that Congress is a much more powerful actor in the formulation of foreign policy than is realized. While Moe and Teel make a very convincing case for the importance of Congress in domestic policy making (in the sections of their article not included in this excerpt), their review of the foreign policy making literature is not nearly so inclusive as their review of domestic policy making literature, nor does it distinguish among different types of issue areas.

H. Bradford Westerfield contends, in an article published in 1966, that the Executive's ascendancy over Congress in foreign policy has risen to new heights. Professor Westerfield observed in 1969, however, that he would revise this article if he were to write it again. The author noted the greatly changed stance of the Congress in foreign policy matters such as the ABM missile debate, in which the Senate failed by a margin of only one vote to override the President's policy. Congress's increasing opposition to President Nixon's Vietnam policy in 1970 lends further weight to Westerfield's revised outlook. In the following article, Aaron Wildavsky makes a strong case for the thesis that the President is much stronger in determining foreign than domestic policy. Edward Kolodziej sketches recent changes in the organization of the primary presidential agency for foreign affairs, the National Security Council. In comparing the Nixon administration's prospects for centralized control of foreign policy making with the past record of recent presidents, Kolodziej casts doubt on the hope that a great deal of change will occur in this area.

C. Wright Mills contends that the professional military have autonomous power to shape fundamental aspects of foreign policy, but Samuel P. Huntington argues that the military play a secondary role in foreign policy making. Neil Sheehan's account of the Joint Chiefs of Staff supports the viewpoint of those who argue that the influence of the professional military has increased with the advent of the Nixon administration. (Incidentally, J. E. Harr's examination of the socioeconomic background of Foreign Service Officers, found in section III. D, contains similar data for the military as well.)

Any consideration of the military establishment must deal with the civilian policy makers of the Defense Department, as well as the professional military. Samuel P. Huntington describes the rise of civilian groups, expert in military matters, within the Defense Department. This new civilian elite has challenged the predominance of military professionals in every field, including military strategy, according to Huntington. All writers on the subject are agreed that Robert McNamara was able to increase the control of the Defense Department by the Secretary of Defense in a way unrivaled by any of his predecessors. Robert J. Art describes the decision making structure initiated by McNamara which helped him gain increased control of the Pentagon. In considering the topic of civilian versus military control of the Pentagon, one must ask what difference it makes who has such control. If the civilian and military leaders share a common outlook on the basic tenets of American military policy, as C. Wright Mills contends in his book, *The Power Elite*, it would seem to make little difference which of the two groups is more powerful. Whether Mills' thesis is correct, however, is a matter that cannot be resolved here.

No discussion of the role of the military establishment in American foreign policy would be complete without reference to the question: is there a military-industrial complex? Mark Pilisuk and Thomas Hayden argue the affirmative in this case, while Patrick M. Morgan takes the negative. The reader will note that neither of these articles is based on a great deal of data, and it is amazing that American social scientists have not done more research on this topic.

The State Department, which is probably thought of by the public at large as the principal executive department in foreign policy making, is discussed in three articles. Stewart Alsop, a leading Washington columnist, argues that the department is actually of secondary importance in foreign policy making. Alsop's opinion was supported by the experience of Presidents Kennedy and Johnson, who tried to get the State Department to assert itself as the primary foreign policy agency, but found the Department unable to assume this role. In the Nixon administration, the State Department has clearly been relegated to a subordinate role, with the appointment of a Secretary inexperienced in foreign relations, and the delegation of new powers to the National Security Council.

John Ensor Harr has compiled data on the background of the Foreign Service, the career professionals of the State Department, and concludes that the Department, like the professional military, is becoming more democratic in a socioeconomic sense. Andrew M. Scott contends that the "culture" of the State Department tends to make the State Department a less effective organization, because this "culture" serves the short-term interests of the Foreign Service at the expense of the long-term needs of the Department.

In a "cold war," intelligence agencies are key actors. David Wise and Thomas Ross, two modern-day "muckraking" journalists, describe the structure of our principal intelligence agencies. They also criticize the operation of these agencies, and the CIA in particular. Lyman B. Kirkpatrick, a former executive director of the CIA, attempts to refute a number of the principal points raised by Wise and Ross, in the excerpts from his memoirs on his service in the CIA published herein. However, Kirkpatrick often seems to be talking past Wise and Ross, as in the case of his discussion of the extent of Congressional control over the CIA budget. The unfortunate truth is that we do not know a great deal about the inner politics of the CIA, because those individuals who have spent a substantial amount of time working for the CIA are not likely to divulge anything substantial about its operations for fear of damaging national security. As a result, the rebuttals of Wise and Ross which exist are not terribly powerful. Likewise, critics of the CIA, even though they may make a case as seemingly compelling as that made by L. Fletcher Prouty (a retired Air Force colonel, now a Washington banker), in his discussion of the role of the CIA in Vietnam, are handicapped in that they are unable to probe as deeply into the intelligence agencies as they are into less security-conscious foreign policy making organs of the federal government.

Congress
and Foreign Policy Making

JAMES A. ROBINSON

WEIGHT OF INFLUENCE

In considering Congress' participation in the total foreign policy-making process, it is useful to have in mind a model of policy processes. We shall adopt one which conceives of the decision process in terms of seven functions which are performed in the making of any decision. These include the *intelligence* function, i.e., the gathering of information, which may include either information which suggests a problem for policy-makers' attention or information for the formulation of alternatives. A second function is the *recommendation* of one or more possible policy alternatives. A third is the *prescription* or enactment of one among several proposed alternative solutions. A fourth is the *invocation* of the adopted alternative, and a fifth is its *application* in specific situations by executive or enforcement officers. A sixth stage of the decision process is the *appraisal* of the effectiveness of the prescribed alternative, and the seventh is the *termination* of the original policy. The latter stages present the opportunity to gather new information, to evaluate the original policy, and to consider whether a new problem has arisen requiring new information, recommendations, or prescription. Then the decision process may begin again.

To consider the weight of influence which different roles and institutions within the total policy-making process exercise, it is useful to see which of these functions are primarily performed by legislatures as against executives. Although we lack the historical analysis, it would be interesting to have data to indicate whether there have been shifts in the predominant participation of executives and legislatures in each of these seven functions. A judgment, not based upon as hard evidence as one would like to have, is that the legislative branch of the U.S. government is no more predominant in any one of these seven decision functions than it was, say, fifty years ago. For example, consider the intelligence function. It is not obvious what the primary sources of information were for Congress

From *Congress and Foreign Policy Making*, Dorsey Press, 1967, pp. 6-15, 64-69. Reprinted by permission.

fifty years ago, but it does seem relatively clear that its primary source of information now is the executive branch. If one examines reports and studies of legislative committees, he will readily find that the data in them are from, and most of their bibliographic references are to, sources within the executive branch. It is customary that bills and resolutions referred to committees of Congress are almost invariably submitted to the executive for comment and analysis. Executive witnesses ordinarily open testimony in hearings on any bill or resolution. With respect to foreign relations, anyone who has observed hearings before either Foreign Affairs or Foreign Relations has noted the difference in attendance of Congressmen at a hearing on, say, the Mutual Security Bill when the Secretary of State or the Joint Chiefs of Staff testify and when private and nongovernmental groups testify.

Many people have commented on the "information revolution" of the 20th century. The effect of the information revolution on executive-legislative relations is several-fold. First, it has increased by many times the amount of information which is available to policy-makers about the problems they confront. Although all decision-making has not been reduced to highly rational, computational techniques, rough observation indicates a great increase in the possibilities of comparing proposed means to given ends much more precisely than fifty or a hundred years ago. This fact probably has reduced the amount of guessing and judgment required when information about the problem is lacking. Second, the executive branches of government have learned to specialize more than legislatures, and in specializing have developed resources for the accumulation of large amounts of factual data about policy problems. It is not clear why Congress or other legislative bodies have not developed more bureaucratic and staff support, but it seems plausible that their failure to do so has put them at a disadvantage vis-a-vis the executive departments which have had the superior resources for handling the vast new amounts of information available to the total policy-making process.

This alteration in the intelligence function, which is a product of the 20th century and which is changing the role of information in policy-making year by year, has had substantial effect on other parts of the decision process. Consider the recommendation function. The executive branch, because of its superior information, is in a preferred position for identifying social and political problems. Thus, it can structure the agenda for the total decision process, including the agenda of the legislative branch. One notes, in this connection, the apparent increase in the tendency of Congress, including its leaders, to expect the executive to assume the initiative in identifying problems and proposing solutions for them. Thus, Democrats complained that Dwight D. Eisenhower was not a "strong President" who gave "leadership" to the legislative branch. What is a general tendency in policy-making is acute with respect to foreign affairs. In international relations the executive has always had an advantage constitutionally and the information revolution has accentuated it. In addition to possessing an advantage in the identification of problems, the executive has primacy in the formulation of alternatives. As a result there is an increasing inclination to rely on the executive for the presentation of proposals to deal with problems. Congress' role, then, becomes less and less one of the initiation of policy alternatives and more and more the modifier, negator, or legitimator of proposals which originate in the executive.

The work nearest to a historical survey of the relative importance of Congress and the Presidency in the initiation of legislation is Lawrence Chamberlain's study of 90 bills enacted between 1880 and 1945.[1] The 90, unfortunately, do not contain any foreign policy measures other than immigration and national defense bills. Unfortunately, also, the means by which the sample of 90 were chosen were unsystematic. They appear to be the author's conception of important legislation during that period. Nevertheless, one gets some very interesting relationships if he tries to graph the relative importance of Congress and the Presidency in initiating these 90 bills over time. For example, Congress was the primary initiator prior to 1900 and then there was a sharp decline in its role concurrent with the Presidency of Theodore Roosevelt and then a slight increase again until 1925 when there is another peak of Congressional initiation almost as high as that of 1900. Then Congress' role drops off again and remains relatively low until the end of the survey in 1945. On the other hand, the Presidency, which was low as an initiator of legislation in 1900 and remains so through 1930 then takes an upturn through the 1930's before it begins to drop off. Corresponding with the decline of Congress and the increase of the Presidency in the initiation of legislation there is an overlapping trend which shows an increase in joint participation of Congress and the Presidency. Thus, a summary view of relative participation of Congress and the Presidency in the initiation of legislation in the 20th century looks like this: Congress declines as the Presidency participates jointly with Congress in the initiation of legislation. An extension of Chamberlain's study from 1945 to 1960 would be expected to show that joint collaboration has given way to virtually exclusive initiation by the executive.

*   *   *

SCOPE OF INFLUENCE

"Scope" refers to the number and kinds of issues, policies, or values affected by the holder of influence. In this case, the question is what foreign policy issues does Congress participate in deciding or affecting?

The Senate possesses a classic constitutional advantage over the House by virtue of the requirement that Presidential appointments of Ambassadors receive the advice and consent of the Senate. The Senate has never rejected a Presidential nomination for an ambassadorial post, "although," as Senator Humphrey has said, "on several occasions Senate opposition was sufficient to induce the President to withdraw his nominee." On other occasions, a Senator's persistent opposition may lead a nominee to decline appointment, even when the Senate confirms him. This was the outcome of Wayne Morse's campaign against Clare Booth Luce, whom the President nominated as Ambassador to Brazil, in 1959. We have no way of knowing how the "rule of anticipated reaction"[2] has worked to cause the President to consider, before making a nomination, whether it would be acceptable to the Senate. On the whole, it seems fair to say, that the Senate has not actively used the confirmation of appointments as an opportunity to influence foreign policy. Senator William Fulbright has inquired into the diplomatic preparation and language competency of nominees, but in the one case in which he chose to oppose the nomination on grounds of competency, the Senate upheld the President.

On another occasion the Senate used the confirmation proceeding to give unprecedented support to a Presidential nominee who had been embarrassed by the President himself. In 1959, President Eisenhower chose Undersecretary of State Christian Herter to succeed John Foster Dulles as Secretary of State. However, Mr. Eisenhower and his press secretary, James Hagerty, created the impression that the appointment was made with reluctance and with reservations. Under the leadership of Chairman Fulbright and Majority Leader Lyndon Johnson, the Committee on Foreign Relations suspended its rule that nominations lay over six days before being acted on within the Committee. Instead, within four hours and thirteen minutes after receiving the nomination from the President, the Senate unanimously confirmed Mr. Herter, and Senate leaders publicly expressed their support and satisfaction with the nominee. Nevertheless, this is an uncommon occurrence.

In addition to the authority to confirm certain Presidential nominees, the Senate also has the unique constitutional authority to give its advice and consent to treaties. This was once the primary opportunity for the Senate to participate in foreign policy, although the initiative rested with the executive. Nevertheless, the mechanisms of foreign policy have been altered, especially in the last twenty-five years. The executive agreement, introduced in quantity to handle tariff changes under the Reciprocal Trade Agreements Program, is much the more common form of internation activity. Further, foreign aid, in its many forms, has become a much more salient instrument of foreign policy than the treaty.

The scope of Congressional influence in foreign policy extends especially to appropriations, and in this field the House of Representatives is traditionally regarded as having the advantage over the Senate. One of the most notable post-World War II changes in the foreign policy values affected by Congress is the appropriation of money. The major foreign policies since 1947 have been foreign aid, sometimes called European Recovery, Point IV, technical assistance, foreign economic operations, mutual security, and most recently AID (Act for International Development). These programs have cost vast amounts of money, second in size only to the outlay of sums for defense. The effect has been to enlarge the scope of the House's influence on foreign policy. Former Speaker Martin recalls that in the 1920's foreign policy was a less expensive business. "For one week the House Foreign Affairs Committee debated to the exclusion of all other matters the question of authorizing a $20,000 appropriation for an international poultry show in Tulsa. This item, which we finally approved, was about the most important issue that came before the Committee in the whole session."[3]

The effect of Congressional influence on appropriations is consistently to reduce or maintain executive requests for foreign policy allotments. Rare is the occasion when Congress will enlarge an executive request for or initiate an expenditure for foreign policy.

One subject on which Congress has dominated the executive is immigration. Chamberlain's survey of the origins of legislation from 1880 to 1945 included nine immigration statutes. In each case he assigned Congress the preponderant influence in determining the policy. Generally speaking, Congress has preferred a more restrictive immigration policy than the President, and Congress has ordinarily favored admitting new immigrants roughly in proportion to the distribution of foreign nationalities within the United States. Although Presidents have vetoed legislation affecting immigration, Congress has been united enough to override the veto, as in 1952, when the McCarran-Walter Act was adopted. The one occasion when Congress took the initiative more "liberally" than the executive was in the repeal of the Chinese Exclusion Acts in 1943. In this case, the executive was reluctant to push the repeal, not for lack of sympathy for the objectives, but out of concern for whether there was sufficient support in Congress to complete repeal. Failure to succeed once the venture was undertaken, which would have been embarrassing for U.S. relations with China and the rest of Asia, was the concern of the executive.

The scope of Congressional influence also extends to the policy-making process within the executive. As we shall see in a later chapter much of Congress' foreign policy activity is in determining the organizational arrangements of the policy-making process, as distinguished from affecting substantive foreign policy by legislation. For example, during 1949-58, more than half the Senate bills and resolutions reported by the Foreign Relations Committee dealt with administrative and organizational machinery in the executive branch. This legislation included such issues as where the International Cooperation Administration should be located, in or out of the Department of State.

DOMAIN OF INFLUENCE

Measuring influence is a combination of gauging the degree of participation in making decisions, the scope or values affected by those decisions, and the extent of the consequences of and the number of persons affected by the decisions. Lasswell and Kaplan defined "domain" in terms of the number of persons affected. It is useful to add something more in computing the importance of the decision. Only to consider the number affected is to ignore the consequences of the influence. Although this raises the difficult problems associated with ranking the intensity of preferences of people and ranking value consequences, one can state the problem even if he can not satisfactorily solve it.

Congressional influence in foreign policy tends to be influence "on the periphery," as Senator Fulbright is supposed to believe. When House or Senate take the initiative, they do so on marginal and relatively unimportant matters. The scope of their influence may be broad in that it is related to several basic values—wealth, power, etc.—but the domain, the impact on those values, is much slighter than the executive's. Consider the most notable case of Congressional initiative in foreign policy in recent years, the Monroney Resolution. The scope of the resolution's influence included the economies of underdeveloped countries, the more efficient use of surplus local currencies owned by the United States, and the possible reduction of the amount of U.S. foreign aid. Yet the International Development Association, created as a result of the impetus of the resolution, was capitalized at only $1 billion and involved only a third that amount for the United States. Further, as we shall note below, one explanation for why this attempt at Congressional initiative suceeded was that it was a marginal issue to which little cost was attached.

On the other hand, the most famous unsuccessful attempt at Congressional initiative, the Bricker Amendment to the Constitution, was viewed by the executive as containing potentially threatening consequences. Had Senator Bricker's proposed amendment been ratified, its impact could hardly have been evaluated in terms of the number who would have been affected by it. Yet the alleged consequences of the Senator's designs for changing the treaty-making process were considerable, and the executive opposed it categorically.

The view that Congress originates marginal proposals is supported by comparing the content of bills initiated in Congress with those initiated by the executive. This is done in greater detail in a subsequent chapter. At this point it is worth noting that quantitatively Congress initiates more foreign policy proposals than the executive. In the period 1949-58, 80 per cent of the Senate bills and resolutions reported by the Committee on Foreign Relations originated with Senators and 20 per cent with the executive. In historical research of this kind it is difficult to identify all the executive-initiated bills and resolutions. We are confident that the 20 per cent is a minimum figure of executive measures, but a somewhat larger number may be more accurate, inasmuch as it is a common occurrence for a legislator to receive a suggestion from one of the departments and in turn seek its help in drafting his proposal. Nevertheless, the data would have to be very inaccurate to deny the proposition that many foreign policy proposals initiate in Congress. Yet none of these are the measures which command the greatest amount of time of the Committee or occupy the attention of the "attentive publics." Foreign aid, fundamental international commitments, participation in international organizations—these bills with the greatest domain originate with the executive.

SUMMARY

To summarize, Congressional participation in foreign policy decisions is principally in the recommendation and prescription stages of the decision process. Recommendations of important measures frequently are initiated by the executive rather than the legislative branch. Thus, in the prescription stage Congress is legitimating, amending, or vetoing executive proposals. The scope of Congressional influence varies with the constitutional provisions governing the making and conduct of foreign relations. The Senate, with an advantage in confirming diplomatic appointments and approving treaties has not exploited the former and is finding the latter less and less an important instrument of policy. The House, with an advantage deriving from its constitutional position with respect to appropriations, awaits the executive budget and reacts to it by legitimating or cutting it, but rarely by raising it. In the initiation and determination of immigration policies Congress has consistently prevailed over the executive, and the scope of Congressional influence also extends to the organization of the executive for making and executing policy. Finally, the domain of Congressional influence, especially when it is initiative, tends to be on marginal and relatively less important matters.

*   *   *

COMPARISON AND SUMMARY

We have . . . reviewed twenty-two foreign policy decisions of the past thirty years. We must repeat our earlier admission that this is a poor sample of U.S. foreign policies, yet it represents nearly all the published case studies of individual foreign policy acts. The inadequacies of this collection of cases for purposes of generalizing about the role of Congress in making foreign policy are revealed in Table 1. One shortcoming of the sample is that all but two of these policies were decided over relatively long periods of time. Only the Korean decision and the decision not to intervene in Indo-China were taken in a matter of days rather than weeks. "Decision time" is often mentioned by writers on this subject as one of the factors affecting the extent of Congressional participation in foreign affairs. The need to act with "dispatch," it has been hypothesized, excludes the legislature which is characterized as a "deliberative" body as opposed to the swifter, more decisive "executive." The decision to resist aggression in Korea certainly comports with this hypothesis. Indeed, the President's reason for not consulting Congress was the need to move quickly. What about Indo-China? In this case, the Congressional leaders "vetoed" the request for a joint resolution in less than two hours. However, this decision may not be an exception to the hypothesis because, if Congressional leaders had consented to such a resolution, several weeks might have been required to hold hearings and consider the matter on the floor, as in the longer case of the Formosan Resolution. Still it is regrettable that we do not have more cases of "short decision time" to compare with the twenty with long decision time.

TABLE 1

CONGRESSIONAL INVOLVEMENT AND DECISION CHARACTERISTICS*

	Congressional Involvement (High, Low, None)	Initiator (Congress or Executive)	Predominant Influence (Congress or Executive)	Legislation or Resolution (Yes or No)	Violence at Stake (Yes or No)	Decision Time (Long or Short)
1. Neutrality Legislation, the 1930's	High	Exec	Cong	Yes	No	Long
2. Lend-Lease, 1941	High	Exec	Exec	Yes	Yes	Long
3. Aid to Russia, 1941	Low	Exec	Exec	No	No	Long
4. Repeal of Chinese Exclusion, 1943	High	Cong	Cong	Yes	No	Long
5. Fulbright Resolution, 1943	High	Cong	Cong	Yes	No	Long
6. Building the Atomic Bomb, 1944	Low	Exec	Exec	Yes	Yes	Long
7. Foreign Service Act of 1946	High	Exec	Exec	Yes	No	Long
8. Truman Doctrine, 1947	High	Exec	Exec	Yes	No	Long
9. The Marshall Plan, 1947-48	High	Exec	Exec	Yes	No	Long
10. Berlin Airlift, 1948	None	Exec	Exec	No	Yes	Long
11. Vandenberg Resolution, 1948	High	Exec	Cong	Yes	No	Long
12. North Atlantic Treaty, 1948-49	High	Exec	Exec	Yes	No	Long
13. Korean Decision, 1950	None	Exec	Exec	No	Yes	Short
14. Japanese Peace Treaty, 1952	High	Exec	Exec	Yes	No	Long
15. Bohlen Nomination, 1953	High	Exec	Exec	Yes	No	Long
16. Indo-China, 1954	High	Exec	Cong	No	Yes	Short
17. Formosan Resolution, 1955	High	Exec	Exec	Yes	Yes	Long
18. International Finance Corporation, 1956	Low	Exec	Exec	Yes	No	Long
19. Foreign Aid, 1957	High	Exec	Exec	Yes	No	Long
20. Reciprocal Trade Agreements Act, 1958	High	Exec	Exec	Yes	No	Long
21. Monroney Resolution, 1958	High	Cong	Cong	Yes	No	Long
22. Cuban Decision, 1961	Low	Exec	Exec	No	Yes	Long

*The assignment of each case to different categories represents a "judgment" rather than a "calculation" on the part of the author.

Another respect in which this sample is atypical is that it includes too few cases of Congressional initiative. Even if one has difficulty in identifying precisely the percentage of executive initiated as opposed to legislative initiated policies (as we indicated in Chapter 1 sometimes occurs), one needs a significant number of decisions of both kinds in order to explore the conditions under which Congress is more or less likely to be the initiator. In this sample, there are only three cases of Congressional initiative: Repeal of Chinese Exclusion, the Fulbright and Monroney Resolutions. The Vandenberg Resolution, usually regarded as a case of Senatorial initiative, was in fact a response to an appeal from the executive. Immigration, as noted earlier, has been an issue on which Congress has for many decades not only been the principal initiator of policy but also has possessed preponderant influence. We will note shortly the relationship between initiative and influence; here we might only comment that the absence of attempts of executive initiative may be a recognition of a low probability of success and a consequent decision to leave the field to Congress. The Fulbright Resolution was a concurrent resolution requiring the approval of both houses, the Monroney Resolution was a simple resolution needing only the endorsement of the Senate. Resolutions, as distinguished from bills, carry less legal authority, and some writers have asserted that they are therefore more convenient and more appropriate forms for Congress to use in attempts to influence international affairs. We shall examine this hypothesis on a much larger number of cases in Chapter 3.

The case studies which are available for summary also are rather heavily overloaded with policies expressed through bills and resolutions as distinguished from policies not requiring legislation or from legislative influence expressed through Congressional investigations or informal participation by Congressional leaders (such as in the Indo-China and Cuban decisions). Seventeen of the twenty-two cases involved legislation, resolutions, or formal approval of a treaty or a nomination. The five foreign policies expressed in nonlegislative fashion may be commented on briefly and compared. In two of them (the Cuban and Indo-China decisions) Congressional leaders preferred not to involve United States armed forces. In the Korean and Berlin decisions, legislation was not immediately required and Congress did not participate at all. The decision to aid Russia is slightly ambiguous; the executive did not ask for authority to include Russia in Lend-Lease, but some Congressmen tried without avail to amend the Lend-Lease Act to exclude Russia. As in the Indo-China case, an attempt at legislation was made but it failed. Future case studies might usefully explore means of influencing foreign policy other than formal legislative actions.

Perhaps the most serious respect in which these twenty-two cases are not a sample of all foreign policies is that they are almost all "successful" policies, successful in the sense that the initiator succeeded in obtaining adoption of the policy. The Indo-China decision is an exception, in that the executive lost to Congress, and the neutrality legislation is partially an exception, in that Congress was six years in yielding to executive pleas on this issue. (The Vandenberg

Resolution, the third case in which Congress had preponderant influence even when the executive initiated, differs from these two in that Vandenberg and the executive worked co-operatively and not competitively.) It would be interesting and useful to have a larger number of episodes in which Congress or the executive attempted to achieve an objective but was thwarted by the other party.

Our comparisons of the cases thus far have been essentially criticisms of the sample and have not yielded much in the way of new generalizations. Given the nature of the sample, it is difficult to compare many different types of cases. Nevertheless, a few interesting points may be tentatively advanced on the basis of these data. First, note the relative involvement of Congress in cases without threat of violence as opposed to cases in which potential or actual violence is present. Table 2 displays the data and indicates that Congress is more likely to be highly involved in nonviolent as opposed to potentially or actually violent cases. And if one considers preponderant influence as opposed to extent of involvement, Congress is more likely to be influential in nonviolent as opposed to potentially violent cases. As Table 3 shows, five of the six decisions in which Congress predominated were nonviolent. Only in the request for force in Indo-China was Congress predominant in a potentially violent case. The implication of this for Congress' exclusive Constitutional authority to declare war is obvious. In spite of its legal advantage, the *actual* locus of influence in our collection of cases of potential violence now resides with the executive.

One other relationship remains to be presented, and this is the connection between initiative and influence. In Chapter 1 we dwelt on initiative as a form of influence distinguished from legitimation or the veto or amendment. Table 4 summarizes the cases of initiation and preponderant influence. Although our sample of Congressional influence is small, note that in the three cases Congress took the initiative it prevailed. Of course, we know of exceptions, e.g., the Bricker Amendment, but it suggests the need to identify conditions of successful Congressional initiative. Nor is this to overlook the fact that the executive can

TABLE 2
CONGRESSIONAL INVOLVEMENT AND VIOLENCE

Involvement	Violence	
	No	*Yes*
None	2	2
Low	2	2
High	11	3

TABLE 3
PREPONDERANT INFLUENCE AND VIOLENCE

Influence	Violence	
	Yes	*No*
Executive	6	10
Congress	1	5

TABLE 4

INITIATOR AND PREPONDERANT INFLUENCE

Initiator	Influence	
	Executive	*Congress*
Executive	16	3
Congress	0	3

bargain with Congress to amend acts of legislative initiative, e.g., the Monroney Resolution, just as Congress can alter executive proposals.

Similarly, when the executive initiates, it too has a high rate of success; in these twenty-two cases it prevailed in nineteen. These data, however inadequate as a sample, suggest the importance of studying initiation as a prime element of influence. For the initiator chooses both the problem or issue for the agenda of the political system *and* the first alternative for debate. Great advantages consist in defining the problem and proposing alternatives. As Professor E. E. Schattschneider phrased it in his presidential address to the American Political Science Association, "The definition of alternatives is the supreme instrument of power; the antagonists can rarely agree on what the issues are because power is involved in the definition. He who determines what politics is about runs the country because the definition of the alternatives is the choice of conflicts, and the choice of conflicts allocates power."

NOTES

[1] *The President, Congress, and Legislation* (New York: Columbia University Press, 1946).

[2] This rule, given a name by Professor Carl J. Friedrich, refers to the phenomenon of one actor's modifying his behavior in anticipation of how another actor would respond if one's behavior were not modified. See *Constitutional Government and Democracy*, (Boston: Little, Brown and Co., 1941), pp. 589-91.

[3] Joe Martin, *My First Fifty Years in Politics*, as told to Robert J. Donovan (New York: McGraw-Hill, 1960), p. 49.

Congress as Policy Maker:
A Necessary Reappraisal

RONALD C. MOE and STEVEN C. TEEL

Traditionally, the President has acted from a position of constitutional and political strength in foreign affairs. The Congress, on the other hand, has tended to have a more limited and ambiguous role in foreign policy making. It is widely assumed that congressional influence has been on the decline and that the shift away from initiation of public policies toward a role of legitimating and amending executive initiatives has been most pronounced in foreign affairs.[1] Such an assumption requires, however, that in some previous period congressional influence in foreign policy was greater than it is today. Sometime in the past there must have been a "golden era." If such an era existed prior to World War II, no one has written about it.[2] What evidence we have of Congress' role prior to the War is impressionistic and hardly suggests that this was the high point of congressional influence, power, and prestige.[3]

While it is true that the President's power in foreign affairs has vastly increased since World War II, this increase has not been at the expense of Congress. Quite the contrary, both the President and Congress have found their powers and responsibilities increased. Although Robert Dahl, writing in 1950, did not view the congressional role in foreign policy as in the ascendency,[4] more recent writers have suggested that the period from 1945 to 1955 was really the "golden era."[5] The diminution of congressional influence, they argue, coincides with the 1960's and what Holbert Carroll calls the international "new environment" which is uncongenial to legislative institutions.[6]

Much of the lament of Carroll, Fulbright,[7] and others, over the plight of Congress is directly attributable to their feelings on the Vietnamese War. They bemoan Congress' seeming inability to influence general policy. While acknowledging the possibility that Congress, on balance, has increased its strength since World War II, they suggest that increments of power have flowed, not to the institution itself, but to several of its committees and are most visible on

Reprinted with permission from the *Political Science Quarterly* 85 (September 1970), pp. 463-67.

peripheral issues and points of detail. The goal of those who currently champion the cause of a strong Congress is to be included in the general or strategic policy-making as well as the details of policy and executive actions. Whether these proponents of balance between the President and Congress will hold to their positions after the Viet Namese War is settled is only problematical.[8]

While there is no general agreement as to the relative standings of the President and Congress in initiating foreign policy legislation, or about trends presently underway, there are a large number of legislative case studies to provide assistance in our evaluation.

The case studies of foreign affairs tend to give credence to Cecil Crabb's observation: "A striking phenomenon associated with the control of foreign relations in recent American history is the expanded role of Congress in virtually all phases of external affairs. . . ."[9] Much of the increased role played by Congress in foreign policy is related to its constitutional monetary powers. Few major policies envisioned by the executive can be implemented without appropriations from Congress. The pre-eminence of the appropriations process since World War II has also altered the relative strength of the two chambers in influencing policy with the House gaining relative to the Senate.[10]

Contrary to the general view, both chambers of Congress have been involved in great policy decisions as well as the slower process of modification of existing policies. The Senate, for its part, is constitutionally required to participate in the process of treaty-making and case studies of its activities in this regard, such as with the Japanese Peace Treaty of 1952,[11] the North Atlantic Treaty,[12] and American participation in the United Nations[13] attest to the vigor it brings to the task. The House, particularly the Appropriations Committee, has found its views often anticipated in Administration proposals.[14]

Many areas of foreign policy are frequently labeled, individually, as "peripheral." Collectively, however, they constitute a major portion of our foreign policy. Congress is generally credited with major or dominant influence in economic aid policy,[15] military assistance,[16] agricultural surplus disposal,[17] and locational decisions,[18] to name only several policy areas. In addition, immigration and tariff policies, discussed previously, are generally thought of as part of foreign policy and there is considerable evidence to indicate that Congress remains a major actor in these fields.

To Senator Fulbright, and others, who argue that Congress ought to abdicate its interest in short-term policies and day-to-day operations, and instead concentrate its attention on longer-range, more basic questions, Richard Fenno offers the following rejoinder:

> To relegate Congress to the making of broad policy decisions and to oversight in terms of broad program management is to prescribe precisely those tasks which Congress is least capable of performing. To criticize Congress for intervening in a specific and detailed fashion is to attack it for doing the only

thing it can do to effectively assert its influence. Specifics and details are indispensable handles which Congressmen use to work inductively toward broader kinds of oversight judgments.[19]

The simple fact is that most broad foreign policy positions taken by this country have been developed, not from a comprehensive model of a better world order, but rather from an incremental evolution of often vague and ambiguous precepts applied pragmatically to a changing world situation. What the critics fail to see is that the oversight function of Congress, with its penchant for detail, cannot be arbitrarily divorced from the policy-making process, whether narrow or broad. To conclude, the evidence does not substantiate the thesis that Congress is declining as a participant in foreign policy-making or that its present, decentralized structure weakens its vis-a-vis the executive. Congress, constitutionally, is required to play a less visible role than is the executive. Having said this, however, the case studies indicate that the contemporary Congress is very much capable of conceptual innovation, legislation modification and energetic oversight.

NOTES

[1] James A. Robinson, *Congress and Foreign Policy Making* (Homewood, Illinois: The Dorsey Press, 1967), pp. 173-75.

[2] Lawrence A. Chamberlain, *The President, Congress, and Legislation* (New York: Columbia University Press, 1946), did not even see fit to discuss "foreign policy" as a separate category of presidential-congressional relations.

[3] See Holbert N. Carroll, *House of Representatives and Foreign Affairs* (rev. ed.; Boston: Little, Brown and Co., 1966), chap. 1; Albert C. F. Westphal, *The House Committee on Foreign Affairs* (New York: Columbia University Press, 1942), pp. 13-26; Joseph Martin, *My First Fifty Years in Politics* (New York: McGraw-Hill Book Co., 1960), p. 49.

[4] Robert Dahl, *Congress and Foreign Policy* (New York: Harcourt Brace and Co., 1950), p. 58.

[5] See, for example, H. Bradford Westerfield, "Congress and Closed Politics in National Security Affairs," *Orbis* (Fall 1966), p. 747 [also next entry this text].

[6] Carroll, pp. 363-68.

[7] Senator William Fulbright's attitude toward executive discretion in foreign affairs has shifted in recent years. This is most evident in his attitude toward foreign aid. In 1964 he argued that specific restrictions on the use of foreign aid ought to be minimized. *Old Myths and New Realities* (New York: Random House, 1964), pp. vii-viii. By 1966, however, he had changed his tone. "I think it prudent for the Congress to retain its full authority to review the authorization as well as the appropriation of funds for foreign aid." *The Arrogance of Power* (New York: Random House, 1966), p. 236.

[8] In point of fact, Congress is not uniformly viewed as impotent in general policy-making. Lyndon B. Johnson, for one, might argue the point. He would probably agree with his predecessor who said: "The Congress looks more powerful sitting here than it did when I was ... one of a hundred in the Senate." Theodore Sorenson, *Kennedy* (New York: Harper and Row, 1965), p. 346.

[9] Cecil V. Crabb, Jr., *American Foreign Policy in the Nuclear Age* (New York: Harper and Row, 1965), p. 91.

[10] Carroll, chap. 14; Crabb, pp. 22-26.

[11] Bernard C. Cohen, *The Political Process and Foreign Policy: The Making of the Japanese Peace Settlement* (Princeton: Princeton University Press, 1957), chaps. 8, 11.

[12] R. H. Heindel, T. V. Kaljawi, and F. Wilcox, "The North Atlantic Treaty in the United States Senate," *American Journal of International Law* XLIII (October 1949), pp. 633-65.

[13] Cecil V. Crabb, *Bipartisan Foreign Policy: Myth or Reality* (Evanston, Ill.: Row, Peterson and Co., 1957), pp. 44-53.

[14] Richard F. Fenno, Jr., *The Power of the Purse* (Boston: Little, Brown and Co., 1966), p. 362. Also, H. Field Haviland, Jr., "Foreign Aid and the Policy Process: 1957," *American Political Science Review* LII (September 1958), pp. 689-724.

[15] John D. Montgromery, *The Politics of Foreign Aid* (New York: Praeger, 1962), pp. 219-221. Michael K. O'Leary, on the other hand, denies extensive congressional influence in economic aid policy. *The Politics of American Foreign Aid* (New York: Atherton Press, 1967), pp. 89-90.

[16] See, for example, William Adams Brown, Jr., and Redvers Opie, *American Foreign Assistance* (Washington, D.C.: Brookings Institution, 1953), part 5.

[17] Peter A. Toma, *The Politics of Food For Peace* (Tucson: University of Arizona Press, 1967), chap. 2.

[18] Theodore J. Lowi, "Bases in Spain," *American Civil-Military Decisions*, Harold Stein, ed. (University, Alabama: University of Alabama Press, 1963), pp. 669-703.

[19] Richard F. Fenno, Jr., review of Joseph P. Harris, "Congressional Control of Administration," in *American Political Science Review* LVIII (September 1964), p. 674.

Congress
and Closed Politics
in National Security Affairs

H. BRADFORD WESTERFIELD

About a decade ago I began to discern and describe a typical pattern in the formation of U.S. national security policies in the continuing era of the Cold War. This policymaking process—except perhaps in periods of heavy U.S. military casualties—tended, according to my interpretation, to unfold in the following sequence:

First, the Administration, drawing ideas from a variety of sources, would nearly make up its collective mind about the policy it wanted to pursue—before the issues involved could be dramatized in public to any considerable extent.

Second, a cluster of *ad hoc* oppositionists would begin to form, largely on the initiative of those who were losing within the Administration. They would be able to take advantage of the diffusion of authority and responsibility in the media and in Congress, and, no matter where they were located in the Executive branch or in what cause they sought support, they could be reasonably sure to find collaborators somewhere outside the Executive. Some of these might be in the form of semi-permanent allies, perhaps particular congressional subcommittees, journalists or academics; others might be issue-hunting opportunists glad to find ammunition for personal or partisan advantage.

Third, this oppositionist agitation would mount, using particularly the various devices available to congressmen for promoting adverse publicity. There might also be serious threats of reprisals against the Administration in other fields should it insist on pursuing its policy in this one.

Fourth, the Administration would feel impelled to promote a counter-cluster, a "support cluster," on behalf of its own crystalizing policy.

Fifth, in the ensuing controversy, more or less public, the preponderant power to shape the decision, at least in peacetime, would almost always rest with those who had already privately gained the upper hand on the issue within the Administration. If they, presumably with the cooperation or at least the implicit backing of the President, had the determination and skill to use the political

From *Orbis* 10, Fall 1966, pp. 737-53. Reprinted by permission of Trustees of the University of Pennsylvania.

tools available to such a strategically located cluster, they would win out in the larger domestic controversy. This sequence could be insured by a customary shrewd Administration practice of granting the concessions, mostly nominal, necessary to conciliate key factions in Congress and among the "attentive public" and thereby maintain a reservoir of confidence in the general wisdom and reasonableness of U.S. leaders in national security affairs. Such a reservoir of confidence can be tapped at various times for support of particular Administration policies.

Except in the case of the most general, long-standing policies, the consensus the Administration must preserve above all others is faith in its leadership capabilities—not fixation on and approval of all its particular policies, because the unpredictability of world affairs makes it likely that the Administration will want a relatively free hand to change its particular policies. Awareness of this long-term need, arising from the external environment, for flexibility via consensus-support ought to make an Administration responsive to many demands for concessions to conciliate potential oppositionists, even at some cost in the . . . rationality of policy; but the sustained image of reasonableness and receptivity should insure that the concessions in particular instances would not have to be great.

On the whole, then, my model emphasized in "stage five" that, at least in peacetime, the policy position which was emerging dominant within the Administration before the issue was thrown open to "outside publics" would still prevail, after all the tumult had died down, as the position of the U.S. government. Congressmen and others would have been able to throw their weight into the scales—but enough would line up with the preponderant Administration position so that the scales would settle back mostly along that prior slant, if reasonable political skill and determination were shown.

Of course the rule of anticipated reactions would be operative here. The drama sketched above would often not need to be acted out in full. At least in circumstances where there was a reasonable prospect that the issue might be transferred to another arena in which the balance of clusters would be somewhat different, the participant factions within the Administration would probably anticipate an ultimate need to strike a compromise—a one-sided compromise, to be sure, along the lines already suggested—and would often therefore be willing to do so in advance and in private, rather than precipitate public controversy. Thus even the frequent avoidance of outside debate would not wholly preclude influence from outside. At least the small segments of our citizenry that we term the most "attentive" publics, who would make themselves heard if alerted to the issue, would often have some influence even when they were not alerted, because of the presumption that otherwise the institutions and habits of a pluralistic polity would eventually produce leaks to them—except when decisions had to be extremely compressed in time or else were so routinized as to be considered by virtually all the insiders to be not susceptible of controversy outside.

One must note, however, that when insiders anticipated the reactions of outsiders there could be some misperception and consequent blundering.

II

It is important to note that this model of a typical policymaking process in national security affairs would not, at least in peacetime, expect the outer publics to undertake initiatives that would from the outset determine the basic line the policy would ultimately take. Nor would the model look to congressmen for such initiatives; congressmen appear as just one somewhat privileged category of outsiders. Like the others, they may exert initiative in offering ideas, but whether the ideas are adopted in the crucial formative stage and are meshed into the semi-crystallized policy alternatives for possible subsequent exposure to public debate is determined from the inside.

Receptivity to ideas from the outside may vary greatly from time to time and from place to place in the Executive branch. But suffusing the entire process in peacetime, it has seemed to me, has been a vague awareness by the participants of how few electoral resources can be mustered by the various outside advocates of new policy ideas. The congressman in peacetime is almost immune from electoral sanctions in picking and choosing among foreign policy causes—at least among the causes that a politician drawn from the middle classes in his particular district would conceivably have a personal inclination to support. The President and his appointees have a somewhat similar immunity. All the participants in the peacetime foreign policy process are largely on their own, safe in this field from the electorate. The ideas of the outsiders are to be judged "on the merits" as evaluated by the insiders; no one, inside or out, can truly display massive, determined public support for particular foreign policies (except perhaps for the most general ones that are endorsed by nearly everyone in government). But the President and his Administration draw strength from the special reservoir of prevalent confidence in their leadership; this gives them broad discretion to choose which policy streams to absorb, which deflect, and which dam up.

There is scant evidence, in the polls or elsewhere, for the view that in peacetime the mass public cares enough about particular national security policies—as distinguished from a candidate's general image of competence in that area—to make an electoral impact.

Wartime is probably different. The domestic political lesson of Korea—that the American mass public will powerfully resist the use of protracted limited war as an instrument of U.S. foreign policy when the war involves substantial American casualties—appears to be moving toward reconfirmation in Viet Nam. American bloodshed—apparently *only* American bloodshed—can arouse the mass public long enough to make wide electoral impact. The pressure to "get it over with" may then take the form preponderantly of demands to expand the war (as in the Korean case) or preponderantly of demands for abandonment of the war (as increasingly about Viet Nam); in either direction it is a pressure that can be expected to culminate in an electoral payoff. But the dates for such payoffs are fixed—coming only once every second year in early November. For a President, insofar as he may be willing to jeopardize his party and much of the rest of his program, the moment of truth can be postponed nearly four years in his first term, and throughout his second term.

If these residual electoral constraints were to become the only surviving effective constraints on Executive discretion in national security affairs, the consent of the governed would be so emptied of meaning that one would be reluctant to call the foreign policymaking process democratic. It would, for comparison, transcend even the discipline of the British system and approximate that of Gaullist France. (At least in Britain the majority party can replace its chieftain, without waiting eight years.) One must look beyond elections for the features of our national security policymaking system that have kept it, even though Executive-dominated, nonetheless broadly responsive to outside influences day-by-day and month-by-month, not just during occasional brief intervals every two or four years in wartime. I would suggest that there are at least four factors that in the past have moderated Executive supremacy in the operation of the model I described:

First, many important decisions in national security affairs can be postponed and have been postponed. Not everything that is important needs to be treated as a crisis, nor has it been. As time has elapsed in the determination of a policy, the chances that someone would open it up to wider influences have grown.

Second, there has been a realistic presumption of "permeability." All the participants in the decision-making process have been inclined to assume that there would eventually be leaks; thus, they have had an incentive to adjust their original preferences and adopt policies that would turn out to be politically and administratively feasible.

Third, we have had an extraordinarily complex sifting process along the road to the White House. The concept of the "availability" of a Presidential candidate has denoted a process of surviving such a formidable range of potential vetoes—and gaining the nomination and winning the election involves surviving so many more potential vetoes-that it has been reasonable for us to assume that no one would reach the White House who would be personally disposed to utilize ruthlessly the full powers of the office. His self-will would long since have partly atrophied through sheer habituation to responsiveness, both to organized groups and to the mass electorate.

Fourth, it may also have been vitally important that a President has had to obtain frequent formal legislative enactments from Congress in national security affairs. A President has needed not only the periodic support of the electorate and some symbolic endorsement from congressmen as part of the continual national and international process of solidaristic image-building, but also numerous concrete enactments without which many important policies could not be pursued constitutionally. This need for legislation has powerfully reinforced the other incentives for a President to take care to keep filled the reservoir of confidence in his general trustworthiness in foreign affairs—and to that end to conciliate and absorb as wide as possible a circle of potential oppositionists, even when, in the immediate instance, they could be overridden.

The central question in the remainder of this article is whether these safeguards still prevail and will continue to prevail in the near future.

III

The first and third factors serving to limit Presidential powers are firmly rooted. There seems no reason to suppose that the hurdles along the road to the White House will take less of a toll in the self-will of future Presidents. Nor do I share the alarmist view that all important national security policy decisions are made under crisis conditions or are even likely to be handled so swiftly that there would not be enough time to open them up to some outside influence. But here we come to a nub of the matter: How much time is consumed in the formation of a particular Executive policy before the presumption of permeability (safeguard number two) becomes operative and helps to shape the participants' behavior? If permeability as a whole should tend to decline, then a longer and longer span of the policymaking process would elapse, even in the absence of the excuse of "crisis," before outside influences would have to be taken into account.

There are signs of a marked decline in permeability. It has long been exceedingly difficult for outsiders to exert major influence over foreign affairs unless their actual or potential collaborators could also become entrenched somewhere inside the Executive branch (except in those special cases where a group may be able to bypass the government entirely and act directly on its own overseas). For dealing with the government, a principal requirement is information, not only about the substantive problem but also about the specific, relevant policymaking process, including its timing; and to secure this information, groups on the outside are likely to find themselves much more dependent on allies or potential allies on the inside than is the case in most domestic affairs. The insiders are in a position, for a time, to practice "closed politics," i.e., to utilize the security system in its various manifestations (clearances and classifications) and to restrict the range of influences that can directly affect decisions by limiting the number and variety of actual *ad hoc* participants.

The legitimizing assumption of such a pattern, if there can be one in democratic terms when "closure" is long maintained, would have to be found somewhere along the line of the notion of "virtual representation." The practice would depend for constitutional democratic rationalization upon the dubious assumption that all worthy viewpoints are represented directly—albeit not proportionately—by the presence of some of their adherents inside the policymaking circles in the Executive branch, a presence that would supposedly be insured through frequent cooptation of outsiders by insiders, subject of course to the presumably necessary disciplines of secrecy. Defenders of such a tightly closed pattern might concede that many outsiders, including some congressmen, notably those on special committees, might have sufficient expertise to have a right to insist on being allowed to participate—if expertise were all that were needed. But these defenders of closed politics would contend also that expeditiousness, flexibility and some overall consistency are needed in a great power's foreign policies, and only the relatively hierarchical processes of the Executive branch (free to exclude such outside influences as it feels it must) can manage to resolve foreign and defense policy conflicts even temporarily and make decisions that are administratively feasible. Hence, we should have a kind of "virtual representation," "cooptative representation," subject only to the limited public accountability of occasional elections.

One must admit a large measure of truth in this image of the requirements of national security in the Cold War era, and recognize that quite a wide range of opinion could continue to be coopted. Closed politics has certainly been mitigated by a steady proliferation of contract research and consultantships. McGeorge Bundy seems to have been particularly adept at the function of keeping channels open for fresh ideas to flow all the way to the President. One might also note that even in domestic affairs most representation that can be said to be truly influential is largely cooptative and "virtual"; elective representation is mostly supplemental. The will of Executive policymakers can rarely be overcome by real pressure from outside on anything.

But one distinctive feature of national security policymaking is that the outsiders can even be kept from knowing what it is they do not have direct influence on—as long as the insiders can stick together and keep the issue "closed." The appearance of a solid front gives oppositionist outsiders no handle, and hence no encouragement. If they persist, they must feel they are beating their heads against a stone wall. Some near-anarchists may delight in this, but more sober citizens are likely to feel demoralized in their opposition. Consider the rapidity with which opposition built up in the United States to the Truman Administration's policy after the Chinese entered the Korean War. The domestic oppositionists found encouragement in General MacArthur's overt defection and in his assurances that the military services were honeycombed with fellow dissenters. Contrast that with the solidarity on Viet Nam of the Kennedy-Johnson Administration and principal members of Congress, until Senator Fulbright finally broke loose in the winter of 1965-1966—a full year after the onset of the major war and more than four years after the start of substantial U.S. troop commitments in Viet Nam.

The U.S. government's solidarity on Viet Nam had been somewhat forced, but it was nonetheless rather effective. For example, I am persuasively assured that throughout the autumn of 1965 Defense Secretary McNamara was urging the President to experiment with a "peace offensive," substantially akin to the effort eventually undertaken at Christmas. But when the peace marchers gathered in Washington at Thanksgiving to make a similar plea they evidently had no idea that they had an *ad hoc* ally near the top. They felt like martyrs. To be sure, they persisted, and some of them enjoyed it, and the President presumably was somewhat moved. The agitation was not in vain. But on a less compelling issue it would have been abandoned much earlier, in the face of the apparently impervious closed wall of the Executive, with no visible chink to chip away at. This should be cause for concern, irrespective of one's judgment of the substance of Administration policy in Viet Nam, which I personally have favored.

John Stuart Mill long ago reminded us that it is this smothering of new ideas generated from outside—perhaps eventually becoming so stifling that there will be little on the outside worth coopting by almost any standards—that is the greatest long-run danger posed by what we call closed politics. This we would confront if the only safeguard were to become the occasional accountability of elections. We are not yet at that point: Presidents are still bred to be responsive, and a crisis atmosphere is not all-pervasive. Permeability exists, but there are signs that it is declining.

For example, the coercive sanctions of the security system are perfected. They contribute, along with other factors, to a persistent, and perhaps growing, like-mindedness—an Establishmentarianism, if you will, or at most a set of compatible Establishmentarianisms. Recruitment patterns are among the factors that tend to confirm and perpetuate like-mindedness. So is the existence of a doctrine, or at least a set of compatible doctrines; I call it "containment until mellowing." It is more precise than most of the doctrines in our diplomatic history. We hear less frequently the old chorus that "America doesn't have a foreign policy"; now we do have one. Having a doctrine makes indoctrination feasible—and it has happened. Some decided gains result; completely open minds may be empty minds. But filling them in too firm a mold may produce closed minds.

Another factor contributing to like-mindedness is the persistent affinity of intellectuals, including national security intellectuals, for the Democratic Party. The Republican Party is acceptable as their channel of influence only when the GOP controls the White House and their only alternative would be the wilderness; even then major cadres of national security intellectuals prefer the wilderness. But to stay in the wilderness with Republicans, telling them what to cry out, is to go virtually beyond the pale. Instead, the intellectuals persist in quiet appeals for cooptation by the Democratic Administration, trying to preserve at least a front of like-mindedness with it; even Senator Robert Kennedy's "government-in-exile" is slow to form and duly muted. Truman's Cold Warriors never die, nor do they fade away.

A more permanent factor—the Republicans after all will return to power some day—tending toward reduced permeability is the steady, marked improvement in the intra-Executive facilities for communication and intelligence. With these improvements, especially in the Defense Department, goes a declining need to use the press for sheer communication within the government, a declining need for officials to "trade" information in return for access to columns and broadcasts. Indeed, increasingly the exchanges that are made with the communications media are in return for nonpublication: the journalists are allowed to preen themselves on being "in on the know" in return for not letting their audience in on it also. Newsmen not only fear being ostracized by their news sources, but as they become more specialist and sophisticated they tend to become more inhibited themselves: to understand all is to forgive all and tell no tales. They mix with diplomats and choose their words like diplomats—unless, of course, they happen to be syndicated columnists who have to sell their own stories and hence like to spice them up, but columnists often spread themselves thin and avoid the chores of depth reporting. Press coverage of the crucial formative stages of policymaking has tended to decline, very noticeably under President Johnson. And if an intra-Executive controversy finally surfaces at all, the press can largely be managed to support the jelling Administration line.

All of these factors that tend to reduce permeability are still reversible. The most confining of all may have only begun to set in: a change in basic habituation from a presumption of early appeal in the policymaking process to the outside to a presumption that such appeals will be very rare and very late. Resort to publicity might increasingly come to seem "unthinkable" to the insiders, even to those who feel they are losing out on a particular policy decision within the confines of the Executive branch. An Administration would then be free, if it chose, to coast along (at least between wartime elections) until some external event occurred that was an unconcealable failure. The "U-2" or "Bay of Pigs" syndrome might become standard.

But, to repeat, we are not there yet.

IV

One reason we are not, I suggested above, is that there has been continuing need for Administrations to reach out to Congress for formal legislative enactments in order to conduct foreign relations.

Constituents' stimuli to congressmen to exert themselves on behalf of specific national security policies have been spasmodic and diffuse in peacetime; congressmen have been essentially free to take them up or leave them. In time of protracted limited war the constituents' prodding mounts persistently—but congressmen have been too unsure of their own competence, constitutional and personal, to question the judgment of the Commander-in-Chief in wartime. Historically, in protracted limited wars congressmen have always come around to doing so; but since 1917 men in public life have not easily made distinctions between the image of national solidarity needed in total war and the more fractured one that may perhaps suffice for limited war.

It has been the Administration itself that has usually had to galvanize congressional action, largely in order to obtain legislation that seemed indispensable.

Political scientists have commonly defined a number of functions of Congress: a *deliberative* function, a *legislative* function (sometimes factoring out an appropriations or financing function), an *oversight* function, and a *service* function for constituents. Suffusing all these functions is a *ceremonial legitimizing* function, through which Congress affixes a kind of "Great Seal of National Unity," and also a *ventilation* or exposure function, which even when retrospective in posture is often prospective in purpose, aiming to shape the precedents for future Executive action by adding a "legislative history" to the behavior pattern they suggest. All these functions are available to congressmen in national security affairs.

It is important to observe that in the heyday of conspicuous congressional influence upon postwar foreign affairs—the first decade after World War II, the first decade of the Cold War—all these functions regularly culminated in major legislative enactments which were indeed indispensable to the basic foreign and defense policies of the Administrations. Far-reaching treaties had to be ratified. Novel, venturesome programs of overseas action had to be formally authorized and the agencies established for them. Habitual ceilings on various kinds of appropriations had to be raised and new patterns of expectation and political tolerance inculcated. Administrations saw no real choice but to elicit some extensive congressional participation in the making of foreign policy; the necessary enactments could not be obtained by mere rubber-stamping and usually could not be extracted by *faits accomplis*. Indeed, after Truman's experience with Korea, it became part of the lore of U.S. national security politics that a President had better obtain a formal predated congressional authorization for him to deploy U.S. forces for combat, in each separate locale where he might anticipate a need to use the powers that had widely been supposed to be his anyway as Commander-in-Chief.

In the course of grinding out the requested national security legislation, congressmen found themselves provided with a focus for the exercise of deliberative, oversight, service, ventilation, and legitimizing functions. All the major functions of Congress were vitalized by the constant stimulus the Administration provided for the legislative function. Even if—except during the Korean War—constituents' prodding was slight, congressmen had career incentives to adopt active roles in national security affairs because one could be sure that the Administration would keep a publicity spotlight of the "semi-managed" press focused upon the foreign and defense policy debates. One would be visible, whether as a Vandenberg or a Walter George or an Otto Passman.

But the need for legislation has been declining, a trend that is more significant than commonly realized.

There was a gradual routinization of national security policy from about 1955 to 1965 that markedly reduced the Administration's need to enlist congressional participation in major new departures. By the first months of Eisenhower's second Administration the Cold War treaty structure had virtually been

completed; almost all the major instruments of America's international involvement (various military options, foreign aid, propaganda, undercover activities
and the like) had been authorized and institutionalized. A pattern of appropriations had been established for them to which all the participants were becoming
accustomed. Disputes about marginal increments here and there could be
considered important by enthusiasts and specialists, but increasingly the
Administrations felt they could afford to stand pat with their own preferences
and let various minor schools of opposition cancel each other out.

Most revealing was the Senate Foreign Relations Committee's frustration and
near abdication of its legislative function. The Foreign Relations Committee had
been the very pillar of congressional involvement in national security policy in
the first postwar decade, when Administrations needed it for novel treaties and
authorizations. By the early 1960's it was left floundering and bored when there
was little new to be done—not much besides the annual foreign aid authorization. Even that survived only because the House Foreign Affairs Committee
was determined to have something to do, and because Administrations decided
that on balance it was worth the painful effort to repeat a full authorizing stage
every year in order to put some limits on the discretion of the House Appropriations Committee, since the members of that committee would not allow
themselves to be bypassed by long-term authorizations for Treasury borrowing
("backdoor financing").

Thanks to the Administration's decision to continue to seek the annual foreign
aid authorizations, this channel for foreign policy influence by specialist
legislators remained open. But in the decade after 1955 the Administration's
critics in the Senate Foreign Relations Committee—although they became more
numerous—were too divided among themselves to be able to make effective use
of it. Partly, to be sure, this was a problem of maverick personalities and
Hamlet-like leadership. Unable to make much headway on behalf of his own
policy preferences, Chairman Fulbright began to object to the fact that the
foreign aid authorization was becoming an annual catch-all of congressmen's
foreign policy proposals. But what other legislative handle did congressmen
have? Was not this better than nothing? Yet Fulbright and most of the members
of the Senate Foreign Relations Committee were becoming so frustrated and
bored with the annual wrangle that by the early 1960's they would have
preferred virtually to abdicate this surviving legislative function to the Appropriations Committees, if the House Foreign Affairs Committee and the Administration would have permitted them to do so. Senators have other, easier ways to
hold the limelight. Mere membership on the Foreign Relations Committee, for
example, gives license for zestful entrepreneurship in generating publicity on
behalf of one's favorite causes, largely uninhibited by personal responsibility for
building the consensus that would be needed to put them into effect. Senators
are tempted to avoid the frustrations of legislation and to content themselves in
national security affairs with posturing like a House of Lords or an array of

syndicated columnists. But House members lack such free-lance opportunities—so the weary routine persisted.

Annual authorizations are an appropriate vehicle for exercise of an oversight function at least—but here again Senators generally abdicated because they were unwilling to bother with the minutiae of supervision of largely routinized policies and programs. Especially after Democrats regained the White House in 1961 and partisan incentives for oversight were reversed and on balance much reduced (available expertise being scarce for the GOP), it was hard to find members of Congress who cared enough to equip themselves for meaningful oversight. Only a few scattered subcommittees really took this task seriously, and they were mostly in the House of Representatives and hence, except for Otto Passman's subcommittee, were barely visible. Passman's industriousness, though perhaps mistargeted, did bring him a vast fund of information and some concessions from the Administration—but for the most part he was ridiculed in the press, overrridden elsewhere in Congress, bypassed by an expansion of P.L. 480 to offset his cuts in foreign aid, and simply outlasted. After all, his effective tenure always depended on Appropriations Committee Chairman Clarence Cannon, and Cannon was already seventy-six years old when he first set Passman up as subcommittee chairman; one could expect they would not hold the stage very long.

Now that their partnership is ended, the Administration is learning to look to the House of Representatives instead of the familiar Senate to form its buffers on foreign aid. Annual authorizations are probably no longer needed to restrain the House Appropriations subcommittee; still the Administration may benefit from their continuation because it helps to sustain the House Foreign Affairs Committee, with its traditionally loyal Democratic majority, for possible future counter-publicity uses against the increasingly alienated and obstreperous Senate Foreign Relations Committee.

With the decline of the legislative function in an era of routinized foreign policy and the slowness of Congress to develop the oversight function, the Administration has sought from Congress a continuation of the old ceremonial legitimizing function that was part of the role of Vandenberg and George and is even more the role of Everett Dirksen today. But for most of the members of the Senate Foreign Relations Committee in the 1960's this symbolization of national unity was a role too dull and perhaps too demeaning, especially in view of their discontent with many of the policies. If major changes could not easily be wrought, there was an inclination to turn one's attention to one's other committee dealing with domestic affairs, which were becoming exciting—at least until the Viet Nam war began in earnest for Americans and the constituents helped to push the members' attention back to foreign affairs.

But when they did, the members of Congress were still reluctant to reassert themselves through a legislative or a narrowly supervisory function. The most concerned among them aspired to a deliberative function. Partly because half of the members of the Foreign Relations Committee are ex-teachers, the myth of the Great Debate is extraordinarily slow in dying, even in the minds of men who ought to know better. The Senate is not now organized for sustained floor debates on nonlegislative issues. Some Senators who wished that it were—at least for a debate on the war—knew that it was not and hence would not trouble their speechwriters; others, adhering to the creed of wartime solidarity whatever the war, kept silent precisely because the subject was a war; still others resigned themselves to silence because of the usual unwillingness of the press to give full coverage to a mere Senate debate. Senators Fulbright and Morse and others tried again and again to spark a great debate, but even with the cooperation of the *New York Times* they essentially failed—as long as they relied on their own limited newsworthiness.

Finally, summoning up their courage to defy the Administration in wartime and suppressing some personal distaste for the "Grand Inquest" ventilation and exposure function of spotlighted television hearings, the aroused Democrats on the Foreign Relations Committee resolved in March 1966 to arrange for others to conduct the debate and attract the audience, while the Senators themselves looked on and offered interpellations. The ensuing hearings were in part an expression of a congressional deliberative function—as the Senators themselves increasingly took advantage of the free television time at some expense to the witnesses. But basically it was a ventilation and exposure function in which the Senators' own limited competence was conceded and the platform for persuasion was provided principally to others.

The distinction may not be important. Attentive opinion was aroused and, since this is wartime, such an arousal, if repeated, could have an electoral payoff. That prospect might serve to restrain future Executive behavior. To be sure, Democratic congressmen too would suffer if the President persisted and the war turned out to be unacceptable to "swing" voters. In this instance, the political bargaining calculus had to be complex and unreliable. But individual Senators might be able to stake out defensible positions for themselves; and the Committee as a whole, by the congenial academic seminar device of presenting conflicting authorities, could preserve what is left of its internal group life. Indeed the whole exercise, even if not often repeated, would be at least a catharsis for the committee and for the attentive public. If frequently repeated, it might be powerfully influential—thanks to the heightened attentiveness of the public in wartime.

The Senate Foreign Relations Committee, and therewith Congress as a whole, may thus be in the process of finding for itself a more important role in national security affairs than it has had since the middle Eisenhower years. But such a development would be a consequence of the war, rather than of any sufficiency the seminar device would have for congressional influence on national security affairs in peacetime. If we are not to return soon after Viet Nam—as we did a few years after Korea—to something approaching Executive supremacy in the modifications of established policies, for which fresh legislative cooperation does not have to be earnestly solicited by the Administration, we shall need Senators and Representatives who are personally motivated to assert themselves regardless of their constituents' apathy or divided counsels—and who are willing to pay attention to details in legislation and oversight. May I be so bold as to suggest that congress needs men like Otto Passman, but devoted to a better cause. It will not be enough for the Senate Foreign Relations Committee to be a national-security version of the Joint Economic Committee, fine and balanced and scholarly though that committee is. Deliberation and ventilation are not enough. We will need some persistent drive for legislative participation if the long-term tendencies toward closed politics are to be held in check. In 1966 Fulbright and the majority of his committee finally did come around to favoring the requirement of annual authorizations for foreign-aid—but they still did not prepare themselves enough to make constructive use of the opportunity it affords.

V

It is not easy to discern where adequate career incentives for such efforts may lie. A demonstration of competence in national security affairs (apart from any particular policy orientation) probably does have some electoral reward for a congressman nowadays, even in peacetime. Surely for those members of the Senate who aspire to the White House the need to establish such a reputation is a very real incentive. Perhaps some similar criterion will emerge for election to the central leadership positions within Congress itself; such a development, at least in the Senate, may be a predictable long-run response to America's deep involvement in international affairs.

Other incentives might be created to encourage congressmen to participate in national security decisions. It would be worth the effort of political scientists as well as the members themselves to explore the possibilities of providing incentives, with more attention to the substance of influence than the glamor of posturing.

But for the most part, I suppose we shall have to depend on the sheer appeal of the subject matter to attract a goodly number of self-motivated congressmen. In the generation that has come of age since World War II, this prospect offers reasonable hope. A promising number of younger congressmen does evince a desire to play an activist role in foriegn affairs and defense. Much will depend on whether nongovernmental outsiders recognize the importance for their own future of encouraging and assisting the efforts of these congressmen, rather than bypassing them in favor of more convenient channels of direct access to the Executive whenever the latter are open.

To be sure, enterprises on Capitol Hill are often maladroit. But if gradual desuetude were to set in there and even the constitutional, institutional, and traditional authority of Congress were to become habitually closed off from the policymaking process of the Executive branch in national security affairs, there

is little reason to suppose that other less formally legitimized outside influences
(e.g., press and attentive public) would continue long thereafter to retain
important access on their own. Even the Executive would be likely to find its
vast freedom of action double-edged: A practice of winning consent by fiats,
scarcely democratic, would probably undermine confidence in the Administration's leadership, and would eventually impair its collaboration with outsiders
even in spheres where the Administration realized the need for it.

The Two Presidencies

AARON WILDAVSKY

The United States has one President, but it has two presidencies; one presidency is for domestic affairs, and the other is concerned with defense and foreign policy. Since World War II, Presidents have had much greater success in controlling the nation's defense and foreign policies than in dominating its domestic policies. Even Lyndon Johnson has seen his early record of victories in domestic legislation diminish as his concern with foreign affairs grows.

What powers does the President have to control defense and foreign policies and so completely overwhelm those who might wish to thwart him?

The President's normal problem with domestic policy is to get congressional support for the programs he prefers. In foreign affairs, in contrast, he can almost always get support for policies that he believes will protect the nation—but his problem is to find a viable policy.

Whoever they are, whether they begin by caring about foreign policy like Eisenhower and Kennedy or about domestic policies like Truman and Johnson, Presidents soon discover they have more policy preferences in domestic matters than in foreign policy. The Republican and Democratic parties possess a traditional roster of policies, which can easily be adopted by a new President— for example, he can be either for or against Medicare and aid to education. Since existing domestic policy usually changes in only small steps, Presidents find it relatively simple to make minor adjustments. However, although any President knows he supports foreign aid and NATO, the world outside changes much more rapidly than the nation inside—Presidents and their parties have no prior policies on Argentina and the Congo. The world has become a highly intractable place with a whirl of forces we cannot or do not know how to alter.

THE RECORD OF PRESIDENTIAL CONTROL

It takes great crises, such as Roosevelt's hundred days in the midst of the depression, or the extraordinary majorities that Barry Goldwater's candidacy

From *TRANS-action* 3, December 1966, pp. 7-14. Copyright © December 1966 by TRANS-action, Inc., New Brunswick, New Jersey.

willed to Lyndon Johnson, for Presidents to succeed in controlling domestic policy. From the end of the 1930's to the present (what may roughly be called the modern era), Presidents have often been frustrated in their domestic programs. From 1938, when conservatives regrouped their forces, to the time of his death, Franklin Roosevelt did not get a single piece of significant domestic legislation passed. Truman lost out on most of his intense domestic preferences, except perhaps for housing. Since Eisenhower did not ask for much domestic legislation, he did not meet consistent defeat, yet he failed in his general policy of curtailing governmental commitments. Kennedy, of course, faced great difficulties with domestic legislation.

In the realm of foreign policy there has not been a single major issue on which Presidents, when they were serious and determined, have failed. The list of their victories is impressive: entry into the United Nations, the Marshall Plan, NATO, the Truman Doctrine, the decisions to stay out of Indochina in 1954 and to intervene in Vietnam in the 1960's, aid to Poland and Yugoslavia, the test-ban treaty, and many more. Serious setbacks to the President in controlling foreign policy are extraordinary and unusual.

Table I, compiled from the Congressional Quarterly Service tabulation of presidential initiative and congressional response from 1948 through 1964, shows that Presidents have significantly better records in foreign and defense matters than in domestic policies. When refugees and immigration—which Congress considers primarily a domestic concern—are removed from the general foreign policy area, it is clear that Presidents prevail about 70 percent of the time in defense and foreign policy, compared with 40 percent in the domestic sphere.

WORLD EVENTS AND PRESIDENTIAL RESOURCES

Power in politics is control over governmental decisions. How does the President manage his control of foreign and defense policy? The answer does not

TABLE I
Congressional Action on Presidential Proposals
From 1948-1964.

Policy Area	Congressional Action		Number of Proposals
	% Pass	% Fail	
Domestic policy (natural resources labor, agriculture, taxes, etc.)	40.2	59.8	2499
Defense policy (defense, disarmament, manpower, misc.)	73.3	26.7	90
Foreign Policy	58.5	41.5	655
Immigration, refugees	13.2	86.0	129
Treaties, general foreign relations, State Department, foreign aid	70.8	29.2	445

Source: Congressional Quarterly Service, *Congress and the Nation,* 1945-1964 (Washington, 1965)

reside in the greater constitutional power in foreign affairs that Presidents have possessed since the founding of the Republic. The answer lies in the changes that have taken place since 1945.

The number of nations with which the United States has diplomatic relations has increased from 53 in 1939 to 113 in 1966. But sheer numbers do not tell enough; the world has also become a much more dangerous place. However remote it may seem at times, our government must always be aware of the possibility of nuclear war.

Yet the mere existence of great powers with effective thermonuclear weapons would not, in and of itself, vastly increase our rate of interaction with most other nations. We see events in Assam or Burundi as important because they are also part of a larger worldwide contest, called the cold war, in which great powers are rivals for the control or support of other nations. Moreover, the reaction against the blatant isolationism of the 1930's has led to a concern with foreign policy that is worldwide in scope. We are interested in what happens everywhere because we see these events as connected with larger interests involving, at the worst, the possibility of ultimate destruction.

Given the overriding fact that the world is dangerous and that small causes are perceived to have potentially great effects in an unstable world, it follows that Presidents must be interested in relatively "small" matters. So they give Azerbaijan or Lebanon or Vietnam huge amounts of their time. Arthur Schlesinger, Jr., wrote of Kennedy that "in the first two months of his administration he probably spent more time on Laos than on anything else." Few failures in domestic policy, Presidents soon realize, could have as disastrous consequences as any one of dozens of mistakes in the international arena.

The result is that foreign policy concerns tend to drive out domestic policy. Except for occasional questions of domestic prosperity and for civil rights, foreign affairs have consistently higher priority for Presidents. Once, when trying to talk to President Kennedy about natural resources, Secretary of the Interior Stewart Udall remarked, "He's imprisoned by Berlin."

The importance of foreign affairs to Presidents is intensified by the increasing speed of events in the international arena. The event and its consequences follow closely on top of one another. The blunder at the Bay of Pigs is swiftly followed by the near catastrophe of the Cuban missile crisis. Presidents can no longer count on passing along their most difficult problems to their successors. They must expect to face the consequences of their actions—or failure to act—while still in office.

Domestic policy-making is usually based on experimental adjustments to an existing situation. Only a few decisions, such as those involving large dams, irretrievably commit future generations. Decisions in foreign affairs, however, are often perceived to be irreversible. This is expressed, for example, in the fear of escalation or the various "spiral" or "domino" theories of international conflict.

If decisions are perceived to be both important and irreversible, there is every reason for Presidents to devote a great deal of resources to them. Presidents have to be oriented toward the future in the use of their resources. They serve a fixed term in office, and they cannot automatically count on support from the populace, Congress, or the administrative apparatus. They have to be careful, therefore, to husband their resources for pressing future needs. But because the consequences of events in foreign affairs are potentially more grave, faster to manifest themselves, and less easily reversible than in domestic affairs, Presidents are more willing to use up their resources.

THE POWER TO ACT

Their formal powers to commit resources in foreign affairs and defense are vast. Particularly important is their power as Commander-in-Chief to move troops. Faced with situations like the invasion of South Korea or the emplacement of missiles in Cuba, fast action is required. Presidents possess both the formal power to act and the knowledge that elites and the general public expect them to act. Once they have committed American forces, it is difficult for Congress or anyone else to alter the course of events. The Dominican venture is a recent case in point.

Presidential discretion in foreign affairs also makes it difficult (though not impossible) for Congress to restrict their actions. Presidents can use executive agreements instead of treaties, enter into tacit agreements instead of written ones, and otherwise help create *de facto* situations not easily reversed. Presidents also have far greater ability than anyone else to obtain information on developments abroad through the Departments of State and Defense. The need for secrecy in some aspects of foreign and defense policy further restricts the ability of others to compete with Presidents. These things are all well known. What is not so generally appreciated is the growing presidential ability to *use* information to achieve goals.

In the past Presidents were amateurs in military strategy. They could not even get much useful advice outside of the military. As late as the 1930's the number of people outside the military establishment who were professionally engaged in the study of defense policy could be numbered on the fingers. Today there are hundreds of such men. The rise of the defense intellectuals has given the President of the United States enhanced ability to control defense policy. He is no longer dependent on the military for advice. He can choose among defense intellectuals from the research corporations and the academies for alternative sources of advice. He can install these men in his own office. He can play them off against each other or use them to extend spheres of coordination.

Even with these advisers, however, Presidents and Secretaries of Defense might still be too bewildered by the complexity of nuclear situations to take action—unless they had an understanding of the doctrine and concepts of deterrence. But knowledge of doctrine about deterrence has been widely diffused; it can be picked up by any intelligent person who will read books or listen to enough hours of conversation. Whether or not the doctrine is good is a separate question; the point is that civilians can feel they understand what is going on in defense policy. Perhaps the most extraordinary feature of presidential action during the Cuban missile crisis was the degree to which the Commander-in-Chief of the Armed Forces insisted on controlling even the smallest moves. From the positioning of ships to the methods of boarding, to the precise words and actions to be taken by individual soldiers and sailors, the President and his civilian advisers were in control.

Although Presidents have rivals for power in foreign affairs, the rivals do not usually succeed. Presidents prevail not only because they may have superior resources but because their potential opponents are weak, divided, or believe that they should not control foreign policy. Let us consider the potential rivals—the general citizenry, special interest groups, the Congress, the military, the so-called military-industrial complex, and the State Department.

COMPETITORS FOR CONTROL OF POLICY

The Public

The general public is much more dependent on Presidents in foreign affairs than in domestic matters. While many people know about the impact of social security and Medicare, few know about politics in Malawi. So it is not surprising that people expect the President to act in foreign affairs and reward him with their confidence. Gallup Polls consistently show that presidential popularity rises after he takes action in a crisis—whether the action is disastrous as in the Bay of Pigs or successful as in the Cuban missile crisis. Decisive action, such as the bombing of oil fields near Haiphong, resulted in a sharp (though temporary) increase in Johnson's popularity.

The Vietnam situation illustrates another problem of public opinion in foreign affairs: it is extremely difficult to get operational policy directions from the general public. It took a long time before any sizable public interest in the subject developed. Nothing short of the large scale involvement of American troops under fire probably could have brought about the current high level of concern. Yet this relatively well developed popular opinion is difficult to interpret. While a majority appear to support President Johnson's policy, it appears that they could easily be persuaded to withdraw from Vietnam if the administration changed its line. Although a sizable majority would support various initiatives to end the war, they would seemingly be appalled if this action led to Communist encroachments elsewhere in Southeast Asia. (See "The President, the Polls, and Vietnam" by Seymour Martin Lipset, *TRANS-action*, Sept/Oct 1966.)

Although Presidents lead opinion in foreign affairs, they know they will be held accountable for the consequences of their actions. President Johnson has maintained a large commitment in Vietnam. His popularity shoots up now and again in the midst of some imposing action. But the fact that a body of citizens do not like the war comes back to damage his overall popularity. We will support your initiatives, the people seem to say, but we will reserve the right to punish you (or your party) if we do not like the results.

Special Interest Groups

Opinions are easier to gauge in domestic affairs because, for one thing, there is a stable structure of interest groups that covers virtually all matters of concern. The farm, labor, business, conservation, veteran, civil rights, and other interest groups provide cues when a proposed policy affects them. Thus people who identify with these groups may adopt their views. But in foreign policy matters the interest group structure is weak, unstable, and thin rather than dense. In many matters affecting Africa and Asia, for example, it is hard to think of well-known interest groups. While ephemeral groups arise from time to time to support or protest particular policies, they usually disappear when the immediate problem is resolved. In contrast, longer-lasting elite groups like the Foreign Policy Association and Council on Foreign Relations are composed of people of diverse views; refusal to take strong positions on controversial matters is a condition of their continued viability.

The strongest interest groups are probably the ethnic associations whose members have strong ties with a homeland, as in Poland or Cuba, so they are rarely activated simultaneously on any specific issue. They are most effective when most narrowly and intensely focused—as in the fierce pressure from Jews to recognize the state of Israel. But their relatively small numbers limits their significance to Presidents in the vastly more important general foreign policy picture—as continued aid to the Arab countries shows. Moreover, some ethnic groups may conflict on significant issues such as American acceptance of the Oder-Neisse line separating Poland from what is now East Germany.

The Congress

Congressmen also exercise power in foreign affairs. Yet they are ordinarily not serious competitors with the President because they follow a self-denying ordinance. They do not think it is their job to determine the nation's defense policies. Lewis A. Dexter's extensive interviews with members of the Senate Armed Services Committee, who might be expected to want a voice in defense policy, reveal that they do not desire for men like themselves to run the nation's defense establishment. Aside from a few specific conflicts among the armed services which allow both the possibility and desirability of direct intervention, the Armed Services Committee constitutes a sort of real estate committee dealing with the regional economic consequences of the location of military facilities.

The congressional appropriations power is potentially a significant resource, but circumstances since the end of World War II have tended to reduce its effectiveness. The appropriations committees and Congress itself might make their will felt by refusing to allot funds unless basic policies were altered. But this has not happened. While Congress makes its traditional small cuts in the military budget, Presidents have mostly found themselves warding off congressional attempts to increase specific items still further.

Most of the time, the administration's refusal to spend has not been seriously challenged. However, there have been occasions when individual legislators or committees have been influential. Senator Henry Jackson in his campaign (with the aid of colleagues on the Joint Committee on Atomic Energy) was able to gain acceptance for the Polaris weapons system and Senator Arthur H. Vandenberg played a part in determining the shape of the Marshall Plan and so on. The few congressmen who are expert in defense policy act, as Samuel P. Huntington says, largely as lobbyists with the executive branch. It is apparently more fruitful for these congressional experts to use their resources in order to get a hearing from the executive than to work on other congressmen.

When an issue involves the actual use or threat of violence, it takes a great deal to convince congressmen not to follow the President's lead. James Robinson's tabulation of foreign and defense policy issues from the late 1930's to 1961 shows dominant influence by Congress in only one case out of seven—the 1954 decision not to intervene with armed force in Indochina. In that instance President Eisenhower deliberately sounded out congressional opinion and, finding it negative, decided not to intervene—against the advice of Admiral Radford, chairman of the Joint Chiefs of Staff. This attempt to abandon responsibility did not succeed, as the years of American involvement demonstrate.

The Military

The outstanding feature of the military's participation in making defense policy is their amazing weakness. Whether the policy decisions involve the size of the armed forces, the choice of weapons systems, the total defense budget, or its division into components, the military have not prevailed. Let us take budgetary decisions as representative of the key choices to be made in defense policy. Since the end of World War II the military has not been able to achieve significant (billion dollar) increases in appropriations by their own efforts. Under Truman and Eisenhower defense budgets were determined by what Huntington calls the remainder method: the two Presidents estimated revenues, decided what they could spend on domestic matters, and the remainder was assigned to defense. The usual controversy was between some military and congressional groups supporting much larger expenditures while the President and his executive allies refused. A typical case, involving the desire of the Air Force to increase the number of groups of planes is described by Huntington in *The Common Defense;*

The FY [fiscal year] 1949 budget provided 48 groups. After the Czech coup, the Administration yielded and backed an Air Force of 55 groups in its spring rearmament program. Congress added additional funds to aid Air Force expansion to 70 groups. The Administration refused to utilize them, however, and in the gathering economy wave of the summer and fall of 1948, the Air Force goal was cut back again to 48 groups. In 1949 the House of Representatives picked up the challenge and appropriated funds for 58 groups. The President impounded the money. In June, 1950, the Air Force had 48 groups.

The great increases in the defense budget were due far more to Stalin and modern technology than to the military. The Korean War resulted in an increase from 12 to 44 billions and much of the rest followed Sputnik and the huge costs of missile programs. Thus modern technology and international conflict put an end to the one major effort to subordinate foreign affairs to domestic policies through the budget.

It could be argued that the President merely ratifies the decision made by the military and their allies. If the military and/or Congress were united and insistent on defense policy, it would certainly be difficult for Presidents to resist these forces. But it is precisely the disunity of the military that has characterized the entire postwar period. Indeed, the military have not been united on any major matter of defense policy. The apparent unity of the Joint Chiefs of Staff turns out to be illusory. The vast majority of their recommendations appear to be unanimous and are accepted by the Secretary of Defense and the President. But this facade of unity can only be achieved by methods that vitiate the impact of the recommendations. Genuine disagreements are hidden by vague language that commits no one to anything. Mutually contradictory plans are strung together so everyone appears to get something; but nothing is decided. Since it is impossible to agree on really important matters, all sorts of trivia are brought in to make a record of agreement. While it may be true, as Admiral Denfeld, a former Chief of Naval Operations, said, that "On nine-tenths of the matters that come before them the Joint Chiefs of Staff reach agreement themselves," the vastly more important truth is that "normally the *only* disputes are on strategic concepts, the size and composition of forces, and budget matters."

Military-Industrial

But what about the fabled military-industrial complex? If the military alone is divided and weak, perhaps the giant industrial firms that are so dependent on defense contracts play a large part in making policy.

First, there is an important distinction between the questions "Who will get a given contract?" and "What will our defense policy be?" It is apparent that different answers may be given to these quite different questions. There are literally tens of thousands of defense contractors. They may compete vigorously for business. In the course of this competition, they may wine and dine military officers, use retired generals, seek intervention by their congressmen, place ads in trade journals, and even contribute to political campaigns. The famous TFX controversy—should General Dynamics or Boeing get the expensive contract?—is a larger than life example of the pressures brought to bear in search of lucrative contracts.

But neither the TFX case nor the usual vigorous competition for contracts is involved with the making of substantive defense policy. Vital questions like the size of the defense budget, the choice of strategic programs, massive retaliation vs. a counter-city strategy, and the like were far beyond the policy aims of any company. Industrial firms, then, do not control such decisions, nor is there much evidence that they actually try. No doubt a precipitous and drastic rush to disarmament would meet with opposition from industrial firms among other interests. However, there has never been a time when any significant element in the government considered a disarmament policy to be feasible.

It may appear that industrial firms had no special reason to concern themselves with the government's stance on defense because they agree with the national consensus on resisting communism, maintaining a large defense establishment, and rejecting isolationism. However, this hypothesis about the climate of opinion explains everything and nothing. For every policy that is adopted or rejected can be explained away on the grounds that the cold war climate of opinion dictated what happened. Did the United States fail to intervene with armed force in Vietnam in 1954? That must be because the climate of opinion was against it. Did the United States send troops to Vietnam in the 1960's? That must be because the cold war climate demanded it. If the United States builds more missiles, negotiates a test-ban treaty, intervenes in the Dominican Republic, fails to intervene in a dozen other situations, all these actions fit the hypothesis by definition. The argument is reminiscent of those who defined the Soviet Union as permanently hostile and therefore interpreted increases in Soviet troops as menacing and decreases of troop strength as equally sinister.

If the growth of the military establishment is not directly equated with increasing military control of defense policy, the extraordinary weakness of the professional soldier still requires explanation. Huntington has written about how major military leaders were seduced in the Truman and Eisenhower years into believing that they should bow to the judgment of civilians that the economy could not stand much larger military expenditures. Once the size of the military pie was accepted as a fixed constraint, the military services were compelled to put their major energies into quarreling with one another over who should get the larger share. Given the natural rivalries of the military and their traditional acceptance of civilian rule, the President and his advisers—who could claim responsibility for the broader picture of reconciling defense and domestic policies—had the upper hand. There are, however, additional explanations to be considered.

The dominant role of the congressional appropriations committee is to be guardian of the treasury. This is manifested in the pride of its members in cutting the President's budget. Thus it was difficult to get this crucial committee to recommend even a few hundred million increase in defense; it was practically impossible to get them to consider the several billion jump that might really have made a difference. A related budgetary matter concerned the planning, programming, and budgeting system introduced by Secretary of Defense McNamara. For if the defense budget contained major categories that criss-crossed the services, only the Secretary of Defense could put it together. Whatever the other debatable consequences of program budgeting, its major consequence was to grant power to the secretary and his civilian advisers.

The subordination of the military through program budgeting is just one symptom of a more general weakness of the military. In the past decade the military has suffered a lack of intellectual skills appropriate to the nuclear age. For no one has (and no one wants) direct experience with nuclear war. So the usual military talk about being the only people to have combat experience is not very impressive. Instead, the imaginative creation of possible future wars—in order to avoid them—requires people with a high capacity for abstract thought combined with the ability to manipulate symbols using quantitative methods. West Point has not produced many such men.

The State Department

Modern Presidents expect the State Department to carry out their policies. John F. Kennedy felt that State was "in some particular sense 'his' department." If a Secretary of State forgets this, as was apparently the case with James Byrnes under Truman, a President may find another man. But the State Department, especially the Foreign Service, is also a highly professional organization with a life and momentum of its own. If a President does not push hard, he may find his preferences somehow dissipated in time. Arthur Schlesinger fills his book on Kennedy with laments about the bureaucratic inertia and recalcitrance of the State Department.

Yet Schlesinger's own account suggests that State could not ordinarily resist the President. At one point, he writes of "the President, himself, increasingly the day-to-day director of American foreign policy." On the next page, we learn that "Kennedy dealt personally with almost every aspect of policy around the globe. He knew more about certain areas than the senior officials at State and probably called as many issues to their attention as they did to his." The President insisted on his way in Laos. He pushed through his policy on the Congo against strong opposition with the State Department. Had Kennedy wanted to get a great deal more initiative out of the State Department, as Schlesinger insists, he could have replaced the Secretary of State, a man who did not command special support in the Democratic party or in Congress. It may be that Kennedy wanted too strongly to run his own foreign policy. Dean Rusk may have known far better than Schlesinger that the one thing Kennedy did not want was a man who might rival him in the field of foreign affairs.

Schlesinger comes closest to the truth when he writes that "the White House could always win any battle it chose over the [Foreign] Service; but the prestige and proficiency of the Service limited the number of battles any White House would find it profitable to fight." When the President knew what he wanted, he got it. When he was doubtful and perplexed, he sought good advice and frequently did not get that. But there is no evidence that the people on his staff came up with better ideas. The real problem may have been a lack of good ideas anywhere. Kennedy undoubtedly encouraged his staff to prod the State Department, But the President was sufficiently cautious not to push so hard that he got his way when he was not certain what that way should be. In this context Kennedy appears to have played his staff off against elements in the State Department.

The growth of a special White House staff to help Presidents in foreign affairs expresses their need for assistance, their refusal to rely completely on the regular executive agencies, and their ability to find competent men. The deployment of this staff must remain a presidential prerogative, however, if its members are to serve Presidents and not their opponents. Whenever critics do not like existing foreign and defense policies, they are likely to complain that the White House staff is screening out divergent views from the President's attention. Naturally, the critics recommend introducing many more different viewpoints. If the critics could maneuver the President into counting hands all day ("on the one hand and on the other"), they would make it impossible for him to act. Such a viewpoint is also congenial to those who believe that action rather than inaction is the greatest present danger in foreign policy. But Presidents resolutely refuse to become prisoners of their advisers by using them as other people would like. Presidents remain in control of their staff as well as of major foreign policy decisions.

HOW COMPLETE IS THE CONTROL?

Some analysts say that the success of Presidents in controlling foreign policy decisions is largely illusory. It is achieved, they say, by anticipating the reactions of others, and eliminating proposals that would run into severe opposition. There is some truth in this objection. In politics, where transactions are based on a high degree of mutual interdependence, what others may do has to be taken into account. But basing presidential success in foreign and defense policy on anticipated reactions suggests a static situation which does not exist. For if Presidents propose only those policies that would get support in Congress, and Congress opposes them only when it knows that it can muster overwhelming strength, there would never by any conflict. Indeed, there might never by any action.

How can "anticipated reaction" explain the conflict over policies like the Marshall Plan and the test-ban treaty in which severe opposition was overcome only by strenuous efforts? Furthermore, why doesn't "anticipated reaction" work in domestic affairs? One would have to argue that for some reason presidential perception of what would be successful is consistently confused on domestic issues and most always accurate on major foreign policy issues. But the role of "anticipated reactions" should be greater in the more familiar domestic situations, which provide a backlog of experience for forecasting, than in foreign policy with many novel situations such as the Suez crisis or the Rhodesian affair.

Are there significant historical examples which might refute the thesis of presidential control of foreign policy? Foreign aid may be a case in point. For many years, Presidents have struggled to get foreign aid appropriations because of hostility from public and congressional opinion. Yet several billion dollars a year are appropriated regularly despite the evident unpopularity of the program. In the aid programs to Communist countries like Poland and Yugoslavia, the Congress attaches all sorts of restrictions to the aid, but Presidents find ways of getting around them.

What about the example of recognition of Communist China? The sentiment of the country always has been against recognizing Red China or admitting it to the United Nations. But have Presidents wanted to recognize Red China and been hamstrung by opposition? The answer, I suggest, is a qualified "no." By the time recognition of Red China might have become a serious issue for the Truman administration, the war in Korea effectively precluded its consideration. There is no evidence that President Eisenhower or Secretary Dulles ever thought it wise to recognize Red China or help admit her to the United Nations. The Kennedy administration viewed the matter as not of major importance and, considering the opposition, moved cautiously in suggesting change. Then came the war in Vietnam. If the advantages for foreign policy had been perceived to be much higher, then Kennedy or Johnson might have proposed changing American policy toward recognition of Red China.

One possible exception, in the case of Red China, however, does not seem sufficient to invalidate the general thesis that Presidents do considerably better in getting their way in foreign and defense policy than in domestic policies.

The National Security Council: Innovations and Implications

EDWARD A. KOLODZIEJ

During his campaign for the presidency, Richard Nixon promised "to restore the National Security Council to its preeminent role in national security planning." Less than a month after assuming office his Administration announced the first important shifts in the process of making national security policy. A preliminary analysis of the nature and implications of the Nixon Administration's innovations indicates that these changes deserve more attention from scholars and practitioners than they have received until now. They are bound to change basic relations among the agencies and offices of the Executive Branch and Congress and will conceivably transform the structure and process of influence, decision, and action through which security and foreign policy is made.

It is still too early to make any definitive statements about the Nixon NSC, but some of the initial discussion of the innovations in procedure and organization appears advised, at the very least, in order to stimulate more systematic examination and evaluation of this unique institution of presidential decision making in foreign policy.

The Nixon Administration has more formally defined the national security system than its immediate predecessors, although not as elaborately as the Eisenhower regime. The National Security Council stands again at the apex of the system. Under Presidents John Kennedy and Lyndon Johnson, the NSC was sharply reduced as an advisory body. Writing to the Jackson Committee in September 1961, McGeorge Bundy, President Kennedy's Special Assistant for National Security Affairs, downgraded the NSC:

> The National Security Council has never been and should never become the only instrument of counsel and decision available to the President in dealing with the problems of national security. . . . The National Security Council is one instrument among many.

From *Public Administration Review* 29, November-December 1969, pp. 573-85. Reprinted by permission of the author and ASPA.

President Kennedy preferred to deal directly, and often individually, with his cabinet and subcabinet officers and white House staff, and would on occasion plunge deeply into the bureaucratic depths to surface information or a novel perspective. Decisions were usually reached in small, informal groups whose members were often only incidentally statutory or advisory members of the NSC. To elicit public confidence, the NSC still served to legitimize decisions taken elsewhere, as during the Cuban missile crisis, or meetings were held to assure advisors of their access to the President.

President Johnson followed a similar pragmatic approach. In place of the legally based NSC, the "Tuesday lunch" group gradually developed into an authoritative, if somewhat crude, policy tool. The Secretaries of State and Defense and the President's Special Assistant for National Security usually attended, joined later by the Press Secretary, the Director of the Central Intelligence Agency, and the Chairman of the Joint Chiefs of Staff. Others were periodically invited to these weekly sessions, depending on the issue or the President's pleasure. Procedures were relaxed. Often no formal records were kept of decisions and the agenda for each lunch was not always precisely defined nor fully staffed beforehand.

The new NSC changes clearly favor the Eisenhower model. Building on the legal foundation of the NSC, a set of supplementary mechanisms have been fashioned to channel information and advice to the President. The President has designated "the National Security Council as the principal forum for consideration of national security policy issues requiring presidential decisions." As under the Administrations of Presidents Kennedy and Johnson, however, membership is restricted to a select group, including as statutory members, the Vice-President, the Secretaries of State and Defense, and the Director of the Office of Emergency Preparedness. To this group have been added the Special Assistant for National Security, the Chairman of the JCS, the Director of Central Intelligence, and the Under Secretary of State, who has enlarged operational responsibilities within the Nixon system.

Keeping the group small meets the criticism levelled at the Eisenhower Administration that the effectiveness of the NSC as a forum for debate and discussion declined as its size enlarged. The restricted composition of the Council enhances the status of its members and can conceivably strengthen their voice in their agencies. This effect will critically depend, however, on how the relative influence of the President's top advisors within the inner NSC circle is perceived by the foreign and security bureaucracies, the Congress, and the public. This problem is especially important with respect to the relation of the President to his Secretaries of State and Defense and to his Assistant for National Security Affairs.

As Figure 1 indicates, policy papers coming before the NSC normally pass through a two-layered filter of interdepartmental committees. At the lowest level are the NSC Interdepartmental Groups, chaired by an appropriate Assistant

FIGURE 1
National Security System of the Nixon Administration

President

Assistant to the President for National Security Affairs (NSA) and Executive Secretary, National Security Council Staff	National Security Council (NSC) *Membership:* 1. Statutory: Vice President Secretary of State Secretary of Defense Director, Office of Emergency Preparedness	Department of State
National Security Council Staff (28) 1. Office of Assistant to President (5) 2. Operations (13) 3. Assistants for Programs (6) 4. Planning (4)	2. Advisory and Invited: Assistant to President for NSA CIA Director, JCS Chairman Under Secretary of State *Functions:* Principal Forum for National Security Issues	Secretary of State

NSC Ad Hoc Groups *Membership:* Appointed by President *Functions:* To deal with particular problems, including those which transcend regional boundaries	NSC Review Groups *Membership:* Assistant to President for NSA (Chairman), Representatives of Secretary of State, Secretary of Defense, CIA Director, JCS Chairman, other agency officers as invited *Functions:* 1. Review issues for NSC consideration 2. Present alternatives, including cost data 3. Present agency view	NSC Under Secretaries Committee *Membership:* Under Secretary of State, assisted by Under Secretary for Political Affairs, Deputy Secretary of Defense, Assistant to President for NSA, other ranking agency officers as invited *Functions:* 1. Consider issues referred by NSC Review Group 2. Consider operational matters arising from NSC IGs, Secretary of State or others which, while important, do not merit NSC review 3. Consider issues jointly sent by Under Secretary of State and Assistant to President for NSA	Under Secretary of State Under Secretary for Political Affairs

NSC Interdepartmental Groups (IGs) *Membership:* Appropriate Assistant Secretary of State (Chairman), Representatives of Assistant to President for NSA, CIA Director, JCS Chairman, other agency officers as invited (IGs are organized as to topic or to geographic region)	*Functions:* 1. Discuss and decide interdepartmental issues 2. Prepare NSC policy paper 3. Prepare NSC contingency papers for potential crises	Assistant Secretaries

Secretary of State and including representatives of the President's Special Assistant for National Security Affairs, the Secretary of Defense, the CIA head, the JCS Chairman, and other agencies at the discretion of the chairman. Interdepartmental Groups are categorized according to their regional and functional concerns. Regional Interdepartmental Groups are responsible for policy in the areas of Latin America, Europe, Africa, Near East and South Asia, and East Asia and the Pacific. Functional Interdepartmental Groups focus on foreign aid, trade policy, monetary problems, strategic posture, military-political issues, *et al.*

Interdepartmental Groups have three main functions: (a) the preparation of policy papers, (b) the initiation of contingency plans for potential crisis areas, and (c) the resolution of interdepartmental issues appropriate to the Assistant Secretary level. Interdepartmental Groups directly submit policy papers and plans, so-called National Security Study Memoranda, to a newly constituted NSC Review Group, headed by the President's Assistant for Security Affairs and comprised of members from the same agency as the Interdepartmental Groups. The Review Group screens papers for the NSC agenda. It also attempts to assure that they present realistic options or alternatives, including cost data, and that they accurately represent agency and departmental views, however divergent they may be or however they may conflict with National Security staff recommendations. The Review Group may also receive submissions directly from executive agencies or from NSC Ad Hoc Groups established by the President for particular tasks.

The systematic and continuous generation of policy studies is to be one of the distinctive features of the new NSC system. While it adopts the Eisenhower Administration's comprehensive approach to policy formation, it is responsive to the criticisms raised both about the Eisenhower and about the Kennedy-Johnson systems. The Review Group and Interdepartmental Groups assume many of the duties previously discharged by the Eisenhower Planning Board and its informal drafting committees, purposes that were relatively neglected in the Kennedy years.

First, the policy initiation and review process is institutionalized and routinized. Responsibilities are fixed in the Interdepartmental Groups and, specifically, in their chairman. Planning within the NSC is consequently given more weight and prestige, whereas it tended to be slighted in fact, if not explicitly by design, in the Kennedy-Johnson emphasis on day-to-day operations.

Second, the continuous generation of policy papers encourages the development of an overall rationale for United States security and foreign policy. As policy is tested by experience, an established method exists authoritatively to review, update, and revise announced objectives and action guidelines. The Kennedy-Johnson Administrations eschewed such mechanisms. The Kennedy National Security Action Memoranda were essentially directives, not policy and planning documents, and were concerned more with immediate and already crystalized issues than with future contingencies; moreover, the National Policy Papers lacked, as did many other policy documents of the Kennedy-Johnson system, direct and explicit presidential backing. National Security Study Memoranda respond to both shortcomings. They are supposed to identify both short- and long-range issues, leaving operational matters to a separate, but closely related, channel of NSC activity; moreover, those memoranda receiving the NSC stamp of approval are invested with presidential authority.

Third, the evolving set of policy papers serves as a management tool in two ways:

(a) Those below are informed about the views of the President and his top advisors. The NSC is to function as a clearly defined, visible, and potentially definitive source of communication and direction. The deliberate ambiguity of the Kennedy-Johnson system, with its multiple vehicles for presidential decision and action, tended to produce confusion at the lower echelons of the bureaucracy regarding official governmental policy. Coordination of interdepartmental action then depended more heavily on the direct intervention of the White House staff and often on the active participation of the President himself.

(b) In contrast to a pragmatic policy process, a comprehensive and codified system attempts to elicit agency recommendations for change within an already identifiable framework of perceptions, conceptualizations, and assumptions about the preferred means and ends of the administration in office. An adopted NSC paper ostensibly becomes an important control mechanism, establishing a set of norms of conduct for agencies and officials charged with its execution.

Fourth, the process of working together in more orderly and defined relations is implicitly valued as an end in itself. Agency officials are expected to meet regularly to discuss long-range planning and the means to achieve commonly defined objectives. Those up and down the chain of command are to be periodically confronted with each other's viewpoints, perspectives, and problems. These patterns of relationship can be seen as gradually developing into instruments calibrated to presidential needs for information, decision, and action. In this connection, the Interdepartmental Groups are given important contingency planning responsibilities and can potentially function as the nucleus of a crisis management team. If the system works, the Interdepartmental Groups could meet the persistent criticism that the modern national security system, since its inception under the Truman Administration in 1947, has been largely unable to meet more than one crisis at a time.

Whether the Nixon NSC can achieve these commendable objectives remains to be seen. On first inspection the present NSC system is vulnerable to many of the objections raised about the Eisenhower procedures. To meet some of these problems the Eisenhower effort to produce a Basic National Security Memorandum—criticized for its vagueness and failure to offer adequate guidelines for governmental operations—has not been reinstated, although an annual foreign policy review is envisioned.

Papers are to be more selective and to identify policy options for the President. They are not to present him with a predetermined consensus, a charge made most often of the Eisenhower Administration's use of the NSC. With the inclusion of cost data (and the presence of systems analysts on the White House staff to analyze them), papers issuing from the Review Group are to resemble more the policy documents commissioned by former Secretary of Defense Robert S. McNamara than the blander publications of the Eisenhower Planning Board. The Review Group requirement to identify policy alternatives aims at the tendency of agencies to compromise their differences or to form tacit treaties before submitting their views to the formal and authoritative NSC process. The creation of a large, experienced White House staff under the Special Assistant, comprising almost 30 members, most with long years in government departments, aims at insuring an independent staff review which reflects a presidential viewpoint within the NSC. Papers reaching the Review Group that fail to meet the options standard can be supplemented or revised by NSC staff initiative—and some already have. The delegation of executive authority to the chairman of the Interdepartmental Groups can also foster the identification of divergent positions, encourage innovation, or not unduly stifle it, and facilitate the flow of policy papers within the system. The availability of additional forums, like the Review Group, the Interdepartmental Groups, and finally the NSC, can offer some incentive to the agencies to press their cases within the NSC system rather than seek indirect redress from Congress or strive for accords with other agencies, a practice that tends to keep issues from reaching the President before they become crises.

*   *   *

As the Chief Executive, the President must set his house in order before he can expect to order the Executive Branch. The recent and significant changes in the NSC system suggest a determination at the presidential level to control the governmental agencies concerned with foreign and security policy and to direct their energies to presidential purposes. It is still too early to know how effectively these efforts will be. At this juncture, however, the principal unresolved questions are whether the innovations have gone far enough, especially with respect to the defense establishment and to the problem of developing a more integrated planning-program-budgeting system at the presidential level; and whether they have gone too far in shifting the focus of policy planning and operations from the Secretary of State and the Department of State to the President's White House staff and, specifically, to the Assistant for National Security Affairs.

The Military Ascendancy

C. WRIGHT MILLS

As the United States has become a great world power, the military establishment has expanded, and members of its higher echelons have moved directly
into diplomatic and political circles. General Mark Clark, for example, who has
probably had more political experience while on active duty than any other
American warlord, "believes in what he calls the 'buddy system'—a political man
and a military man working together," of which he has said: "In the past, many
American generals were inclinded to say of politics: 'To hell with it, let's talk
politics later.' But you can't do it this way any more."

In 1942, General Clark dealt with Darlan and Giraud in North Africa; then he
commanded the Eighth Army in Italy; then he was occupation commander for
Austria; and, in 1952, he became US Commander in newly sovereign Japan, as
well as head of the US Far East Command and UN Commander in Korea.
General George C. Marshall, after being the President's personal representative to
China, became Secretary of State (1947-49), then Secretary of Defense
(1950-51). Vice Admiral Alan G. Kirk was Ambassador to Belgium in the late
'forties and then to Russia. In 1947, the Assistant Secretary of State for
occupied areas was Major General John H. Hildring who dealt "directly with the
military commanders who control the execution of policy in Germany, Austria,
Japan and Korea"; Brigadier General Frank T. Hines was Ambassador to
Panama; and General Walter Bedell Smith was Ambassador to Russia. General
Smith later became the head of the Central Intelligence Agency (1950-53), then
Under Secretary of State (1953-54). As occupation commander in Germany,
there was General Lucius D. Clay; of Japan, General MacArthur. And no
diplomat, but a former Army Chief of Staff, General J. Lawton Collins, went to
troubled Indo-China in 1954 "to restore some order" in an area which he said
"had essential political and economic importance for Southeast Asia and the free
world."

Moreover, while still in uniform as well as out of it, high-ranking officers have engaged in policy debate. General Omar Bradley, one of the most articulate deniers of undue military influence in civilian decisions, has appeared before Congressional committees, as well as before broader publics, in support of policies involving economic and political as well as strictly military issues. General Marshall, for example, has submitted arguments against the Wagner-Taft resolution which favored increased immigration to Palestine and its further development as a Jewish homeland. With Generals Bradley, Vandenberg, and Collins, as well as Admiral Sherman, General Marshall has also defended before Congressional committees the Truman administration against Republican attack upon its Far-Eastern policy, and the ousting of General MacArthur from his Far-Eastern command.

General Bradley has made numerous speeches which in their context were readily interpreted, by Senator Taft and Hanson Baldwin among others, as relevant to the political issues of the 1952 Presidential elections. "This speech," wrote Hanson Baldwin, "helped put General Bradley and the Joint Chiefs of Staff into the political hustings where they have no business to be." Senator Taft, who accused the Joint Chiefs of Staff of being under the control of the political administration and of echoing their policies rather than rendering merely expert advice, was himself supported by General Albert Wedemeyer, as well as by General MacArthur. Another general, Bonner Fellers, was on the Republican National Committee.

In the 1952 election, in direct violation of U.S. Army Regulation 600-10, General MacArthur, in public speeches, attacked the policies of the duly elected administration, delivered the keynote address at the Republican convention, and made it clear that he was open to the Presidential nomination. But another general, Eisenhower, also not retired, was successfully supported for this role. Both of these generals, as well as what might be considered their political policies, were supported by other military men. There is no doubt about it: there are now Republican and Democratic generals. There are also, as we now know well, officers who are for or against individual Senators—such as McCarthy—and who in their military positions lean one way or the other to reveal it or to hide it.

In 1954, a notable array of high military—headed by retired Lt. General George E. Stratemeyer with retired Rear Admiral John G. Crommelin as Chief of Staff—offered their names in an effort to rally ten million signatures for a McCarthy petition. This occurred in the context of the military ascendancy at a time when the words of Old Soldier MacArthur had not faded:

> We of the military shall always do what we are told to do. But if this nation is to survive, we must trust the soldier once our statesmen fail to preserve the peace. (1953)

> I find in existence a new and heretofore unknown and dangerous concept that the members of our armed forces owe primary allegiance and loyalty to

those who temporarily exercise the authority of the Executive Branch of government rather than to the country and its Constitution which they are sworn to defend. No proposition could be more dangerous. (1951)

But more important perhaps than the straightforward assumption of political roles, the private advice, or the public speeches, is a more complex type of military influence; high military men have become accepted by other members of the political and economic elite, as well as by broad sectors of the public, as authorities on issues that go well beyond what has historically been considered the proper domain of the military.

Since the early 'forties, the traditional Congressional hostility toward the military has been transformed into something of a "friendly and trusting" subservience. No witness—except of course J. Edgar Hoover—is treated with more deference by Senators than the high military. "Both in what it did and in what it refused to do," we read in an official government account, "the wartime Congress co-operated consistently and almost unquestioningly with the suggestions and the requests from the Chief of Staff." And in the coalition strategy, while the President and the Prime Minister "decided," theirs were choices approved by the military and made from among alternatives organized and presented by the military.

According to the Constitution, the Congress is supposed to be in charge of the support and governing of the armed might of the nation. During times of peace, prior to World War II, professional politicians in the Congress did argue the details of military life with the military, and made decisions for them, debating strategy and even determining tactics. During World War II, Congressmen "voted" for such items as the Manhattan Project without having the slightest idea of its presence in the military budget, and when—by rumor—Senator Truman suspected that something big was going on, a word from the Secretary of War was enough to make him drop all inquiry. In the postwar period, the simple fact is that the Congress has had no opportunity to get real information on military matters, much less the skill and time to evaluate it. Behind their "security" and their "authority" as experts, the political role of the high military in decisions of basic political and economic relevance has become greatly enlarged. And again, it has been enlarged as much or more because of civilian political default—perhaps necessarily, given the organization and personnel of Congress—than by any military usurpation.

No area of decision has been more influenced by the warlords and by their military metaphysics that that of foreign policy and international relations. In these zones, the military ascendancy has coincided with other forces that have been making for the downfall of civilian diplomacy as an art, and of the civilian diplomatic service as an organized group of competent people. The military ascendancy and the downfall of diplomacy has occurred precisely when, for the first time in United States history, international issues are truly at the center of the most important national decisions and increasingly relevant to virtually all decisions of consequence. With the elite's acceptance of military definitions of world reality, the professional diplomat, as we have known him or as we might imagine him, has simply lost any effective voice in the higher circles.

Once war was considered the business of soldiers, international relations the concern of diplomats. But now that war has become seemingly total and seemingly permanent, the free sport of kings has become the forced and internecine business of people, and diplomatic codes of honor between nations have collapsed. Peace is no longer serious; only war is serious. Every man and every nation is either friend or foe, and the idea of enmity becomes mechanical, massive, and without genuine passion. When virtually all negotiation aimed at peaceful agreement is likely to be seen as "appeasement," if not treason, the active role of the diplomat becomes meaningless; for diplomacy becomes merely a prelude to war or an interlude between wars, and in such a context the diplomat is replaced by the warlord.

The Rise of Military Influence in the Nixon Administration

NEIL SHEEHAN

Although the lines of power within the Nixon Administration's Defense Department have not yet been definitively drawn, the influence of the Joint Chiefs of Staff appears to have grown appreciably.

The new Secretary of Defense, Melvin R. Laird, has substantially vitiated the effect of the elaborate machinery constructed by former Defense Secretary Robert S. McNamara to impose aggressive civilian management and control over the military from the top, knowledgeable sources say.

Mr. Laird is not dismantling the machinery, but he has weakened its impact by changing the character and role of two of its major components, the sources say.

The changed components are the Office of International Security Affairs, which is the Pentagon's foreign policy section; and the Office of Systems Analysis, created to oversee all weapons programs and strategic planning.

The counsel of the Joint Chiefs is being heard and considered as it has not been since the end of the Eisenhower era, well informed sources say. The chiefs are initiating proposals instead of reacting to those initiated by the civilian staffs of the Secretary of Defense.

In general, military leaders are pleased with the way things are going under the Republican Administration.

One example of the increased influence of the chiefs cited by military sources is the rate at which American troops are being withdrawn from Vietnam. Although Mr. Laird is pushing for disengagement as quickly as possible, the Joint Staff, the operating agency of the chiefs, is understood to be controlling the detailed planning involved. Gen Creighton W. Abrams, the American military commander in Vietnam, is being allowed, after review and concurrence by the chiefs, to determine more or less the rate at which South Vietnamese forces can take over responsibilities from the Americans and thus free United States troops for withdrawal.

From *The New York Times*, June 30, 1969. © 1969 by The New York Times Company. Reprinted by permission.

Another example is the reversal of the civilian defense position on the Spanish base issue after Mr. Laird took over. Under Paul C. Warnke, the former head of the Office of International Security Affairs, the office had adopted a position paper that expressed considerable skepticism about the military value of the air bases in Spain and recommended that no further commitments be made to retain them.

This position was subsequently reversed at the request of the Joint Chiefs. The old agreement and its commitment was extended until September, 1970, and Spain was given a $50-million arms aid grant and a $35-million credit from the Export-Import Bank to purchase weapons here.

The commitment to Spain is unclear, but the prolonged agreement contains a provision that "a threat to either country, and to the joint facilities that each provides for the common defense, would be a matter of concern to both countries and each country would take such action as it may consider appropriate."

The extent to which the newfound influence of the chiefs will affect politico-military policy and defense spending is still unclear, however. The organizational check on their power within the Pentagon has been replaced to some degree by the growing antimilitary mood in Congress and the country.

This climate is exerting pressure on President Nixon to hold down military spending and is strengthening the ability of outside agencies like the Bureau of the Budget to do the cutting.

LAIRD ECONOMY MOVE

And despite the public compatibility with military views that Mr. Laird has displayed on such issues as the antiballistic missile controversy, he is said to be very conscious of the need for economy.

The defense secretary is understood to have quietly warned the chiefs that Congress simply will not accept any major increases in the current $80-billion defense budget and that for the first time since the Eisenhower era the Defense Department will have to do its planning for the 1971 fiscal year budget with a preconceived ceiling in mind.

Informed observers do not believe that Mr. Laird intends to relinquish civilian control over the Pentagon to the military.

They think that as a professional politician he means to retain control by establishing cordial working relationships with the military and thus to be able to work out mutually acceptable compromises on key problems.

Mr. McNamara, the professional manager, believed that only a hardnosed civilian staff responsive to his direction could achieve real civilian control.

Conversations with senior and working level officials in and outside the Pentagon disclose several reasons for the increased weight of the Joint Chiefs in the bureaucratic equation.

The two principal reasons are:

1. A personal inclination by Mr. Laird and his chief civilian aides to seek and carefully listen to military judgment in decision-making.
2. The new National Security Council machinery that provides a clearly defined channel for the Joint Chiefs to express their views.

FIVE SERVICE LEADERS

The Joint Chiefs of Staff consist of five armed forces leaders, including the chairman. They are Gen. Earle G. Wheeler, chairman; Gen. William C. Westmoreland, Army Chief of Staff; Admiral Thomas H. Moorer, Chief of Naval Operations; Gen. John P. McConnell, Air Force Chief of Staff; and Gen. Leonard C. Chapman, Commandant of the Marine Corps.

The conversations with Pentagon officials reveal that while the power of the Joint Chiefs has increased, the influence of the Pentagon's civilian-run Office of International Security Affairs has declined both within and outside the Defense Department.

Its decline is attributed to the fact that Mr. Laird, unlike his predecessors, has not actively sought a foreign policy role and to the loss of the maverick independence on foreign policy matters that the International Security Office preserved under former Secretaries McNamara and Clark M. Clifford.

The office then played a key role in turning around the Johnson Administration's Vietnam war policy and often outweighed the State Department in formulating foreign policy.

Now, under the new Assistant Secretary for International Security Affairs, Warren Nutter, a former foreign policy adviser to Barry Goldwater, and men of like political views he has brought in to assist him, the office inclines to positions similar to those of the Joint Chiefs on foreign policy questions.

SYSTEMS ANALYSIS DECLINE

As a result, the State Department pays much less attention to it in the interagency bargaining through which policy documents are drawn up for eventual submission to the National Security Council.

A third major development has been the very noticeable weakening in bureaucratic muscle of the Office of Systems Analysis, which held a pivotal position under Mr. McNamara and Mr. Clifford.

Like the international security office, the systems' analysis office has a combined civilian-military staff but is run by civilians and is an operating arm of the Secretary of Defense.

The cost effectiveness and strategic analysis in the systems analysis office, irritably dubbed "the whiz kids" by the military, review all weapons proposals by the military.

Very frequently under Secretaries Clifford and McNamara, the reviews were so different in content from the original proposals that they constituted independent weapons programs, and the systems analysis office also often instituted its own strategic studies on both conventional and nuclear war.

The systems analysis technique compares alternative weapons systems and strategies in terms of their cost in money and manpower and their military effectiveness in meeting potential enemy threats and the nation's foreign policy commitments. The comparisons are made primarily through the use of statistical and mathematical data.

REVERSAL OF ROLES

The Joint Staff, the chief's operating arm, and the individual armed services, which each of the chiefs except the chairman heads in a separate capacity, found themselves continually reacting to papers initiated by systems analysis personnel.

"The whole system was designed to keep the chiefs off balance," one well-informed source said.

Now the roles have been reversed. The Joint Staff and the services are initiating most of the position papers and the systems analysis office has been largely reduced to commenting on the papers.

"If you can initiate the paper, that gives you one leg up in the bureaucracy," the source commented.

Secretary Laird and his Deputy Secretary, David Packard, have indicated some skepticism about the value of the systems analysis approach by paying considerably less attention to its reviews than Mr. McNamara did, knowledgeable officials say.

Significantly, they have also continued to delay nominating a permanent Assistant Secretary to head the office and have reduced its work load. Where systems analysis formerly did a sizable number of major studies each year, it is scheduled to do only two this year—one on nuclear forces and the other on general purpose (conventional warfare) forces.

"Hopefully we can do it right the first time and save some money," Mr. Packard was quoted as saying in a recent interview to explain the reversal of roles between systems analysis and the Joint Staff. "Now an awful lot of people are going over the same thing time after time," he added.

Some informed observers speculate, however, that the downgrading of the systems analysis office may prove somewhat temporary, a kind of internal public relations effort by Mr. Packard and Mr. Laird to mollify the Joint Chiefs and to establish cordial working relations, and that they may later come to rely on it more as a tool to exert civilian control.

But the McNamara era also taught the military to establish its own capability in this field by educating officers in this quantitative analytical technique. The Joint Staff and the individual services are now much better equipped to counter systems analysis arguments.

Mr. Laird and Mr. Packard have clearly created an atmosphere within the department in which the chiefs feel much more comfortable and efficacious, knowledgeable sources say.

The civilian staffs at the working level are under implicit instructions to try to work out compromise solutions with the military and to arrive at what Mr. Laird refers to as common "defense positions." Under Mr. McNamara, "the marching orders were to be tough and skeptical," one informed observer noted.

Consequently, the chiefs are understood to feel a lessening of overall bureaucratic pressure. They were glad to see the departure of Mr. Warnke, the former Assistant Secretary for International Security Affairs, whom some are said to have regarded as "a unilaterial disarmer."

Now senior civilian officials in international security, before arriving at their own positions, will sometimes telephone their counterparts on the Joint Staff and ask for advice on foreign policy questions.

Where there is disagreement with the chiefs on a specific issue, the dissenting views are now included in the basic document, instead of being footnoted, as they often were under Mr. McNamara—an important bureaucratic distinction. "It's easy to overlook footnotes," one officer said.

The National Security Council system also has precise machinery for the chiefs to present a formal separate view to the President. They do not have to hope that the chairman, General Wheeler, will manage to work it in at the Tuesday lunches that constituted President Johnson's policy-making group.

Mr. Laird has also expanded the Secretary's regular Monday morning meeting with his Assistant Secretaries, the service secretaries and the chiefs. Under Mr. McNamara these meetings tended to be formal half-hour sessions that dealt with technical items, like 500-pound bomb production, and the civilians did most of the talking.

Now the meetings last an hour to an hour and a half and range over all issues facing the department that week, such as the strategy to be adopted at committee hearings on Capitol Hill, major weapons programs, manpower, training or the latest analysis of the situation in Vietnam. "There's no end to what's discussed," one source said.

The chiefs have been encouraged and join freely in the discussion, offering their advice.

Mr. Laird meets again separately with them each Monday afternoon, and he frequently spends other long hours with them in the chief's council chamber in the bowels of the Pentagon, colloquially referred to as "the tank," talking over such matters as the nuclear threat posed by the Soviet SS-9 missile, the conditions under which Okinawa should revert to Japan and other matters of current concern.

Informed sources say that the chiefs, as separate heads of their services, also now have direct access to Deputy Secretary Packard on major budget and weapons program management questions, the details of which he usually handles. They normally see him accompanied by their civilian service secretary.

Mr. Packard has made clear in these meetings that he wants to be as "helpful" as possible, sources say, and the chiefs are said to find this "a much quicker and clearer" way of doing business than through the complicated staff procedure Mr. McNamara insisted upon.

Mr. Laird and Mr. Packard have coined a term for their approach to relations with the military. They call it "participatory management."

But the questions remains: Which side will participate most?

Power, Expertise, and the Military Profession

SAMUEL P. HUNTINGTON

THE DECLINE IN POWER

Immediately after World War II the air was full of alarms about the growing power of the military. These subsided somewhat during the early 1950's. They reappeared at the end of the decade, however, and they were given a major stimulus from President Eisenhower in January, 1961. "In the councils of government," the retiring President warned, "we must guard against the acquisition of unwarranted influence, whether sought or unsought, by the military-industrial complex. The potential for the disastrous rise of misplaced power exists and will persist." The President's words highlighted an increasing concern with the relations between the military and big business, the role of military leaders in shaping foreign policy decisions, their struggles to get more of the taxpayers' dollars, their opposition to disarmament and support for more belligerent foreign policies and their links with Radical Right extremists. In the words of one author: ". . . the sober and shocking and little-realized truth is that today it is less possible than ever before to place any kind of effective check on the Military." If these views were held only by an extremist minority, they would not be worthy of attention. Eisenhower's farewell address, however, endowed them with respectability, and they are now widely held by many reasonable and moderate commentators. In addition, the fears of military power expressed by groups within the United States interact with and help reinforce images of military dominance widely held by intellectual and political groups abroad.

This image of military dominance is false and dangerous. In actual fact, the power of the military profession "in the councils of government" has decreased steadily since World War II. It has reached its postwar nadir under the vigorous leadership of President Kennedy and Secretary of Defense McNamara at the very time, paradoxically, that concern about the growth of military power has been on the upswing. This concern is rooted in the traditional American tendency to view control in *quantitative* rather than *institutional* terms. Before World War II the United States solved the problem of civilian control by maintaining only minimal military forces. Since World War II, however, substantial military forces

From *Daedelus* 92, Fall 1963, pp. 793-801. Reprinted by permission.

have been necessary, and about 10 per cent of the gross national product has been devoted to military purposes. Hence, it seems logical to assume that civilian control is threatened. The strength of civilian control, however, depends not on the size of the armed forces, but on the strength of the political institutions and ideology of the country. The Soviet Union devotes about 18 percent of its GNP to military purposes. Yet civilian control is effective because communist political institutions and ideology make it effective. Only when the Party was divided against itself in the succession struggle did the military get a foot in the door of power; and when the succession crisis was over, they were quickly ejected. Similarly, in the United States civilian control depends not on how much of the GNP is devoted to military purposes but on the unity, coherence and strength of political institutions and political leadership, and on the attitudes which leaders and public have toward military power.

Between 1939 and 1942, a revolution took place in American civil-military relations. Generals and admirals moved from political isolation into the seats of power. This revolution, however, directly reflected traditional American attitudes that war and peace were two distinct states. In peace, the military should be small in size and divorced from power. In war, however, the goal is victory, and hence military needs should be overriding. As a result, top military leaders played a far more important role in the United States in World War II than they did in any other major belligerent except Japan. The President and the Joint Chiefs of Staff formulated strategy. The Secretaries of State, War and Navy played marginal roles. Unlike the military chiefs, they did not regularly attend the great wartime planning conferences between Roosevelt and Churchill. Congress voluntarily relinquished its control functions. "The War Department, or . . . General Marshall," as one congressman observed, "virtually dictated the budgets." The military were less powerful in economic mobilization than they were in strategy and foreign policy, but even there their power steadily grew during the war. The Joint Chiefs, Admiral Leahy remarked in 1945, were "under no civilian control whatever." Toward the close of the war, the activities and interests of the military extended far beyond military operations. This situation was tolerable, however, because the military exercised their power with the consent and enthusiastic support of the President, the Congress, and the people: they wielded power but they wielded it to achieve the goals desired by the political community as a whole.

World War II thus marked the high point of military influence. Since 1945, the power of the military profession has steadily declined. Military leaders and military institutions were less powerful in the Truman Administration than they were during World War II. They were less powerful under Eisenhower than they were under Truman. They are less powerful now under Kennedy than they were under Eisenhower. This constant decline in the power and influence of the military profession is the single most important trend in American civil-military relations during the past fifteen years. The decline has been marked by a number of changes in the relations between military and civilian groups.

1. Decline in Political Influence of the Top Leaders of the Military Profession

In the years immediately after World War II the great military commanders of the war were popular heroes and major political figures in their own right. The Truman Administration was politically weak and needed the help of the great soldier-statesmen of World War II—Marshall, Eisenhower, Bradley—to secure support for its policies in Congress and among the public at large. Marshall served the administration as Secretary of State and Secretary of Defense, Eisenhower and Bradley as presiding officers of the Joint Chiefs, Eisenhower as Supreme Commander in Europe. The single most important foreign policy issue of Truman's second term—the conduct of the Korean War—was essentially a debate between MacArthur on the one hand, and Marshall and Bradley on the other.

The election of Eisenhower created a different, if somewhat paradoxical, situation. A military man was now President, but for this very reason the influence of other military men was limited. Eisenhower, of course, waged a continuing and successful battle to keep down the military budget, which aroused considerable opposition among his Chiefs of Staff. But what could they do? No military man on active duty could compete with the prestige of General Eisenhower, and the prestige of *General* Eisenhower was the principal weapon of *President* Eisenhower in imposing restrictions on military spending. Admiral Radford was the only military officer who played a significant role in policy-making, and he was one officer who also shared the administration's budgetary outlook.

At the close of his term of office President Eisenhower reportedly expressed doubts about the ability of his successor—Kennedy or Nixon—who would lack his military experience and reputation to exercise effective control over the military. President Kennedy, however, demonstrated that the ability to control and to lead can derive as much from political skill as from military knowledge. The top military leaders of the 1960's, moreover, are the products of a peacetime military bureaucracy rather than of wartime military command. This does not mean that they are any less worthy than their predecessors: General Taylor is certainly one of the most brilliant and able leaders the American military profession has produced. But they lack the independent-political appeal of their predecessors. In 1948 the Chiefs of Staff were wartime heroes; in 1963 it is doubtful if one American in a hundred could name the five Chiefs of Staff. The military leaders now are the creatures of the politicians, and, as the experience of Admiral Anderson demonstrates, if one of them does stray out of line he can be easily dropped by the administration.

2. The Decreasing Role of Military Men in the Civilian Agencies of Government

The development of the Cold War immediately after World War II caught the government unprepared with personnel to staff its new foreign affairs activities.

The civilians who had joined the government during the war were heading back to their peacetime jobs. Where was the government to find men able, dedicated, willing to serve and at least partially familiar with foreign policy problems? The obvious source was the military. As a result, military officers were appointed to key State Department offices, ambassadorial posts and positions in other foreign affairs agencies. Although the number of military officers occupying civilian positions declined after 1946 and 1947, it remained high throughout the Truman Administration.

Unlike Truman, Eisenhower was able to enlist the services of large numbers of businessmen for his administration. Although he initially appointed several top military officers to civilian positions, the overall participation of military officers in civil office declined significantly during the later years of his administration. Under Kennedy this tendency was intensified. In Kennedy's first two years no professional military officer was appointed to a top civil position in the government. The officers had performed a notable service in stepping into the breach in the early years of the Cold War, when civilians were either unqualified or unwilling to serve. By the 1960's, however, the foreign assistance, overseas information and intelligence agencies had developed their own professional staffs. The State Department, which had suffered under the attacks of McCarthy and the administrative indifference of Dulles, was beginning to refurbish the professional skills and esprit of the Foreign Service. Below the top levels of the foreign affairs and defense agencies, there was an increasing interchange of personnel as military officers were temporarily assigned to the State Department and other civilian agencies, and representatives of these agencies temporarily worked for the Department of Defense. This, however, was an educational device designed to improve understanding and coordination. Unlike the massive movement of military men into civilian posts in the 1940's, it reflected strength rather than weakness in the civilian agencies.

3. The Increasing Expertise and Influence of Civilian Groups in the Formation of Military Policy

Not only have the military retreated from the civilian side of foreign policy, but a variety of civilian groups have moved into the military sphere and have begun to play a major role in the determination of strategy and military policy. Most important among these groups are the so-called "defense intellectuals," the physical scientists and the civil servants of the Department of Defense. The involvement in military policy of the first two groups was a direct result of the changing nature of war and strategy; it was evidence of one way in which the decrease in the differences between military and civilian skills could serve to limit the power of the military. It was also persuasive evidence of the extent to which innovation in strategy and technology was dependent on the actions of groups outside the military hierarchy.

The increasing complexity of war and the decreasing relevance of the traditional distinctions between sea, land and air warfare caused military officers to lag behind in the development of strategic ideas relevant to deterrence. Most of the significant writings on strategy produced after World War II were produced by civilians. Increasing attention was paid to strategy in the universities, in the various centers for the study of foreign and military policy problems such as the Council on Foreign Relations, and in specialized research organizations such as RAND. Experts such as Brodie, Kaufmann, Kissinger, Wohlstetter, Schelling and Kahn took the lead in articulating theories of stabilized deterrence, limited war, tactical nuclear war, arms control and civil defense. Divorced from service interests and trained in the exact or social sciences, they were able to bring a fresh approach to the problems of strategy. During the Eisenhower Administration, their role was largely critical. In the Kennedy Administration, they moved into the White House and the Pentagon. They were able, in a sense, to beat the military at their own game. Traditionally, the professional military officer is supposed to be contemptuous of the ignorance of civilians on military problems and strategy. One striking aspect of the McNamara Pentagon, however, has been the allegation that the civilian "whiz kids" are unduly contemptuous of the military officers for *their* backwardness and ignorance.

The natural scientists are a second civilian group challenging the military on their home ground. Their entrance into military affairs followed inevitably from the atomic bomb. In 1946 they played a major role, on both sides, in the struggle over civilian vs. military control of atomic energy. In the early 1950's, some scientists were leading figures in the development of thermonuclear weapons. Others took the lead in pushing continental defense and low-yield nuclear weapons. Subsequently, sputniks and space again brought the scientists to the center of the scene. A Special Assistant to the President for Science and Technology was appointed, and the office of the Director of Research and Engineering was established in the Department of Defense. The latter official supervises all military research and development. In the debates of the late 1950's and early 1960's concerning technology, space activities, nuclear testing, arms control, disarmament and even weapons development, the role of the scientists was as important or more important than that of the soldiers.

A third civilian group lacks the glamor or public prestige of the defense intellectuals or the physical scientists. In the fifteen years following the unification of 1947, however, the civil servants in the Department of Defense also quietly gained in power and influence. Military officers are normally rotated through top staff positions in tours of three or four years. By the late 1950's, however, some top civil servants had been with the central defense establishment since its creation in 1947. Continuity of service gave them experience, knowledge, contacts and power. The civilian scientists and defense intellectuals primarily play a critical, innovating role in military matters. The civil servants in the office of the Secretary of Defense, on the other hand, primarily play a restricting, controlling role. As a result, the growth of their power is a popular target for criticism by military leaders.

In addition to these three groups of civilians, the top political leadership of the Department of Defense is becoming more knowledgeable in military policy and strategy. These leadership positions are normally occupied by bankers, lawyers, industrialists and educators. Over the course of years, however, each political party has built up a reservoir of talent with experience in military matters. At the end of the Eisenhower Administration, "most civilian leaders in the Pentagon had spent periods of 4 to 8 years in defense work, if not in the same post." The Kennedy Administration, in turn, did not start from scratch but included executives like Gilpatric and Nitze, who had held responsible positions under Truman. The next Republican administration presumably will have its share of Eisenhower appointees. Thus, after fifteen years of Cold War, civilians are playing more and more important roles in shaping military policy. In the late 1940's, few civilians would have dared challenge the wisdom of the Joint Chiefs on strategy. Those who did carried little weight. In the early 1960's, initiative and leadership on strategic matters were shared among a variety of groups, some military, but many civilian.

4. Centralization of Authority over Military Policy in the Executive Branch

Historically, Congress has played an important role in determining the size and weapons of the armed forces and in sharing responsibility through its treaty and war-making powers for their use. After World War II, however, the power to determine the military budget, force levels, weapons and uses of the armed forces became securely lodged in the administration, that is, in top leadership of the executive branch of the government. This decline in the power of Congress also meant a decline in the power of the military professionals. So long as Congress could act independently on force levels, the commanders could appeal executive decisions to Congress with the expectation that they might well be overruled. After World War II military leaders continued to look to Congress to correct unfavorable executive decisions. Frequently Congress heeded these appeals and added additional sums to the military budget. In almost every case, however, the President wielded an effective veto over the congressional action by impounding the appropriated funds or by refusing to authorize larger forces. Congressional groups, of course, can lobby with the administration and harass it in a variety of ways. But the administration can, if it wishes, always have the last word.

5. Continued Divisions Among the Military

The above-mentioned factors have all contributed to a marked rise in civilian authority vis-à-vis the military professionals. Conceivably these developments might have been counterbalanced by other changes on the military side of the equation. By and large, however, they were not. In particular, the single most significant factor abetting the rise of civilian influence was the continued division of the military against itself. Interservice controversy, intraservice divisions, interprogram rivalries all helped to weaken the voice of the military. On few, if any, major issues did the military professionals develop a coherent military viewpoint. Split among themselves, they invited civilian intervention into military affairs. When they were able to compromise their differences and agree on a common program, the result was often so obviously a political compromise that civilian leaders were justified in tearing it apart on grounds of sound military logic. This competition went on not only in the Joint Chiefs of Staff but also in the broader reaches of the "military-industrial complex." Those fearful of the power of the complex assume that it is an entity acting with a singleness of purpose. In actuality, however, it is more of an arena than a unity. It is divided against itself and quite incapable of unified action. The services compete with each other over strategy, weapons and budgets. Corporations compete with each other for defense contracts. Scientific and technical advisory groups offer conflicting advice. Local communities and congressional representatives clash with administration leaders and the chiefs of staff. The lines of conflict and alliance are continually changing. Seldom, if ever, are they drawn on a civilian vs. military basis.

Throughout the Cold War years the determination of military policy has remained firmly in the hands of the civilians. Three major revisions of overall strategy occurred in 1950, 1953 and 1961. In each case, the political leadership of the government took the initiative in changing strategy and supplied the basic ideas and concepts. Most of the other important changes in American policies and programs have been inaugurated by civilians. Civilian Pentagon leaders have not hesitated to overrule military chieftains on the need for particular types of weapons. Inevitably, the pressure from the military is for the proliferation of programs and expenditures. But as the history of the Eisenhower Administration demonstrates, an administration can keep military spending down if it wishes to. Military expenditures (in constant dollars) were less in the last year of the Eisenhower Administration than they were in any earlier year in that administration.

McNamara's Control
of the Pentagon

ROBERT J. ART

TYPES OF DECISIONS

We began this book by asking two basic questions. First, why did Secretary of Defense Robert McNamara choose the General Dynamics Corporation to develop the TFX airplane when the chief of staff of the Air Force and the chief of Naval Operations both recommended that he select the Boeing Company to do the job? Second, why was he able to make and carry out such a decision when these two military chiefs had traditionally been the final authorities responsible for selecting sources to develop major weapon systems for their respective services?

We have answered the first question. In discussing the specific reasons for his choice, we saw that McNamara's institutional role and his analytical approach to making decisions led him to make such a choice. Furthermore, we saw that his analytical approach reinforced his institutional role. His institutional perspective required that he look at all the programs of the Defense Department in their relationships to each other. His cost-effectiveness technique made it possible for him to do so. As secretary of Defense, McNamara had ultimate responsibility for making certain that the country had integrated, balanced, and effective forces. He employed a technique of analysis (1) that required him to consider alternative ways of satisfying a military requirement, (2) that required him to calculate the cost of each alternative, (3) that required him to weigh the military effectiveness of each alternative, and (4) that required him to compare all alternatives in terms of their cost and effectiveness. By using such a technique, McNamara accomplished something that no secretary of Defense before him had done. He developed the ability to make informed decisions on which of the choices before him would contribute the most to integrating and balancing military instruments of force.

From Robert J. Art, *The TFX Decision*, pp. 157-66. Copyright © 1968 by Little, Brown and Company (Inc.). Reprinted by permission.

Intuition and hunches—the major methods of his predecessors—were still necessary for making decisions; but these two could now be based upon a more complete, detailed knowledge both of what the military requirements were and of the options available to meet them. In systematically looking for and comparing options, McNamara acquired the information necessary to do his job effectively.

Secretary McNamara's goal did not differ from that of his military chiefs. He, as they, wanted to provide the country with the "best" possible defense. He, as they, believed that this was done by creating integrated and balanced forces. He, as they, thought that such forces required "adequate" and "suitable" weapon systems. However, what Secretary McNamara defined as "adequate" (the General Dynamics proposal), the service chiefs defined as satisfactory but less than desirable. What Secretary McNamara defined as "suitable" (the biservice approach), the service chiefs defined as possible but undesirable. The differences were thus not over the goals to be achieved but rather over the means by which to achieve them.

In the TFX case, McNamara argued, first, that paying more for a weapon system *than was necessary in order to meet the military requirement* would mean that fewer resources would be available to spend on other weapon systems necessary to meet other military requirements. In so arguing, Secretary McNamara did not assert that the cheapest weapon system was always the "best" choice for meeting a particular requirement. The cheapest system might not yield the performance necessary to carry out a mission effectively. To choose the cheapest in such a case would mean in reality to choose the most expensive, both because the requirement would not have been met and because additional resources would have to be committed to meet the still unmet requirement. Rather, in picking the General Dynamics proposal, McNamara asserted one of his major management principles for running the Defense Department: that in a situation where each of two weapon systems meets the requirements, it is good *military* judgment to select the cheaper one.

Secretary McNamara argued, second, that making the TFX a biservice or common program, *when doing so would not prevent the two services from meeting their requirements,* would enable him to buy still more planes, if that proved necessary, than would have been possible had he chosen two completely different aircraft for the two services. In so arguing, Secretary McNamara did not assert that all new development programs should be carried out on a biservice or a triservice basis. In some situations such programs could prevent the services from meeting their requirements. Again, such a choice, though it might appear to save money, could in the end be costlier. Rather, in making the TFX a biservice program, McNamara asserted a second of his major management principles for running the Defense Department: where one weapon system meets the requirements of several services, it is good *military* judgment to make the program a biservice one.

By his source selection and biservice decisions, McNamara in effect said to the two services: if you pay more than you have to for this weapon system, you will have fewer resources to purchase the other things that you need now or will need in the future. He thereby pressed them to consider, first, how much performance they really needed in a weapon system, not how much they ideally wanted, and, second, what effect choosing the more or the less expensive program would have on their present programs and future options. By these two basic decisions in the TFX program, Secretary McNamara required each service to consider what effect its development program would have not only on that of the other service but also on those of the entire Defense Department. Neither their experiences nor their institutional roles had predisposed the service chiefs to make such calculations. McNamara, in effect, asked each service chief to assume the perspectives of the secretary of Defense. That McNamara encountered so much opposition to the two basic TFX decisions was proof of how little accustomed the services were to considering such factors, and of how difficult their institutional perspectives made such a task for them.

CONTROL OVER DECISIONS

Secretary McNamara, however, did more than ask the services to do things that they had never really tried. He also succeeded in making them do those things, where others before him had usually failed. This raises the second basic question of this book: how did McNamara make the services do what they had often claimed as their aim but had never worked for? How did he assert his authority over what had been considered military prerogative: the right to choose weapons and to select their producers?

First, he centralized the process of decision-making by deciding himself whenever it became evident to him that others would not make the kinds of decisions he wanted. Second, he altered certain elements in the decision-making process in order to make it produce in the future the types of decisions he wanted. By centralizing and altering the decision-making process, McNamara gained effective control over the key decisions that were being made in the Defense Department. He thus enlarged the effective power of the secretary of Defense both to make more decisions and to do so in areas hitherto untouched by persons in that office. He did so within the Defense Department generally and in the TFX case specifically.

Centralizing the Process

Centralizing decision-making power within the Office of the Secretary of Defense did not begin with McNamara. It had been a gradual development ever since the Department of Defense had been created in 1947. What was new with McNamara was the efficiency and the effectiveness with which he accelerated this postwar trend. In part this acceleration was due to McNamara's own brilliance; in part, to the ability of the assistants he brought with him. But in larger part it was brought about by the curious reversal of positions that he produced within the Defense Department.

The revolutionary manner in which McNamara made his decisions (revolutionary, that is, for the Defense Department), transformed the "expert" career bureaucrat into the "novice" and the "inexperienced" political appointee into the "professional." By demanding that decisions be made through a cost-effectiveness analysis, McNamara freed himself from the secretary's usual dependence on the experience and knowledge of the military officer and the career civil servant. By demanding something that only he and his small personal staff possessed the experience and competence to do, McNamara declared insufficient or invalid, or both, the customary criteria for making decisions and the traditional grounds for justifying them.

In the TFX case, McNamara refused to accept the judgment of the services either that a biservice program was not feasible or that the Boeing Company was preferable. Particularly in the latter case, McNamara asserted his independence from the bureaucracy. He refused to accept a decision sanctified by the repeated ratification of people who took very little time or trouble to make their decisions. Only one person other than Air Force Secretary Zuckert had even bothered to read the Fourth Evaluation Group Report. Most had not even glanced at it. Instead they had relied on an oral briefing that optimistically described the performance of the Boeing plane, but omitted the Report's critical analysis of the risks and difficulties involved in attempting to achieve such performance. On the Fourth Round the members of the Source Selection Board did not receive this 400-odd page, highly technical report until the morning of the day they made their decisions. Thus the biservice and source selection decisions were centrally imposed from the top down rather than "bubbling-up" from below. They were *McNamara's* decisions.

Altering the Process

There was, however, a danger to McNamara in making decisions in such a manner. In reversing the unanimous recommendation of his military officers, McNamara laid himself open to the charge of ignoring the judgment of experts who supposedly knew most about these matters. Such charges were made by Defense Department officials and by congressmen. In order to make certain that he would not be put in such a position again, McNamara resolved to strengthen his control over the process by which sources for the development of advanced weapon systems are selected. He did so in two ways. First, he made it impossible that he would ever again have to reverse the recommendation of his military officers by making it their function to *advise* him on the selection of sources rather than to *recommend* one to him. He would no longer have to overrule the military's recommendations because they could no longer make any. Second, he made clear through new regulations that the secretary of Defense was responsible for selecting the source, though he might choose to delegate the

authority to one of the service secretaries. Through both changes McNamara
canceled the ability of the Source Selection Board to make decisions for him. He
"rigged" the decision-making procedures in order to prevent them from blocking
the outcomes he wanted. Figure 1 illustrates these two changes in the System
Selection procedure by showing the correspondence between the old and new
procedures.

FIGURE 1

System Source Selection Procedure

NEW (after April 6, 1965)		OLD (before April 6, 1965)
Source Selection Authority (Secretary of Defense or Service Secretary) *makes* source selection decision. ↑	corresponds to	Air Force secretary *reviews* and *approves* SSB decision. ↑
Source Selection Advisory Council *evaluates* material of SSEB. ↑	corresponds to	Source Selection Board (SSB) *recommends* and *selects* a source. ↑
Source Selection Evaluation Board (SSEB) evaluates contractors' proposals.	corresponds to	Source Selection Evaluation Group evaluates contractors' proposals.

*   *   *

CONCEPTIONS OF THE OFFICE

In the TFX program, then, Secretary of Defense McNamara innovated both in
the types of decisions that he did make and in the manner in which he made and
carried them out. Both types of innovations stemmed from a conception that
McNamara had of his office—a conception unlike that of any of his predecessors,
except perhaps for that of James Forrestal. In making such novel decisions and
in enforcing them, McNamara in effect not only asserted that a secretary of
Defense can make and overrule decisions on *military* as well as financial and
administrative grounds. He also asserted that because any analytic technique can
yield only so much information, it is necessary for a decision maker to make
judgments and that his perspective as secretary of Defense made *his* judgments
the most valuable and valid for the requirements of *his* job. In order to innovate
McNamara had to take the initiative. In his own words:

> I think that the role of public manager is very similar to the role of a
> private manager; in each case he has the option of following one of two
> major alternative courses of action. He can either act as a judge or a leader.
> In the former case, he sits and waits until subordinates bring to him
> problems for solution, or alternatives for choice. In the latter case he
> immerses himself in the operations of the business or governmental activity,

examines the problems, the objectives, the alternative courses of action, chooses among them, and leads the organization to their accomplishment. In the one case, it's a passive role; in the other case, an active role. . . . *I have always believed in and endeavored to follow the active leadership role as opposed to the passive judicial role.*

I'm here to originate and stimulate new ideas and programs, not just to referee arguments.

In the TFX controversy that is exactly what he did.

A Military-Industrial Complex
Does Exist

MARC PILISUK and THOMAS HAYDEN

... [There are] three grounds for denying that a military-industrial complex prevents peace:

1. it is held that the *scope* of decisions made by any interest group is quite narrow and cannot be said to govern anything so broad as foreign policy;
2. it is held that the "complex" is not *monolithic, not self-conscious*, and *not coordinated*, the presumed attributes of a ruling elite;
3. it is held that the military-industrial complex does not wield power if the term "power" is defined as the ability to realize its will even against the resistance of others and regardless of external conditions.

These formulations, to repeat, are made neither explicitly nor consistently in the new literature. But they crystallize the basic questions about definition which the new literature raises. Moreover, they are quite definitely the major contentions made by academic criticisms of power elite theory .... Since their critiques are mainly directed at the work of C. Wright Mills,[1] it is with Mills that we will begin to analyze the theories which claim there *is* a military-industrial complex blocking peace.

THE THESIS OF ELITE CONTROL

Mills is by far the most formidable exponent of the theory of a power elite. In his view, the period in America since World War II has been dominated by the ascendance of corporation and military elites to positions of institutional power. These "commanding heights" allow them to exercise control over the trends of the business cycle and international relations. The Cold War set the conditions which legitimize this ascendance, and the decline and incorporation of

From Mark Pilisuk and Thomas Hayden, "Is There a Military-Industrial Complex Which Prevents Peace?: Consensus and Countervailing Power in Pluralistic Systems," *Journal of Social Issues*, Volume XXI, No. 3 (1965), pp. 67-117. Reprinted by permission of the publisher and author. This article has been revised in Marc Pilisuk's *International Conflict and Public Policy*, to be published by Prentice-Hall, Inc., Englewood Cliffs, New Jersey.

significant left-liberal movements, such as the CIO, symbolizes the end of opposition forces. The power elite monopolizes sovereignty, in that political initiative and control stem mainly from the top hierarchical levels of position and influence. Through the communications system the elite facilitates the growth of a politically indifferent mass society below the powerful institutions. This, according to the Mills argument, would explain why an observer finds widespread apathy. Only a small minority believes in actual participation in the larger decisions which affect their existence and only the ritual forms of "popular democracy" are practiced by the vast majority. Mills' argument addresses itself to the terms of the three basic issues we have designated, i.e., scope of decision power, awareness of common interest, and the definition of power exerted.

By *scope*, we are referring to the sphere of society over which an elite is presumed to exercise power. Mills argues that the scope of this elite is general, embracing all the decisions which in any way could be called vital (slump and boom, peace and war, etc.). He does not argue that *each* decision is directly determined, but rather that the political alternatives from which the "Deciders" choose are shaped and limited by the elite through its possession of all the large-scale institutions. By this kind of argument, Mills avoids the need to demonstrate how his elite is at work during each decision. He speaks instead in terms of institutions and resources. But the problem is that his basic evidence is of a rather negative kind. No major decisions have been made for 20 years contrary to the policies of anti-communism and corporate or military aggrandizement; *therefore* a power elite must be prevailing. Mills might have improved his claims about the scope of elite decisions by analyzing a series of actual decisions in terms of the premises which were *not* debated. This could point to the mechanisms (implicit or explicit) which led to the exclusion of these premises from debate. By this and other means he might have found more satisfying evidence of the common, though perhaps tacit, presuppositions of seemingly disparate institutions. He then might have developed a framework analyzing "scope" on different levels. The scope of the Joint Chiefs of Staff, for instance, could be seen as limited, while at the same time the Joint Chiefs could be placed in a larger elite context having larger scope. Whether this could be shown awaits research of this kind. Until it is done, however, Mills theory of scope remains open to attack, but, conversely, is not subject to refutation.

Mills' theory also eludes the traditional requirements for inferring monolithic structure, i.e., consciousness of elite status, and coordination. The modern tradition of viewing elites in this way began with Mosca's *The Ruling Class* in a period when family units and inheritance systems were the basic means of conferring power. Mills departs from this influential tradition precisely because of his emphasis on institutions as the basic elements. If the military, political, and economic *institutional orders* involve a high coincidence of interest, then the groups composing the institutional orders need not be monolithic, conscious, and coordinated, yet still they can exercise elite power. This means specifically that a military-industrial complex could exist as an expression of a certain fixed ideology (reflecting common institutional needs), yet be "composed" of an endless shuffle of specific groups. For instance, 82 companies have dropped out of the list of 100 top defense contractors, and only 36 "durables" have remained on the list in the years since 1940. In terms of industry, the percentage of contracts going to the automotive industry dropped from 25 percent in World War II to 4 percent in the missile age. At the same time, the aircraft companies went from 34 to 54 percent of all contracts, and the electronics industry from 9 to 28 percent (Peck and Scherer, 1962). Mills' most central argument is that this ebb-and-flow is not necessarily evidence for the pluralists. His stress is on the unities which underlie the procession of competition and change. The decision to change the technology of warfare was one which enabled one group to "overcome" another in an overall system to which both are fundamentally committed. Moreover, the decision issued from the laboratories and planning boards of the defense establishment and only superficially involved any role for public opinion. The case studies of weapons development by Peck and Scherer, in which politics is described as a marginal ritual, would certainly buttress Mills' point of view.

Making this institution analysis enables Mills to make interesting comments on his human actors. The integration of institutions means that hundreds of individuals become familiar with several roles: General, politician, lobbyist, defense contractor. These men are the power elite, but they need not know it. They conspire, but conspiracy is not absolutely essential to their maintenance. They mix together easily, but can remain in power even if they are mostly anonymous to each other. They make decisions, big and small, sometimes with the knowledge of others and sometimes not, which ultimately control all the significant action and resources of society.

Where this approach tends to fall short, is in its unclarity about how discontinuities arise. Is the military-industrial complex a feature of American society which can disappear and still leave the general social structure intact? Horst Brand has suggested a tension between financial companies and the defense industries because of the relatively few investment markets created by defense.[2] Others are beginning to challenge the traditional view that defense spending stimulates high demand and employment. Their claim is that the concentration of contracts in a few states, the monopolization of defense and space industry by the largest 75 or 100 corporations, the low multiplier effect of the new weapons, the declining numbers of blue-collar workers required, and other factors, make the defense economy more of a drag than a stimulant.[3] Mills died before these trends became the subject of debate, but he might have pioneered in discussion of them if his analytic categories had differentiated more finely between various industries and interest groups in his power elite. His emphasis was almost entirely on the "need" for a "permanent war economy" just when that need was being questioned even among his elite.

However, this failure does not necessarily undermine the rest of Mills' analysis. His institutional analysis is still the best means of identifying a complex without calling it monolithic, conscious and coordinated. Had he differentiated more exactly he might have been able to describe various degrees of commitments to an arms race, a rightist ideology constricting the arena of meaningful debate, and other characteristics of a complex. This task remains to be done, and will be discussed at a later point.

Where Mills' theory is most awkward is in his assertions that the elite can, and does, make its decisions against the will of others and regardless of external conditions. This way of looking at power is inherited by Mills, and much of modern sociology, directly from Max Weber. What is attributed to the elite is a rather fantastic quality: literal omnipotence. Conversely, any group that is *not* able to realize its will even against the resistance of others is only "influential" but not an elite. Mills attempts to defend this viewpoint but, in essence, modifies it. He says he is describing a tendency, not a finalized state of affairs. This is a helpful device in explaining cracks in the monolith—for instance, the inability of the elite to establish a full corporate state against the will of small businessmen. However, it does not change the ultimate argument—that the power elite cannot become more than a tendency, cannot realize its actual self, unless it takes on the quality of omnipotence.

When power is defined as this kind of dominance, it is easily open to critical dispute. The conception of power depicts a vital and complex social system as essentially static, as having within it a set of stable governing components, with precharted interests which infiltrate and control every outpost of decision-authority. Thereby, internal accommodation is made necessary and significant change, aside from growth, becomes impossible. This conception goes beyond the idea of social or economic determinism. In fact, it defines a "closed social system." A "closed system" may be a dramatic image, but it is a forced one as well. Its defender sees events such as the rise of the labor movement essentially as a means of rationalizing modern capitalism. But true or false as this may be, did not the labor movement also constitute a "collective will" which the elite could not resist? An accommodation was reached, probably more on the side of capital than labor, but the very term "accommodation" implies the existence of more than one independent will. On a world scale, this becomes even more obvious. Certainly the rise of communism has not been through the will of capitalists, and Mills would be the first to agree. Nor does the elite fully control technological development; surely the process of invention has some independent, even if minor, place in the process of social change.

Mills' definition of power as dominance ironically serves the pluralist argument, rather than countering it. When power is defined so extremely, it becomes rather easy to claim that such power is curbed in the contemporary United States. The pluralists can say that Mills has conjured up a bogeyman to explain his own failure to realize his will. This is indeed what has been done in review after review of Mills' writings.

* * *

But is Mills' definition the only suitable one here? If it is, then the pluralists have won the debate. But if there is a way to designate an irresponsible elite without giving it omnipotence, then the debate may be recast at least.

* * *

...Perlo ... draws interesting connections between the largest industrial corporations and the defense economy, finding that defense accounts for 12 percent of the profits of the 25 largest firms.[4] He adds the factor of foreign investment as one which creates a further propensity in favor of a large defense system, and he calculates that military business and foreign investments combined total 40 percent of the aggregate profits among the top 25. He draws deeper connections between companies and the major financial groups controlling their assets.

This kind of analysis begins to reveal important disunities within the business community. For instance, it can be seen that the Rockefellers are increasing their direct military investments while maintaining their largest foreign holdings in extremely volatile Middle Eastern and Latin American companies. The Morgans are involved in domestic industries of a rather easy-to-convert type, and their main foreign holdings are in the "safer" European countries, although they too have "unsafe" mining interests in Latin America and Africa. The First National City Bank, while having large holdings in Latin American sugar and fruit, has a more technical relation to its associated firms than the stock-owner relation. The Mellons have sizeable oil holdings on Kuwait, but on the whole are less involved in defense than the other groups. The DuPonts, traditionally the major munitions makers, are "diversified" into the booming aerospace and plutonium industries, but their overseas holdings are heavily in Europe. Certain other groups with financial holdings, such as Young and Eaton interests in Cleveland, have almost no profit stake in defense or foreign investments. On the other hand, some of the new wealth in Los Angeles is deeply committed to the aerospace industry.

Perlo makes several differentiations of this sort, including the use of foreign-policy statements by leading industrial groups. But he does not have a way to predict under what conditions a given company would actively support economic shifts away from the arms race. These and other gaps, however, are not nearly as grave as his lack of analysis of other components of the military-industrial complex. There is no attempt to include politicians, military groups and other forces in a "map" of the military-industrial complex which Perlo believes exists. This may be partly because of the book's intent, which is to document profiteering by arms contractors, but for whatever reason, the book is not theoretically edifying about the question we are posing. Nor does it refute the pluralist case. In fact, it contains just the kind of evidence that pluralist arguments currently employ to demonstrate the absence of a monolith.*

REVISING THE CRITERIA FOR INFERRING POWER

After finding fault with so many books and divergent viewpoints, the most obvious conclusion is that current social theory is currently deficient in its explanation of power. We concur with one of Mills' severest critics, Daniel Bell, who at least agrees with Mills that most current analysis concentrates on the "intermediate sectors," e.g., parties, interest groups, formal structures, without attempting to view the underlying system of "renewable power independent of any momentary group of actors."[5] However, we have indicated that the only formidable analysis of the underlying system of renewable power, that of Mills, has profound shortcomings because of its definition of power. Therefore, before we can offer an answer of our own to the question, "Is there a military-industrial complex which blocks peace?", it is imperative to return to the question of power itself in American society.

We have agreed essentially with the pluralist claim that ruling-group models do not "fit" the American structure. We have classified Mills' model as that of a ruling-group because of his Weberian definition of power, but we have noted also that Mills successfully went beyond two traps common to elite theories, *viz.*, that the elite is total in the scope of its decisions, and that the elite is a coordinated monolith.

But we perhaps have not stressed sufficiently that the alternative case for pluralism is inadequate in its claim to describe the historical dynamics of American society. The point of our dissent from pluralism is over the doctrine of "counter-vailing power." This is the modern version of Adam Smith's economics and of the Madisonian or Federalism theory of checks-and-balances, adapted to the new circumstances of large-scale organizations. Its evidence is composed of self-serving incidents and a faith in semi-mystical resources. . . .

To take the more immediate example of the military sphere, the pluralist claim is that the military is subordinate to broader, civilian interests. The first problem with the statement is the ambiguity of "civilian." Is it clear that military men are more "militaristic" than civilian men? To say so would be to deny the increasing trend of "white-collar militarism." The top strategists in the Department of Defense, the Central Intelligence Agency and the key advisory positions often are Ph.D.'s. In fact, "civilians" including McGeorge Bundy, Robert Kennedy, James Rostow and Robert McNamara are mainly responsible for the development of the only remaining "heroic" form of combat:

---

*This article has been revised in Marc Pilisuk's *International Conflict and Public Policy*, in press (Prentice-Hall). The revised article discusses more compelling evidence cited in Seymour Melman's *Pentagon Capitalism* (1970), Richard Barnett's *The Economy of Death* (1969), and William Domhoff's data on ruling elites.

counter-insurgency operations in the jungles of the underdeveloped countries. If "militarism" has permeated this deeply into the "civilian" sphere, then the distinction between the terms becomes largely nominal.

. . . The intrusion of civilian professors into the military arena has been most apparent in more than 300 universities and non-profit research institutions which supply personnel to and rely upon contracts from the Department of Defense. About half of these centers were created to do specialized strategic research. One of these, the RAND Corporation, was set up by Douglas Aviation and the Air Force to give "prestige type support for favored Air Force proposals."[6] When RAND strategy experts Wohlstetter and Dinerstein discovered a mythical "missile gap" and an equally unreal preemptive war strategy in Soviet post-Sputnik policy, they paved the way for the greatest military escalation of the cold war era, the missile race.

The civilian strategists have frequently retained an exasperating measure of autonomy from the services which support them. . . . That the civilian and military planners of military policy sometimes differ does not detract from the argument. What must be stressed is that the apparent flourishing of such civilian agencies as RAND (it earned over 20 million dollars in 1962 with all the earnings going into expansion and has already spawned the nonprofit System Development Corporation with annual earnings exceeding 50 million dollars) is no reflection of countervailing power. The doctrine of controlled response under which the RS 70 fell was one which served the general aspirations of each of the separate services; of the Polaris and Minuteman stabile deterrent factions, of the brushfire or limited war proponents, guerilla war and paramilitary operations advocates, and of the counterforce adherents. It is a doctrine of versatility intended to leave the widest range of military options for retaliation and escalation in U.S. hands. It can hardly be claimed as victory against military thought. The fighting may have been intense but the area of consensus between military and civilian factions was great.

CONSENSUS

All that countervailing power refers to is the relationship between groups who fundamentally accept "the American system" but who compete for advantages within it. The corporate executive wants higher profits, the laborer a higher wage. The President wants the final word on military strategies, the Chairman of the Joint Chiefs does not trust him with it, Boeing wants the contract, but General Dynamics is closer at the time to the Navy Secretary and the President, and so on. What is prevented by countervailing forces is the dominance of society by a group or clique or a party. But this process suggests a profoundly important point; that *the constant pattern in American society is the rise and fall of temporarily-irresponsible groups.* By temporary we mean that, outside of the largest industrial conglomerates, the groups which wield significant power to influence policy decisions are not guaranteed stability. By irresponsible we mean that there are many activities within their scope which are essentially unaccountable in the democratic process. These groups are too uneven to be described with the shorthand term "class." Their personnel have many different characteristics (compare IBM executives and the Southern Dixiecrats) and their needs as groups are different enough to cause endless fights as, for example, small vs. big business. No one group or coalition of several groups can tyrannize the rest as it demonstrated, for example, in the changing status of the major financial groups, particularly the fast-rising Bank of America which has been built from the financial needs of the previously-neglected small consumer.

However, it is clear that these groups exist within consensus relationships of a more general and durable kind than their conflict relationships. This is true, first of all, of their social characteristics. . . . [D]ata from Suzanne Keller's compilation of military, economic, political and diplomatic elite survey materials in *Beyond the Ruling Class* (1963) and from an exhaustive study of American elites contained in Warner, et al., *The American Federal Executive* (1963) . . . suggest an educated elite with an emphasis upon Protestant and business-oriented origins. Moreover, the data suggest inbreeding with business orientation in backgrounds likely to have been at least maintained, if not augmented, through marriage. The consistencies suggest orientations not unlike those which are to be found in examination of editorial content of major business newspapers and weeklies and in more directly sampled assessments of elite opinions.

The second evidence of consensus relationships, besides attitude and background data indicating a pro-business sympathy, would come from an examination of the *practice* of decision making. By analysis of such actual behavior we can understand which consensus attitudes are reflected in decision-making. Here, in retrospect, it is possible to discover the values and assumptions which are defended recurrently. This is at least a rough means of finding the boundaries of consensus relations. Often these boundaries are invisible because of the very infrequency with which they are tested. What are visible most of the time are the parameters of conflict relationships among different groups. These conflict relationships constitute the ingredients of experience which give individuals or groups their uniqueness and varieties, while the consensus relations constitute the common underpinnings of behavior. The tendency in social science has been to study decision-making in order to study group differences; we need to study decision-making also to understand group commonalities.

Were such studies done, our hypothesis would be that certain "core beliefs" are continuously unquestioned. One of these, undoubtedly, would be that efficacy is preferable to principle in foreign affairs. In practice, this means that violence is preferable to non-violence as a means of defense. A second is that private property is preferable to collective property. A third assumption is that the particular form of constitutional government which is practiced within the

United States is preferable to any other system of government. We refer to the preferred mode as limited parliamentary democracy, a system in which institutionalized forms of direct representation are carefully retained but with fundamental limitations placed upon the prerogatives of governing. Specifically included among the areas of limitation are many matters encroaching upon corporation property and state hegemony. While adherence to this form of government is conceivably the strongest of the domestic "core values," at least among business elites, it is probably the least strongly held of the three on the international scene. American relations with, and assistance for, authoritarian and semi-feudal regimes occurs exactly in those areas where the recipient regime is evaluated primarily upon the two former assumptions and given rather extensive leeway on the latter one.

The implications of these "core beliefs" for the social system are immense, for they justify the maintenance of our largest institutional structures: the military, the corporate economy, and a system of partisan politics which protects the concept of limited democracy. These institutions, in turn, may be seen as current agencies of the more basic social structure. The "renewable basis of power" in America at the present time underlies those institutional orders linked in consensus relationships: military defense of private property and parliamentary democracy. These institutional orders are not permanently secure, by definition. Their maintenance involves a continuous coping with new conditions, such as technological innovation and with the inherent instabilities of a social structure which arbitrarily classifies persons by role, status, access to resources, and power. The myriad groups composing these orders are even less secure because of their weak ability to command "coping resources," e.g., the service branches are less stable than the institution of the military, particular companies are less stable than the institutions of corporate property, political parties are less stable than the institution of parliamentary government.

In the United States there is no ruling group. Nor is there any easily discernible ruling institutional order, so meshed have the separate sources of elite power become. But there is a social structure which is organized to create and protect power centers with only partial accountability. In this definition of power we are avoiding the Weber-Mills meaning of *omnipotence* and the contrary pluralist definition of power as consistently *diffuse*. We are describing the current system as one of overall "minimal accountability" and "minimal consent." We mean that the role of democratic review, based on genuine popular consent, is made marginal and reactive. Elite groups are minimally accountable to publics and have a substantial, though by no means maximum, freedom to shape popular attitudes. The reverse of our system would be one in which democratic participation would be the orienting demand around which the social structure is organized.

Some will counter this case by saying that we are measuring "reality" against an "ideal," a technique which permits the conclusion that the social structure is undemocratic according to its distance from our utopian values. This is a convenient apology for the present system, of course. We think it possible, at least in theory, to develop measures of the undemocratic in democratic conditions, and place given social structures along a continuum. These measures, in rough form, might include such variables as economic security, education, legal guarantees, access to information, and participatory control over systems of economy, government, and jurisprudence.

The reasons for our concern with democratic process in an article questioning the power of a purported military-industrial complex are twofold. First, just as scientific method both legitimizes and promotes change in the world of knowledge, democratic method legitimizes and promotes change in the world of social institutions. Every society, regardless of how democratic, protects its core institutions in a web of widely shared values. But if the core institutions should be dictated by the requisites of military preparedness, then restrictions on the democratic process, i.e., restrictions in either mass opinion exchange (as by voluntary or imposed news management) or in decision-making bodies (as by selection of participants in a manner guaranteeing exclusion of certain positions), then such restrictions would be critical obstacles to peace.

Second, certain elements of democratic process are inimical to features of military oriented society, and the absence of these elements offers one type of evidence for a military-industrial complex even in the absence of a ruling elite. Secretary of Defense Robert McNamara made the point amply clear in his testimony in 1961 before the Senate Armed Services Committee:

Why should we tell Russia that the Zeus development may not be satisfactory? What we ought to be saying is that we have the most perfect anti-ICBM system that the human mind will ever devise. Instead the public domain is already full of statements that the Zeus may not be satisfactory, that it has deficiencies. I think it is absurd to release that level of information. (Military Procurement Authorization Fiscal Year 1962).

Under subsequent questioning McNamara attempted to clarify his statement that he only wished to delude Russian, not American, citizens about U.S. might. Just how this might be done was not explained.

A long established tradition exists for "executive privilege" which permits the President to refuse to release information when, in his opinion, it would be damaging to the national interest. Under modern conditions responsibility for handling information of a strategic nature is shared among military, industrial, and executive agencies. The discretion regarding when to withhold what information must also be shared. Moreover, the existence of a perpetual danger makes the justification "in this time of national crisis," suitable to every occasion in which secrecy must be justified. McNamara's statement cited above referred not to a crisis in Cuba or Viet Nam but rather to the perpetual state of cold war crisis. And since the decision about what is to be released and when, is subject to just such management the media became dependent upon the agencies for timely leaks and major stories. This not only adds an aura of omniscience to the agencies, but gives these same agencies the power to reward "good" journalists and punish the critical ones.

The issues involved in the question of news management involve more than the elements of control available to the President, the State Department, the Department of Defense, the Central Intelligence Agency, the Atomic Energy Commission or any of the major prime contractors of defense contracts. Outright control of news flow is probably less pervasive then voluntary acquiescence to the objectives of these prominent institutions of our society. Nobody has to tell the wire services when to release a story on the bearded dictator of our hemisphere or the purported brutality of Ho Chi Minh. A frequent model, the personified devil image of an enemy, has become a press tradition. In addition to a sizeable quantity of radio and television programming and spot time purchased directly by the Pentagon, an amount of service, valued at $6 million by *Variety*, is donated annually by the networks and by public relations agencies for various military shows. Again, the pluralistic shell of an independent press or broadcasting media is left hollow by the absence of a countervailing social force of any significant power.[7]

... Several shared premises, unquestioned by any potent locus of institutionalized power were described as:

a. Efficacy is preferable to principle in foreign affairs (thus military means are chosen over non-violent means);
b. Private property is preferable to public property; and
c. Limited parliamentary democracy is preferable to any other system of government.

At issue is the question of whether an America protecting such assumptions can exist in a world of enduring peace. Three pre-conditions of enduring peace must be held up against these premises.

The first is that enduring peace will first require or will soon generate disarmament. Offset programs for the reallocation of the defense dollar require a degree of coordinated planning for the change inconsistent with the working assumption that "private property is preferable to public property" in a corporate economy....

If one pools available projections regarding the offset programs, especially regional and local offset programs, necessary to maintain economic well-being in the face of disarmament in this country, the programs will highlight two important features. One is the lag time in industrial conversion. The second is the need for coordination in the timing and spacing of programs. One cannot reinvest in new home building in an area which just been deserted by its major industry and left a ghost town. The short-term and long-term offset values of new hospitals and educational facilities will differ in the building and the utilization stages and regional offset programs have demonstrable interregional effects.[8] Plans requiring worker mobility on a large scale will require a central bank for storing job information and a smooth system for its dissemination. Such coordination will require a degree of centralization of controls beyond the realm which our assumption regarding primacy of private property would permit. . . . Gross intransigence has already been seen even on the contingency planning for non-defense work by single firms like Sperry Rand which have already been severely hurt by project cutbacks. And the prospect of contingency planning will not be warmly welcomed in the newer aeroframe industry (which is only 60% convertible to needs of a peace-time society).[9] Private planning, by an individual firm for its own future does occur, but, without coordinated plans, the time forecast for market conditions remains smaller than the lag time for major retooling. A lag time of from six to ten years would not be atypical before plans by a somewhat over-specialized defense contractor could result in retooling for production in a peace-time market. In the meantime, technological innovations, governmental fiscal or regulatory policies, shifts in consumer preferences, or the decisions by other firms to enter that same market could well make the market vanish. Moreover, the example of defense firms which have attempted even the smaller step toward diversification presents a picture which has not been entirely promising.[10] Indeed, one of several reasons for the failures in this endeavor has been that marketing skills necessary to compete in a private enterprise economy have been lost by those industrial giants who have been managing with a sales force of one or two retired generals to deal with the firm's only customer. Even if the path of successful conversion by some firms were to serve as the model for all individual attempts, the collective result would be poor. To avoid a financially disastrous glutting of limited markets some coordinated planning will be needed.

The intransigence regarding public or collaborative planning occurs against a backdrop of a soon-to-be increasing army of unemployed youth and aged, as well as regional armies of unemployed victims of automation. Whether one thinks of work in traditional job market terms or as anything worthwhile that a person can do with his life, work (and some means of livelihood) will have to be found for these people. There is much work to be done in community services, education, public health, and recreation, but this is people work, not product work. The lack of countervailing force prevents the major reallocation of human and economic resources from the sector defined as preferable by the most potent institutions of society. One point must be stressed. We are not saying that limited planning to cushion the impact of arms reduction is impossible. Indeed, it is going on and with the apparent blessing of the Department of Defense.[11] We are saying that the type of accommodation needed by a cutback of $9 billion in R & D and $16 billion in military procurement requires a type of preparation not consistent with the unchallenged assumptions.

Even the existence of facilities for coordinated planning does not, to be sure, guarantee the success of such planning. Bureaucratic institutions, designed as they may be for coordination and control, do set up internal resistance to the very coordination they seek to achieve. The mechanisms for handling these bureaucratic intransigencies usually rely upon such techniques as bringing participants into the process of formulating the decisions which will affect their own behavior. We can conceive of no system of coordinated conversion planning which could function without full and motivated cooperation from the major corporations, the larger unions, and representatives of smaller business and industry. Unfortunately, it is just as difficult to conceive of a system which would assure this necessary level of participation and cooperation. This same argument cuts deeper still when we speak of the millions of separate individuals in the "other America" whose lives would be increasingly "administered" with the type of centralized planning needed to offset a defense economy. The job assignment which requires moving, the vocational retraining program, the development of housing projects to meet minimal standards, educational enrichment programs, all of the programs which are conceived by middle-class white America for racially mixed low income groups, face the same difficulty in execution of plans. Without direct participation in the formulation of the programs, the target populations are less likely to participate in the programs and more likely to continue feelings of alienation from the social system which looks upon them as an unfortunate problem rather than as contributing members. Considering the need for active participation in real decisions, every step of coordinated planning carries with it the responsibility for an equal step in the direction of participatory democracy. This means that the voice of the unemployed urban worker may have to be heard, not only on city council meetings which discuss policy on the control of rats in his dwelling, but also on decisions about where a particular major corporation will be relocated and where the major resource allocations of the country will be invested. That such decision participation would run counter to the consensus on the items of limited parliamentary democracy and private property is exactly the point we wish to make.

Just as the theoretical offset plans can be traced to the sources of power with which they conflict, so too can the theoretical plans for international governing and peace-keeping operations be shown to conflict with the unquestioned beliefs. U.S. consent to international jurisdiction in the settlement of claims deriving from the nationalization of American overseas holdings or the removal of U.S. military installations is almost inconceivable. Moreover, the mode of American relations to less-developed countries is so much a part of the operations of those American institutions which base their existence upon interminable conflict with Communism that the contingency in which the U.S. might have to face the question of international jurisdiction in these areas seems unreal. Offers to mediate, with Cuba by Mexico, with North Viet Nam by

France, are bluntly rejected. Acceptance of such offers would have called into question not one but all three of the assumptions in the core system. International jurisdictional authority could institutionalize a means to call the beliefs into question. It is for this reason (but perhaps most directly because of our preference for forceful means) that American preoccupation in those negotiations regarding the extension of international control which have taken place, deal almost exclusively with controls in the area of weaponry and police operations and not at all in the areas of political or social justice.

The acceptance of complete international authority even in the area of weaponry poses certain inconsistencies with the preferred "core beliefs." Non-violent settlement of Asian-African area conflicts would be slow and ineffective in protecting American interests. The elimination, however, of military preparedness, both for projected crises and for their potential escalation, requires a faith in alternate means of resolution. The phasing of the American plan for general and complete disarmament is one which says in effect: prove that the alternatives are as efficient as our arms in protection of our interests and then we disarm. In the short term, however, the effectiveness of force always looks greater.

The state of world peace contains certain conditions imposed by the fact that people now compare themselves with persons who have more of the benefits of industrialization than they themselves. Such comparative reference groups serve to increase the demand for rapid change. While modern communications heighten the pressures imposed by such comparisons, the actual disparities revealed in comparison speak for violence. Population growth rates, often as high as three percent, promise population doubling within a single generation in countries least able to provide for their members. The absolute number of illiterates as well as the absolute number of persons starving is greater now than ever before in history. Foreign aid barely offsets the disparity between declining prices paid for the prime commodities exported by underdeveloped countries and rising prices paid for the finished products imported into these countries.[12] All schemes for tight centralized planning employed by these countries to accrue and disperse scarce capital by rational means are blocked by the unchallenged assumptions on private property and limited parliamentary democracy. A recent restatement of the principle came in the report of General Lucius Clay's committee on foreign aid. The report stated that the U.S. should not assist foreign governments "in projects establishing government owned industrial and commercial enterprises which compete with existing private endeavors." When Congressman Broomfield's amendment on foreign aid resulted in cancellation of a U.S. promise to India to build a steel mill in Bokaro, Broomfield stated the case succinctly: "The main issue is private enterprise vs. state socialism. . . ." Moreover, preference for forceful solutions assures that the capital now invested in preparedness will not be allocated in a gross way to the needs of underdeveloped countries. Instead, the manifest crises periodically erupting in violence justify further the need for reliance upon military preparedness.

We agree fully with an analysis by Lowi[13] distinguishing types of decisions for which elite-like forces seem to appear and hold control (redistributive) and other types in which pluralist powers battle for their respective interests (distributive). In the latter type the pie is large and the fights are over who gets how much. Factional strife within and among military industrial and political forces in our country are largely of this nature. In redistributive decisions, the factions coalesce, for the pie itself is threatened. We have been arguing that the transition to peace is a process of redistributive decision.

Is there, then, a military-industrial complex which prevents peace? The answer is inextricably imbedded into the mainstream of American institutions and mores. Our concept is not that American society contains a ruling military-industrial complex. It can accommodate a wide range of factional interests from those concerned with the production or utilization of a particular weapon to those enraptured with the mystique of optimal global strategies. It can accommodate those with rabid desires to advance toward the brink and into limitless intensification of the arms race. It can even accommodate those who wish either to prevent war or to limit the destructiveness of war through the gradual achievement of arms control and disarmament agreements. What it cannot accommodate is the type of radical departures needed to produce enduring peace.

NOTES

[1] C. Wright Mills, *The Power Elite* (New York: Oxford University Press, 1959).

[2] Horst Brand, "Disarmament and American Capitalism," *Dissent*, Summer 1962, pp. 236-51.

[3] Seymour Melman, ed., *A Strategy for American Security* (New York: Lee Offset Incorporated, 1963); and Amitai Etzioni, *The Hard Way to Peace* (New York: Collier, 1962).

[4] Victor Perlo, *Militarism and Industry* (New York: International Publishers, 1963).

[5] Daniel Bell, *The End of Ideology* (Glencoe, Ill.: Free Press, 1959).

[6] Saul Friedman, "The RAND Corporation and Our Policy Makers," *The Atlantic Monthly*, September 1963, pp. 61-68.

[7] John M. Swomley, Jr., "The Growing Power of the Military," *The Progressive*, January 1959.

[8] Thomas Reiner, "Spatial Criteria to Offset Military Cutbacks." Paper presented at the University of Chicago Peace Research Conference, November 18, 1964.

[9] James J. McDonagh and Steven M. Zimmerman, "A Program for Civilian Diversifications of the Airplane Industry," in *Convertibility of Space and Defense Resources to Civilian Needs.* (Subcommittee on Employment and Manpower, U.S. Senate, 88th Congress. [Washington, D.C.: U.S. Government Printing Office, 1964].

[10] H.E. Feron and R.C. Hook, Jr., "The Shift from Military to Industrial Markets," *Business Topics*, Winter 1964, pp. 43-52.

[11] Arthur Barber, "Some Industrial Aspects of Arms Control," *The Journal of Conflict Resolution* 7, 1963, pp. 491-95.

[12] David Horowitz, *World Economic Disparities: The Haves and the Have-Nots* (Santa Barbara, Calif.: Center for Study of Democratic Institutions, 1962).

[13] Theodore J. Lowi, "American Business, Public Policy, Case-Studies, and Political Theory," *World Politics* 16, July 1964, pp. 676-715.

Politics, Policy,
and
the Military-Industrial Complex

PATRICK M. MORGAN

For our purposes I think it is useful to offer this preliminary classification of the possible relationships between the purveyors of violence and civilian authorities.

1. Warrior societies—where the essential business of society is war and where military prowess is the basis for wealth, status, and political position. A good example might be ancient Sparta or the various barbarian hordes that often threatened and destroyed civilizations in the Mediterranean, the Middle East, and China.
2. Societies where the armed forces or individual military leaders use their control over the means of violence to take control of the government. Examples would include Rome during much of her imperial political history, the coup-ridden states of Latin America, etc.
3. Societies with civilian rule in which martial values, war and conquest, are emphasized. This is essentially a modern-day variant of (1) and includes such states as the three Axis powers of World War II.
4. Societies where the military, as a threat to take over the government, is a powerful interest group to be conciliated, which often means permitting military control over segments of the society or over a certain portion of the budget to remain relatively undisturbed. Many medieval kings, Chinese emperors, and Latin American Presidents have found themselves in this position.
5. Societies where the military has no observable ambition to control the government but is still a significant interest group. Any system with large standing military forces will at least fall in this category, and thus at a minimum the U.S. and U.S.S.R. may be placed here as would some other West and East European states.
6. Societies where the military is relatively uninfluential. One thinks of Switzerland and Austria as examples.

From Patrick M. Morgan, "Politics, Policy, and the Military-Industrial Complex," in Omer L. Carey, *The Military-Industrial Complex and U.S. Foreign Policy*. Reprinted by Permission of Washington State University Press © 1969. This article has been substantially abridged.

7. Societies without any real armed forces. Certain "primitive" societies of this type have existed, and some modern states such as Costa Rica would also be included.

This classification enables us to catalogue the various streams of criticism directed at the U.S. military-industrial complex. Those prey to Orwellian fears clearly expect that this country will eventually qualify for categoriess (1) or (3). The "it could happen here" theme of *Seven Days in May* would find us in danger of falling into category (2). Tom Hayden and many of his supporters see the U.S. as a "militarized society" that is already in category (3). . . . However, most critics would place the U.S. in (5) and would argue that the influence of the military establishment is not only substantial but also excessive. They range in viewpoint from those who wish to cut defense spending in favor of other programs and other values—say civil rights, poverty programs, urban redevelopment—to those of pacifist persuasions who wish to move the nation into category (7) and perceive almost any level of military spending as excessive.

In terms of what the critics have in mind the phrase "military-industrial" is misleading. In brief the idea is that a huge military establishment today inevitably breeds civilian appendages in industry and our universities to supply much of the research, technology, and sophisticated weaponry deemed essential for deterrence and defense. These civilian institutions and numerous citizens prosper on the manna of massive defense expenditures. This tendency in turn produces a political component—a corps of local, regional, and national politicians whose political self-interests now dictate promotion of or at least acquiescence in such spending on behalf of their constituents. The result is a complex: a large collection of workers, local businessmen, important industries, university officials, scientists, generals, and politicians who at the least constitute a massive interest or pressure group within the political process. Very often the space program is also included because many of these projects are military in nature or have military implications and because the technology, hardware, and program management skills involved are relevant for national defense operations. Thus there is a good deal of overlap in the lists of prime contractors for the Pentagon and NASA. Some critics also include the intelligence community in the complex. In part this inclusion is because of the CIA's covert military operations in the past, but primarily it is due to the fact that these critics tend to define the complex in terms of a "hard-line" orientation toward foreign policy problems in the government which they think has been shaped not only by military influence but also by the intelligence agencies which allegedly share this viewpoint.

Though I have perhaps overstated the case a bit, there clearly is something like a complex. Defense spending generates employment for some 7½ million persons directly, or 10.3 per cent of the total work force. Many of our largest corporations do a sizable amount of business with the Pentagon, though typically this is only a small fraction of their overall operations (the auto companies, for example, derive 2-5 per cent of their business from the Pentagon or NASA). In addition, a number of large corporations in the fields of aerospace, electronics, engines, etc. are heavily dependent on government contracts for from 60 per cent to all of their business. Disbursements from the Pentagon to colleges and universities have been running close to $400 million per year. Finally, there is the steady flow of funds to RAND, the Hudson Institute, the Institute for Defense Analysis, and other think-tanks.

In any area where a major base is to be closed or where a major employer has cut back operations for failure to secure defense contracts, civic leaders and local businessmen mobilize rapidly to try to secure a reversal of the harmful decisions. At the national level many of the strongest supporters of defense spending—Henry Jackson, Mendel Rivers, Richard Russell—are elected from areas that benefit heavily from these disbursements. The Senate and House Armed Services Committees contain many members elected from the first ten states on the list of Pentagon spending by state.

What helps sustain the image of a "complex" is the fact that a network of personal ties and related experiences helps link many of these elements together. Over 2000 ex-high ranking officers are employed in firms doing a significant amount of business with the Pentagon. Over seventy Congressmen are on active status in the reserves, and over sixty own stock in aerospace and related companies. Many staff members on Congressional Armed Services Committees formerly carried on similar or related work in the Pentagon. And there are frequent social contacts that supplement these ties.

Unfortunately, those who point with alarm often simply assume that the complex is a powerful political influence and let it go at that. They take it as given that a fat contract for a particular firm, involvement in Vietnam, or the decision to build the ABM demonstrates the political muscle of the complex. The evidence cited almost always has to do with the traditional tactics of pressure groups—campaign contributions, buttonholing Congressmen, public relations work, and the like. But if this is all that can be offered then the dangers posed by the complex become primarily a function of its size, and it becomes the burden of the critic to demonstrate that defense spending could be drastically cut without damage to national security. I think it is not necessary to go in this direction, but that it is possible to lay some preliminary groundwork for attempts to assess the power and influence of the complex by a different approach.

The starting point must be an attempt to distinguish the set of major political decisions primarily responsible for bringing into being a continuously high rate of defense spending from all the lesser legislative and administrative decisions about when, where, and how to spend the money. Examples of the former would be the decision to enter the Korean War, adoption of what is often referred to as the McNamara Doctrine, the decision to go to the moon in this decade, the series of decisions that drew the U.S. militarily into Vietnam, and two administrations' commitments to a thin ABM system. The latter then include the decisions on the precise levels of spending each year, on weapons systems and mixes, on contracts, on the location of bases, etc.

I strongly suspect that a detailed analysis of the fundamental decisions—those which required new higher levels of military and related spending to be implemented—would not uncover any undue level of military-industrial influence within the government. A recent careful study of the Korean decision indicates that the political officials who dominated the process by which massive intervention was selected from among the possible alternatives were moved by such considerations as the need to establish and maintain the credibility of American commitments and the alleged lessons of recent history about the dangers of unresisted aggression.[1]

It is unlikely that adoption of the McNamara Doctrine would be found to be the result of pressures from any complex for increased defense spending. Rather, it was the culmination of a long period in which scientists, intellectuals, and leading Democrats had openly expressed dismay over the doctrine of Massive Retaliation and the state of the nation's defenses. Kennedy successfully campaigned on a platform stressing missile and other security gaps in our defense posture, which rejected policies instituted originally by ex-General Eisenhower and Admiral Arthur Radford. Much of the new defense orientation had to be brought in and imposed on the reluctant military chiefs who often found only the increased spending to their liking.

The decision to embark on a race to the moon, I think, can best be viewed as a glamor project very much in keeping with the Alliance for Progress, the Peace Corps, and similar decisions by an administration intent on giving itself and the nation a dynamic, imaginative, progressive image. It promised substantial payoffs in terms of international prestige and domestic morale, and it appealed to the technological, problem-solving orientation of American culture which attracts us to vast projects of an essentially engineering nature.

The decisions concerning Vietnam also cannot be described as initiated or controlled by the complex. The key civilian officials outside the Pentagon in both the Kennedy and Johnson Administrations, including the two Presidents, held views on the nature of American national interests and the challenges to those interests in the 1960s that ultimately played the decisive role. Even General Shoup can go no farther than to refer to military "encouragement" as the "Johnson Administration hastened" into Vietnam. Military influence has been primarily concerned with the conduct of the war, and even there civilian officials have injected themselves into such decisions as the selection of bombing targets, and have often rejected military requests for massive increases in U.S. forces and a greater escalation of the level of violence.

I think the ABM decisions may ultimately be seen in much the same light. For example, I think the politics of Mr Nixon's decision can be most persuasively explained by the following tentative interpretation. The new President made several initial moves which eventually severely curtailed his freedom of action.

First, he selected as Secretary of Defense a man already known to be in favor of the ABM who would inevitably recommend one when the time came. An early Nixon decision against ABM would then have cut the ground from under a key cabinet member by rejecting his judgment, and it would have occurred just after a Nixon television spectacular designed to assure the nation that he and we could have every confidence in each member of the cabinet. Columnists, reporters, and editorialists would have had a field day.

He then compounded the error by forcing himself into an early decision with the setting of a deadline. That left no room for "long and careful restudy of the problem," no time for the procrastination Presidents find useful on difficult decisions until a bit of coalition-building can take place that will see them through the Congress. And it gave ABM opponents every incentive to do a little coalition-building of their own. Suddenly the anti-ABM campaign was in full swing, headed by important and, in some cases, ambitious Democrats and in the glare of nationwide publicity. Now no minority President, particularly one with a minority party in Congress, and no President facing a host of would-be-Presidents in the Senate, can afford to lose his first major test of strength. A Nixon decision against ABM whether for strategic, diplomatic, budgetary, or whatever reasons would inevitably have been interpreted instead as a Presidential retreat in the face of Congressional opposition, as a political defeat of the first order. The spectacle of an administration on the run would have increased the prospects for endless Presidential haggling with a Congress controlled by the opposition and thus a steady erosion of Nixon's political position. In other words, political considerations very different from those that would arise out of complex-related pressures may well have left the President with very little choice other than to propose the Safeguard System.

In much the same way it is possible to interpret President Johnson's decision to build the Sentinel System as a response to political pressures other than any that may have been initiated by the complex. At the time the decision was announced several analysts suggested that it was designed to remove any "ABM-gap" and "security gap" ammunition from Republican guns for the upcoming campaign, that the ABM was aimed more at the Republicans than the Chinese.

If we turn, necessarily briefly, to the decisions on "when, where, and how" to spend the money we would be on much better grounds for assuming that something in the way of "excessive" political influence by a military-industrial complex is involved. Most of the examples cited by critics refer to these kinds of decisions. Defense contractors engage in constant lobbying, provide favors for Congressmen and jobs for ex-Pentagon officials. In return they often obtain practically risk-free contracts, freedom from the strictures of competitive bidding, use of government property, and frequent opportunities for over-charging on numerous items. Pentagon officials also lobby heavily in Congress and have numerous favors to dispense. They are in turn blessed with uniquely favorable appropriations hearings, a sympathetic Congressional ear for many a pet service project, and opportunities to continue programs that have long since outlived their usefulness. Congressmen who are influential in determining levels of military spending often secure large chunks of the appropriations for their states and districts. They also get to announce Pentagon contracts which will provide new business for their particular areas.

What we are dealing with here is something like the pork barrel bills writ large. Decisions already made will cause very large sums to be spent, and the result is a race for the gravy. Most critics assume that this race, and the political influence wielded for success in it, is an accurate reflection of the process by which the gravy was made available in the first place. As far as I can determine this is not really true. In casting about for historical analogies I am struck by the similarity between this situation and the building of the railroads in this country—in which decisions made on other considerations were converted into magnificent opportunities for personal and corporate profit in the guise of advancing the national interest.

Two additional qualifications must be mentioned. First, it is not easy to demonstrate that the entire process by which weapons and other equipment are acquired is dominated by the influence of special interests. For example, a recent study of the TFX decision concluded that is was impossible to demonstrate that undue political influence determined the selection of General Dynamics over Boeing despite stringent efforts to prove this by Congressional opponents of McNamara's decision.[2]

Second, the mere existence of lobbying, personal contacts, supersalesmanship by companies and pressures from local officials is not enough to support the claim that we are in the grip of an overly powerful complex of interests. To a considerable extent such activities are the stuff of politics, part of the process by which money gets spent on schools, food stamps, or health and through which commerce, drugs, or the stock market are regulated. Thus the most persuasive argument of the critics is not that these activities are harmful by their very existence, but that they are inherently dangerous in the area of national defense because of the size and number of the interests involved. Unfortunately this is only an assumption, and its persuasiveness has tended to inhibit careful analysis to determine if it is true.

NOTES

[1] Glenn Paige, *The Korean Decision* (New York: Free Press, 1968).
[2] Robert J. Art, *The TFX Decision* (Boston: Little Brown, 1968). pp. 3-8.

The Sad State of State

STEWART ALSOP

... Vietnam ... provides a striking example of the urge of all Washington departments and agencies to shoulder the State Department aside and to get into the foreign policy act. The little country, as this is written, is crawling with representatives of at least three dozen Washington departments, bureaus, and agencies.

To cite one specific example, the provincial town of Mytho in the Mekong Delta in 1964 harbored precisely one representative of the American civilian bureaucracy—a very young and very junior State Department man, whose office was his jeep. A couple of years later, there were more than twenty American civilians from half a dozen departments and agencies in the place—more than three times the number of French civilian officials in Mytho when the colonial era was in full flower. They had all the appurtenances of the American official abroad—offices, vehicles, villas, and organization charts to establish the pecking order.

"One of the things that truly startled me when I first came here," Under Secretary Katzenbach has said, "was to learn that no less than 80 percent of the people officially representing the United States overseas were working for agencies other than the Department of State."

Before the war the United States was actually represented in foreign lands by the State Department, but after the war "abroad" became bureaucratically fashionable, and every department bureau, and agency wanted to get into the act. Moreover, the various MAAG (Military Advisory Assistance Groups) and other military missions abroad helped to solve one of the oldest of military problems: what to do with the military when they have no war to fight.

A "slot" could always be found for Colonel So-and-so or Commander Such-and-such in an MAAG or as an attaché in an embassy. The trouble was, of course—and still is—that a great many countries all over the world were soon fairly pullulating with Americans in uniform, conspicuous in their large new American cars. This has been very helpful to the Communist propagandists, whose favorite theme is "American neocolonialism."

The military are the most conspicuous members of American missions abroad. But they need never be lonely. As Briggs writes: "In addition to the propaganda, handout, and skulduggery agencies, all abundantly overstaffed, practically every executive department in Washington has permanent or temporary representation abroad." The representatives abroad, in order to prove their usefulness, keep up a massive correspondence, mostly by cable, with the home office, while the home office keeps them happy and busy with queries like the one about the bats and noxious birds. It is surprising that any serious diplomatic work ever gets done at all.

The State Department could hardly have stemmed entirely the urge of its bureaucratic rivals to get into the foreign policy act. The department has always been a weak sister politically—it has no natural political constituency in the United States, and it thus swings less weight on Capitol Hill than, say, the Civil Aeronautics Bureau or the Bureau of Indian Affairs. Moreover, with the exception of Christian Herter, the postwar Secretaries of State have had very little interest in the mechanics of the conduct of foreign policy.

The late John Foster Dulles was especially prone to regard the entire State Department much as the Roman generals regarded the *impedimenta* of wives, prostitutes, and traders who accompanied their armies on the march—as unavoidable but annoying excess baggage. Once, while attending a Pan-American meeting of foreign ministers in Brazil, Dulles made an important decision which deeply involved American policy in Europe. An aide suggested that the decision be conveyed to the appropriate regional desks of the State Department in Washington.

"Why?" Dulles inquired in mild surprise. "I'm here.'"

Dulles regarded the whole business of administering the State Department, or defending its interests in Washington's unending imperial wars of the bureaucracy, as no business at all of his, and in varying degrees other Secretaries of State have adopted a similar attitude. One result is that, in the post-war years, other bureaucratic empires, from the Pentagon and the CIA to the Agriculture or Treasury Departments, have forced on the beleaguered State Department a series of nonaggression treaties staking out their role in the conduct of foreign policy.

An American embassy abroad is thus festooned with bureaucrats from outside the State Department, ranging from the "spooks" of the CIA to specialists in shrimp production from the Fish and Wildlife Service. Under the circumstances, the ambassador, the official representative of the President of the United States, has no easy task remaining the master in his own house, since most of these supernumeraries look to their own agencies or departments for orders and promotions.

Soon after he became President, John F. Kennedy wrote a letter to each American ambassador firmly instructing him to be chief of his own mission henceforth, in fact as well as name. Under this dispensation all communication with Washington was to be routed through the ambassador's office, and to be approved by him. Thus the practice of completely bypassing the chief of mission, to which the CIA and the military had been particularly prone, was supposedly ended. This Kennedy order did help to make an ambassador, theoretically at least, *primus inter pares*. But the effectiveness with which an ambassador rides herd on his "country team" depends very heavily still on his personality. To be master in his own house he must be willing to be cordially detested by a lot of the people he sees every day.

In 1954, in compliance with the recommendations of a distinguished committee appointed by President Eisenhower and headed by Dr. Henry Wriston, the State Department endured the most disastrous in an unending series of "reforms" and "reorganizations." About 2,400 State Department employees of one sort or another—civil servants, administrators, specialists, and so on, most of whom had never served abroad and had little or no experience in diplomacy—were made Foreign Service Officers as by the touch of a magic wand. The size of the Foreign Service was thus tripled, from around 1,200 people pre-Wriston to around 3,600 today.

This "democratization" of the Foreign Service had a shattering effect on the morale of the service, already harried by the attacks of Joseph R. McCarthy. In the McCarthy era, a Foreign Service Officer had to endure being widely regarded as a homosexual, or a traitor, or quite possibly a homosexual traitor.

To the beleaguered members of the Foreign Service, there was nothing even faintly amusing about the McCarthy era. With some lapses which he later regretted, Secretary of State Dean Acheson ("the red Dean," McCarthy called him) stood up bravely to the attack. John Foster Dulles, by contrast, unwisely supposed that McCarthy could be appeased, and as a result some very able Foreign Service Officers were cast to the wolves. The most conspicuous was John Davies, a brilliant Far Eastern specialist, who was dismissed and denied his pension rights in 1954. His chief sin lay in having expressed views on China policy sharply at variance with those of Republican doctrine, in those days of the "unleashing" of Chiang Kai-shek.

The sacrifice of Davies, and other similar surrenders to McCarthyism, certainly did not improve morale. At the time, in a courageous letter of protest to Charles Saltzman, the Eisenhower-appointed Under Secretary of State for Administration, veteran FSO Robert Joyce summed up sentiment in the Foreign Service:

> The feeling is widespread in the Foreign Service that Davies was not a loyalty or security risk or any kind of risk other than a public relations risk. . . . I need not add that there is a deep feeling of revulsion at the fact that Davies was summarily dismissed without a pension at the age of forty-seven and with a wife and four young children.

In those days, the Foreign Service regarded itself as a *corps d'élite*, and the external attack by McCarthy and his fellow Neanderthals had a unifying internal effect, as Joyce's indignant letter suggests. The FSOs who survived McCarthy's attacks and Dulles' too-frequent surrenders to McCarthy had a sense of having been through the fire together. Wrisonization destroyed the *esprit de corps*—the *esprit* of a *corps* can hardly survive if the size of the *corps* is arbitrarily tripled overnight. Many of the Wristonees turned out to be able people, and even the old-guard FSOs agree that an occasional transfusion of new blood into the Foreign Service is badly needed. But this was more a drowning than a transfusion, and almost everyone now agrees that the net result was badly to demoralize the morale of the service.

With the size of the Foreign Service tripled overnight, there were not enough good jobs to go round. This is truer today than ever. Many able Foreign Service Officers and Wristonees who were young men at the time of Wristonization are now reaching the age when they ought to become chiefs of mission—or else mark down their life story as a failure.

STATE DEPARTMENT HIERARCHY

The number one and number two men are of course the Secretary and Under Secretary. Number three is the Under Secretary of State for Political Affairs; number four, the Deputy Under Secretary for Administration; and number five, the Deputy Under Secretary for Political Affairs.

... The Policy Planning Council is still officially a part of the top hierarchy. When it was headed by George Kennan, and later by Paul Nitze (it was then called the Policy Planning Staff), it was the central policy-making organ of the American Government. Kennan kept wanting to retire to an ivory tower (or rather to his farm in Pennyslvania) to contemplate his navel and think large thoughts about foreign policy, but because he was so brilliantly able, he kept being dragged back into the day-to-day business of dealing with crises. He played a key role in all the major decisions of the late nineteen-forties, and after Nitze took over from him on New Year's Day, 1950, Nitze also played a key role, notably in planning and arranging the secret negotiations which preceded the Korean settlement.

Since those days, the Policy Planning Council has been gently subsiding into obscurity. John Foster Dulles consulted policy planners Robert Bowie and Gerard Smith quite often, but he regarded policy planning as exclusively his function. Under Dean Rusk, the Council has become more moribund than ever before.

At the next hierarchical level, there are five "functional" bureaus (Economic Affairs, for example, and Education and Cultural Affairs) and five geographic bureaus . . . [all headed by Assistant Secretaries] .

The system of "clearances and concurrences" shares with the committee system the responsibility for the enormous amount of waste motion in the process of foreign policy making. In theory, of course, the system makes sense.

Its purpose is to let the right hand know what the left hand is doing. A policy on British Guiana that seems fine to the Bureau of Inter-American Affairs may seem perfectly horrible to the Bureau of European Affairs. And the Pentagon, the CIA, perhaps even Treasury and Commerce, have a legitimate interest in foreign policy decisions. The trouble is that the whole system has gotten out of hand.

One reason is that there are too many people in the State Department. Everyone who has ever had any experience at all with the department agrees on that point. Hans Morgenthau, George Kennan, and Ellis Briggs have all suggested that the department could operate more efficiently with half as many people, while Dean Acheson, William Atwood and others have proposed a more modest cutback of about a quarter of the staff.

The trouble is not only that there are too many people in the State Department; there are too many *able* people. A bureaucracy hums along happily enough if it consists very largely of drones, content to shuffle their papers and collect their pay checks. But the presence of large numbers of intelligent and able people produces near-chaos. An able man wants to earn his salary, and when something important is afoot, he wants to get into the act. Getting into the act means attending the meetings of the committees and "task forces" (another, more activist-sounding name for committees) dealing with the major crises of the moment.

These committees thus keep getting bigger and bigger. To cite one example, in the early Kennedy period, a "task force" assigned to dealing with the Berlin crisis started with a half-dozen men, and grew as the crisis deepened to more than sixty. Because all the able and intelligent people attending them want to have their say, instead of sitting dumbly on the sidelines, the meetings become more and more interminable.

*   *   *

The high level of intelligence helps to account for the fact that morale in the Service has probably never been lower—not even in the McCarthy days. An intelligent man well into middle age, or approaching it, hates to spend most of his time in waste motion. "The system" ensures that an FSO—especially if he is on Washington duty—does just that. There are FSOs who share the despair of George Kennan, who wrote in the nineteen-fifties that "only some form of catastrophe—natural disaster, financial collapse, or the atomic bomb—could dismantle [the system] or reduce it to healthier proportions."

Secretary of State Dean Rusk's approach to the business of running the State Department has much in common with that of John Foster Dulles, who at first wanted to remove himself physically from the department by taking an office in the White House. Rusk's idea was that he should occupy himself with policy matters, while his Under Secretary ran the department.

His first Under Secretary, Chester Bowles, actually performed a useful job in shaking up the department, helping to restore the authority of ambassadors over their "country team," and appointing able younger men to top positions. But then Bowles committed the sin of being right about the Bay of Pigs disaster while almost everybody else (including President Kennedy) was wrong; and the more unforgivable sin of making widely known the fact that he had been right. Moreover, day-to-day administration was by no means Bowles' forte. After Bowles was edged out, his successor, George Ball, tried his hand at running the department, and also performed usefully for a while. But Ball is an able and articulate man with strong convictions, and as time went by he found the job of running the department increasingly unfascinating. Thus a vacuum was created, into which Crockett and the administrators deftly moved.

When Ball was replaced by former Attorney General Nicholas deB. Katzenbach, Katzenbach was predictably appalled by his first exposure to "the system." He was baffled by the office symbols which are essential to communication by anyone caught up within its toils: "For a while I confused S slant S (S/S) with S slant S dash S (S/S-S) until I discovered that one was on one side of the hall and the other one on the other. But I confess I remain intrigued by S slant S dash EX (S/S-EX)." He was amazed that it required twenty-nine signatures to clear one routine dealing with the non-earth-shaking subject of milk exports.

Policy-making is, after all, the chief function of the Secretary of State and his alter ego, the Under Secretary. Foreign policy is so insanely complex a matter nowadays that a man deeply involved in the making of it has very little time left over to worry about who should be DCM (Deputy Chief of Mission) in Rangoon. Even so, it seems unlikely that the vacuum would have been so complete, or the triumph of the administrators so final, if Dean Rusk had been a different sort of man.

. . . Dean Rusk has played a passive role. It is interesting to compare his long reign in the State Department with Robert McNamara's long, now ended reign in the Department of Defense.

In his years in the Pentagon, McNamara basically altered both the strategic doctrines of the United States and the methods by which those doctrines are shaped and determined. Aside from his unwavering line on Vietnam, Dean Rusk has left behind him no memorial whose merits will be argued by future historians—no Marshall Plan, no NATO, not even a SEATO or an Eisenhower Doctrine. No important new departure in foreign policy is clearly identified with his name. As for "the system," the State Department's policy-making mechanism, it is what it was before Rusk became Secretary of State—except that it has become even more cumbersome.

Everybody who has been exposed to "the system" agrees that *something* had to be done about it, that somehow the State Department has got to find a way to respond less slowly and bureaucratically to the enormous challenges which confront this country abroad. Most of those who have been exposed to the system agree at least on the broad outlines of what needs to be done.

Ex-Ambassador Attwood, in an article in the *Atlantic Monthly*, came up with conclusions with which few would quarrel:

> Revitalizing State would be difficult, but it would not be impossible under a reform-minded Secretary with full White House backing and a sympathetic Congress. The recommendations I have made . . . can be summarized as follows:
>
> 1. Get rid of deadwood and trim overstaffed posts and bureaus.
> 2. Promote FSOs on merit rather than seniority.
> 3. Make salary scales comparable with those offered by private industry.
> 4. Minimize the production and distribution of paper.
> 5. Personalize (that is, decomputerize) personnel assignments.
> 6. Dismantle the AID bureaucracy, and put foreign economic assistance under the State Department.
> 7. Coordinate the activities of all federal agencies concerned with foreign affairs.

All these things certainly need to be done, though they would certainly take some doing. Another thing that needs very badly to be done, in this writer's opinion, is to return to the Foreign Service control over the Foreign Service. One of the Foreign Service's career ambassadors—a Foy Kohler, a Charles Bohlen—should be made directly responsible, under the Secretary of State, for running the Foreign Service. The administrators should be returned to the equivalent of pants-pressing—they should be sternly told that their job is to support the Foreign Service, not to run it.

For the pride and the prestige of the Foreign Service, which have been so badly eroded over the years, must be restored. The poor old Foreign Service has been regularly castigated as an "elite." It used to *be* an "elite," before Wristonization "democratized" it, and it was an elite that produced a great many men of very superior ability and great independence of thought—Robert Murphy, Charles Bohlen, George Kennan, Llewellyn Thompson, Foy Kohler. An "elite," after all, is a useful thing to have around—the word is defined in the dictionary as "the choice or best part, as of a body or class of persons." That rather accurately describes the kind of Foreign Service we need.

The Class Background
of the Foreign Service

JOHN ENSOR HARR

Probably no other professional group in the United States has as strong and persistent an image of being closely tied to particular social and regional origins as the FSO corps.

The idea that diplomatic careers are the preserve of the sons of the upper classes in the northeastern United States, mostly graduates of the Ivy League colleges, has its roots, of course, in historical fact. Warren Ilchman states that before the Rogers Act of 1924 combined the Diplomatic and Consular Services, the diplomats had very definite feelings of "social superiority" over the consuls. "The man who entered the Diplomatic Service, with very few exceptions, had private means of support. Flowing from this were a host of social prejudices."[1]

Since the wage scale was inadequate, private means were necessary. Doubtless an important attraction for men of private means to enter the Diplomatic Service was the cultural affinity of upper class Americans, particularly those on the eastern seaboard, for Europe. The profession of diplomacy had been developed and established in Europe, and Europe was the world center of diplomacy. American diplomats were inclined to feel that the world of the consul was "pedestrian." "While the diplomat did not avoid routine, he lived in a much more prestigious and exciting world. He met the 'best people' in each capital and was part of the social life of the *Corps Diplomatique*. Even in dreary Central American posts, he was still an honored part of the European colony."[2] Of the men who entered the Diplomatic Service between 1914 and 1922, Ilchman reports, more than half were born in the nine northeastern states. More than 70 percent attended residential private secondary schools, compared to almost the same percentage of consuls who attended public schools. A greater percentage of the diplomats had college degrees (85 percent to 69), and there was a "vast difference" in the colleges attended: "Harvard, Yale, and Princeton provided 63.8 percent of all diplomats, 32.4 percent attending the first alone."[3]

From John Ensor Harr, *The Professional Diplomat* (copyright © 1969 by Princeton University Press): pp. 171-188, minus all tables, save Table 21. Reprinted by permission. This chapter has been abridged, mainly through removal of most tabular material.

The process that Ilchman has called the "democratization" of the Foreign Service definitely began with the merger brought about by the Rogers Act, and the beginnings of salaries and allowances that made it possible for men without private income to contemplate diplomatic careers.

The reality has changed substantially, but the image of the diplomat as the effete easterner has persisted, for several probable reasons. Certainly one is social distance. The doctor and the lawyer are familiar figures to virtually every American, but the diplomat is not. The widespread antipathy for many decades in the American heartland toward foreign involvements undoubtedly has helped perpetuate the striped pants stereotype.

The elitist ideology of the FSO corps contributes to the perpetuation of the upper class image of the Service. Even though the goal since the Rogers Act has been an aristocracy of talent instead of birth, this has not entirely gotten through to the public, since the nature of the talent is not easily demonstrable as with the doctor and the lawyer; thereby credence has been given to the image of a privileged caste. And, even though the reality behind the image has changed, the issue of the "representativeness" of the FSO corps is alive today.

My purpose in this chapter is to examine the reality of the social origins and characteristics of FSOs (as determined in the 1966 "Survey of the Diplomatic Profession"—SDP) in comparison, where comparable data are available, to other groups—graduating college seniors, military leaders, civilian federal executives, business leaders, and the total U.S. population.[4]

PLACE OF BIRTH

. . . [D]espite the changes brought about by the Rogers Act and subsequent measures, the FSO corps is not nearly as representative of the regional breakdown of American population as civilian federal executives. Although the percentage born in the northeast declined from 53 percent before the Rogers Act to 43 or 44 percent in later periods, this is still far above the actual population. The FSO corps is underrepresented in the midwest, southwest, and the south, with the largest gap in the south. The military has a similar pattern, except that its concentration is in the south. Using Janowitz' 1950 sample of military leaders, it can be seen that only about half the proportion of military officers, as compared to FSOs, come from the northeast in contrast to considerably more than double the proportion from the south.[5]

*   *   *

FATHER'S OCCUPATION AND INCOME

The backgrounds of FSOs may still be largely concentrated in urban northeastern settings, but entrance is certainly not restricted to the sons of the affluent or even of the middle class. Perhaps the most telling proof of "democratization" is the striking pattern of family income, shown in Table 1 in comparison to the foreign service group in the NORC survey. The heavy concentration of the SDP respondents in the lower end of the income spectrum shows how decisive the shift has been since the pre-Rogers Act days when a man had to have some wealth to undertake a diplomatic career. Clearly the diplomatic profession, like other professions, has become an avenue of upward mobility for those from lower socio-economic strata, particularly in the case of lateral entrants. Using different categories, Janowitz shows a similar trend for Army officers.

TABLE 1

Family Income (percent)[6]

	NORC Foreign Service	SDP lateral entrants	SDP exam. entrants	Total SDP
Less than $5,000	17.0	45.7	29.5	35.4
5,000 to 7,499	23.5	24.1	22.1	22.8
7,500 to 9,999	12.7	12.7	12.2	12.5
10,000 to 14,999	13.6	8.5	17.6	14.3
15,000 to 19,000	8.6	3.8	2.9	3.2
20,000 and over	13.3	2.4	12.2	8.7
Not sure	11.4	2.8	3.8	3.1
Totals	100	100	100	100
Number	(327)	(212)	(375)	(587)

Despite the definite trend toward opening up the military and Foreign Service elites to all social strata, neither appears to be as open as business leadership. . . . The Warner and Abegglen survey of business leaders shows greater percentages of sons from two lower income groups—white collar and workingman—than either the military or the Foreign Service. The latter, however, shows 11 percent from a working-class background, compared to only 5 percent of the military officers. In keeping with the heavily urban background of FSOs, only 4 percent list their father's occupation as farmer. Lateral entrants show a much greater percentage than examination entrants from the "small business" background, and a slightly greater percentage from a working-class background. To account for the very large percentages of lateral entrants at the low end of the income spectrum, "small business" for the most part must have been very small.

PARENT'S EDUCATION

Here we . . . compare the SDP sample and the NORC college seniors by level of education of fathers and mothers. The distribution is remarkably close in the two samples, whether the educational level of fathers or of mothers is compared. The most striking result is the extraordinarily high educational level of mothers, higher than fathers in both groups if professional education is excluded.

The northeast has remained even more disproportionate as a place of education for FSOs than as a birthplace. Although the proportion of FSOs attending college in the northeast had declined over the years, it is still more than twice the proportion of population in the northeast.

* * *

. . . Still, the figures . . . are not surprising, given the fact that 44 percent of the FSOs were born in the northeast, and other considerations such as the prevalence of highly regarded graduate schools in the northeast and the traditions some of them have of providing candidates for the Foreign Service. Obviously young men from the midwest, south, and southwest leave their home regions to attend schools in the northeast, possibly because they believe the schools in that region will prepare them better for a Foreign Service career.

Writing of the period up to 1939, Ilchman points to the continued importance to the democratized Foreign Service of Harvard, Princeton, and Yale, which provided 63.8 percent of the members of the old Diplomatic Service. He reports that these three schools sent 36 percent of FSO recruits in 1926-30, 40 percent in 1931-35, and 26 percent in 1936-39. State universities provided 25 percent in 1936-39, up from the 9 percent to the Diplomatic Service.

The big three of the Ivy League are still very important recruitment sources for the Foreign Service, but proportionately less so than before World War II. In a five-year period, 1957 to 1962, Harvard, Princeton, and Yale provided only 15 percent of the newcomers to the FSO corps.

A final indication of the importance of Harvard, Princeton, and Yale is that of 72 degrees held by the officers in the top two grades of the Foreign Service in 1966—the seven Career Ambassadors and 52 career Ministers—30 were taken at these three schools.

RELIGIOUS AFFILIATIONS

Data on religious affiliations are not easy to obtain for comparative purposes. Unfortunately no trend data on religious affiliations of FSOs exist, but it is possible to compare the SDP sample to NORC's college seniors and to military leaders. As reported in the SDP, 68.7% of FSOs are Protestant, 17.8% are Roman Catholic, and 6.2% are Jewish.

Janowitz observes that the military elite historically has been overwhelmingly Protestant, but a trend toward greater representation is evident in the West Point class of 1961. If earlier data on FSOs were available, it is likely that a similar trend from a strongly Anglo-Saxon Protestant group to a more nearly representative one would be evident. As it is, Catholics are still slightly underrepresented in the Service.

The NORC data are interesting, in that less than half the proportion of Jews appears in the "Foreign Service" group as in the total sample, The proportion of Jews actually in the Foreign Service is considerably higher, but is largely composed of lateral entrants.

POLITICAL ORIENTATIONS

The comparison of political orientations of FSOs with those of military officers offers a marked contrast. Nearly 75 percent of FSOs are on the liberal side, choosing either "somewhat liberal" or "liberal" in self-rating their political orientations, while Army and Navy officers show very nearly that percentage on the conservative side, with Air Force officers at about 60 percent.

There are no significant variations among SDP subgroups on this question, with liberal sentiment well distributed by grades and method of entry. Janowitz shows that the most highly ranked military officers show conservative tendencies to a more pronounced degree than the next rank group.

The FSOs also come out as considerably more liberal than the college seniors, either those choosing a "foreign service" career or the total NORC sample. An indication that a diplomatic career has some appeal to those with a liberal political orientation is that the "foreign service" college seniors show up as slightly more liberal than the total NORC sample.

At least part of the difference between the NORC and FSO groups may be accounted for by a difference in the wording of the question. NORC used the word "very" in conjunction with "conservative" and "liberal," which may have caused a tendency to stay near the middle. Note that the largest percentage of any of the groups at an outside position is the nearly one-third of FSOs who regard themselves as "liberal."

Another difference in the wording of the questions was that the military officers did not have the option of choosing "neither liberal nor conservative" as did the NORC and SDP groups. Thus the comparisons should be taken only as roughly indicative; yet the differences are so pronounced that the lack of uniformity in wording is overshadowed. Certainly "conservative" and "liberal" are gross labels, but they do reflect basic orientations, if not specific political content.

RACE AND REPRESENTATIVENESS

It was unnecessary to ask for an identification of race in the SDP, since the answer was already known. It is mainly on racial grounds that the issue of the representativeness of the Foreign Service is alive today.[7]

For a long time the Foreign Service has been able to resist the imposition of geographic quotas. Before the Rogers Act the Consular Service had such quotas, but the Diplomatic Service did not. Repeatedly, as early as 1900, geographic quotas have been proposed, most recently by the Wriston Committee in 1954. By gradually improving its geographical representation, and by such devices as making its written and oral examinations available to candidates throughout the country instead of only in Washington, the Department of State has succeeded in avoiding quotas.

The Service has not succeeded, however, in appointing anything near a representative number of Negroes. Ilchman comments that few Negroes applied and few were appointed in the years up to 1939. There were two Negroes in the FSO corps in 1935, he states, and eight in 1942. In 1967 there were 20 Negroes in the FSO corps, only a little more than one-half of one percent.

The problem was explored fairly thoroughly at the time of the existence of the Herter Committee in a series of meetings with Negro leaders and educators. The conclusion was that no systematic social bias existed, but that young Negroes, especially those from the southern Negro colleges, were culturally disadvantaged in competing with white students in the Foreign Service examination process. A much smaller proportion of Negro applicants than white applicants passed the examinations. Negro students from the first-rate northern universities were not applying for the examination in any appreciable number, either because they were not interested or because they suspected bias.

One result of these meetings was development of a "foreign affairs Scholars program" financed mainly by the Ford Foundation. For each of several years 40 students from minority groups were selected during their junior years to come to Washington as paid interns in State, USIA, and AID. During their senior years, approximately 25 of the 40 were awarded $4,000 scholarships for a year of study in university programs especially useful to those contemplating foreign affairs careers. The students were not obligated to enter government employment, but were expected to take the FSO examination.

It is too early to know what specific effect the program will have on the proportion of Negroes in diplomatic service (the program was terminated in 1967), but undoubtedly the proportion will increase over time. Far from being biased, the State Department can be said to be eager to have qualified young Negro candidates. Ironically, progress may be slow because of the marked increase in mobility in very recent years of the well-educated young Negro college graduates and the fact that the salaries in the lower grades of the Foreign Service are not competitive with those offered by industry.

CONCLUSION

In summary, it is clear that in terms of social origins and characteristics, the FSO corps maintains certain elements of distinctiveness in comparison to other groups, and yet it has moved steadily on the path of becoming more socially representative of American society at large.

There continues to be a strong northeastern regional flavor in terms of birth and education; urban backgrounds are pronounced as are liberal political orientations. Jews are well represented in the Service and Catholics are slightly underrepresented. Negroes are seriously underrepresented, but this is not a problem peculiar to the FSO corps and there are remedial efforts underway. FSOs are likely to have come from a middle or lower income stratum.

It seems clear that the regional flavor is the product of lingering traditions, proximity, and the character of the educational institutions in the northeast, rather than of any systematic bias. For example, it is perhaps significant that the west is overrepresented, in terms of formal education at least, although not to the same degree as the northeast. This suggests that the insularity of the American heartland in respect to the international character of diplomacy is still an operative factor, though a diminishing one.

Ilchman was satisfied that the Service had become democratized in the period up to 1939. In regard to the continued high incidence of the alumni of Harvard, Princeton, and Yale in recruitment into the Service, Ilchman pointed out that any attempt to restrict their entry "would be contrary to democratic presuppositions." That reliance has decreased in the intervening time, and we have the overwhelming evidence of the family income background to support the democratization thesis. Clearly the Service has become an avenue of upward mobility, a fact nonetheless important if the avenue for lower income groups and Jews has been largely the unorthodox one of lateral entry.

The political orientations of FSOs clearly are not the product of social class, although regional overtones may have some significance. One suspects that in the main the liberal leanings of FSOs are the product of individual intellectual commitment, of a kind that would tend to make persons interested in the Foreign Service in the first place and would be reinforced in a diplomatic career with its emphasis on cross-cultural skill and political accommodation.

The distinctive elements aside, FSOs are very much like other important groups in American society in becoming progressively less castelike. The conclusion in the Warner study seems apropos, that "our society, although much like what it has been in past generations, is more flexible than it was; more men and their families are in social motion."[8]

NOTES

[1] *Professional Diplomacy in the United States, 1779-1939* (Chicago: University of Chicago Press, 1961), p. 167.

[2] *Ibid.*, pp. 151-52.

[3] *Ibid.*, pp. 164, 170-71.

[4] Data on military leaders in this chapter is drawn from Morris Janowitz, *The Professional Soldier* (Glencoe, Ill,: The Free Press, 1960), data on civilian federal executives and career Civic Service executives is taken from W. Lloyd Warner, *et al.*, *The American Federal Executive* (New Haven, Conn.: Yale University Press, 1963). The material on business leaders is cited here as it appears in *The American Federal Executive* and *The Professional Soldier*; it actually originated in earlier studies by Warner and Abegglen, about 1952. The data on graduating college seniors comes from major surveys conducted by the National Opinion Research Center (NORC) in 1961 and 1962. At the request of the Herter Committee, NORC obtained data on interest in foreign affairs careers in its 1962 follow-up survey of graduating college seniors. The "NORC Foreign Service" group used in this chapter consists of 327 graduating college seniors who expressed definite interest in foreign affairs careers. The "NORC Total Sample" group consists of a representative sub-sample of 3,397 cases created by NORC for purposes of comparison. See National Opinion Research

Center, "College Graduates and Foreign Affairs," Survey No. 452, The University of Chicago, May 1962 (mimeog.) and Frances Fielder and Godfrey Harris, *The Quest for Foreign Affairs Officers—Their Recruitment and Selection*, Foreign Affairs Personnel Study No. 6 (New York: Carnegie Endowment for International Peace, 1966). The last named source makes extensive presentations of NORC survey results.

[5] Janowitz, *op. cit.*, p. 88.

[6] The FSOs were asked in the SDP to estimate "family income" during the years of their later upbringing, i.e., the high school years. On the average, the FSOs are nearly a generation older than the NORC college seniors; for many of them the years of "later upbringing" would have been the Depression years. It was not possible to adjust the FSO "family income" estimates to 1962 dollars. For all these reasons, the data on the two groups obviously are not directly comparable. However, at least roughly the figures suggest similarity, and in any event support the major point, that neither the bulk of FSOs nor of aspirants to foreign affairs careers come from the more affluent levels of society.

[7] Warner, *op. cit.*, p. 22.

[8] It is also alive in regard to women, but the reason that women are very much underrepresented in the FSO corps is widely understood and accepted. Because of the semi-nomadic existence of FSO's it is virtually impossible for a woman to have a career as an FSO and also be married, a problem that is not true of most professional groups. This tends to depress the number of women recruited through the basic examination process, since the heavy investment in the officer in recruitment and training is very likely to be lost when early in her career she resigns to get married.

Environmental Change and Organizational Adaptation: The Problem of the State Department

ANDREW M. SCOTT

Every organization exists in an environment and interacts with it to some extent. When the environment changes in a significant way, the organization usually goes through a process of adaptation which, allowing for time lag, corresponds in some way to the environmental change. If sufficient adaptation does not take place, strains will develop and the organization will begin to move toward irrelevance, extinction, or some form of abrupt, forced, change. Some organizations adapt to change more readily than others. This article deals with an organization—the Department of State—which has found adaptation extremely difficult.

To note that the Department has been insufficiently adaptive is not to suggest that it has been changeless. The Foreign Service Act of 1946 and the integration of State Department officers into the Foreign Service in 1953, for example, represented efforts to make the Department and the Foreign Service more effective instruments of American foreign policy. Such changes have usually resulted from external rather than internal pressures.

Interestingly enough, during the period since World War II in which the adaptation of the Department of State was altogether inadequate, the foreign affairs system as a whole showed an impressive capacity for adaptation. Foreign aid began in the post-World War II period with the modest goals of relief and rehabilitation. Governmental agencies were brought into existence to administer aid programs and the concept of what might be done with economic aid gradually expanded to encompass the economic rebirth of one continent and the economic development of others. The concept of technical assistance emerged as a response to felt needs, and when it was given funding and organizational support a new instrument of statecraft was born. The United State[s'] Government wanted to carry its story to other nations during the Cold War and so yet another instrument of statecraft, the United States Information Agency, came

From *International Studies Quarterly* 14 (March 1970), pp. 85-94. Reprinted by permission of the author and Wayne State University Press.

253

into being. Various forms of military aid were developed—the use of military advisors, the training of foreign officers in the United States, and development of civic action programs, and so on. Just as new weapons altered the nature of war and the way that men thought about it, they also altered the way that men thought about peace, and this period witnessed the creation of the Arms Control and Disarmament Agency. At the same time the White House was organized to play a more important role in the foreign affairs process. But in the midst of all these developments, the Department of State showed only minimal adaptation.

The starting point for understanding the Department lies in an appreciation of the nature and dominance of the Foreign Service corps. Only 15% of the total number of persons employed by the Department of State are Foreign Service officers, but they set the tone for the whole. The Foreign Service has the characteristics of a typical career service including entry at the bottom, resistance to lateral entry, career tenure and regular advancement through grades if qualified, competition with others for advancement, *esprit de corps*, and a tendency toward corps self-government.

The Foreign Service has developed an internal culture of its own consisting of an interrelated set of ideas, behavioral norms, and operating practices, including several of those enumerated above. The norms and ideology associated with this culture permeate the Department and govern departmental responses in a variety of important areas.

This subculture contains elements which satisfy short-term needs of the career service and individuals in it but which do not necessarily satisfy the long-term needs of the Department of State nor the requirements of American foreign policy. These elements include, for example, hostile or condescending attitudes toward research, planning, management, and "outsiders." Their dysfunctionality often takes the form of promoting attitudes and behavior that tend to insulate the organization from full and free contact with its environment. An organization that is not fully exposed to its environment is under reduced pressure to adapt to it. The short-term functionality of these elements is usually to be found in the way in which they soothe and reassure members of the subculture, protect them from critics and criticism, help smooth interpersonal relations within the Service, and promote discipline and order.

One of the dysfunctional aspects of the Foreign Service subculture is the extent to which it encourages officers to become inward-looking and absorbed in the affairs of the Service. Perhaps all career services tend to do this, but the Foreign Service carries it to an extreme. When an individual finds himself in an environment that places great emphasis upon rank and status, he usually learns to concern himself with matters of assignment, promotion, the impression he makes on fellow officers, the position he takes on shifting alignments in the Service, and the like. Learning to adapt one's behavior and reactions to organizational expectations is an important part of being socialized into an organization. The fully socialized individual would be one who has internalized the organization's norms and learned expected behavior patterns so well that he conforms to them without thought. This degree of socialization would be functional in the sense that if all members were fully socialized the internal affairs of the Service would move smoothly and without a hitch. It would, of course, be highly dysfunctional for American foreign policy.

Given the importance to the individual of the internal workings of the Service, it is understandable that he may become as concerned with these workings, and their relation to his career, as with the organization's success in dealing with the external world. If an officer fails to do well in internal competition he will be directly penalized, but if the organization fails to cope effectively with its environment he may not suffer personally at all because the responsibility for the failure will be diffused throughout the entire organization. It is not surprising, therefore, that an individual may become more concerned with office holding than with organizational accomplishment, more concerned with trying to *be* something rather than with trying to *do* something. There is no invisible hand that makes it inevitable that the internal processes of an organization must produce results that are in harmony with the formal objectives of the organization. The two may easily drift into conflict, and when this happens it is as likely that the formal goals of the organization will suffer as that organizational imperatives will be disregarded. The very absorption with Service matters that socialization encourages, and almost requires, can be counterproductive from the point of view of the conduct of foreign policy.

If an organization is dealing with a relatively stable and unchanging environment, an insulated mode of operation may work fairly well, but if the environment is highly dynamic, as the international environment now is, insulation is likely to entail high costs. For one thing, it hinders the development in the organization of a determination to do what it can to shape events. The attitudes toward planning that are embodied in this particular subculture provide a case in point. The ideology teaches that planning is usually futile because each situation is unique and cannot be anticipated. That being the case, the best that one can do is to play things by ear and improvise creatively when events require it. Ideology, therefore, helps explain why the Department appears incapable of a serious planning effort. From time to time senior departmental officers have decreed that the Department will henceforth engage in planning. These efforts have been greeted with profound skepticism and have usually been short-lived.

A nation with widespread interests should be constantly planning for the future. Those responsible for policy must ask what actions should be taken today and tomorrow and next month in order to bring about a desired result some time in the more distant future. If the Department of State is not prepared to undertake this activity, some other organization is likely to try to fill the vacuum. During the McNamara era it was the Department of Defense, to a degree. More important has been the changing role of the President's staff. The White House is not insulated from its environment but is, on the contrary, a focal point for a great many pressures. The members of the White House staff do not belong to the State Department subculture, do not share its attitudes toward planning, and hence are free to engage in that activity. Furthermore, they are at the President's elbow, and a President is likely to feel the need for effective policy planning.

The White House staff has been important in the foreign affairs field since John F. Kennedy assumed office. The explanation for this is to be found only in part in the fact that the Presidents of the 1960's have been strong or interested in foreign affairs. At the outset President Kennedy expected to operate through the State Department and only established the Bundy operation when that expectation was disappointed. Lyndon Johnson had great confidence in Secretary Rusk, but that did not prevent W. W. Rostow from becoming a powerful figure in foreign affairs. Henry Kissinger, foreign affairs advisor to President Nixon, is shaping American policy as visibly as the Department of State and has made a point of drawing certain planning functions to himself and his staff.

Foreign affairs staff members in the White House have become important because the times have demanded action and the Department of State has not been able to gear itself for action. There is significance in President Kennedy's happy daydream of "establishing a secret office of 30 people or so to run foreign policy while maintaining the State Department as a facade in which people might contentedly carry papers from bureau to bureau."

It may seem strange to speak of the Department as insulated from its environment when its officers all over the world file millions of words annually, but the term is nevertheless appropriate. If a scale could be developed showing the extent to which public organizations interact with their environments, the Department would be found toward the lower end of that scale. It is insulated in that the Foreign Service is a career service with little lateral entry. It is insulated in that its members have a high level of interaction with one another and a relatively low level of interaction with significant figures in the outside environment—Congressmen, individuals in other departments and agencies, young people, corporate executives, academicians, and certain categories of foreigners. It is insulated in that it is unresponsive to changing circumstances and to the emergence of new skills, new information, new ideas, and new problems. It is insulated in that it defines what is relevant to its mission in a parochial way. It is insulated in that it has developed ways of explaining away outside criticism and has learned to ignore or sidetrack most demands for change.

It is easy to understand why individuals in an organization may act so as to shield the organization from its environment. When the organization is insulated, the need for disruptive adjustments to the environment is reduced and uncertainty and felt pressures are minimized. Isolation makes life easier. Men can do things the way they are accustomed to doing them and they can think accustomed thoughts. The drive toward isolation can be seen in many organizations but has been particularly apparent in the Department of State. Since changes in the international environment in which it operates are many, complex, and follow one another in rapid succession, the attractiveness of holding that environment at arm's length is particularly great. Since the Washington environment is also complex and changing and, in addition, is somewhat threatening and critical, it is not surprising that the Department should have developed fairly elaborate defense mechanisms.

Structural characteristics of the career system also impede easy adaptation. When entry into the Service is primarily at the bottom, the carriers of new ideas are apt to be young and to be low in rank, status, and influence. Power in the organization will rest in the hands of older men who are likely to be imbued with traditional ideas. During a workshop in 1966 junior Foreign Service officers identified a number of Departmental problems, including the following:

—Assignment to jobs is based more on seniority than on competence;
—The Service is not making use of modern organizational, training, and assignment practices;
—Older officers prevent progressive, adaptive action by younger officers;
—The Service reserves decisions to the highest levels and suppresses ideas from lower levels;
—Fear of criticism and retaliation inhibit dissent and the expression of nonconformist ideas.

Each of these "problems" represents a feature of the Foreign Service system that is functional from the point of view of a senior officer's conception of the smooth operation of the Service, i.e., a seniority system, personalized management, caution and conservatism on the part of senior officers, deference on the part of junior officers, the absence of vigorous debate that might mar interpersonal relations. Yet each of these features is also *dysfunctional* from the point of view of the Service's long-term future and its formal purposes. Order and discipline within the Service are purchased at the cost of imagination, flexibility and organizational drive.

The argument set forth here is that the departmental subculture has served to cripple the Department of State by promoting insulation and by furthering a variety of dysfunctional doctrines. If this line of analysis is correct, it means that the subculture will have to be substantially modified before the Department can play its proper role in foreign affairs. The historical record of the Department would not encourage optimism in this connection. Examples of bureaucratic self-renewal are few and far between, and certainly the Department of State does not have a history of success.

Nevertheless, in recent years there have been stirrings that may prove to be important. In 1967 a group of "Young Turks" in the Foreign Service gained control of the American Foreign Service Association with the idea of using it as an instrument to press for service reform. Some of the reforms that the Association's leadership is concerned with—improved training, more effective use of research, rapid promotion of able younger officers, altered assignment practices—would have the effect of weakening the hold of a number of the dysfunctional doctrines that now tie up the Department.

The leaders of the Association have also indicated that they intend to open the Foreign Service to its environment. One of the ways in which they propose to do this is by giving Foreign Service officers experience in the nongovernmental sectors of the foreign affairs community.

The concept of a foreign affairs community is interesting and potentially significant. There are many individuals who work professionally in foreign affairs outside the government. Together with those in the government, they comprise what might be termed a "foreign affairs community." Members of this community who are not in the government represent a resource that governmental agencies could utilize more fully. Conversely, members of the community in the government represent a resource from the point of view of businesses engaging in overseas activity, foundations concerned with international affairs, banks, nongovernmental organizations with international interests, and academic institutions. If the degree of lateral movement of personnel among the various sectors of the community could be substantially increased, this would be a net gain for all concerned. The attractiveness of Foreign Service would certainly be increased and its competitive position would be improved if movement in and out of the Service were made much easier. At present the young man considering the Foreign Service is asked to choose a way of life once and for all because the decision to go into the Service usually forecloses other options. An able young man would be more likely to opt for the Service if he knew that he could move out of it for a few years with comparative ease and then back in if he chose. Perhaps, in time, young men may be able to plan for a career in foreign affairs that will involve relatively easy movement among the various sectors of the foreign affairs community. An individual's career would not have to be tied to a particular organization, such as the Foreign Service, but could be planned with an eye to the broad arena of foreign affairs. Perhaps also, in time, the Foreign Service and the other governmental services will be merged into a single foreign affairs service. This would do a good deal to overcome the tendency toward parochialism and would certainly open up the Foreign Service.

The leaders of the Foreign Service Association are interested in opening up the Service by making greater use of the principle of lateral entry. This would have a number of advantages, particularly if it could be coupled with short terms of service. At present the Foreign Service does not have enough technical specialists. Given the Service's predisposition toward the "generalist," such specialists are not likely to be developed within the Foreign Service and must therefore be recruited from outside. Many of the specialist candidates for appointment might not be interested in giving up their professional careers in order to spend a large part of their lives abroad but might be interested in entering the Service for four or five years. The adoption of a different philosophy with regard to lateral entry would make it easier for the Service to draw on the vast reservoir of trained men in the middle years of their lives. More important, these men might be a valuable leaven in the Foreign Service since they would be likely to have perspectives at variance with those normally found in the Service.

Some FSO's have misgivings about the extension of lateral entry on the ground that it will tend to undermine the concept of a career service. Their instincts are probably right. The guild-like characteristics of the Service would be strained by extensive use of lateral entry. If a choice must be made between a closed Service, on the one hand, and an open, adaptive Service on the other, however, there can be no doubt where the long-term interests of the nation and of the Department of State lie.

One of the features of the Young Turk rebellion that makes it encouraging is that it has received the backing of the Secretary of State and of Under Secretary Elliot Richardson. The Under Secretary has endorsed a number of ideas of the American Foreign Service Association, has instituted some changes, and is considering others. If a working alliance can be achieved between top appointive officials in the Department and the dissident elements in the Foreign Service, the entire situation in the Department could become malleable. Together they might be able to do that which neither could do alone.

The external environment in which the Department of State must operate is going to become more rather than less demanding with the passage of time. The Department is charged with conducting the foreign policy of one of the world's most powerful nations, and the insulation and dysfunctionality that were irritating but tolerable in the era before World War II are too costly and dangerous to be tolerated any longer. The costs associated with non-adaptation, errors made, imagination not exercised, problems not understood, and opportunities overlooked are not borne by the Department alone but by many people, in the United States and elsewhere, whose destinies are shaped to some extent by the successes and failures of the Department.

The Invisible Government

DAVID WISE AND THOMAS B. ROSS

There are two governments in the United States today. One is visible. The other is invisible.

The first is the government that citizens read about in their newspapers and children study about in their civics books. The second is the interlocking, hidden machinery that carries out the policies of the United States in the Cold War.

This second, invisible government gathers intelligence, conducts espionage, and plans and executes secret operations all over the globe.

The Invisible Government is not a formal body. It is a loose, amorphous grouping of individuals and agencies drawn from many parts of the visible government. It is not limited to the Central Intelligence Agency, although the CIA is at its heart. Nor is it confined to the nine other agencies which comprise what is known as the intelligence community: the National Security Council, the Defense Intelligence Agency, the National Security Agency, Army Intelligence, Navy Intelligence, Air Force Intelligence, the State Department's Bureau of Intelligence and Research, the Atomic Energy Commission and the Federal Bureau of Investigation.

The Invisible Government includes, also, many other units and agencies, as well as individuals, that appear outwardly to be a normal part of the conventional government. It even encompasses business firms and institutions that are seemingly private.

THE INTELLIGENCE COMMUNITY

... [T]he principal members of the intelligence community [are]: Army Intelligence, the Office of Naval Intelligence, Air Force Intelligence, the Atomic Energy Commission, the Federal Bureau of Investigation, the State Department's Bureau of Intelligence and Research, the National Security Agency, the Defense Intelligence Agency, as well as the CIA.

Condensed from Chapters 1, 13-15, 17-18 of *The Invisible Government*, by David Wise and Thomas B. Ross. Copyright © 1964 by David Wise and Thomas B. Ross. Reprinted by permission of Random House, Inc.

Army Intelligence

The Army G-2 is the oldest of the nation's intelligence services, with a tradition dating back to World War I. In World War II it carried off several coups: the capture intact of a high-level Nazi planning group in North Africa; the advance seizure of a map of all enemy mines in Sicily; and the capture of the entire Japanese secret-police force on Okinawa. On a bureaucratic level, it did battle with the OSS and the ambitious intelligence men of the Army Air Corps. After the war the G-2 absorbed many of the OSS operatives under a directive by President Truman. But it lost air intelligence when the Air Force was created as a separate service. The Army yielded further ground after the formation of the DIA, but retained four vital functions: (1) technical intelligence on the types, quantity and quality of army weapons of foreign powers; (2) the attaché system, which tries to estimate the size, organization and deployment of foreign armies through the efforts—mainly overt—of Army representatives in the major United States embassies; (3) the Counter Intelligence Corps, which is charged with detecting and preventing treason, espionage, sabotage, gambling, prostitution and black marketeering; (4) the Army Map Service, which is responsible for meeting most of the government's mapping needs.

Office of Naval Intelligence

The ONI is the smallest of the intelligence branches of the three services. Its total complement amounted to 2,600 men in 1961,[1] and the number has undoubtedly declined as the DIA has absorbed more and more of the service intelligence functions. The Navy maintains no separate counter-intelligence unit such as the Army's CIC. But it makes use of an attaché system, and it deploys intelligence men at all of its installations, ashore and afloat. The principle mission of the ONI is to collect information on foreign naval forces. It keeps a special weather eye on the Soviet submarine fleet and compiles elaborate dossiers on the world's major beaches, harbors and ports.

Air Force Intelligence

The A-2 is the most mechanically sophisticated of the service intelligence operations. It employs the latest electronic gear to determine the missile, bomber, satellite and radar potential of the Soviet Union. The Electronics Division, through its Reconnaissance, Equipment and Control Branches, gathers the electronic intelligence (a separate chapter will deal with the startling advances that have been made in this field). Under a Pentagon directive in 1961, the Air Force controls all reconnaissance satellites orbiting the Soviet Union. A Target Division is responsible for sorting out the intelligence intake and maintaining a current list of potential enemy targets. It also compiles and publishes the *Bombing Encyclopedia,* a compendium of target information. The A-2 conducts a world-wide attaché system through its International Liaison Division. It also maintains a Military Capabilities Branch and a Wargame Branch in the Threat Assessments Division of its Directorate of Warning and Threat Assessment.

Atomic Energy Commission

The AEC is responsible for making estimates of the atomic-weapons capabilities of the Soviet Union and other nuclear powers. Since 1948 the United States has maintained round-the-clock monitoring of the atmosphere to detect radioactive particles from atomic tests. Samples are collected by the U-2 and other high-flying aircraft. From an analysis of the samples, the AEC can determine not only the fact that atomic explosions have taken place but also the type and power of the weapons detonated. The AEC also plays an important role in assessing test-ban proposals. It carries out intensive experimentation in ways to shield atomic explosions from detection and ways to pierce the shielding devised by other nations.

Because of the law which set it up and its close relationship to the Joint Committee on Atomic Energy in the Congress, the AEC is one of the most independent branches of the Invisible Government. One of Eisenhower's parting admonitions to Kennedy was: "You may be able to run lots of things around here. But one of them you can't run is the AEC."

Federal Bureau of Investigation

As the investigative arm of the Department of Justice, the FBI is responsible, among its other duties, for catching spies. In this phase of its work—as opposed to its conventional criminal investigations—the FBI is an intelligence agency, and as such, part of the Invisible Government. The assistant to J. Edgar Hoover, the FBI director, sits on USIB, and the FBI has a liaison man who reports to work at the CIA headquarters in Langley [Virginia] every day.

Actual counter-espionage work is conducted by the FBI's hush-hush division Number 5. This is the Domestic Intelligence Division, headed by William C. Sullivan. It is in charge of espionage, sabotage and subversion cases.

In Miami, New York and Washington, there are FBI agents permanently assigned to counter-espionage. A squad supervisor is assigned to intelligence in each of the FBI's fifty-five field offices in the United States. Agents who normally conduct ordinary criminal investigations are assigned to espionage cases when necessary.

About 20 percent of the 650,000 cases investigated by the FBI in 1963 were espionage-internal security cases, although the exact figure is classified.

"Over the years," Hoover told a House committee in 1962, "no phase of American activity has been immune to Soviet-bloc intelligence attempts. The Soviets have attempted to obtain every conceivable type of information. The targets have been all-encompassing and have included aerial photographs, maps and charts of our major cities and vital areas, data regarding the organization of our military services and their training programs, technical classified and unclassified information concerning nuclear weapons, planes, ships and submarines. Of prime interest to the Soviets is information concerning U.S. military bases, including missile sites and radar installations."

* * *

Since 1950 a total of thirty-four Soviet and seventeen Communist-bloc diplomats have been expelled from the United States for a variety of reasons. . . . [M]any of the espionage efforts of Soviet agents operating as diplomats seem bumbling and almost amateurish. There is a long record of such cases.

By contrast, Soviet "illegals"—spies operating under deep cover—are skilled experts and therefore much harder for the FBI to detect. They slip into the country with false documents, pass for ordinary Americans, and enjoy no embassy protection.

The FBI's counter-espionage work is concentrated within the continental United States. Although the bureau operated in the Western Hemisphere and cracked Nazi espionage rings in South America during World War II, espionage and counter-espionage abroad became the province of the CIA and the military intelligence organizations after the war. Contrary to popular belief, however, the FBI does have some agents overseas. They are assigned to American embassies, usually under the cover of "legal attachés."

The FBI had 14,239 employees in 1964 (of whom 6,014 were agents), but its budget of $146,900,000 ranked it as one of the smaller units of the Invisible Government, even though its counter-espionage work is vital to national security.

Bureau of Intelligence and Research

INR, the State Department's intelligence agency, is really misnamed, in the view of one of its former directors, Roger Hilsman.

"To be frank with you," he told a House Appropriations Subcommittee in 1961,

> I am uneasy about this word "intelligence" in the title of the bureau. It is, in a real sense, not really an intelligence agency as you think of the word and it does not collect as such.
>
> It is analysis—research and analysis is its function as an agency. [But] it has functions relating to the intelligence community. Normally, quick data comes from the other collection agencies, and from the diplomatic reporting which is not part of our bureau, but the embassies overseas.

As Hilsman indicated, INR relies upon the information of others—the diplomatic service, the CIA, the military attachés and the published documents and maps of foreign nations. INR analyzes this information for the use of the Secretary of State and the other branches of the intelligence community.

Its main function on USIB is to make sure that the final intelligence estimates reflect the political, social and economic facts of life, as seen from the State Department's viewpoint.

The absence of cloak-and-dagger in INR is reflected in the fact that it is the only member of USIB whose intelligence budget is part of the public record. It employs about 350 persons and spends approximately $2,800,000 annually (the figures vary slightly from year to year). It produces over 16,000 pages of social, political, economic and biographic analyses each year. By its own estimate, 40 to 60 percent of the raw data for these analyses come from the diplomatic reports of United States embassies abroad. INR also makes use of the scholarly output of the universities and periodically commissions a study by the academic community. It briefs the Secretary of State every day.

INR, the FBI, the AEC and the intelligence branches of the military services represent the lesser agencies of the Invisible Government. The big ones, in terms of men, money and influence, are the National Security Agency, the Defense Intelligence Agency and the CIA.

The National Security Agency

Probably the most secretive branch of the Invisible Government is the National Security Agency. Even more than the CIA, the NSA has sought to conceal the nature of its activities.

The CIA's functions were revealed in general outline by Congress in the National Security Act of 1947. But the NSA's duties were kept secret in the classified presidential directive which established the agency in 1952.

The only official description of its activities is contained in the *U. S. Government Organization Manual*, which states vaguely: The National Security Agency performs highly specialized technical and co-ordinating functions relating to the national security."

Nevertheless, it is no secret that the NSA is the nation's code-making and code-breaking agency. It is impossible, however, to receive official confirmation of that obvious fact. Unlike Allen Dulles and other high-ranking CIA men who have occasionally talked to the press and on television, NSA officials have refused to grant interviews under any circumstances.

As a sub-agency of the Defense Department, the NSA is watched over by the deputy director of defense research and engineering. But the various men who have held this post have been similarly uncommunicative.

During the Eisenhower years, the job of overseeing the NSA was held by military men. The Kennedy and Johnson Administrations turned to civilians with broader scientific expertise. In 1963, the assignment was taken on by Dr. Eugene G. Fubini, a fifty-year-old Italian-born physicist.

Fubini was confirmed by the Senate without difficulty despite a challenge from Senator Thurmond, the South Carolina Democrat. During the Armed Services Committee hearings on June 27, 1963, Thurmond questioned Fubini closely on his political affiliations in Italy prior to his emigration to the United States in 1939.

Fubini admitted that he had been a dues-paying member of the GUF, the Fascist student organization in the universities. But he explained that membership was "almost a compulsory thing" in Mussolini's Italy, and that he finally left his homeland in political protest.

Fubini made it clear, to Thurmond's evident relief, that he had never been associated with Communist or Socialist movements. His biographical data also underscored the fact that he had served ably as a scientific consultant and technical observer with the U.S. Army and Navy in Europe during World War II.

After the war Fubini joined the Airborne Instruments Laboratory of Long Island, New York. He worked on several classified electronic projects and rose to become the vice-president of the company. By the time he joined the Pentagon in 1961 he was thoroughly impressed with the need for tight security. He became convinced that a mass of vital national secrets was being given to the Russians through careless public disclosure.

Fubini and his staff maintained a long list of security violations which appeared in the press and elsewhere. Prominent on the list were public statements by Defense Secretary McNamara and his deputy, Roswell Gilpatric. In their zeal to defend administration policy, notably in McNamara's television extravaganza after the Cuban missile crisis, Fubini felt his bosses were sometimes imprudent about national security.

Fubini's dedication to security was matched by the agency he inherited. The NSA's U-shaped, three-story steel-and-concrete building at Fort Meade, Maryland, is surrounded by a double barbed-wire fence ten feet high. The fences are patrolled night and day, and guards with ready machine guns are posted at the four gatehouses.

The interior, including the longest unobstructed corridor in the world (980 feet long and 560 feet wide), is similarly patrolled. The building is 1,400,000 square feet, smaller than the Pentagon but larger than the CIA's Langley headquarters. It houses high-speed computers and complicated radio and electronic gear. It is said to have more electric wiring than any other building in the world.

Special security conveyor belts carry documents at the rate of a hundred feet a minute and a German-made pneumatic tube system shoots messages at the rate of twenty-five feet a second.

The NSA headquarters was built at a cost of $30,000,000 and was opened in 1957. It contains a complete hospital, with operating rooms and dental offices. It also houses eight snack bars, a cafeteria, an auditorium and a bank. All of the building's windows are sealed and none can be opened.

Comparable precautions have been taken with NSA employees. They are subject to lie-detector tests on application and intensive security indoctrination on acceptance. Periodically, the indoctrination briefing is repeated and employees are required to sign statements that they have reread pertinent secrecy regulations.

Even so, the NSA has had more than its share of trouble with security violations. In 1960 two young mathematicians, William H. Martin and Bernon F. Mitchell, defected to Russia. They held a news conference in Moscow, describing in detail the inner workings of the NSA. They were soon discovered to be homosexuals, a fact which led indirectly to the resignation of the NSA's personnel director, and the firing of twenty-six other employees for sexual deviation.

It also led on May 9, 1963 to a vote by the House, 340 to 40, to give the Secretary of Defense the same absolute power over NSA employees as the Director of Central Intelligence had over his employees. Under the legislation, which was introduced by the Un-American Activities Committee, the Secretary of Defense was authorized to fire NSA employees without explanation and without appeal if he decided they were security risks. The bill also required a full field investigation of all persons before they were hired.

The legislation was attacked by several congressmen.

Thomas P. Gill, the Hawaii Democrat, warned that the bill opened the way to "arbitrary and capricious action on the part of government administrators. . . . There has been much said about danger to the national security. Democracy itself is a dangerous form of government and in its very danger lies its strength. The protection of individual rights by the requirement of due process of law, which has long endured in this nation of ours, is a radical and dangerous idea in most of the world today.

"This dangerous concept is outlawed in the Soviet Union, in Red China, in Castro's Cuba, indeed, in all of the Communist bloc and many of those countries aligned with it. I think we might well ask: How does one destroy his enemy by becoming like him?"

Edwin E. Willis, the Louisiana Democrat and a member of the Un-American Activities Committee, defended the bill on ground that the NSA "carries out the most delicate type intelligence operations of our government. . . . The National Security Agency plays so highly specialized a role in the defense and security of the United States that no outsider can actually describe its activities. They are guarded not only from the public but from other government agencies as well. The Civil Service Commission, which audits all government positions, is not allowed to know what NSA employees do."

If the bill was so important for the NSA, Willis was asked, why shouldn't it be applied to all other sensitive agencies?

"As to the other agencies," Willis replied, "we will have to take them one at a time."

Although the Martin and Mitchell case stirred the House to action, it was only one of several sensational security scandals to hit the NSA.

In 1954 Joseph Sydney Petersen was tried and convicted on charges of misusing classified NSA documents. He was accused of taking and copying documents to aid another nation. In the court papers the government said Petersen "copied and made notes from classified documents indicating the United States' success in breaking codes utilized by The Netherlands." The Dutch Embassy in Washington admitted it had exchanged "secret intelligence" with Petersen on the assumption that he had acted with the knowledge of his superiors.

In 1959, during his visit to the United States, Khrushchev bragged that he had obtained top-secret American codes and had intercepted messages from President Eisenhower to Prime Minister Nehru. "You're wasting your money," Krushchev remarked to Allen Dulles. "you might as well send it direct to us instead of the middleman, because we get most of it anyway. Your agents give us the code books and then we send false information back to you through your code. Then we send cables asking for money and you send it to us."

On July 22, 1963, *Izvestia* published a letter from Victor Norris Hamilton, a naturalized American of Arab descent who had sought asylum in the Soviet Union. Hamilton said he had worked for a division of the NSA which intercepted and decoded secret instructions from Arab countries to their delegations at the United Nations. Hamilton claimed UN Ambassador Henry Cabot Lodge had sent a letter to the division thanking them for the information. The Pentagon admitted Hamilton had been an employee of the NSA and said he had been discharged in 1959 because he was "approaching a paranoid-schizophrenic break." (The NSA has an unusually high rate of mental illness and suicide.)

An even graver security breach at the NSA was also disclosed in July of 1963. Army Sergeant First Class Jack E. Dunlap committed suicide when he realized he had been discovered selling top-secret NSA documents to Soviet officials. Dunlap reportedly received $60,000 during a two-year period for disclosing United States intelligence on Russian weapons advances, the deployment of their missiles and troops, as well as similar information about the NATO countries.

The playboy sergeant, who had a wife and five children, spent the money on several girl friends, two Cadillacs and frequent trips to the race track. A Pentagon official described the case as "thirty to forty times as serious as the Mitchell and Martin defections."

These security violations revealed a mass of information about the NSA. And most of it was indirectly confirmed by the Pentagon in its contradictory statements on the case, and by the House Un-American Activities Committee in issuing a public report stressing the seriousness of the Martin and Mitchell defection. Out of it all a painstaking enemy analyst could have derived the following picture of the National Security Agency:

NSA was divided into four main offices. The Office of Production (PROD) attempted to break the codes and ciphers and read the messages of the Soviet Union, Communist China, other Communist countries, United States Allies and neutral nations.

The Office of Research and Development (R/D) carried out research in cryptanalysis, digital computing and radio propagation. It also developed new communications equipment.

The Office of Communications Security (COMSEC) produced U.S. codes and tried to protect them. And the Office of Security (SEC) investigated NSA personnel, conducted lie-detector tests and passed on the loyalty and integrity of employees.

While the NSA was reading the secret communications of over forty nations, including the most friendly, it shared some of its secrets through a relationship between its United Kingdom Liaison Office (UKLO) and its British counterpart, the GCHQ. The NSA, at least according to Martin and Mitchell, also provided code machines to other nations and then intercepted their messages on the basis of its knowledge of the construction and wiring of the machines.

The NSA gathered its raw information through more than 2,000 intercept stations around the world. They were designed to pick up every electronic emanation and communication in the Communist bloc: countdowns at missile sites, tell-tale sounds of industrial construction, military orders for troop movements, and air defense instructions to radar installations and fighter-plane squadrons.

In addition, the NSA sent its eavesdropping equipment along on flights by the U-2 and other aircraft over the Soviet Union (until 1960) and over Communist China. Separate flights, called ELINT (for electronic intelligence) missions, skirted Communist borders, picking up the location and characteristics of enemy radar stations. Occasionally, the planes would play "foxes and hounds," feinting toward or into Soviet defenses so as to analyze the nature of the response on nearby U.S. radar screens and listening·gear.

The NSA also practiced what is known in the trade as "audio surveillance" and in layman's terms as "bugging," or "telephone tapping."

It was clear that the United States had come a long way from that day in 1929 when Secretary of State Henry L. Stimson closed the "black chamber," the State Department's primitive code-breaking section, with the explanation:
"Gentlemen do not read each other's mail."

The Defense Intelligence Agency

The DIA, the newest member of the Invisible Government and the most powerful competitor of the CIA, owes its existence to the post-Sputnik "missile gap" controversy of the late 1950s.

As the Soviets demonstrated the range and accuracy of their missiles in a series of spectacular space shots, the Air Force demanded that the United States embark on a massive ICBM program of its own. Almost weekly in the period between 1957 and 1960 the Air Force went before the United States Intelligence Board to argue that the Russians were deploying hundreds of ICBMs and were tipping the military balance of power in their favor.

To substantiate the claim, Air Force photo-interpreters introduced scores of pictures taken by the U-2 spy plane, which started to fly over the Soviet Union in 1956.

"To the Air Force every flyspeck on film was a missile," a CIA man remarked scornfully. Allen Dulles, relying on the independent interpretation of the photos by the CIA's Research Division, challenged two thirds of the Air Force estimates.

USIB's meetings were dominated by long and bitter arguments over the conflicting missile estimates. The situation reflected the perennial problem of interservice rivalry. Each service tended to adopt a self-serving party line and pursue it relentlessly. At budget time each year the Air Force would see endless numbers of Soviet missiles and bombers; the Navy would detect the latest enemy submarines just off the East Coast; and the Army would mechanize a few dozen more Russian divisions.

Overwhelmed by the constant bickering, USIB and the civilian leaders of the Pentagon were anxious to find some mechanism for resolving the conflict. They turned the problem over to a Joint Study Group which was set up in 1959 to conduct a sweeping investigation of the intelligence community.

The group was composed of military men, active and retired, and career intelligence officials in the State Department, the Defense Department and the White House. It was headed by Lyman Kirkpatrick, then the inspector general of the CIA. A polio victim who was confined to a wheel chair, Kirkpatrick was often spotted overseas, pursuing his many investigations.

The Joint Study Group submitted a comprehensive list of recommendations late in 1960. One of the most important called for the creation of the DIA and for the removal of the service intelligence agencies from USIB. The DIA was to serve as the arbiter of the conflicting service estimates and to present its findings to USIB as the final judgment of the Pentagon.

The idea appealed strongly to Thomas S. Gates, Jr., the last Secretary of Defense in the Eisenhower Administration. When the Kennedy Administration took office in January, 1961, Gates forcefully urged McNamara to put the recommendation into effect without delay.

McNamara was quickly persuaded of the wisdom of Gates' advice. After a thorough study of the missile-gap claims, McNamara concluded that there was no foundation in the argument that the United States was lagging behind the Soviet Union in the production or deployment of ICBMs. The study convinced him of the dangers inherent in the fragmented intelligence operation at the Pentagon. He saw great value in subordinating the service intelligence branches to a centralized agency directly under his supervision.

Accordingly, McNamara recommended the speedy creation of the DIA. But Dulles balked at the idea. Despite his many wrangles with the services, Dulles felt it was imperative that they continue to have a voice in the deliberations of the intelligence community. He feared that the creation of the DIA would lead to the elimination of the service intelligence branches from USIB.

Then the CIA would be cut off from direct access to the facts and opinions developed by the military men and would be forced to rely on whatever information the DIA saw fit to give it. Dulles was impressed with the service argument, which ran something like this:

Yes, the services have been guilty at times of analyzing intelligence from a parochial point of view. But other agencies of the government are no less susceptible to self-serving judgments. The function of USIB is to serve as a forum for all viewpoints—even extreme viewpoints. Only then can the Director of Central Intelligence, and through him the President, arrive at comprehensive and objective assessments. Dissent should be aired at the highest possible level and not suppressed outside the orbit of presidential observation.

If the service intelligence branches were removed from USIB, the DIA would become the sole respresentative of the government's biggest producer and biggest consumer of intelligence. And the DIA as an agency subordinate to a political appointee—the Secretary of Defense—would be more vulnerable to political influences than are the services which have a semi-autonomous status by law.

Dulles was particularly worried about the possibility that the DIA would gain a monopoly over aerial reconnaissance. The Defense Department controlled the reconnaissance equipment and Dulles feared that the DIA would be tempted to hoard the photographs produced by the equipment. He was determined to prevent any such thing.

During the U-2 era, the CIA had built up a skilled corps of civilian photo-interpreters and they would surely quit if the Pentagon monopolized aerial photographs. Without interpreters, the CIA would have no way to verify Defense Department estimates. At a time when electronic espionage was bulking ever larger, Pentagon control of aerial reconnaissance could result in Pentagon dominance of the entire intelligence community.

Dulles expressed his misgivings to McNamara, who responded with assurances that the DIA would be only a co-ordinating body and that it would not supplant the intelligence branches of the Army, Navy, and Air Force. Some of Dulles' advisers suspected that the Pentagon had covert ambitions for the DIA which were being suppressed temporarily for tactical reasons. But Dulles felt McNamara's pledge left no ground for him to oppose the DIA. He went along with the proposal. So did John McCone, then head of the AEC.

The DIA was created officially on October 1, 1961. Named as director was Lieutenant General Joseph F. Carroll, who had been the inspector general of the Air Force. Carroll started his career with the FBI and was a leading assistant of J. Edgar Hoover at the time he moved to the Air Force in 1947 to set up its first investigation and counter-intelligence section.

CIA men delighted in pointing out that all of Carroll's experience had been as an investigator and that he had no credentials as a foreign or military intelligence analyst. More to the CIA's liking were Carroll's two subordinates, both of whom had served with the CIA: Major General William W. (Buffalo Bill) Quinn, a former West Point football star, who was named deputy director; and Rear Admiral Samuel B. Frankel, a Chinese- and Russian-speaking expert on the Communist world, who became the DIA's chief of staff.

Both of these men had worked closely with Allen Dulles. Frankel served under him on USIB. Quinn, the G-2 for the Seventh Army in Europe during World War II, acted as personal courier for the information Dulles gathered in Switzerland on Nazi troop movements. (Quinn left the DIA to become the commander of the Seventh Army in November, 1963.)

The original charter for the DIA provided that the new agency was to: (1) draw up a consolidated budget for all the intelligence units within the Pentagon; (2) produce all Defense Department estimates for USIB and other elements of the intelligence community; (3) provide representation on USIB in the person of its director; and (4) develop plans for integrating the intelligence schools run by the various services.

Although the original list of functions seemed relatively modest, an expansion of the DIA's responsibilities was clearly implied in its authorization by McNamara to provide "overall guidance for the conduct and management" of all duties retained by the individual services.

And with the inevitability of Parkinson's Law, the DIA quickly added to its domain. By 1964, when the DIA became fully operational, it had more than 2,500 employees. It had acquired 38,000 feet of Pentagon office space and had submitted a request for a separate $17,000,000 building.

It had succeeded in eliminating the separate service intelligence publications and supplanting them with two of its own; and it had launched a *Daily Digest*, which was viewed by the CIA as duplicatory and competitive to its own *Central Intelligence Bulletin*.

The DIA had also supplanted the J-2, the intelligence staff of the Joint Chiefs of Staff, both on USIB and in supplying information to the Chiefs themselves. It had replaced the services in the production of "order of battle" intelligence— estimates of the size and deployment of enemy forces. And it was occasionally providing information directly to the President without funneling it through USIB. The DIA did so on request in 1963 when Kennedy wanted quick intelligence on whether the Guatemalan Army would be able to handle expected Communist riots.

By 1964 the DIA's control over military intelligence had expanded to such a degree that the services were reduced to the role of providing technical information on enemy weapons, running the attaché system and collecting—but not analyzing—raw intelligence.

* * *

CIA: The Inner Workings

... The CIA is, of course, the biggest, most important and most influential branch of the Invisible Government. The agency is organized into four divisions: Intelligence, Plans, Research, Support, each headed by a deputy director.

The Support Division is the administrative arm of the CIA. It is in charge of equipment, logistics, security and communications. It devises the CIA's special codes, which cannot be read by other branches of the government.

The Research Division is in charge of technical intelligence. It provides expert assessments of foreign advances in science, technology and atomic weapons. It was responsible for analyzing the U-2 photographs brought back from the Soviet Union between 1956 and 1960. And it has continued to analyze subsequent U-2 and spy-satellite pictures. In this it works with the DIA in running the National Photo Intelligence Center.

* * *

The Plans Division is in charge of the CIA's cloak-and-dagger activities. It controls all foreign special operations, such as Guatemala and the Bay of Pigs, and it collects all of the agency's covert intelligence through spies and informers overseas.

* * *

The job of the Intelligence Division is essentially a highly specialized form of scholarship. And 80 percent of its information comes from "open sources": technical magazines, foreign broadcast monitoring, scholarly studies, propaganda journals, and data produced by such visible branches of the government as the U.S. Information Agency, the Agriculture, Treasury, and Commerce Departments, and the Agency for International Development.

The Intelligence Division's function is to take the mass of information available to it and "produce" intelligence, that is, to draw up reports on the economic, political, social and governmental situation in any country in the world. The division is subdivided into three major groups: one makes long-range projections of what can be expected in crisis areas; a second produces a daily review of the current situation; and a third, established by [Ray] Cline shortly after he took over, is supposed to detect the gaps in what the CIA is doing and collecting.

Cline and his subordinates pride themselves on their independence and detachment from operational problems. They maintain that they evaluate information flowing in from the CIA Plans Division on an equal basis with intelligence coming in from elsewhere in the government. They contend that they do not have any ax to grind or any vested interest or operation to protect and, therefore, that they produce the most objective reports of any branch of the government.

The most important of these reports are prepared, sometimes on a crash basis, by the Office of National Estimates (ONE), which acts as the staff of the twelve-man Board of National Estimates (BNE). . . .

"National Intelligence Estimates," Lyman Kirkpatrick, the executive director of the CIA has said,

> are perhaps the most important documents created in the intelligence mechanisms of our government. . . . A national estimate is a statement of what is going to happen in any country, in any area, in any given situation, and as far as possible into the future. . . .
>
> Each of the responsible departments prepares the original draft on that section which comes under its purview. Thus the Department of State would draft the section on the political, economic or sociological development in a country or an area or a situation, while the Army would deal with ground forces, the Air Force with the air forces, and the Navy with the naval forces, and the Department of Defense under the Joint Chiefs of Staff with the guided-missile threat.
>
> The Board of Estimates would then go over the individual contributions very carefully—sometimes very heatedly—and arrive at a common view. Any one of the intelligence services has the right of dissent from the view which will be expressed as that of the Director of Intelligence. [This is known as "taking a footnote."]

These National Intelligence Estimates go to the United States Intelligence Board for review. Under Dulles, . . . [the] board generated its own studies and was under the jurisdiction of the deputy director for intelligence. One of the changes made by McCone was to bring the Board of National Estimates directly under his personal command. McCone then controlled the frequency and subject matter of NIE reports. USIB functioned as an advisory group to McCone and estimates were frequently rewritten at his direction.

The NIE was then transmitted to the President as the estimate of the Director of Central Intelligence. Ultimately, therefore, despite all this vast intelligence machinery, the end product goes to the President as the personal responsibility and personal estimate of one man.

It is in this area that the structure of the Invisible Government is the most complex. The Director of Central Intelligence is the ultimate arbiter of the vital security information, predictions and evaluations that are placed on the desk of the President. He presides over the branches of the intelligence community represented on USIB; but, as has been seen, he also heads the CIA, which is one of these branches. He controls not only the intelligence product of CIA but also the product of the entire Invisible Government. He is therefore both umpire and player, the chairman of the board and a member of it.

In addition to producing the raw material for the national estimates, the CIA also provides the President with a daily top-secret checklist of the major world crises. Copies go to the Director of Central Intelligence and to the Secretaries of State and Defense. Top-ranking men in the CIA's Intelligence Division get to work at 3:00 A.M., to read the overnight cables and compile the checklist.

During the Kennedy Administration, the checklist was presented to the President the first thing each morning by Major General Chester V. (Ted) Clifton, the chief White House military aide. Under President Johnson, McGeorge Bundy initially assumed the responsibility for the morning intelligence briefing.

Special procedures have been established to assure that the President and the three other recipients of the checklist can be reached instantly in an emergency. An Indications Center is manned twenty-four hours a day by representatives of the CIA, the Pentagon and the State Department. It works under the guidance of a Watch Committee, which meets once a week to survey crisis situations and, if necessary, to recommend an immediate convening of the Board of Estimates.

*   *   *

The CIA had been rigorously compartmented in the interests of maximum security. The agency's left hand was purposely prevented from knowing what the right hand was doing. The Intelligence Division would receive all of the covert information collected by CIA agents abroad, but it was kept in ignorance about all clandestine operations. In the parlance of the trade, all cloak-and-dagger schemes were "vest pocketed" by the Plans Division.

*   *   *

Soon after McCone took office [in 1961], he decided to change the system. He set up a three-man study group composed of Lyman Kirkpatrick, General Cortlandt Van Rensselaer Schuyler, executive assistant to Governor Rockefeller, and J. Patrick Coyne, former FBI agent and executive director of the President's Foreign Intelligence Advisory Board.

Perhaps the most important change decided upon by McCone was his instruction to the Plans Division to keep the Intelligence Division continuously posted on all its activities. Thereafter, the Intelligence Division received "sanitized" reports (names of agents removed) on all current operations. The intelligence analysts were thus in a position for the first time to contest the special pleading of the men who were running the operations. On the basis of the large pool of information available to them from all branches of the Invisible Government, they could recommend changes in or complete cancellation of doubtful schemes.

Although there is some interchange of personnel, a natural suspicion exists between the Plans Division, which tends to attract activists and risk-takers, and the Intelligence Division, which tends to attract academic and contemplative types.

In its political complexion, too, the CIA splits roughly along the lines of its major functional responsibilities.

"The DDI side," one veteran CIA official explained, "tends to be liberal: they're at home with people like Schlesinger and Bundy. They tend to be liberal

Democrats and liberal Republicans. The other side of the house has many (types. It tends to get more conservative people, Bissell excepted. Helms I ... politics, he's just a good professional intelligence man. But there are all kinds in CIA, as you'd expect."

A frequent charge against the CIA, justified in part, is that it tends to support right-wing, military governments that it regards as "safe," ignoring more liberal elements that might, in the long run, provide a more effective hedge against Communism.

Viewed in this context, it is significant that officials in the Plans Division are considered by their colleagues to be by instinct and background more conservative than the pure intelligence analysts. It is the agents serving in foreign stations under the DDP, after all, who are most directly concerned in the field with the question of where to throw CIA support in a complex political situation.

While the work of all of these divisions is centered at Langley, the CIA also operates inside the United States in many locations and in many guises. Although few Americans are aware of it, the CIA has offices in twenty cities throughout the country. The National Security Act of 1947, establishing the CIA, stated that "the agency shall have no police, subpena, law-enforcement or internal-security functions." Since the CIA was created to deal exclusively with foreign intelligence, the question might be raised as to why it has field offices across the nation.

The answer CIA officials give is that the offices are needed to collect foreign intelligence domestically, principally from travelers returning from abroad.

* * *

THE SEARCH FOR CONTROL

To maintain the CIA and the other branches of the intelligence establishment, the government spends about $4,000,000,000 a year. The exact figure is one of the most tightly held secrets of the government and it appears in none of the Federal budget documents, public or private. It is unknown, in fact, even to many of the key officials in the Invisible Government. Because the intelligence community is carefully fragmented, those in one branch find it difficult to estimate the budgets of the others.

All of the budgets are pulled together by the director of the International Division of the Budget Bureau. He is assisted by four experts, each of whom handles about $1,000,000,000 of the Invisible Government's money. One assistant checks on the National Security Agency, the second on the CIA, the third on the DIA and military intelligence, and the fourth on overhead reconnaissance.

All of the Invisible Government's hidden money is buried in the Defense Department budget, mainly in the multibillion-dollar weapons contracts, such as those for the Minuteman and Polaris missiles. The Comptroller of the Pentagon knows where the money is hidden, but so carefully is it camouflaged, even his closest assistants are unable to guess at the amount.

It is not startling, then, that even those at the very center of the Invisible Government vary in their estimates of what is being spent. In a private briefing for high-ranking military men in the summer of 1963 McCone offered a figure of $2,000,000,000[2] and estimated that 100,000 persons were involved in intelligence work.

However, McCone appeared to be limiting his estimate to the money spent by the CIA and the other agencies on the more conventional forms of intelligence work. In addition, $2,000,000,000 is spent each year on electronic intelligence (the NSA and aerial spying). When the two forms of intelligence are included, the total budget reaches $4,000,000,000 and the personnel figure amounts to about 200,000.

It is often assumed that the National Security Council controls this vast intelligence establishment. But in practice much of the activity of the Invisible Government is never examined at NSC meetings. Nor is it disclosed to the United States Intelligence Board (which, for example, was not informed in advance of the Bay of Pigs).

The important decisions about the Invisible Government are made by the committee known as the Special Group. Although the composition of the committee has varied slightly, its membership has generally included the Director of Central Intelligence, the Under Secretary of State for Political Affairs (or his deputy), and the Secretary and Deputy Secretary of Defense. In the Kennedy and early Johnson Administrations, the presidential representative—and key man—on the Special Group was McGeorge Bundy. The others members were McCone, McNamara, Roswell Gilpatric, Deputy Secretary of Defense, and U. Alexis Johnson, Deputy Under Secretary of State for Political Affairs.

The Special Group was created early in the Eisenhower years under the secret Order 54/12. It was known in the innermost circle of the Eisenhower Administration as the "54/12 Group" and is still so called by a few insiders. The Special Group grew out of the "OCB luncheon group."[3] It has operated for a decade as the hidden power center of the Invisible Government. Its existence is virtually unknown outside the intelligence community and, even there, only a handful of men are aware of it.

The Special Group meets about once a week to make the crucial decisions— those which are too sensitive or too divisive to be entrusted to USIB. The more grandiose of the Invisible Government's operations have been launched in this exclusive arena. It is here in this hidden corner of the massive governmental apparatus that the United States is regularly committed to policies which walk the tightrope between peace and war.

CIA men generally have the Special Group in mind when they insist that the agency has never set policy, but has only acted on higher authority.

"The facts are," Allen Dulles has declared, "that the CIA has never carried out any action of a political nature, given any support of any nature to any persons, potentates or movements, political or otherwise, without appropriate approval at a high political level in our government *outside the CIA.*"

To the average citizen, Dulles' statement might logically conjure up a picture of the Cabinet, the National Security Council or some special presidential commission meeting in solemn session to debate the wisdom of a dangerous clandestine operation.

But, in fact, some decisions of this type have been made by the Special Group in an informal way without the elaborate records and procedures of other high government committees. And these fateful decisions have been made without benefit of outside analysis. Little detached criticism has been brought to bear on the natural human tendency of the leaders of the Invisible Government to embark upon ventures which might prove their toughness, demonstrate their vision or expand their power.

* * *

It is apparent, then, that the two presidential watchdog committees, the Board of Consultants on Foreign Intelligence Activities of the Eisenhower Administration and the Foreign Intelligence Advisory Board of the Kennedy and Johnson Administrations, have had great difficulty getting to the bottom of things. Both committees were composed of part-time consultants who met only occasionally during the year.

* * *

By 1954 substantial pressure had built up in Congress for a closer scrutiny of the intelligence community. Mike Mansfield, then a freshman senator from Montana, submitted a resolution that would have carried out the Hoover Commission recommendation by creating a Joint Committee on the Central Intelligence Agency. In its final form, the resolution called for a twelve-man committee, six from the Senate and six from the House, and for the appropriation of $250,000 for staff expenditures during the first year.

Thirty-four senators joined Mansfield in sponsoring the resolution. But by the time the proposal came to a vote on April ll, 1956, fourteen of these sponsors had reversed themselves, and the resolution was defeated, fifty-nine to twenty-seven. Thirteen of those who had changed their minds were Republicans evidently reflecting White House pressure. Many of the Democrats who voted against the resolution clearly were worried about disturbing Senator Richard B. Russell, the chairman of the Armed Services Committee, and other Democratic titans who opposed the idea.

Mansfield's language in introducing the resolution was not calculated to please the conservative inner club of the Senate, which enjoyed special relations with the Invisible Government.

"An urgent need exists," Mansfield said,

for regular and responsible Congressional scrutiny of the Central Intelligence Agency. Such scrutiny is essential to the success of our foreign policy, to the preservation of our democratic processes and to the security of the intelligence agency itself. . . .

If we fail to establish some sort of permanent, continuing link between Congress and the CIA, the only result will be growing suspicion. . . . In the first place, the whole concept of peacetime foreign intelligence operations has been alien to the American tradition. . . .

Our form of government . . . is based on a system of checks and balances. If this system gets seriously out of balance at any point the whole system is jeopardized and the way is opened for the growth of tyranny. . . .

CIA is freed from practically every ordinary form of Congressional check. Control of its expenditures is exempted from the provisions of the law which prevent financial abuses in other government agencies. Its appropriations are hidden in allotments to other agencies. . . .

I agree that an intelligence agency must maintain complete secrecy to be effective. However, there is a profound difference between an essential degree of secrecy to achieve a specific purpose and secrecy for the mere sake of secrecy. Once secrecy becomes sacrosanct, it invites abuse.

*   *   *

The CIA's view on whether there should be more Congressional scrutiny was stated officially in a letter to Mansfield from General Cabell on September 4, 1953. "It is our opinion," he wrote, "that, from our point of view, the present ties with Congress are adequate."

Allen Dulles agreed: "Any public impression that the Congress exerts no power over CIA is quite mistaken. Control of funds gives a control over the scope of operations—how many people CIA can employ, how much it can do and to some extent what it can do. . . .

"The chairman of the House [Appropriations] Subcommittee [on the CIA] is Clarence Cannon, and a more careful watchdog of the public treasury can hardly be found."

Whether or not Dulles' judgment held true for other budgetary matters, the eighty-three-year-old Cannon had no great reputation on his subcommittee as a "careful watchdog" of the CIA. In fact, he was such a good friend and great admirer of Dulles that much of the secret CIA hearings during Dulles' tenure were taken up with mutual congratulations. CIA officials came armed with thick black volumes, but the other members of the House Subcommittee never had time to probe deeply into the agency's activities. Some of the members displayed annoyance but could do little about it in view of Cannon's absolute control over the committee.

NOTES

[1] All figures on the number of persons involved in intelligence work are highly classified. But the ONI's figure slipped out through the oversight of a Pentagon censor in testimony released in 1961 by the House Defense Appropriations Subcommittee.

[2] Significantly, many CIA officials estimate that the Soviet Union spends $2 billion a year on its spy apparatus. On the other hand, Soviet Secret Police Chief Alexander N. Shelepin estimated in 1959 that the CIA spent $1.5 billion a year and employed 20,000 persons.

[3] The OCB, the Operations Coordinating Board, was composed of the Undersecretary of State, the Deputy Secretary of Defense, the President's Special Assistant (National Security Affairs), and the directors of CIA, USIA, and the old International Cooperation Administration. They were supposed to make sure the President's decisions were carried out in their departments. The OCB was abolished by President Kennedy in his first month in office.

The Real CIA

LYMAN B. KIRKPATRICK, JR.

While I had never envisaged myself as a financial expert, or a budgeteer, I found myself greatly enjoying the responsibilities of comptroller. The budget division of the Agency was a good one, staffed with able and aggressive individuals, and they were quick to establish a control room and a presentation system that became more and more impressive as this developed. I had of course had experience with the budget at every level, having had to defend my budget first as division chief and then as office chief over the years.

Our intensive work in developing a tight financial control system paid immense dividends when President Johnson announced his economy moves in December 1963. In accordance with the President's orders, we immediately instituted a vast program for savings in the Agency. While the Defense Department, with its massive expenditures got the headlines, I have always felt comparatively speaking that the CIA did as good or a better job in effecting economies.

Hardly had the agony of the first Johnson cutback passed when an even more potentially painful demand was made. Budget advised that all agencies would be allowed an average salary level that could not be exceeded.

A careful study was prepared to see what the average grade level proposed by the Bureau of the Budget would do to the CIA. It was disastrous. There would be no promotions for a long time. It would be impossible to fill any of the vacancies in important categories at high grades. It would severely affect the sound development of the Agency and the effect on morale was unpleasant to contemplate. A vast chart was prepared showing our personnel strengths and proposals in each grade and by each component over a five-year period. When Charles Schulze took over as the new director of the Budget in 1965, he and his then deputy, Elmer Staats, were invited to the CIA headquarters to be briefed on the Agency's system for money and manpower controls. They seemed impressed at what had been done in this "unorthodox" outfit in preparing a manpower control program. In any event, the effect on the Agency was there in black and white and the director of the Budget granted the necessary relief.

There has been a great deal of comment in the press over the years about the CIA's budget and how it is handled. The impression is left that Congress either gives the Agency a blank check, or is munificent in its largesse. Nothing could be further from the truth. The Agency must have its budget approved by the Bureau of the Budget—that is, by the two or three examiners, the chief and deputy chief of the International Division, and the director, deputy director, and an assistant director who all have clearances for all of the CIA's activities. The examiners who work on the CIA budget are always thoroughly acquainted with all that the Agency does or wants to do. The Bureau each year makes many pertinent recommendations, and is consistently tough in keeping the Agency's budget down. And once this hurdle is cleared, the CIA Subcommittee of House Appropriations goes into an equally intense review.

Further, every director of the CIA has insisted on the most meticulous care in recording all of the CIA's expenditures and accounting for every cent spent. When McCone added the cost-analysis system and stepped up improved management methods, the CIA's controls were as good as most in industry or government.

The National Security Council today provides a good forum for discussion of the highest policy matters in international affairs. Its statutory members consist of the Secretaries of State and Defense, the director of the Office of Emergency Planning, and the Vice President. The chairman of the Joint Chiefs of Staff and the director of Central Intelligence are the military and intelligence advisers and observers. It is chaired by the President himself.

The director of Central Intelligence as an intelligence adviser attends each meeting, usually gives an intelligence briefing on the world situation, and frequently is asked to participate by the President. The members of the NSC, particularly the Secretary of State and Secretary of Defense, are not only the two principal consumers of intelligence but also the heads of those departments most directly concerned with intelligence operations.

We need look no further back in our own history than to Pearl Harbor to view the chaos and catastrophe that comes from an intelligence system that lacks centralization, coordination, and a single voice in Washington.

There was an abundance of information available in Washington in November and early December 1941 on Japanese activities that had already alerted the American armed forces in the Pacific. . . .

. . . In the system prevailing in 1941, each intelligence organization reported only to its own chief, who may or may not have had access to the President. That system in effect made the President of the United States his own intelligence officer.

The tragedy of Pearl Harbor is not that there wasn't enough intelligence. There can always be more information in any situation, and hard information on the location of the Japanese task force that was headed for Pearl Harbor of course could have made all of the difference between surprise and alert. The tragedy is the fact that the information that was available was not put in one package so that all of the evidence could be sifted and weighed by an objective and dispassionate group and presented to the President in one package, with one conclusion.

President Roosevelt was put in the position of hearing some information from J. Edgar Hoover and the FBI, some from Secretary of State Hull, some from the Chief of Staff of the Army, George C. Marshall, and some from the Chief of Naval Operations, Admiral Harold R. Stark. In addition, he discussed the matter with a variety of other advisers and counselors. Perhaps most tragic was the fact that there was no group where all views and opinions could be thoroughly reviewed on the highest level. This lack of a high council in Washington was then, and has been on even more recent occasions, one of the grave dangers to our security. The Presidency is too high a post with too awesome power to be permitted informal arrangements for the highest policy decisions.

The creation of the National Security Council by the National Security Act of 1947 provided the President with an advisory body for such high-level deliberations, if he chooses to use it.

At the time of the Cuban missile crisis, a number of possible policy gambits were considered by the top echelon policy-makers in the week which elapsed between the discovery of the missiles and President Kennedy's speech of October 22. The director of Central Intelligence, John McCone, was asked to estimate probable reactions (notably Soviet and Cuban) to the possible United States courses of action. It is notable that the findings of the director and the intelligence community were proved sound in every case.

This situation is a magnificent illustration of the role of the director of Central Intelligence as the principal intelligence officer of the United States. Imagine how much more difficult the situation would have been if there had been no central organization, and no coordinated production of intelligence. If each of the departments had presented its own intelligence, and its own assessment of the situation, as had been done at the time of Pearl Harbor, the NSC would have spent as much of its time weighing and assessing intelligence as it did deliberating over courses of action. As it was, the NSC was confident that all of the intelligence experts, representing their departments, had analyzed with care the incoming reports and that the DCI had presented their combined judgment.

Unfortunately there are still those who do not recognize the merits of the system and who try to reduce the role of the director of Central Intelligence or to divorce him from the Central Intelligence Agency, either of which would set back the system to pre-Pearl Harbor days and seriously endanger the security of the country.

The present system provides the President with an objective, overall presentation of intelligence based upon the total knowledge available to the

United States government. It does not deprive any of the departments of any of their established rights and responsibilities or inhibit their presenting a differing view at either the intelligence or policy level. It has created a voice in the government that can speak without being restrained by either policy problems or budget considerations. It can provide one of the most important contributions to the policy makers as long as the director of Central Intelligence is strong and forceful and has sufficient character not to worry if on occasion the views he is presenting may differ from those of such influential officials as the Secretary of Defense, or Secretary of State, or the chairman of the Joint Chiefs of Staff.

The question is often raised as to why the intelligence function for the government cannot be handled by the Department of State, or the Department of Defense, or both. Is there really a need for a central organization?

The Department of State has a mission that is basically incompatible with intelligence. If it is assumed that it is the President of the United States who makes the foreign policy, then it would be safe also to assume that it is the Secretary of State who is the President's principal staff officer for the development of the foreign policy, and that it is his Department that must do the bulk of the pick-and-shovel work.

If these assumptions are correct then the Department of State should play no greater role in the intelligence system than that of a consumer of information prepared by a central organization, but based on all reporting from all sources. It would be only human if the officials of the State Department wanted success for a policy they had formulated. Therefore their objectivity in processing information reports relating to that policy would be subject to question. This problem would be as true abroad as it is in Washington.

This can be well illustrated by an actual case that happened not long ago, but which for obvious reasons will not be precisely identified.

The United States policy was to put its full support behind the "X" government in country "Y." The ambassador was, as he should be, fully committed to the pursuit of that policy. This obviously affected his reaction to reports that the X government was corrupt, inefficient, dictatorial, and hated by the people. How many times has the United States government decided that it was following a poor policy and changed it without being forced to by events beyond its control? And how many times have United States ambassadors urged Washington to change a policy when they realized it was wrong?

The X case is an apt illustration. Intelligence reports that were assessed as having a high degree of reliability by the collector definitely indicated that the X government was very unpopular and was in danger. The ambassador not only refused to place any credence in the reports, but even tried to prevent their being transmitted back to Washington. When he was convinced that he had no authority to suppress the reports, he cabled Washington attacking the reports as unreliable and dangerous. A week later the X government was overthrown by a coup.

Ones cannot fault the ambassador too harshly for passionately pushing the policy that his government was pursuing. But one would hope that most ambassadors would be more receptive to new information that might suggest modification of a policy.

The ambassador's efforts to suppress information reports that disagreed with his views, however, revealed an abysmal ignorance of the purpose of the intelligence organization, which was there for him to use just as much as it was there to report back to Washington. Because the information that had been produced from clandestine sources did not agree with information that he and his staff had obtained from overt contacts, the ambassador looked on his "spooks"—as he relished calling them at cocktail parties—as antagonists and not part of his own staff.

This is of course another example of incompatibility of intelligence work with diplomacy. The much more important reason for not putting national intelligence in the State Department is that inevitably an intelligence organization will attract attention, as the CIA has, and this in turn would tend to discredit the veracity of the Department of State. Thus, perhaps it is best that State's intelligence work be confined to research in support of policy that is basically all that the present Bureau of Intelligence Research does. In other words, their responsibility is to assemble and present intelligence material from the CIA and other agencies to the policy makers in the department.

Arguments that the production of national intelligence should be turned over to the Department of Defense are equally dangerous. The Department of Defense is charged with providing military security for the United States. The training, interests, attitudes, and conditioning of its personnel are in that area. National intelligence involves much more than purely military security considerations. It must go deeply into the political background of various nations, complicated international arrangements, and the psychology of world leaders, more of whom are civilian than military.

Those responsible for the defense of the United States only naturally want to be prepared to face all possible enemies under every contingency, in any place in the world. No nation could afford this type of defense establishment and consequently there must be a judgment as to what it can afford. It appears logical that such a judgment may be better reached separately from the Defense Department.

The creation of the Defense Intelligence Agency has provided an excellent vehicle for the Defense Department to satisfy its own intelligence requirements, but it is not equipped for the preparation of national intelligence. By its military nature it could never attract the type of civilian intelligence officers that have manned the Central Intelligence Agency for the last two decades.

Finally, should the Defense Department ever receive a national intelligence mandate it would automatically be at sword's point with the State Department, which is responsible for all foreign policy.

Having over the years considered and studied all of these various possibilities, I came to the conclusion that the central intelligence concept provided the most effective method for providing the top policy makers of the government with impartial, objective, and unopinionated intelligence—that is, as far as mortals can produce it. This places on the director of Central Intelligence a particular responsibility for rapport with the policy makers of the government, particularly those in the Department of Defense and State.

All of the Directors of Central Intelligence have been extremely conscious of the relations of intelligence to the policy makers. They have also been aware of their responsibilities to Congress. Yet there have been no two areas of intragovernmental relations on which so much inaccurate information has reached the public. Two of the favorite themes of the press have been that the CIA (and thereby the intelligence system) has been immune from congressional scrutiny and that the Agency has been involved in making (or even worse, subverting) United States foreign policy.

Almost from the start of my career in the Agency I was associated with the organization's congressional relations, and for several years was charged with the responsibility of giving it general supervision on behalf of the director.

Each of the directors with whom I served had a slightly different technique for dealing with Congress, and each in my opinion had excellent relations with Congress almost consistently during their tenure of office. . . . In 1955 Senator Mike Mansfield, then the Majority Whip, introduced a bill for a Joint Committee on the CIA. He had thirty-four co-sponsors for his bill, several of whom withdrew before the final vote. This is the only such bill that reached the floor of the Senate and on April 9, 1956, there was a spirited debate, with the proposal finally defeated by a vote of 59 to 27 and Mansfield abandoned even by the then Majority Leader Lyndon Johnson. Mansfield felt then, as I am sure he does today, that the degree of congressional supervision over the CIA was not sufficient and that a Joint Committee could supply what was missing. He also was gravely concerned that the Agency's influence in the conduct of United States foreign relations was too great and that Congress should be more fully informed of what was going on in the invisible field. It is rather interesting to note that even if John F. Kennedy co-sponsored the initial bill, he opposed a Joint Committee when he became President, as had Eisenhower before him and Johnson since.

Allen Dulles naturally had to face an irate Congress after both the U-2 episode in May 1960 and the Bay of Pigs in April 1961, but in each instance he was able to establish to the satisfaction of the appropriate committees that the Agency was not acting irresponsibly but under the proper control and supervision of the Executive branch. Whether one agrees or disagrees with the wisdom of the activities concerned, there was no doubt that the Agency acted on higher orders.

The real issue in Congress is whether the Senate Foreign Relations Committee should review the work of the CIA. This is the contention of such men as

Senator Mansfield and Senator Eugene McCarthy of Minnesota. Mansfield's original proposal for a Joint Committee on Intelligence was very unpopular in the House where the members feel that they are the minority in any joint committee. Joint Committees are also unpopular with the standing committees and the creation of one for intelligence—or for the CIA—would not result in either the Armed Services or Appropriations Committees yielding their established responsibilities. This would mean that the CIA would be subjected to the review of three different committees.

In the first session of the 90th Congress in January 1967, three members of the Senate Foreign Relations Committee were added to the Joint Armed Services-Appropriations Subcommittee that reviews the CIA's work. A proposal to do this in the previous Congress had met with open hostility on the part of Senator Richard Russell, chairman of the Armed Services Committee, and had been effectively killed when the Senate voted 67 to 28 to refer the resolution to the Armed Services Committee, where it was pigeonholed. Senator Russell changed his mind during the course of 1966 and the broadened representation on the Senate's CIA subcommittee is important evidence of congressional review.

In my opinion it had been most unfortunate that some senators and some congressmen make the CIA the scapegoat for the failure to work out an arrangement for review of the Agency's work among themselves. Their efforts were usually rewarded in that portion of the press hostile to the CIA with articles implying that there was something wrong with the Agency or that congressional supervision was inadequate. This hurt the Agency in the eyes of the public and was not warranted.

I would be the last to maintain that Congress could not have exerted, within the realm of security, more detailed review of the Agency's work. A competent review would depend on whether the congressmen involved were willing to take the time, which might entail two or three days a month, to go over with the Agency what it was doing. Not the least of the effort would be the necessity to obtain a basic knowledge of the extensive and complicated work not only of the CIA but of the entire intelligence system. The present committees can well do this, and some of their members have made a conscientious effort to do so.

But truthfully, in my opinion, the underlying problem in Congress as far as the CIA is concerned, does not concern intelligence but those other things that the CIA may be directed to do by the policy makers. I have no intention of discussing those other things other than to say that I feel in some instances the policy makers have seized on the CIA's apparatus for covert action as a method to solve some of their problems that they cannot solve by diplomacy or direct military action. Unfortunately, the CIA in its youthful enthusiasm has been more than willing to try and accomplish what the policy makers wanted done, and while their successes have been many, their failures have been public. It has been these failures that have attracted unfavorable attention to the Agency and focused the attention of the Foreign Relations Committee on its work. This matter of covert action is a sensitive area for the Agency to be in and should be used only with the greatest caution and under the most extreme emergency requirements. If these conditions were followed, the Agency's reputation would be restored.

In any event, it is the director of Central Intelligence to whom Congress looks for the good conduct of the Agency. Fortunately, each of the directors thus far have enjoyed the confidence of Congress and this has served the organization well.

One of the inevitable problems that the director of Central Intelligence faces is that while he must deal with Congress on many delicate matters and important issues, he is the President's man. This can be awkward at times when intelligence has been accurate but policy has been faulty. For example, during the Suez crisis of 1956 United States intelligence was superb. It carefully followed the deepening problems with the United Arab Republic and was accurate in indicating Nasser's violent reaction to the United States refusal to support the building of the Aswan Dam.

Being well aware of the critical situation, all United States intelligence agencies followed with meticulous care the military activities of the Israelis, the British, and the French in the Middle East. It was an alert Army attaché in Tel Aviv who flashed the warning that the Israelis had mobilized and that this time they definitely were going to attack Egypt through the Sinai Peninsula and that the attack was imminent. This gave Washington time for the Intelligence Watch Committee, the second highest formal body in the Intelligence system, composed of the number-two men in all of the agencies, to study the situation and warn the policy level that this meant war against Egypt. President Eisenhower strenuously urged the three powers to cease and desist but the attack took place.

Following the attack, John Foster Dulles made the statement that "we were not informed," and this was immediately taken by Congress and the press to mean that there had been a major intelligence failure. The Secretary of State meant that the United States government had not been informed by the British, French, or Israelis of their plans. Brother Allen was obviously in no position to correct the misimpression at that time.

The relations of the director of Central Intelligence with the President therefore must be among the closest of the senior echelon in Washington. However, it should never be such that it interferes with or cuts across the President's relations with his Secretaries of State and Defense. Consequently, it is a dangerous practice for the director of Central Intelligence to consult with the President alone on substantive matters, or for that matter on operational matters. There is nothing so highly classified that should not be known by the Secretaries of State and Defense, even though on occasion operational matters in intelligence areas must obviously be confined to a limited number of people in

Washington. However, to even go further and say that operational matters should be confined solely to the President and the Secretaries of State and Defense would deprive them of expert advice from their own staffs that they should be allowed to seek, none of them presumably being experienced in intelligence.

The soundest system for the DCI's relations with the President revolves around the briefings given the National Security Council, or even more limited groups, by the director of Central Intelligence. In this fashion the President and his Secretaries of State and Defense simultaneously hear from the chief intelligence officer of the United States. They can discuss, debate, or disagree with his interpretation and hopefully reach some agreement on the conditions that affect American security. This is especially true when there are, and for the foreseeable future will continue to be, areas of ignorance where intelligence cannot be precise due to the lack of hard facts. No better illustration of this exists than the absence of precise information on the reaction in Hanoi to United States bombings of North Vietnam.

While the director of Central Intelligence is obviously in a position of considerable influence, one should not assume that his role is enviable. If he is to do his job properly he may find himself on occasion expressing a minority viewpoint, or even disagreeing with the President of the United States. This he must do, and assuming that all present are statesmen, the country will benefit therefrom.

Another unenviable assignment for the DCI is that of coordinating the total United States intelligence effort. This involves tying together the work of three of the most important departments in the Cabinet—State, Defense, and Justice—and dealing at several different echelons of the government with organizations that have both departmental and national responsibilities. The law that created the CIA wisely provides that it will have access to all of the information of all of the other agencies. The director is given authority to inspect the files of these other organizations if he so desires. But despite this broad authority, there is an almost inevitable bureaucratic resistance to supervision and coordination from without. The United States Intelligence Board was particularly well used by John McCone to coordinate the total intelligence effort, but one should not assume that this is easily done or can always be accomplished without considerable bureaucratic in-fighting.

The necessity for coordination becomes most obvious in presenting intelligence to the President. If the central intelligence concept is to be successful, then the intelligence should represent the combined wisdom as well as the resources of the total intelligence effort as assembled, collated, analyzed, and produced for the director of Central Intelligence by the CIA.

The coordination role of the director of Central Intelligence has been gradually extended into the budgetary field and more and more the President has been, as he should be, looking to the director to defend not just the CIA budget but the budget for the total United States intelligence effort. This first occurred during the Eisenhower administration, when the President was startled by its size the first time he saw a cumulative budget for the total United States intelligence effort. That budget has now multiplied several times, and one might take this to be an indication of the growth of bureaucracy. But intelligence is a necessity and not a luxury. It is rather ridiculous to try and be penurious about intelligence expenditures as long as there are any gaps in our information.

There have been efforts to put the director of Central Intelligence on the same side of the table as the Bureau of the Budget in examining the budgetary presentations of the other intelligence agencies. This was first presented to Mr. McCone who wisely resisted it and instead used the United States Intelligence Board as the vehicle for coordinating the intelligence budgets. It was always incredible to me that some of the intelligence organizations even then did not recognize the necessity for full cooperation and were not forthcoming with all of the information required. This was undoubtedly a residue of the resentment in the intelligence department of the powerful and centralized position of the director of Central Intelligence.

The President also looks to the director of Central Intelligence as the principal intelligence officer of the United States in dealing with foreign intelligence services and with their governments on intelligence matters. This is extremely important because of the propensity of some foreign intelligence services to try and play off one United States intelligence organization against another. In recent years the skill and experience of the CIA in liaison with foreign intelligence services has been more and more recognized and consequently foreign intelligence services have had less success in trying to divide the United States services.

Finally, the director of Central Intelligence is the personification of the United States intelligence effort to the American people. How exactly this role is to be enacted has not yet been adequately determined. Allen Dulles very wisely moved into the vacuum in the Executive branch of the government on the subject of Communism and spoke often and well on Communist activities in various parts of the world. His views were the only measured sound on the subject in the United States at the time of Senator Joseph McCarthy's accusations. But Mr. Dulles was criticized for this by some who felt that the director of Central Intelligence should be a silent and unseen figure. These people were doing the intelligence agency and the American system a disservice and were equating the CIA only with espionage and operations and were ignoring the fact that it is the largest single research organization on Communism anywhere in the world, and thus can speak on this subject with unequalled expertise. John McCone, in taking over the directorship, had been warned by President Kennedy and his colleagues on the dangers of public speeches and consequently shunned them until his last days in office when he broke his self-imposed rule in order to accept some awards.

While the director of Central Intelligence in no way should compete with either the Secretary of State or the Secretary of Defense in their comments on world situations, diplomatic or military, he nevertheless should be the federal spokesman where the subject is primarily intelligence. Those who maintain that the director of Central Intelligence should be unseen and unheard fail to recognize the realities of life in a free society. It should be recognized by now that whenever there is a scrap of publishable information about the CIA, it will be exploited to the nth degree. Only the stature and image of the director of Central Intelligence, one of the very few public figures in the Agency, can serve to counterbalance the inevitable adverse publicity.

The future of the United States intelligence effort will indeed rest upon the proper application of the legitimate power that the director of Central Intelligence possesses. It is important that he be strong and that his voice be heard at the highest level of the government. Efforts to weaken him or to submerge his influence are contrary to the national interest. It is vital that he report directly to the President and not through any intermediate echelon. It is equally important that the CIA not be subordinate either in fact or through political pressure to any other department or agency. . . .

The Secret Team
and
the Games they Play

L. FLETCHER PROUTY

The hill costumes of the Meo tribesmen contrasted with the civilian clothes of United States military men riding in open jeeps and carrying M-16 rifles and pistols. These young Americans are mostly ex-Green Berets, hired on CIA contract to advise and train Laotian troops.

Those matter-of-fact, almost weary sentences, written late in February by T. D. Allman of *The Washington Post* after he and two other enterprising correspondents left a guided tour and walked 12 miles over some hills in Laos to a secret base at Long Cheng describe a situation that today may seem commonplace to anyone familiar with American operations overseas, but that no more than 10 years ago would have been unthinkable.

To take a detachment of regular troops, put its members into disguise, smuggle them out of the country so that neither the public nor the Congress knows they have left, and assign them to clandestine duties on foreign soil under the command of a non-military agency—it is doubtful that anyone would have dared to suggest taking such liberties with the armed forces and foreign relations of the United States, not to say with the Constitution, to any President up to and especially including Dwight D. Eisenhower.

Indeed, the most remarkable development in the management of America's relations with other countries during the nine years since Mr. Eisenhower left office has been the assumption of more and more control over military and diplomatic operations abroad by men whose activities are secret, whose budget is secret, whose very identities as often as not are secret—in short a Secret Team whose actions only those implicated in them are in a position to monitor.

How determinedly this secrecy is preserved, even when preserving it means denying the United States Army the right to discipline its own personnel, not to say the opportunity to do justice, was strikingly illustrated not long ago by the refusal of the Central Intelligence Agency to provide witnesses for the

---

Reprinted from *The Washington Monthly*, May 1970, pp. 11-13, 16-19. Reprinted by permission of the author and publisher.

court-martial that was to try eight Green Beret officers for murdering a suspected North Vietnamese spy, thus forcing the Army to drop the charges.

The Secret Team consists of security-cleared individuals in and out of government who receive secret intelligence data gathered by the CIA and the National Security Agency and who react to those data when it seems appropriate to them with paramilitary plans and activities, e.g., training and "advising"—a not exactly impenetrable euphemism for "leading into battle"—Laotian troops. Membership in the Team, granted on a "need to know" basis, varies with the nature and the location of the problems that come to its attention.

At the heart of the Team, of course, are a handful of top executives of the CIA and of the National Security Council, most notably the chief White House adviser on foreign policy. Around them revolves a sort of inner ring of Presidential staff members, State Department officials, civilians and military men from the Pentagon, and career professionals in the intelligence services.

And out beyond them is an extensive and intricate network of government officials with responsibility for or expertise in some specific field that touches on national security think-tank analysts, businessmen who travel a lot or whose businesses (e.g., import-export or operating a cargo airline) are useful, academic experts in this or that technical subject or geographic region, and, quite importantly, alumni of the intelligence service—a service from which there are no unconditional resignations.

Thus the Secret Team is not a clandestine super-planning board of super-general staff but, even more damaging to the coherent conduct of foreign affairs, a bewildering collection of temporarily assembled action committees that respond pretty much ad hoc to specific troubles in various parts of the world, sometimes in ways that duplicate the activities of regular American missions, sometimes in ways that undermine those activities, and very often in ways that interfere with and muddle them.

For example, when serious border troubles broke out along the northern frontiers of India, Pakistan, Nepal, and Bhutan in 1962, the CIA brought in U.S. military equipment and manpower, including Special Forces (Green Beret) troops, to train Indian police, despite the fact that the Joint Chiefs of Staff had already sent to New Delhi for the same purpose a special team headed by Gen. Paul Adams, founder and commanding general of the U.S. Strike Command. The CIA operators practically ignored Gen. Adams and Ambassador John Kenneth Galbraith in proceeding with their plans, and there is no evidence that the U.S. Congress ever knew the CIA was in the picture at all.

One source of the Team's power is the speed with which it can act. The CIA's communications system is so extraordinarily efficient, especially by contrast with State's, that the Team can, in a phrase that often gets used at such times, "have a plane in the air" responding to some situation overseas while State is still decoding the cable informing it of that situation.

A few years ago, for example, while the strongest member of an Asian government that the United States was strenuously supporting (call him Marshal X) was lying sick in a Tokyo hospital, word came that a group of discontented young officers was planning a coup in his absence. In a matter of hours, thanks to the Team, Marshal X was on his way home in a U.S. Air Force jet fighter; he arrived at his office in plenty of time to frustrate the plotters.

The power to pull off feats like that is more than operational power; it is in a real sense policy-making power. In this particular case it was the power to commit the United States to the protection and support of Marshal X, even though many officials who dealt with Marshal X's government on a workaday basis regarded him as the most obnoxious member of it.

Calling back "a plane in the air" is not an easy thing to do, and the Team knows and benefits from this fact.

Another source of the Team's power is its ability to manipulate "need to know" classifications. One way to make sure that there is little opposition to your proposed activities is to fail to tell those who might oppose them what those activities are; even men with high-ranking policy-making jobs and the appropriate Top Secret clearances often are kept in the dark about Team plans.

Thus Adlai Stevenson, ambassador to the United Nations, was not informed about the Bay of Pigs invasion plans until the very last minute when rumors about it began to appear in the press; and even then Tracy Barnes, the CIA man sent to brief Stevenson, gave him a vague and incomplete picture of the operation.

After the Bay of Pigs, which some people vainly hoped would end large-scale, paramilitary CIA clandestine operations, President Kennedy appointed a board of inquiry to review the fiasco. Its members were Adm. Arleigh Burke, Allen Dulles, Attorney Gen. Robert Kennedy, and Gen. Maxwell Taylor.

Gen. Taylor, dissatisfied with the role the Eisenhower Administration had assigned to the Army, had retired from the service after his tour as Army Chief of Staff to write *The Uncertain Trumpet*. While serving on the board of inquiry, he became close friends with Robert Kennedy. Dulles and Bobby Kennedy recommended him for the post of Special Military Adviser to the President, and the President later named him chairman of the Joint Chiefs of Staff.

In those posts, by playing the game with the CIA, especially with respect to Vietnam, Taylor was able to preside over a major rebirth of the Army. The Vietnam buildup, whose beginning was engineered by the CIA, ultimately meant the abandonment of Eisenhower's exclusive reliance on Strategic Air Command and missile strategy in favor of the policy Taylor wanted—of developing a capacity to meet brushfire situations with conventional ground forces, Army forces naturally.

The most important respect in which Taylor played the Secret Team game was to acquiesce in giving the CIA operational control of the Green Beret forces in

Vietnam and Laos. The CIA took full advantage of this unprecedented situation, which saw the agency in control of those forces at least through 1963, by using it to stimulate inter-service rivalries. The rivalries led to an increase in the buildup, and the buildup led to more power for the Secret Team.

Because of the favored position of the Army's Green Berets, the other services thought it would be wise for them to have Special Forces of their own in Vietnam. The Air Force had a number of specialized aircraft and crews left over from the Bay of Pigs operation; these were organized into the nucleus of Special Air Warfare units and hurried to Vietnam to work with the CIA.

Not to be outdone by the Army and the Air Force, the Navy created special units known as SEAL (Sea-Air-Land) teams and sent them to Vietnam to work with the Agency.

Such actions resulted in a considerable clandestine buildup of forces in Vietnam long before the official escalation took place. And of course, once those forces were there something had to be done with them.

For example, the Air Force contribution consisted of units of C-123 medium transport aircraft. However, there already were plenty of medium transports in Vietnam—Caribous, under Army control, that had been flown there via the Atlantic, not having enough range to cross the Pacific. Consequently, Defense Secretary Robert McNamara had a squadron of C-123's converted at considerable cost to become defoliant sprayer aircraft.

It may be too much to say that the defoliation program would never have been undertaken if those C-123's hadn't been sitting idly in Vietnam, but there is no doubt that their presence gave the program considerable stimulation.

The CIA is most adept at working in and around and through all levels of the U.S. government. No one, not even the majority of Agency personnel, knows the full extent of agency manipulations within the governmental structure. The Agency can obtain what it desires in any quantity, and often for no cost.

During the depression years of the 1930's, Congress passed a law which was known as the Economy Act of 1932 and, as amended, it is still on the books. This act, whose purpose is to save money and discourage needless spending, permits an agency that needs material to purchase it at an agreed price from another agency by an accounting off-set without spending "new money."

For example, the Department of Agriculture can buy surplus tractors from the Army at a price agreed upon by both parties, even if it is only a dollar each. (Since most such equipment is declared surplus, whether it is or not, by the selling agency, the price usually is low.) By means of authority of this kind, the CIA has learned how to "buy" from all agencies of the government, primarily from the Department of Defense, a tremendous amount of new and surplus equipment—and to take over bases at home and abroad for its own use without appearing to have spent substantial funds and many times without the selling party knowing the true identity of the buyer.

This method of budgetary bypassing works something like this: The Agency creates an Army unit for some minor purpose which the Army and the Defense Department are willing to agree to. The unit is listed on the Army roster as, say, the 1234 Special Supply Company, Fort Wyman (fictional name), New Jersey.

This small and inconspicuous unit is mostly manned by regular Army personnel but will have a few Army personnel who are actually CIA employes with reserve status, and a few CIA career employes. It can serve as a supply receiving point for holding Agency material prior to overseas shipment.

After 1234 has been operating for a time and appears to be a bona-fide Army unit, not only to the rest of the Army personnel at Fort Wyman but also to the real Army people who are serving with it, it will begin to requisition supplies of all kinds and amounts from the Army. This procedures continues for a time, then the unit will begin to requisition in a normal manner items from the Navy and the Air Force.

With these hidden sources of supply, the CIA often can build an arsenal and support clandestine operations in some foreign country without the Department of Defense, much less the Department of State, ever knowing it—though presumably Defense could find out if it took the trouble to scrutinize carefully the activities of its various 1234's.

It was this power and freedom to move forces and equipment quickly without the usual review by proper authority that made possible the first entry of troops and equipment into South Vietnam in the early Sixties. In order to mount a particular operation it considered important, the CIA needed 24 helicopters and it obtained White House permission over strenuous objections from the Pentagon to have them sent to Vietnam.

Sending 24 helicopters anywhere automatically means sending 400 men as well, counting only pilots and gunners and mechanics and cooks and clerks and bakers and rest of the immediate establishment. If the intention is—and the intention always is—to give those 24 helicopters real support, then it involves sending 1,200 men.

Moreover, the statistics are that, in any helicopter squadron, because of maintenance servicing requirements, only half the machines will be operational at any one time. So if 24 operational helicopters are needed, 48 will have to be sent, which means 2,400 men.

But if you're sending a supporting force involving 2,400 men, then the support for them—PX's, movies, motor pools, officers' and enlisted men's clubs, perimeter guards to protect all this, and so on and so on—becomes really extensive, and thousands more men get attached to it. And so it goes.

"Twenty-four helicopters" can, in fact did, ultimately mean a full-scale military involvement.

The CIA also knows how to get research and development contracts it initiates transferred to the Department of Defense when it comes time to make quantity purchases of the new equipment, and then, once DOD has spent the money, requisition that equipment back through outfits like 1234.

Something very much like this happened with the M-16 rifle, which, as the result of the Team's machinations, is now a standard infantry weapon. The reasons the CIA first wanted the M-16 developed are obscure, though perhaps one of them is that it is a "NATO caliber" piece and therefore does not rely on American-made ammunition, and perhaps another is that it is small and light and therefore suitable for use by guerrillas and counter-guerrillas.

In any case, a decision was made that the M-16 was needed in quantity by the CIA for certain operations in Asia, and Fairchild, the aircraft company, was given a research and development contract. At the time, the CIA was unable to elicit any interest at all in the project from the Army, which was fighting a rear-guard action against Secretary McNamara's decision to close its venerated Springfield Arsenal; it refused to look at a weapon that had not gone the Army Ordnance route.

However, the CIA was able to push the M-16 through the office of the Secretary of Defense, over the head of the Army, and then induce the Air Force to put in a procurement order for 60,000 of the M-16's. Not long after the Air Force received delivery of the 60,000 rifles, they vanished mysteriously somewhere overseas.

The Agency's operatives appear in the organizations of many other government agencies. A visitor to the overseas office of a Military Advisory Group that presumably has a staff of 40 might find a hundred men working in the MAAG compound; these are CIA people whose salaries are paid by the Agency so that budget reviews in Washington will not reveal their existence. These people are in addition to the large number of military personnel carried on its budget for the ostensible purpose of cross-training; and this does not count the Special Forces troops.

Sometimes the official military may be unaware of the activities of supposed members of its own MAAG groups or other military organizations. In similar fashion, as revealed by *Los Angeles Times* reporter Jack Foisie, the CIA is using the State Department's AID program as a cover for clandestine operations.

In Laos, the number of agents posing as civilian AID workers totals several hundred. They are listed as members of the AID mission's Rural Development Annex.

In sum, during the last decade the White House's National Security Council apparatus and the CIA—particularly its operational side, which now has nine overseas employes to every one on the intelligence-gathering side—have grown enormously both in size and in influence.

More and more foreign-policy decisions are being made in secret, in response only to immediate crises rather than in accordance with long-range plans, and all too often with very little consultation with professional foreign-policy or military planners.

More and more overseas operations are being conducted in secret, and ad hoc, and with very little control by professional diplomats or soldiers.

And the one organ of government that, on behalf of the people that elected it, should be monitoring these goings-on, is today as ignorant as the public—because Congress submitted to secrecy on a grand scale years ago when it authorized the CIA. It is hard to imagine how or when the Secret Team can be brought into the open and made publicly accountable for its actions.

4

CASE STUDIES:
THE WAR IN VIETNAM

The Vietnamese conflict is the foreign policy area of greatest concern to most Americans in the 1970's. Our involvement in this conflict can be traced back to the end of the second World War, and it is now more than six years since this nation decided to commit an enormous amount of resources toward winning this conflict. James C. Thomson, Jr., a Harvard professor of Far East history, who spent several years in the White House Office and in the Department of State during the Johnson administration, tries to answer the question: how did we involve ourselves in Vietnam? While none of his specific answers to this question can be supported with hard data, each of them is more than ample food for a great deal of thought. Eugene Eidenberg discusses the decision making process which led to the Americanization of the war in 1965. Eidenberg emphasizes the incremental nature of decision making for Vietnam and notes that the series of "small" decisions led to a situation which none of the principal actors would have decided to enter had they known what would come about. Newspaper reporters Hedrick Smith and William Beecher discuss the policy process leading to the President's decision in March 1968 to curtail the bombing of North Vietnam in an attempt to get North Vietnam to the bargaining table. The final item in this section is Hedrick Smith's reconstruction of President Nixon's decision of April, 1970, to invade Cambodia.

Samuel P. Huntington has argued that military policy making is executive in locale and legislative in nature. By this, he means that basic military policy decisions are made within the executive branch of government, but are the result of a competitive process, in which various executive agencies representing differing viewpoints share power with each other. The reader should ask himself whether Huntington's characterization of the policy process describes the

decisions relating to Vietnam which are discussed in the readings in this section
He should further ask himself how the policy making process sketched here
coincides with the various accounts of the nature of power in the foreign policy
making process which have been sketched in previous sections of this volume.

How Could Vietnam Happen?
An Autopsy

JAMES C. THOMSON, JR.

As a case study in the making of foreign policy, the Vietnam War will fascinate historians and social scientists for many decades to come. One question that will certainly be asked: How did men of superior ability, sound training, and high ideals—American policy-makers of the 1960s—create such costly and divisive policy?

As one who watched the decision-making process in Washington from 1961 to 1966 under Presidents Kennedy and Johnson, I can suggest a preliminary answer. I can do so by briefly listing some of the factors that seemed to me to shape our Vietnam policy during my years as an East Asia specialist at the State Department and the White House. I shall deal largely with Washington as I saw or sensed it, and not with Saigon, where I have spent but a scant three days, in the entourage of the Vice President, or with other decision centers, the capitals of interested parties. Nor will I deal with other important parts of the record: Vietnam's history prior to 1961, for instance, or the overall course of America's relations with Vietnam.

Yet a first and central ingredient in these years of Vietnam decisions does involve history. The ingredient was *the legacy of the 1950s*—by which I mean the so-called "loss of China," the Korean War, and the Far East policy of Secretary of State Dulles.

This legacy had an institutional by-product for the Kennedy Administration: in 1961 the U.S. government's East Asian establishment was undoubtedly the most rigid and doctrinaire of Washington's regional divisions in foreign affairs. This was especially true at the Department of State, where the incoming Administration found the Bureau of Far Eastern Affairs the hardest nut to crack. It was a bureau that had been purged of its best China expertise, and of farsighted, dispassionate men, as a result of McCarthyism. Its members were generally committed to one policy line: the close containment and isolation of

From *The Atlantic Monthly* 22, April 1968, pp. 47-53. Copyright © 1968, by The Atlantic Monthly Company, Boston, Mass. Reprinted with permission.

mainland China, the harassment of "neutralist" nations which sought to avoid alignment with either Washington or Peking, and the maintenance of a network of alliances with anti-Communist client states on China's periphery.

Another aspect of the legacy was the special vulnerability and sensitivity of the new Democratic Administration on Far East policy issues. The memory of the McCarthy era was still very sharp, and Kennedy's margin of victory was too thin. The 1960 Offshore Islands TV debate between Kennedy and Nixon had shown the President-elect the perils of "fresh thinking." The Administration was inherently leery of moving too fast on Asia. As a result, the Far East Bureau (now the Bureau of East Asian and Pacific Affairs) was the last one to be overhauled. Not until Averell Harriman was brought in as Assistant Secretary in December, 1961, were significant personnel changes attempted, and it took Harriman several months to make a deep imprint on the bureau because of his necessary preoccupation with the Laos settlement. Once he did so, there was virtually no effort to bring back the purged or exiled East Asia experts.

There were other important by-products of this "legacy of the fifties":

The new Administration inherited and somewhat shared a *general perception of China-on-the-march*—a sense of China's vastness, its numbers, its belligerence; a revived sense, perhaps, of the Golden Horde. This was a perception fed by Chinese intervention in the Korean War (an intervention actually based on appallingly bad communications and mutual miscalculation on the part of Washington and Peking; but the careful unraveling of that tragedy, which scholars have accomplished, had not yet become part of the conventional wisdom).

The new Administration inherited and briefly accepted *a monolithic conception of the Communist bloc.* Despite much earlier predictions and reports by outside analysts, policy-makers did not begin to accept the reality and possible finality of the Sino-Soviet split until the first weeks of 1962. The inevitably corrosive impact of competing nationalisms on Communism was largely ignored.

The new Administration inherited and to some extent shared *the "domino theory" about Asia.* This theory resulted from profound ignorance of Asian history and hence ignorance of the radical differences among Asian nations and societies. It resulted from a blindness to the power and resilience of Asian nationalisms. (It may also have resulted from a subconscious sense that, since "all Asians look alike," all Asian nations will act alike.) As a theory, the domino fallacy was not merely inaccurate but also insulting to Asian nations; yet it has continued to this day to beguile men who should know better.

Finally, the legacy of the fifties was apparently compounded by an uneasy sense of a worldwide Communist challenge to the new Administration after the Bay of Pigs fiasco. A first manifestation was the President's traumatic Vienna meeting with Khrushchev in June, 1961; then came the Berlin crisis of the summer. All this created an atmosphere in which President Kennedy undoubtedly felt under special pressure to show his nation's mettle in Vietnam—if the Vietnamese, unlike the people of Laos, were willing to fight.

In general, the legacy of the fifties shaped such early moves of the new Administration as the decisions to maintain a high-visibility SEATO (by sending the Secretary of State himself instead of some underling to its first meeting in 1961), to back away from diplomatic recognition of Mongolia in the summer of 1961, and most important, to expand U.S. military assistance to South Vietnam that winter on the basis of the much more tentative Eisenhower commitment. It should be added that the increased commitment to Vietnam was also fueled by a new breed of military strategists and academic social scientists (some of whom had entered the new Administration) who had developed theories of counter-guerrilla warfare and were eager to see them put to the test. To some, "counterinsurgency" seemed a new panacea for coping with the world's instability.

*   *   *

So much for the legacy and the history. Any new Administration inherits both complicated problems and simplistic views of the world. But surely among the policy-makers of the Kennedy and Johnson Administrations there were men who would warn of the dangers of an open-ended commitment to the Vietnam quagmire?

This raises a central question, at the heart of the policy process: Where were the experts, the doubters, and the dissenters? Were they there at all, and if so, what happened to them?

The answer is complex but instructive.

In the first place, the American government was sorely *lacking in real Vietnam or Indochina expertise.* Originally treated as an adjunct of Embassy Paris, our Saigon embassy and the Vietnam Desk at State were largely staffed from 1954 onward by French-speaking Foreign Service personnel of narrowly European experience. Such diplomats were even more closely restricted than the normal embassy officer—by cast of mind as well as language—to contacts with Vietnam's French-speaking urban elites. For instance, Foreign Service linguists in Portugal are able to speak with the peasantry if they get out of Lisbon and choose to do so; not so the French speakers of Embassy Saigon.

In addition, the *shadow of the "loss of China"* distorted Vietnam reporting. Career officers in the Department, and especially those in the field, had not forgotten the fate of their World War II colleagues who write in frankness from China and were later pilloried by Senate committees for critical comments on the Chinese Nationalists. Candid reporting on the strengths of the Viet Cong and the weaknesses of the Diem government was inhibited by the memory. It was also inhibited by some higher officials, notably Ambassador Nolting in Saigon, who refused to sign off on such cables.

In due course, to be sure, some Vietnam talent was discovered or developed. But a recurrent and increasingly important factor in the decision-making process was *the banishment of real expertise.* Here the underlying cause was the "closed politics" of policy-making as issues become hot: the more sensitive the issue, and the higher it rises in the bureaucracy, the more completely the experts are excluded while the harassed senior generalists take over (that is, the Secretaries, Undersecretaries, and Presidential Assistants). The frantic skimming of briefing papers in the back seats of limousines is no substitute for the presence of specialists; furthermore, in times of crisis such papers are deemed "too sensitive" even for review by the specialists. Another underlying cause of this banishment, as Vietnam became more critical, was the replacement of the experts, who were generally and increasingly pessimistic, by men described as "can-do guys," loyal and energetic fixers unsoured by expertise. In early 1965, when I confided my growing policy doubts to an older colleague on the NSC staff, he assured me that the smartest thing both of us could do was to "steer clear of the whole Vietnam mess"; the gentleman in question had the misfortune to be a "can-do guy," however, and is now highly placed in Vietnam, under orders to solve the mess.

Despite the banishment of the experts, internal doubters and dissenters did indeed appear and persist. Yet as I watched the process, such men were effectively neutralized by a subtle dynamic: *the domestication of dissenters.* Such "domestication" arose out of a twofold clubbish need: on the one hand, the dissenter's desire to stay aboard; and on the other hand, the nondissenter's conscience. Simply stated, dissent, when recognized, was made to feel at home. On the lowest possible scale of importance, I must confess my own considerable sense of dignity and acceptance (both vital) when my senior White House employer would refer to me as his "favorite dove." Far more significant was the case of the former Undersecretary of State, George Ball. Once Mr. Ball began to express doubts, he was warmly institutionalized: he was encouraged to become the inhouse devil's advocate on Vietnam. The upshot was inevitable: the process of escalation allowed for periodic requests to Mr. Ball to speak his piece; Ball felt good, I assume (he had fought for righteousness); the others felt good (they had given a full hearing to the dovish option); and there was minimal unpleasantness. The club remained intact; and it is of course possible that matters would have gotten worse faster if Mr. Ball had kept silent, or left before his final departure in the fall of 1966. There was also, of course, the case of the last institutionalized doubter, Bill Moyers. The President is said to have greeted his arrival at meetings with an affectionate; "Well, here comes Mr. Stop-the-Bombing . . ." Here again the dynamics of domesticated dissent sustained the relationship for a while.

A related point—and crucial, I suppose, to government at all times—was *the "effectiveness" trap*, the trap that keeps men from speaking out, as clearly or often as they might, within the government. And it is the trap that keeps men from resigning in protest and airing their dissent outside the government. The most important asset that a man brings to bureaucratic life is his "effectiveness," a mysterious combination of training, style, and connections. The most ominous complaint that can be whispered of a bureaucrat is: "I'm afraid Charlie's beginning to lose his effectiveness." To preserve your effectiveness, you must decide where and when to fight the mainstream of policy; the opportunities range from pillow talk with your wife, to private drinks with your friends, to meetings with the Secretary of State or the President. The inclination to remain silent or to acquiesce in the presence of the great men—to live to fight another day, to give on this issue so that you can be "effective" on later issues—is overwhelming. Nor is it the tendency of youth alone; some of our most senior officials, men of wealth and fame, whose place in history is secure, have remained silent lest their connection with power be terminated. As for the disinclination to resign in protest: while not necessarily a Washington or even American specialty, it seems more true of a government in which ministers have no parliamentary backbench to which to retreat. In the absence of such a refuge, it is easy to rationalize the decision to stay aboard. By doing so, one may be able to prevent a few bad things from happening and perhaps even make a few good things happen. To exit is to lose even those marginal chances for "effectiveness."

Another factor must be noted: as the Vietnam controversy escalated at home, there developed *a preoccupation with Vietnam public relations as opposed to Vietnam policy-making*. And here, ironically, internal doubters and dissenters were heavily employed. For such men, by virture of their own doubts, were often deemed best able to "massage" the doubting intelligentsia. My senior East Asia colleague at the White House, a brilliant and humane doubter who had dealt with Indochina since 1954, spent three quarters of his working days on Vietnam public relations: drafting presidential responses to letters from important critics, writing conciliatory language for presidential speeches, and meeting quite interminably with delegations of outraged Quakers, clergymen, academics, and housewives. His regular callers were the late A. J. Muste and Norman Thomas; mine were members of the Women's Strike for Peace. Our orders from above: keep them off the backs of busy policy-makers (who usually happened to be nondoubters). Incidentally, my most discouraging assignment in the realm of public relations was the preparation of a White House pamphlet entitled *Why Vietnam*, in September, 1965; in a gesture toward my conscience, I fought—and lost—a battle to have the title followed by a question mark.

*   *   *

Through a variety of procedures, both institutional and personal, doubt, dissent, and expertise were effectively neutralized in the making of policy. But what can be said of the men "in charge"? It is patently absurd to suggest that they produced such tragedy by intention and calculation. But is is neither absurd nor difficult to discern certain forces at work that caused decent and honorable men to do great harm.

Here I would stress the paramount role of *executive fatigue*. No factor seems to me more crucial and underrated in the making of foreign policy. The physical and emotional toll of executive responsibility in State, the Pentagon, the White House, and other executive agencies is enormous; that toll is of course compounded by extended service. Many of today's Vietnam policymakers have been on the job for from four to seven years. Complaints may be few, and physical health may remain unimpaired, though emotional health is far harder to gauge. But what is most seriously eroded in the deadening process of fatigue is freshness of thought, imagination, a sense of possibility, a sense of priorities and perspective—those rare assets of a new Administration in its first year or two of office. The tired policy-maker becomes a prisoner of his own narrowed view of the world and his own clichéd rhetoric. He becomes irritable and defensive— short on sleep, short on family ties, short on patience. Such men make bad policy and then compound it. They have neither the time nor the temperament for new ideas or preventive diplomacy.

Below the level of the fatigued executives in the making of Vietnam policy was a widespread phenomenon: *the curator mentality* in the Department of State. By this I mean the collective inertia produced by the bureaucrat's view of his job. At State, the average "desk officer" inherits from his predecessor our policy toward Country X; he regards it as his function to keep that policy intact—under glass, untampered with, and dusted—so that he may pass it on in two to four years to his successor. And such curatorial service generally merits promotion within the system. (Maintain the status quo, and you will stay out of trouble.) In some circumstances, the inertia bred by such an outlook can act as a brake against rash innovation. But on many issues, this inertia sustains the momentum of bad policy and unwise commitments—momentum that might otherwise have been resisted within the ranks. Clearly, Vietnam is such an issue.

To fatigue and inertia must be added the factor of internal confusion. Even among the "architects" of our Vietnam commitment, there has been persistent *confusion as to what type of war we were fighting* and, as a direct consequence, *confusion as to how to end that war.* (The "credibility gap" is, in part, a reflection of such internal confusion.) Was it, for instance, a civil war, in which case counterinsurgency might suffice? Or was it a war of international aggression? (This might invoke SEATO or UN commitment.) Who was the aggressor—and the "real enemy"? The Viet Cong? Hanoi? Peking? Moscow? International Communism? Or maybe "Asian Communism"? Differing enemies dictated differing strategies and tactics. And confused throughout, in like fashion, was the question of American objectives; your objectives depended on whom you were fighting and why. I shall not forget my assignment from an Assistant Secretary of State in March, 1964: to draft a speech for Secretary McNamara which would, *inter alia,* once and for all dispose of the canard that the Vietnam conflict was a civil war. "But in some ways, of course," I mused, "it *is* a civil war." "Don't play word games with me!" snapped the Assistant Secretary.

Similar confusion beset the concept of "negotiations"—anathema to much of official Washington from 1961 to 1965. Not until April, 1965, did "unconditional discussions" become respectable, via a presidential speech; even then the

Secretary of State stressed privately to newsmen that nothing had changed, since "discussions" were by no means the same as "negotiations." Months later that issue was resolved. But it took even longer to obtain a fragile internal agreement that negotiations might include the Viet Cong as something other than an appendage to Hanoi's delegation. Given such confusion as to the whos and whys of our Vietnam commitment, it is not surprising, as Theodore Draper has written, that policy-makers find it so difficult to agree on how to end the war.

Of course, one force—a constant in the vortex of commitment—was that of *wishful thinking*. I partook of it myself at many times. I did so especially during Washington's struggle with Diem in the autumn of 1963 when some of us at State believed that for once, in dealing with a difficult client state, the U.S. government could use the leverage of our economic and military assistance to make good things happen, instead of being led around by the nose by men like Chiang Kai-shek and Syngman Rhee (and, in that particular instance, by Diem). If we could prove that point, I thought, and move into a new day, with or without Diem, then Vietnam was well worth the effort. Later came the wishful thinking of the air-strike planners in the late autumn of 1964; there were those who actually thought after six weeks of air strikes, the North Vietnamese would come crawling to us to ask for peace talks. And what, someone asked in one of the meetings of the time, if they don't? The answer was that we would bomb for another four weeks, and that would do the trick. And a few weeks later came one instance of wishful thinking that was symptomatic of good men misled: in January, 1965, I encountered one of the very highest figures in the Aministration at a dinner, drew him aside, and told him of my worries about the air-strike option. He told me that I really shouldn't worry; it was his conviction that before any such plans could be put into effect, a neutralist government would come to power in Saigon that would politely invite us out. And finally, there was the recurrent wishful thinking that sustained many of us through the trying months of 1965-1966 after the air strikes had begun: that surely, somehow, one way or another, we would "be in a conference in six months," and the escalatory spiral would be suspended. The basis of our hope: "It simply can't go on."

*   *   *

As a further influence on policy-makers I would cite the factor of *bureaucratic detachment*. By this I mean what at best might be termed the professional callousness of the surgeon (and indeed, medical lingo—the "surgical strike" for instance—seemed to crop up in the euphemisms of the times). In Washington the semantics of the military muted the reality of war for the civilian policy-makers. In quiet, air-conditioned, thick-carpeted rooms, such terms as "systematic pressure," "armed reconnaissance," "targets of opportunity," and even "body count" seemed to breed a sort of games-theory detachment. Most memorable to me was a moment in the late 1964 target planning when the question under discussion was how heavy our bombing should be, and how extensive our strafing, at some midpoint in the projected pattern of systematic pressure. An Assistant Secretary of State resolved the point in the following words: "It seems to me that our orchestration should be mainly violins, but with periodic touches of brass." Perhaps the biggest shock of my return to Cambridge, Massachusetts, was the realization that the young men, the flesh and blood I taught and saw on these university streets, were potentially some of the numbers on the charts of those faraway planners. In a curious sense, Cambridge is closer to this war than Washington.

There is an unprovable factor that relates to bureaucratic detachment: the ingredient of *cryptoracism*. I do not mean to imply any conscious contempt for Asian loss of life on the part of Washington officials. But I do mean to imply that bureaucratic detachment may well be compounded by a traditional Western sense that there are so many Asians, after all; that Asians have a fatalism about life and disregard for its loss; that they are cruel and barbaric to their own people; and that they are very different from us (and all look alike?). And I *do* mean to imply that the upshot of such subliminal views is a subliminal question whether Asians, and particularly Asian peasants, and most particularly Asian Communists, are really people—like you and me. To put the matter another way: would we have pursued quite such policies—and quite such military tactics—if the Vietnamese were white?

It is impossible to write of Vietnam decision-making without writing about language. Throughout the conflict, words have been of paramount importance. I refer here to the impact of *rhetorical escalation* and to the *problem of oversell*. In an important sense, Vietnam has become of crucial significance to us *because we have said that it is of crucial significance*. (The issue obviously relates to the public relations preoccupation described earlier.)

The key here is domestic politics: the need to sell the American people, press, and Congress on support for an unpopular and costly war in which the objectives themselves have been in flux. To sell means to persuade, and to persuade means rhetoric. As the difficulties and costs have mounted, so has the definition of the stakes. This is not to say that rhetorical escalation is an orderly process; executive prose is the product of many writers, and some concepts—North Vietnamese infiltration, America's "national honor," Red China as the chief enemy—have entered the rhetoric only gradually and even sporadically. But there is an upward spiral nonetheless. And once you have *said* that the American Experiment itself stands or falls on the Vietnam outcome, you have thereby created a national stake far beyond any earlier stakes.

Crucial throughout the process of Vietnam decision-making was a conviction among many policy-makers: that Vietnam posed a *fundamental test of America's national will*. Time and again I was told by men reared in the tradition of Henry L. Stimson that all we needed was the will, and we would then prevail. Implicit in such a view, it seemed to me, was a curious assumption that Asians lacked will, or at least that in a contest between Asian and Anglo-Saxon wills, the non-Asians must prevail. A corollary to the persistent belief in will was a *fascination with power* and an awe in the face of the power America possessed as no nation or civilization ever before. Those who doubted our role in Vietnam were said to shrink from the burdens of power, the obligations of power, the uses of power, the responsibility of power. By implication, such men were soft-headed and effete.

Finally, no discussion of the factors and forces at work on Vietnam policy-makers can ignore the central fact of *human ego investment*. Men who have participated in a decision develop a stake in that decision. As they participate in further, related decisions, their stake increases. It might have been possible to dissuade a man of strong self-confidence at an early stage of the ladder of decision; but it is infinitely harder at later stages since a change of mind there usually involves implicit or explicit repudiation of a chain of previous decisions.

To put it bluntly: at the heart of the Vietnam calamity is a group of able, dedicated men who have been regularly and repeatedly wrong—and whose standing with their contemporaries, and more important, with history, depends, as they see it, on being proven right. These are not men who can be asked to extricate themselves from error.

*   *   *

The various ingredients I have cited in the making of Vietnam policy have created a variety of results, most of them fairly obvious. Here are some that seem to me most central:

Throughout the conflict, there has been *persistent and repeated miscalculation* by virtually all the actors, in high echelons and low, whether dove, hawk, or something else. To cite one simple example among many: in late 1964 and early 1965, some peace-seeking planners at State who strongly opposed the projected bombing of the North urged that, instead, American ground forces be sent to South Vietnam; this would, they said, increase our bargaining leverage against the North—our "chips"—and would give us something to negotiate about (the withdrawal of our forces) at an early peace conference. Simultaneously, the air-strike option was urged by many in the military who were dead set against American participation in "another land war in Asia"; they were joined by other civilian peace-seekers who wanted to bomb Hanoi into early negotiations. By late 1965, we had ended up with the worst of all worlds: ineffective and costly air strikes against the North, spiraling ground forces in the South, and no negotiations in sight.

Throughout the conflict as well, there has been *a steady give-in to pressures for a military solution* and only minimal and sporadic efforts at a diplomatic and political solution. In part this resulted from the confusion (earlier cited) among the civilians—confusion regarding objectives and strategy. And in part this resulted from the self-enlarging nature of military investment. Once air strikes and particularly ground forces were introduced, our investment itself had transformed the original stakes. More air power was needed to protect the ground forces; and then more ground forces to protect the ground forces. And needless to say, the military mind develops its own momentum in the absence of clear guidelines from the civilians. Once asked to save South Vietnam, rather than to "advise" it, the American military could not but press for escalation. In addition, sad to report, assorted military constituencies, once involved in Vietnam, have had a series of cases to prove: for instance, the utility not only of air power (the Air Force) but of supercarrier-based air power (the Navy). Also Vietnam policy has suffered from one ironic by-product of Secretary McNamara's establishment of civilian control at the Pentagon: in the face of such control, interservice rivalry has given way to a united front among the military—reflected in the new but recurrent phenomenon of JCS unanimity. In conjunction with traditional congressional allies (mostly Southern senators and representatives) such a united front would pose a formidable problem for any President.

Throughout the conflict, there have been *missed opportunities, large and small, to disengage ourselves from Vietnam on increasingly unpleasant but still acceptable terms.* Of the many moments from 1961 onward, I shall cite only one, the last and most important opportunity that was lost: in the summer of 1964 the President instructed his chief advisers to prepare for him as wide a range of Vietnam options as possible for postelection consideration and decision. He explicitly asked that all options be laid out. What happened next was, in effect, Lyndon Johnson's slow-motion Bay of Pigs. For the advisers so effectively converged on one single option—juxtaposed against two other, phony options (in effect, blowing up the world, or scuttle-and-run)—that the President was confronted with unanimity for bombing the North from all his trusted counselors. Had he been more confident in foreign affairs, had he been deeply informed on Vietnam and Southeast Asia, and had he raised some hard questions that unanimity had submerged, this President could have used the largest electoral mandate in history to de-escalate in Vietnam, in the clear expectation that at the worst a neutralist government would come to power in Saigon and politely invite us out. Today, many lives and dollars later, such an alternative has become an elusive and infinitely more expensive possibility.

In the course of these years, another result of Vietnam decision-making has been *the abuse and distortion of history.* Vietnamese, Southeast Asian, and Far Eastern history has been rewritten by our policy-makers, and their spokesmen, to conform with the alleged necessity of our presence in Vietnam. Highly dubious analogies from our experience elsewhere—the "Munich" sellout and "containment" from Europe, the Malayan insurgency and the Korean War from Asia—have been imported in order to justify our actions. And more recent events have been fitted to the Procrustean bed of Vietnam. Most notably, the change of power in Indonesia in 1965-1966 has been ascribed to our Vietnam presence; and virtually all prograss in the Pacific region—the rise of regionalism, new forms of cooperation, and mounting growth rates—has been similarly explained. The Indonesian allegation is undoubtedly false (I tried to prove it, during six months of careful investigation at the White House, and had to confess failure); the regional allegation is patently unprovable in either direction (except, of course, for the clear fact that the economies of both Japan and Korea have profited enormously from our Vietnam-related procurement in these countries; but that is a costly and highly dubious form of foreign aid).

There is a final result of Vietnam policy I would cite that holds potential danger for the future of American foreign policy: *the rise of a new breed of American ideologues who see Vietnam as the ultimate test of their doctrine*. I have in mind those men in Washington who have given a new life to the missionary impulse in American foreign relations: who believe that this nation, in this era, has received a threefold endowment that can transform the world. As they see it, that endowment is composed of, first, our unsurpassed military might; second, our clear technological supremacy; and third, our allegedly invincible benevolence (our "altruism," our affluence, our lack of territorial aspirations). Together, it is argued, this threefold endowment provides us with the opportunity and the obligation to ease the nations of the earth toward modernization and stability: toward a full-fledged *Pax Americana Technocratica*. In reaching toward this goal, Vietnam is viewed as the last and crucial test. Once we have succeeded there, the road ahead is clear. In a sense, these men are our counterpart to the visionaries of Communism's radical left: they are technocracy's own Maoists. They do not govern Washington today. But their doctrine rides high.

Long before I went into government, I was told a story about Henry L. Stimson that seemed to me pertinent during the years that I watched the Vietnam tragedy unfold—and participated in that tragedy. It seems to me more pertinent than ever as we move toward the election of 1968.

In his waning years Stimson was asked by an anxious questioner, "Mr. Secretary, how on earth can we ever bring peace to the world?" Stimson is said to have answered: "You begin by bringing to Washington a small handful of able men who believe that the achievement of peace is possible.

"You work them to the bone until they no longer believe that it is possible.

"And then you throw them out—and bring in a new bunch who believe that it is possible."

Americanizing the War in Vietnam

EUGENE EIDENBERG

... [T] he decisions on Vietnam in 1965 were conditioned by earlier commitments and events. First, a basic "decision of principle" had been made by the president that this nation would do what it could to stabilize the military and political situation in South Vietnam. Indeed, according to the administration, this was what the American commitment was all about. In doing so, however, the United States government found itself struggling against the forces of militarism, corruption, and chaos that have torn at South Vietnam all during this war. The American dilemma has been to justify massive support for a government and social system that had neither the superficial trappings of democracy nor the more fundamental characteristics of a viable nation-state. Second, the president had received the almost unanimous support of the Congress for the committing of substantial resources in Vietnam. Third, Lyndon Johnson had won an overwhelming personal and political victory in the election of 1964. Fourth, military and political conditions in South Vietnam were deteriorating at an accelerating pace. Of these four factors, the firm administration commitment to "hold" in South Vietnam until some military and political stability could be created, and the internal conditions of Vietnam itself, were the considerations most important to the decisions to be made in 1965.

Debate focused on the deteriorating political and military trends in South Vietnam, and these did not suggest a clear and persuasive line of action for the administration. The disputes over what specific actions to take in providing military assistance to South Vietnam should be understood as a normal condition in any highly stressful decisional situation. When the stakes are high, and outcomes of action uncertain, there is a predictable reserve against plunging into a radical course of action. The merits and counter-arguments are heard and reheard as the president seeks a course that will produce desired results in a situation over which he does not have complete information or control. One

From Allen Sindler, editor, *American Political Institutions and Public Policy*, pp. 104-121. Copyright © 1969 by Little, Brown and Company (Inc.). Reprinted by permission.

White House staff assistant said: "At the time of decision, the president has to make a 100 per cent action commitment on 51 per cent of the information. Unfortunately, there is rarely any middle ground between 'yes' and 'no.' "

The president himself saw the issues in Vietnam rather starkly and heroically. Though specific actions may have been the products of incomplete information, Lyndon Johnson saw South Vietnam near total collapse and was prepared to do what he could to prevent it. However, the widely shared decision to stay in Vietnam did not mean that the people who helped make the decision shared any notions of what it meant operationally. One national security advisor to the president stated: "No one, including the president, knew what it would take to hold in Vietnam. The hard fact is that the government was not asking what the implications of holding in Vietnam were. Long-range planning is very difficult in the heat of the day-to-day situation."

Altogether, the 1965 decisions were the operational consequences of the antecedent choice to hold made in 1964; and they were narrowly defined incremental changes in response to the administration's view of events taking place in Vietnam itself. Several forces restricted the president's freedom to quickly escalate or de-escalate American involvement.

First was the unprecedented election vitory which could be viewed simply as a defeat for Goldwater's escalation policies and a victory for the announced Johnson policy of restricted American military involvement. But LBJ's landslide election could also be read as furnishing high support for any course the president decided was in the nation's best interest. By the end of January, 1965, there was a general feeling in the nation (Gallup reported a ratio of 4-1) that South Vietnam was losing to the Viet Cong; that American influence ought to be used to find peace through negotiations if possible (Gallup reported 8 out of 10 favored this course); but that if the issue came to either being pushed out of the country or forced into military crisis, opinion was 4-3 in favor of sending American troops to prevent the loss. In short, the president could count on majority backing should stronger action be required.

A substantial limit on rapid escalation, however, was the prospect of so losing control of events that general or possibly nuclear war might result. Two prior presidents (Eisenhower and Kennedy) had carefully attempted to delimit American actions in Vietnam in order to avoid a Soviet-American confrontation. Since the advent of nuclear weapons, all presidents have shouldered the awesome obligation of keeping a ready defense while also stabilizing international tensions sufficiently to prevent recourse to a nuclear strike. As suggested earlier, in Vietnam the president had to see that American action did not suddenly become so threatening or provocative to China or Russia that one or both would become directly involved. Indeed, the cataclysmic risks inherent in primary reliance on the nation's nuclear capacity was a major reason for America's development of the flexible response capability first made operational in the Vietnam situation. No doubt there was strong feeling within the military and in the administration that this capability ought to be given a chance to cope with events in Southeast Asia.

Finally, an important factor militating against precipitous American action was the general predisposition to avoid any decisions that might eliminate too many future options. Calvin Coolidge's observation is relevant, if a little dated. He was fond of saying that when a problem came down the road he would jump in a ditch, and "nine times out of ten it will pass you by." Lyndon Johnson's style may not have been to jump in the ditch, but certainly by temperament, he resisted extreme action in any direction on the theory that it would unnecessarily lose friends and foreclose future alternatives.

THE BOMBING DECISION

If early 1964 saw a deterioration in South Vietnam, by the end of the year the situation was reaching critical proportions. The administration, knowing that a continued American "holding operation" was inadequate, searched for alternatives. A high-ranking intelligence official observed: "There was a major mounting of more military threats than the South Vietnamese army could handle—there was a rupture in the delicate equilibrium between threats and capability to respond. By early 1965, South Vietnam was perilously close to defeat—not a defeat of the sort the French suffered at Dien Bien Phu in 1954—but a Waterloo defeat of attrition and collapse. The will to resist was increasingly reduced. The South Vietnamese army was being whipsawed by more threats than it could meet."

Then at 2:00 A.M. Sunday, February 7, 1965, Saigon time, the Viet Cong attacked American and South Vietnamese installations in the Pleiku area in central South Vietnam, killing 7 and wounding 109 Americans. In addition, sixteen American helicopters and six American fixed-wing planes were damaged or destroyed by mortar fire. The United States retaliated by launching air strikes from three aircraft carriers, the *Ranger*, the *Hancock*, and the *Coral Sea*, steaming about 100 miles off the South Vietnamese shore, against the barracks and staging areas in southern North Vietnam. The president announced that American dependents of civilian and military personnel were being withdrawn from Vietnam.

In rethinking the choices for extending the American commitment in Vietnam, the president's inner circle of national security advisors felt that ". . . the retaliatory bombing tactic—and eventually the continuous bombing of military targets in the North—was less of an Americanization of the war and [was] a step less likely to get us irreconcilably involved than was the commitment of large numbers of troops." The administration was still not seriously thinking about American troops taking over the war, although that alternative was being discussed more frequently. There remained the hope that air power would coerce Hanoi to cease their infiltration of the South, and perhaps would even bring them to the negotiating table.

The judgment that tactical bombing against the supply routes running from the North into the South would effectively reduce the flow of men and materials was very controversial. Studies on the effect of Allied bombing on German industrial production during World War II show that bombing can have the unintended result of raising the enemy's morale while only marginally affecting his production capacity. In Vietnam, the tactical bombing of supply routes involved as targets not production plants, but trails, bridges, columns of trucks, and streams of people on foot and on bicycles carrying supplies and weapons on their backs. American critics argued that no bombing strategy could be effective against such targets, and that the attempted disruption of the supply routes simply solidified morale in the North and made America's conduct of the war a target for negative world opinion.

Nevertheless the administration saw the issue differently. The Central Intelligence Agency was reporting the movement of North Vietnamese regular troops into the South over the trails and roads that had been in preparation for over a year. Walt Rostow, in an interview with this author, dated the start of the decisional process as follows: "The time of decision came for the president when in the latter half of 1964, Hanoi helped support a radical increase in Viet Cong main forces; switched over to heavy weaponry; opened the Laos trails; and used them to introduce regular North Vietnamese forces."

Despite Rostow's assertions, debate over the activity from the North during this period has been considerable. The State Department's white paper, "Aggression from the North: The Record of North Vietnam's Campaign to Conquer South Vietnam" (published in February, 1965) reported only 5,000 regular North Vietnamese troops in the South. Taken by itself, that datum does not suggest why the South Vietnamese were in such precarious condition. However, the intelligence community, evaluating the events at Pleiku and the increased movement of men and materiel from the North, concluded that the North Vietnamese government was moving "to finish South Vietnam off. The immediate impetus for a decision was the recognition that either we fished or cut bait—or South Vietnam was lost."

On February 11 and 24, further retaliatory strikes by American and South Vietnamese aircraft were undertaken. On February 25, Secretary Rusk emphasized in a news conference this nation's view on responsibility for military activity in the South: "North Vietnam . . . has directed and supplied the essential military personnel and arms . . . aimed at the overthrow of the government of South Vietnam. . . . The evidence of North Vietnam's direct responsibility for this aggression has been repeatedly presented. . . ." On February 28, American and South Vietnamese officials announced that President Johnson had decided to open continuous limited air strikes against North Vietnam in order to stem the flow of men and arms to the South and to "bring about a negotiated settlement." The bombing decisions had been made.

The United States government neither announced nor acknowledged that any major shift in its policy had occurred. During a March 13 news conference the president observed, ". . . the incidents have changed, in some instances the equipment has changed, in some instances the tactics and perhaps the strategy in a decision or two have changed . . . [but] our policy is still the same. . . ." Clearly, however, whether the bombing decision was labeled a change of tactics or something more, it sharply affected the world's and our own view of what American policy was. It marked a turning point in the line of American policy that had been building for at least five years, and it signified an increase in the scale of the war's violence. The bombing decisions meant to those in the Johnson administration who participated in them that "we had once and for all cast our lot in favor of major action." For the president's national security team, "the war began in February of 1965."

It is significant that the commitment to bombing was essentially an operational decision reached in the crisis context of how to save the South. There is no indication, either in the published record or from the interviews conducted for this study, that the decision makers were seriously estimating the costs of staying in Vietnam. The assumption was that we would stay and that somehow the cost would be worth the payoff once our goals were achieved: the viability of South Vietnam as a nation-state, the return of North Vietnamese to their homeland, and the suppression of the Viet Cong insurgency. But how the United States government viewed the commitment of North Vietnamese was never made clear. How long were the North Vietnamese prepared to supply the South at the expense of heavier and heavier bombing? How much manpower would the North devote to the war in the South? Were the North's leaders prepared to match the United States at every stage of the war's intensification? The United States believed the North was prepared for a long war of attrition, but if we demonstrated that we would stay in Vietnam as long as necessary, then the North's will to endure would ultimately be broken.

THE TROOP DECISIONS

The bombing had no depressing effect on North Vietnam's determination to prosecute the war. Hanoi rejected an American offer to negotiate, calling it a trick, and the first three months of 1965 saw a sharp increase in sabotage and terrorism incidents. The American position, Secretary Rusk indicated, was that negotiations would begin only when Hanoi showed that it was ". . . prepared to stop doing what it is doing and what it knows it is doing against its neighbor." Six months earlier the United States had refused an attempt, organized by the Secretary General of the United Nations, U Thant, to set a meeting with Hanoi in Burma, on the grounds that such talks would destroy the morale of the South Vietnamese government.

In short, the North Vietnamese were not prepared to admit the American assertion that they had troops in the South and were therefore helping to prolong the war, and the United States would not permit negotiations to start as long as they felt South Vietnam's military and political situation was not as strong as it should be. The confluence of these factors eliminated chances for serious talks between the two sides for three-and-one-half years.

The relationship between the political instability in Saigon and the deteriorating military situation, even after United States bombing was begun, is difficult to uncover. The decision makers in Washington acted on the intelligence estimates of the time: "[T]he continuing whipsawing of the South's forces was a prime contributor to the political instability in the South, not the other way around." Another commentator, Theodore Draper, wrote: "The crisis in 1965 in South Vietnam was far more intimately related to South Vietnamese disintegration than to North Vietnamese infiltration. . . . In effect the South Vietnamese crisis of 1965 was essentially a reprise of the 1963 crisis, not a totally new phenomenon as argued by the State Department."[1] Whatever its sources, the political disintegration in the South stimulated the Viet Cong and Hanoi to increase their pressure for the final victory that increasingly seemed within their grasp. It is at this point that the presence of North Vietnamese regular troops in the South became more apparent; Assistant Secretary William Bundy reported that by the spring of 1965 intelligence disclosed that four regular North Vietnamese army regiments were in the South.

In May, the CIA's leading Vietnam authority returned to Washington and reported to McGeorge Bundy in the White House, ". . . the atmosphere of defeat in South Vietnam is palpable. Unless there is a major increase in the size of the army in the field there will be a complete military collapse in the South." The CIA estimate was verified and given urgency by the military chiefs, who were growing alarmed over the deepening military crisis. The decision for the president was rapidly becoming a question, as Walt Rostow described it to this author, ". . . of whether to pull out 25,000 troops or do what was necessary to prevent the disintegration of South Vietnam that was coming from the expansion of the North's effort through regiment-sized units being moved South."

McGeorge Bundy received a series of CIA estimates in the spring of 1965 assessing the consequences for all of Asia if the United States withdrew from Vietnam. These "reaction estimates" argued forcefully that a United States withdrawal would leave China as the only world power with influence in Southeast Asia, and would seriously threaten United States strategic interests. Secretary of Defense McNamara had articulated these concerns in a speech in March, 1964, after his return from a visit to South Vietnam. "Its location [Southeast Asia] across East-West air and sea lanes flanks the Indian subcontinent on one side and Australia, New Zealand, and the Philippines on the other; and dominates the gateway between the Pacific and Indian oceans. In Communist hands, this area would pose a most serious threat to the security of the United States and the family of free world nations to which we belong." The estimates also took a careful look at the fate of other Southeast-Asian nations (Thailand, Cambodia, Laos, Malaysia, to name only four) should Hanoi be allowed to demonstrate that a "war of national liberation" could succeed. An intelligence officer intimately involved in the Vietnam issue said: ". . . at root in Vietnam is a test case of the invincibility of wars of national liberation supported externally, but conducted as an internal insurgency operation. . . . In fact this was one of the ways the issue was put to the president when he was considering American responses on the issue." Finally, the estimates stressed the maintenance of the American commitment as a test of its pledge and obligation and of its military strength and flexibility. As Walt Rostow said at a later date in an interview, "American interest in South Vietnam in large part stems from a serious threat to the credibility of our commitment. We made one, started to follow through on it, and then had to decide to go all the way or back down. The meaning of our deterrent capability is at stake."

Again, the estimates were based on evaluations of the costs of getting out, with no questions asked about the costs of staying in. Why those critical questions were not asked leads one to the basic views on Vietnam of the president and the administration's other leading spokesmen. Writing in *The New York Times* in May of 1968, Eliot Fremont-Smith argues that President Johnson took a "poorly calculated and incoherently justified step" (in Americanizing the war), which was brought on in part by his dated cold-war view of international relations. The president and his advisors paid insufficient attention to the costs of staying because they were convinced we had to stay, no matter what the cost. In this view, after all, nothing less than the protection of South Vietnam from external oppression, the containment of Communist China, and the defeat of the tactics of wars of national liberation were at stake.

The president characteristically took his time in reaching a final decision on the question of American troops. "When the president takes a problem," one of his aids said, "he will walk around it for a long time. He conducts a series of discussions; will talk about it with old friends; wait until he has a feel for every facet . . . it is a process that takes a long time." It is probable that the "decisions" to use troops were made in a technical sense in the spring of 1965, although they were not announced until midsummer. The "walking around" also allowed time in which to develop support for an emerging but not yet completely visible policy.

One sign of the growing American commitment in Southeast Asia was the president's May 4 request for a $700 million supplemental appropriation to cover military expenditures, "especially in Vietnam," for fiscal 1965. (At the end of 1964 approximately 25,000 American troops were in Vietnam; by March, 1965, that number had reached 35,000 and by June, 1965, there were nearly 75,000. From the end of 1963 to mid-1965—eighteen months—American forces had grown threefold.) President Johnson told a gathering in the East Room of the White House, comprised of members of the House and Senate Appropriations,

Foreign Relations, and Armed Services committees, "This is in no way a routine appropriation. For each member of Congress who supports this request is voting to continue our effort to try to halt communist aggression . . . This is the firm and irrevocable commitment of our people and our nation, whatever the risk and whatever the cost." Three days after submitting his request, Johnson received and signed the measure, which had been pased by the House, 408-7, and the Senate 88-3.

A commitment as extensive as 75,000 troops and several billion dollars annually, it was soon seen, was inadequate to reverse the deteriorating situation in Saigon. "By June," William Bundy recalled, "it was clear to all the president's senior advisors that we would have to up the level of American troops. . . . This is the fork in the road when we crossed into another kind of commitment." In late June: "A serious policy review was begun. Planning papers and policy review papers were prepared in the State and Defense Departments to be added to the reaction estimates being circulated from the CIA at the highest levels of the government." In early July, McNamara returned to Vietnam for a very intensive first-hand look, accompanied by Henry Cabot Lodge, Jr., who had just accepted assignment to his second tour as ambassador to South Vietnam, replacing Maxwell Taylor. At a July 9 press conference, Johnson indicated that the McNamara trip was likely to be a prelude to an increase in American forces. "We have lost in the neighborhood of some 300 men in the period since I have been president. We expect that it will get worse before it gets better. . . . Our manpower needs there are increasing, and will continue to do so, . . . Whatever is required I am sure will be supplied."

On July 13, the president stated that American military commanders in Vietnam had been given authority "to use American forces . . . in the ways which [they] consider most effective to resist the communist aggression. . . . [T]hey will be available for more active combat missions when the Vietnamese government and General Westmoreland agree that such active missions are needed." These words confirmed that the American presence was about to change from support for the South Vietnamese Army to assumption of the offensive in the ground war. And, Johnson forewarned, ". . . it is quite possible that new and serious decisions will be necessary in the near future."

Upon McNamara's return in late July the president entered a week of "intensive consultation with his senior foreign policy team." William Bundy said, of this week,

> we looked very much down the pike, much more than had been the case to this point in our involvement in Vietnam. For the first time we began to have some planning for financial and manpower needs. The immediate choice was to double our force levels . . . with an idea that we would have to go to 200,000 . . . but the president meant to look at each stage prior to execution . . . we envisaged the possiblity of future decisions expanding the scope of our involvement.

On July 28, in a televised press conference, the president announced the results of his intensive week of consultations. He reviewed the history of the war and described his conviction that America's presence in Vietnam was important not only to protect South Vietnam but also to save all of non-communist Asia from "... the grasping ambition of Asian communism." He mentioned the mounting military pressure on South Vietnam and then gravely announced:

> I have asked the commanding general, General Westmoreland, what more he needs to meet this mounting aggression. He has told me. We will meet his needs. . . . I have today ordered to Vietnam . . . certain . . . forces which will raise our fighting strength from 75,000 to 125,000 men almost immediately. Additional forces will be needed later, and they will be sent as requested.

Such momentous decisions obviously were not made lightly. For in Americanizing the war, the Johnson administration not only accepted the less than predictable costs of a major land war in Asia on difficult terrain against an elusive enemy, but it also bet that Soviet and Chinese involvement would remain at acceptable levels. The effects of its policies on the triangular relationships between the United States, the Soviet Union, and Communist China remained a paramount American concern. As with the bombing decisions, it was mandatory that the American course of action should avoid provoking a direct confrontation with Russia or China. In addition, the United States had to be sensitive to the delicate relations among the communist nations Russia, China, and North Vietnam.

Secretary of State Rusk gave the administration's 1965 view regarding the relationship between North Vietnam and China. He told the Senate Foreign Relations Committee that China was the source of the doctrine for the war in South Vietnam, whereas Hanoi was simply the instrument of that doctrine (the war of national liberation). To others, however, the matter was not that simple. Russia has been the major supplier of heavy weapons for the North Vietnamese, carefully protecting its interests in Southeast Asia lest China become the only communist power influential with the nations of Indochina. For its part, China had been careful to maintain its contribution to the effort in fear of having North Vietnam (a traditional enemy of the Chinese) permanently look to the Soviet Union for aid. American policy frequently has been criticized for its failure to exploit these traditional and modern rivalries.

American policy also risked closing the gap between Russia and China, which had been growing with their ideological, political, and economic disputes. Americanizing the war minimized America's capacity to exploit the rift between the two world communist powers, and threatened to reverse its growing rapprochement with Russia, a development kindled by the Nuclear Test Ban Treaty of 1963.

Johnson's 1964 decision to hold the line in Vietnam thus gave birth to a second round of implementing decisions. In February, 1965, the bombing started with a highly selective list of targets approved personally by the president. Through the spring and summer there were small increases in troop levels, but the decision to Americanize the war on July 28 meant that force levels would be maintained at whatever strength was necessary to deny South Vietnam to the North in the short run, and to secure the South militarily for the long run.

SOME GENERAL LESSONS

The Options

Judged by hindsight, the bombing and troop decisions of 1965 followed with a qualified inevitability the fundamental decision "to hold" made earlier. Once the latter decision was made, the tactical (and even strategic) military decisions depended not on the policy initiatives of American decision makers, but rather on the uncertain capacity of the South Vietnamese to withstand the mounting military, terrorist, and political pressure from North Vietnam and from the Viet Cong in the South. When was that basic decision to hold made? Some of the president's foreign policy aides place the date as early 1964, others as later that year when the crisis developed in the South. In a recent book, Tom Wicker, a political analyst on *The New York Times*, says that Johnson made the decision 48 hours after assuming the presidency. "I am not going to lose Vietnam," the president is reported to have said. "I am not going to be the president who saw Southeast Asia go the way China went." Once this goal was defined, all subsequent problems were perceived only in the narrowed context of alternatives that would most efficiently achieve it. It was not until March, 1968, when the president de-escalated the bombing of the North and withdrew from the campaign for re-election, that there was any sign that the basic premise of America's effort was being questioned or altered. In the intervening three-and-one-half years American policy was a continuous effort to achieve for the South Vietnamese a goal they were increasingly unable to achieve for themselves, and perhaps one that had never been within their reach.

The direction of American policy on Vietnam was supported by virtually every senior national security advisor to the president. As viewed by the administration, the operational choices facing the president in 1964 were: (1) to maintain present levels of American involvment with military advisors; (2) to move toward a withdrawal of American forces; (3) to move toward a limited and graduated response that would permit North Vietnam to pull back before the war reached unacceptable proportions; and (4) to hit North Vietnam and the Viet Cong very hard with one or more overwhelming military strikes. The men around the president saw options 1 and 2 as identical in their consequences (a surrender of the South to the North), and never seriously considered them. Option 4 was held to involve excessive risk of a general war. This left the limited and graduated response strategy (option 3) as the choice of all the senior advisors at the time the decisions were being made.

The tragedy in the events that have followed the exercise of that option is that it was adopted precisely because it was thought to minimize the chances of a large-scale or prolonged war. Either no one close to the president considered the implications of the graduated response should North Vietnam and the Viet Cong refuse to yield, or American intelligence about North Vietnam's capacity and will to resist was badly in error. From 1965 on, the decisions to add targets to the bombing list, or to increase the troop commitments became "simply of a tactical sort . . . ," to use the words of a high State Department official. Under different circumstances, and perhaps with different leadership, the alternatives in Vietnam might have been more varied and the choices made among them could have led to a peaceful settlement of the dispute. However, once Johnson made that decision of principle, subsequent American policy in Vietnam was made all but inevitable.

Another close participant said of the mid-1965 troop decisions, ". . . these were a series of incremental decisions that seemed justified at the time. We all faced the tough question of trying to assess the cost/benefit ratio of withdrawing or going on at each stage, and the conclusion was that no matter what the cost might be now, it would not be as expensive as allowing it to go." A member of the CIA with expert knowledge of the Vietnam question said: "There can be argument over whether American involvement is right had we known what the cost would be, but I'd be very suprised if anybody could have said at any point prior to 1967 what these costs would in fact be." Perhaps it was faulty intelligence or the difficulty in fighting guerrilla wars or an outdated "cold-war" ideology that persuaded America that it was critical to fight a war it could not win. Whatever the reason, by now it is clear to all observers that the cost of "staying the course" in Vietnam far exceeded any estimates that were available to the decision makers when they made the choice to continue the war.

The United States expected that its show of force and determination would persuade North Vietnam to seek a negotiated settlement to the war. The American misunderstanding is made evident by the gap between the original conception of what would constitute a sufficient show of force and determination and what has actually been required. In 1965 the administration was talking about forces as great as 200,000 men; by early 1968 American troops in the field had passed the 500,000 mark. In 1965, restricted but continuous bombing of "military" targets in the North to slow the infiltration of men and materiel was begun; in 1967-1968 the North Vietnamese capital of Hanoi and the port city of Haiphong had become regular targets for the American air force. In 1965, American troops were committed to "buying time" for the South Vietnamese to develop a viable nation politically, socially, and economically; in early 1968, the

North Vietnamese and the Viet Cong mounted attacks against the major cities of the South which demonstrated that the military security for the population centers of the South still had not been achieved.

The nagging difficulty with America's Vietnam policy is the administration's recognition that "there can be no such thing as a purely military solution to the war in Vietnam," while at the same time its military policy made more elusive the political conditions necessary for a solution. A basic contradiction of American policy has perhaps doomed it to failure from the start. On the one hand, the need to secure the allegiance of the Vietnamese by instituting social and economic reform in the South has been emphasized. It was always assumed that at some point the South Vietnamese would have to bear the burden of their own defense, which could be achieved only if the civilian population supported the government. However, the military policy of searching out and destroying the enemy and his support facilities (more often than not, the villages and hamlets of the countryside) ultimately had to alienate many thousands of innocent civilians who were brutalized, uprooted, and harassed by government and American forces naturally suspicious of potential enemies among the civilian populace, as well as by marauding Viet Cong forces. Moreover, allowing for the quagmire of South Vietnamese politics, American efforts to coerce or otherwise bring about reform of the South Vietnamese government were feeble and ineffective.

Decision Making

America's involvement in a major land war in Vietnam came, as George Ball wrote, despite the administration's strong predilection to avoid such an entanglement. "It was the result of a process, not a single decision," an observation which takes on added meaning if we consider McGeorge Bundy's contrast of America's policy on the Cuban missile crisis of 1962 and on Vietnam. "The Cuban situation," urges Bundy,

> was in response to privately held information over which we had complete control. Secondly, Cuba 1962 concentrated the processes of government so that every decision was made by the president and everyone knew it . . . there was a focusing of the process. Vietnam was the product of slowly-building pressures, both external and internal to American government and to the real situation in Southeast Asia. The issues of Vietnam in 1965 didn't ripen according to any grand strategic plan.

Bundy makes an important point, but it should not obscure the judgment that Johnson's faith that his policies would bring Hanoi to the bargaining table was a version of a "grand strategic plan."

Once the choice was made to "stay the course" in Vietnam, subsequent choices were confined to tactics and means in a strategic commitment not seriously open to review. That same commitment led the administration to focus on short-run operational concerns at the expense of long-range planning. It also foreclosed options which were not to be made available again until three frustrating years of inconclusive fighting had passed and American public opinion had become increasingly disenchanted with the war. When in 1968 Johnson announced he would not run again, he became the victim of his earlier neglect to consider fully the implications and costs of an indeterminate and deepening American involvement in Vietnam.

The typically incremental nature of governmental decision making also has to be considered in attempting to comprehend American policy in Vietnam. The scale and character of America's military presence in 1964 and in 1968 provide stark contrast, but the current stage was reached by successive steps, each of which seemed at the time a reasonable extension of the previous level of activity and an appropriate response to changing events. Johnson was particularly committed to incremental policy making prior to his election in 1964 in his own right, because he was anxious to establish links of continuity to the policies of John F. Kennedy.

The evolution of Johnson's policy on Vietnam took place in an official environment strongly supporting that policy. Among those who had the president's ear there were few dissenting views, and many of them, with the conspicuous exception of Undersecretary of State George Ball, took the direction of urging even greater military efforts. It was LBJ's style to rely heavily, on Vietnam policy and other matters, on the judgment of a small number of personally trusted advisors, rather than, as Eisenhower did, on the National Security Council. In this, Johnson was more like Kennedy, who disliked, in McGeorge Bundy's words, "scheduled decision making," and who preferred to work with "small ad hoc groups formed to meet special problems."

Presidents vary in how they structure receipt of the information and advice they desperately need, but none can escape the ultimate responsibility for decision making thrust on them by the modern American system of government. "The buck stops here," stated the motto on Truman's presidential desk. As President Kennedy observed, ". . . the president must finally choose . . . he bears the burden . . . the advisors may move on to new advice." Also, the personal views of the presidential incumbent, as distinguished from the organization of his decision making process, may at times have decisive effects. Tom Wicker has argued that Johnson's hard-line, cold war attitudes on international communism and his newness in the presidential office led him to narrow his options too early and too inflexibly, i.e., his commitment to "stay the course" in Vietnam was overly explicit and premature. Others have urged that had John Kennedy lived, he would have extricated the United States from its enlarging commitment in Vietnam.

Since history cannot be rerun, no definitive responses to these assertions can be had. The Vietnam involvement, however, was predicated on a view of America's role in resisting communist aggression which was by no means peculiar to President Johnson and the men around him. Indeed, even today the growing disillusionment of the American public is caused less by our involvement in Vietnam than by its inconclusiveness and indefiniteness. Furthermore, the intent of the Johnson policy, however poorly it worked out in practice, was to avoid involvement in a major war, which was and remains a goal widely shared by Americans. It is one thing, therefore, to suggest that Vietnam policy under Johnson was flawed by important miscalculations and misperceptions, but quite another to argue that the policy defects derived from Johnson's personal attitudes or that the policy undoubtedly would have been changed for the better had John Kennedy not been assassinated.

NOTE

[1] Theodore Draper, *Abuse of Power,* New York, The Viking Press, 1967, p. 85.

The Vietnam Policy Reversal of 1968

HEDRICK SMITH and WILLIAM BEECHER

On the cold and cheerless early morning of Feb. 28, 1968, the Chairman of the Joint Chiefs of Staff, Gen. Earle G. Wheeler, landed at Andrews Air Force Base after an urgent mission to Saigon. Pausing only to change into a fresh uniform, he hurried through the rain to the White House to deliver a report and make a request.

The report was designed to encourage an anxious President and his beleaguered advisers, but it served only to shock them into extended debate.

The request—for more troops—was designed to bring military victory at last in the eight-year American military effort, but it led instead to a fateful series of decisions that stand in retrospect as one of the most remarkable turnabouts in United States foreign policy.

The month of March, 1968, became a watershed for a nation and a Government in turmoil. The Johnson Administration, by pulling back from the brink of deeper commitments and moving toward disengagement set a course that affects the daily decisions of the Nixon Administration.

Many of the ingredients of decision then—troop strength and what to do about bombing North Vietnam—are still live issues, and many of the principal actors involved a year ago are participants in yet another crucial policy debate on Vietnam.

On that day at the end of February, President Johnson and his closest aides assembled for breakfast around the Chippendale table in the elegant family dining room on the second floor of the Executive Mansion. Before rising from the table, they had set in motion the most intensive policy review of the Johnson Presidency—and one of the most agonizing of any Presidency.

The wrenching debate began almost by accident and then gained a momentum all its own. One dramatic record of its progress appeared in the 12 versions of a Presidential speech that evolved during the month—the last draft pointing in the opposite direction from the first.

From *The New York Times*, March 6 and 7, 1969. © 1969 by The New York Times Company. Reprinted by permission.

The entire episode also provided a remarkable demonstration of how foreign policy is battled out, inch by inch, by negotiation rather than decision. The turnabout emerged through sharp confrontations and subtle, even conspiratorial, maneuvering—with compromises struck for bureaucratic purposes and with opponents in agreement for contrary reasons.

At the time of that breakfast meeting, President Johnson had been thinking for about two months about not seeking re-election. His principal advisers had little inkling of his thoughts, and the President himself had no expectation that the tensions in the Government would shatter the consensus of his inner circle.

Clark M. Clifford, appointed but not yet sworn in as Secretary of Defense, was to play the pivotal role in the Vietnam reassessment, but it was not a one-man show.

Mr. Clifford had to be persuaded. He immediately came under pressure from a faction of civilian dissenters at the Pentagon who believed the war was deadlocked, questioned American óbjectives and felt that time to salvage American policy was fast running out.

When the debate was over, the President had set the Government on the path toward peace negotiations and disengagement from the war. He had imposed a limit on the military commitment to South Vietnam, ordered a reduction in the bombing of North Vietman, and offered to negotiate with the Hanoi regime. And he had coupled the offer with the announcement of this withdrawal from the 1968 political campaign.

The replacement of the quest for military victory with the search for compromise might have been reversed by North Vietnam if it had not—to almost everyone's surprise—responded favorably to Mr. Johnson's offer. Furthermore, the hawkish faction in the White House inner circle sought to resist the new trend until the Johnson Administration left office in January.

THE TET DRIVE ASSESSED

The catalytic event in the policy reappraisal—and the centerpiece of General Wheeler's vivid report—was the enemy's Lunar New Year offensive, which began Jan. 30, 1968, and swelled into coordinated assaults on 36 South Vietnamese cities and included, in Saigon, a bold penetration of the United States Embassy compound.

Confident and secure one day, Gen. William C. Westmoreland, then the American commander in Saigon, found himself on the next dealing with a vast battle the length of South Vietnam.

The psychological impact on Washington had outrun the event: The capital was stunned. But General Wheller, with murals of the American Revolution behind him, offered a more reassuring picture to the White House breakfast on Feb. 28.

The Tet attacks had not caused a military defeat, he said. The enemy had been thrown back with heavy losses and had failed to spark a popular uprising against the South Vietnamese regime. Not only had the Government in Saigon and its army survived the hurricane, he continued, but the offensive has "scared the living daylights," out of non-Communists, and they were beginning to cooperate.

On the other hand, the general said that more—many more—American troops were needed because the allied forces were off balance and vulnerable to another offensive.

General Westmoreland felt, General Wheeler reported, that massive reinforcements would guard against a quick repetition of the Tet offensive and would allow the allies to regain the initiative, to exploit the enemy's losses and to "speed the course of the war to our objectives."

General Wheeler gave the Westmoreland request his personal endorsement. It added up to 206,000 more men.

"IT WAS ROUGH AS A COB!"

General Westmoreland, who did not actually use the figure, regarded the proposal as a planning paper. But President Johnson and other officials, knowing that, as a matter of administrative technique, no request became formal until the President had decided how many troops would be sent, treated the Westmoreland paper as a request. Even without a precise total they sensed how much was being sought. The "shopping list" outlined by General Wheeler called for three more combat divisions, with sizable air, naval and land support.

Once the plan was fed through the Pentagon computers the precise number emerged. It became so secret that to this day some officials will not utter it—a reminder of the President's wrath when it did leak to the press during the March debate.

The sheer size of the request—a 40 per cent increase in the 535,000-man force committed to Vietnam—stunned Mr. Johnson and the civilians around him, though the initial impulse was to see how the commander's needs might be filled.

"It was a hell of a serious breakfast," one participant recalled. "It was rough as a cob!"

Some of the participants believed that a substantial troop increase could well revive arguments for widening the war—for giving General Westmoreland permission to go after enemy sanctuaries on the ground in Cambodia and Laos, and perhaps even in North Vietnam.

The President was wary about a massive new commitment. Had he not gone to extraordinary lengths to send half a million men to Vietnam without calling up reserves or imposing economic controls? Every year the generals had come to him—sometimes more than once a year—with the plea for "a little bit more to get the job done." Now, with the nation sharply divided over the war, they were asking for mobilization.

They had confronted Mr. Johnson with a dilemma. The gist of the Wheeler-Westmoreland report, in the words of one breakfast guest, was blunt: "We've got to have a big infusion of troops or we can't achieve our objectives."

No one at that breakfast table that day advocated lowering objectives. It was a time, however, when many pressures for a change of course were converging on the White House.

SPREADING DOUBTS ABOUT WAR

The Tet offensive had punctured the heady optimism over the military progress reported to Congress by General Westmoreland and by Ellsworth Bunker, the Ambassador to South Vietnam, in November, 1967. Not only had the pool of disenchantment spread by late February to fence-sitters in Congress, to newspaper offices and to business organizations. It had also reached the upper echelons of the Government.

If tolerance of the war had worn thin, so had the nation's military resources—so thin, indeed, that there was almost nothing more to send to Vietnam without either mobilizing, enlarging draft calls, lengthening the 12-month combat tour or sending Vietnam veterans back for second tours of duty—all extremely unappealing.

Congress was in such ferment that the process of legislation was partly paralyzed. The dollar was being battered by the gold crisis in Europe and inflation at home.

More fundamentally, the nation was seriously divided. The fabric of public civility had begun to unravel as opinion on the war polarized.

RUSK BREAKS A PRECEDENT

President Johnson chose his long-time friend, Clark Clifford, to head a task force to advise him on the troop request. It quickly became a forum for debating the entire rationale for the war.

At 10:30 A.M. on Friday, March 1, in the East room of the White House, Mr. Clifford took the oath of office as the sucessor to Robert S. McNamara. Three hours later he gathered the task force around the oval oak table in the private Pentagon dining room of the Secretary of Defense.

Secretary of State Dean Rusk, for the first time in his seven years at State, went to the Defense Department for a formal meeting.

The others present were all, like Mr. Rusk, veterans of arguments on Vietnam policy—Walt W. Rostow, the President's assistant for national security affairs, Richard Helms, Director of Central Intelligence; General Wheeler, General Maxwell D. Taylor, former Chairman of the Joint Chiefs of Staff, former Ambassador to Saigon and a Presidential adviser on Vietnam, Paul H. Nitze, Deputy Secretary of Defense; Under Secretary of State Nicholas deB. Katzenbach; Paul C. Warnke, Assistant Secretary of Defense for International Security Affairs; Phil G. Goulding, Assistant Secretary of Defense for Public Affairs; William P. Bundy, Assistant Secretary of State for East Asian Affairs, and, for financial advice, the Secretary of the Treasury, Henry H. Fowler.

None of the civilians present advocated a flat commitment of 206,000 more men, nor did they want to reject the request out of hand. Several insiders later suggested that a smaller request, for 30,000 to 50,000 men, would probably have been granted and the Administration crisis would have been avoided, or at least delayed.

Instead there was an early collision in the task force over war strategy and the possibilities of victory. There were, of course, shadings of viewpoint on most questions, but two broad coalitions emerged:

One favored continuation of General Westmoreland's strategy of wearing down the enemy by intense military pounding. The argument's assumption was that the Tet situation was less a setback than an opportunity. By boldly seizing the initiative, according to this view, the allies could decimate and demoralize the enemy and open the way to a favorable settlement.

The other group challenged the very premises of the old strategy. Its members urged a less aggressive ground war, called for new efforts to open negotiations and, implicitly, laid the groundwork for political compromise.

FOUR EXPONENTS OF CONTINUITY

The exponents of continuity were Mr. Rusk, and Mr. Rostow and Generals Wheeler and Taylor. Mr. Rusk, by then the stanchest defender of the war in public, patiently bore the heat of criticism. Tall, unbending, composed, he was, in his own words, "the iceman."

Mr. Rostow and General Taylor, who had gone to Vietnam early in 1961 as President Kennedy's personal envoys and who came back advocating intervention, were even more opposed to "letting up the pressure." Mr. Rostow, athletic and ebullient, funneled the news from Saigon to the President.

The advocates of change were Messrs. Nitze, Warnke, and Katzenbach, and later—most powerfully—Mr. Clifford. Mr. Helms, thoughtful and angular, was neutral on policy questions. The weight of his C.I.A. analysis called into question military judgments, past strategy and the quest for victory implicit in so many earlier decisions.

Although Mr. Clifford was never alone, his eventual role was remarkable because it was wholly unexpected.

He came into government with a reputation as a hawk, as a trusted, loyal "back-room" counselor to Mr. Johnson who had steadfastly supported Administration policy. In December, 1965, he had opposed the 36-day bombing pause then advocated by his predecessor. One man acquainted with the circumstances of the Clifford appointment said later:

"I am sure the President felt, 'Here is a good, strong, sturdy supporter of the war, and that's what I need.' McNamara was wobbling—particularly on the bombing issue. I think the President felt Clifford was strong and sturdy."

But Mr. Clifford had begun to have doubts during a trip in August, 1967, to Vietnam and allied countries contributing troops to the war. On his return he confided to the President that he was deeply uneasy at having discovered that the American view of the war was not fully shared by Australia, New Zealand, Thailand and the Philippines.

Disturbed he was, but he remained a supporter of Administration policy. He was encouraged by secret diplomatic efforts in August, 1967, and again in January, 1968, to get negotiations with Hanoi started on the basis of the so-called San Antonio formula.

That proposal, made public by President Johnson in a speech in the Texas city on September 30, 1967, offered to halt the bombing of North Vietnam provided it would lead promptly to productive talks and "assuming" that Hanoi would not take military advantage of the cessation.

At Mr. Clifford's Senate confirmation hearings on Jan. 25, 1968, he had added the important interpretation that this meant that the President would tolerate "normal" levels of infiltration from North to South Vietnam.

The president had not cleared Mr. Clifford's remarks in advance and, as a result, according to one informed source, "all hell broke loose at the White House and the State Department."

Secretary Rusk was said to have argued for two days with President Johnson against giving Administration endorsement to the interpretation. He was overruled. On Jan. 29 the State Department said Mr. Clifford's remarks represented United States policy.

He plunged into the minutiae of Vietnam like a lawyer taking a new case. He had private talks with Mr. McNamara, whose own misgivings had sharpened in his final months at the Pentagon.

As a newcomer with limited knowledge, Mr. Clifford had to rely on civilian subordinates more than had his brilliant and experienced predecessor. The large faction of dissenters from Administration policy was quick to seize the opportunity to press its views. The Tet offensive, recalled one dissenter, "gave us something we could hang our arguments on, something to contradict the beguiling upward curve on the progress charts" from Saigon.

With the lid off, the new Secretary discovered a nest of "hidden doves" at the Pentagon, including his deputy, Mr. Nitze; Assistant Secretaries Warnke, Alain C. Entoven, Goulding and Alfred B. Fitt; the Under Secretaries of the Army, Navy and Air Force—David E. McGiffert, Charles F. Baird and Townsend W. Hoopes; a few younger generals and colonels and a score of young civilians brought in by Mr. McNamara, principally Dr. Morton H. Halperin, Dr. Les Gelb and Richard C. Steadman.

The men who clearly had the greatest impact on the new Secretary's thinking were Messrs. Nitze, Warnke and Goulding—perhaps Mr. Warnke more than the others.

"Warnke was deeply upset about Vietnam and he was persuasive," a colleague said. "His style and Mr. Clifford's meshed." As a measure of their mutual confidence, Mr. Clifford chose Mr. Warnke as a law partner when both left the Government.

When the Clifford task force got under way, a number of officials took the troop request as evidence of panic on General Westmoreland's part. But ranking officers who were in Saigon headquarters during and after the Tet offensive assert that there was no thought of asking for many more troops until shortly before General Wheeler's visit late in February.

"The President asked General Wheeler to go out to Vietnam to find out what General Westmoreland thought he could use," a Pentagon official said. Civilian officials were irritated by this approach. "It was a mistake to ask a damned-fool question like that," a State Department official remarked.

The Joint Chiefs of Staff had their own reasons for favoring a massive increase and a reserve call-up. For months they had been deeply concerned that the strategic reserve had been dangerously depleted and they had been looking for a chance to reconstitute it by persuading the President to mobilize National Guard units.

Another view was held by Ambassador Bunker, who never fully endorsed the troop request and who wanted first priority for re-equipping and expanding the South Vietnamese Army—a suggestion endorsed by Pentagon civilians.

The Wheeler-Westmoreland plan presented to the task force called for 206,000 men by June 30, 1969—roughly 100,000 within a few months and two later increments of about 50,000 men each. The first segment was to come from available active-duty units in the United States; the rest were to come from the reserves.

In the view of the Joint Chiefs, only the full number would assure victory. The implication was that with 206,000 more men, the war would "not be terribly long," as one Pentagon civilian put it—but there was no precise forecast.

At this point Mr. Warnke, in his nasal Massachusetts accent, read a C.I.A. paper that challenged the military thesis head on. Hanoi, he said, would match American reinforcements as it had in the past, and the result would simply be escalation and "a lot more killing" on both sides.

Besides, the task force was told, the financial costs would be immense. The proposed scale of reinforcements would add nearly $10-billion to a war already costing $30-billion a year.

As an alternative, Mr. Warnke urged a turn toward deescalation—a pullback from General Westmoreland's aggressive search-and-destroy tactics and the abandonment of isolated outposts like the besieged Marine garrison at Khesanh. He said that American forces should be used as a mobile shield in and around population centers and that more should be demanded from the South Vietnamese Army.

The sheer complexity of the troop issue began to raise doubts in Mr. Clifford's mind.

QUESTIONS OTHERS AVOIDED

"Part of it was Clark's intelligent questioning and part of it was his naiveté," a colleague recalled. "He asked about things that others more familiar with the details would not have asked.

"He just couldn't get the figures straight on troops. He drove Bus Wheeler mad. He would say, 'Now I understand you wanted 22,000 men for such and such,' and Wheeler would point out this didn't include the support elements, and if you added them, it would be 35,000 in all.

"This happened again and again every time Clark wanted to get the numbers down as low as possible, and it had a psychological impact on him," the source added.

The first weekend in March was consumed by a study of the papers drafted for the task force and by questions. "It was meet all day, sandwiches in for lunch, sandwiches in for dinner," a participant recalled.

Word was passed to President Johnson that the review "wasn't going well" and had hit a "discordant note." But Mr. Clifford's doubts had not hardened into convictions by the time he handed the President his first report on March 5.

A short, unsigned, four-or-five-page memorandum, it recommended giving General Westmoreland 50,000 more troops in the next three months and set out a schedule for readying the rest of the 206,000 men for dispatch over the next 15 months.

FROM DIVERGENT POINTS OF VIEW

Characteristically, the President's advisers disagreed on the recommendation's significance. The Pentagon saw it as a move "to get the pipeline going"—general approval of the troop request; State Department officials viewed it as part of a process of "whittling down" the 206,000 figure.

Although Mr. Clifford had passed along the report, he was uneasy about it. He was worried that if the President approved the first batch of troops, that action would move him irrevocably toward the whole 206,000. But the Secretary did not challenge the report directly; he tried to stall, suggesting that the task force check General Westmoreland's reaction to be sure the "mix" of forces was right.

General Wheeler wanted to move ahead, but others, including Mr. Rusk and Mr. Rostow, were willing to have the issue studied further, so the task force carried on for several more days.

This seemed to suit Mr. Johnson's mood, too. His instinct, a White House aid explained later, was to delay implementing the plan. "He kept putting off making an initial decision," the aide said.

For the President had heard the grumbles in Congress over the danger to the dollar from the gold drain and from the rising costs of the war. Politicians were alarmed by the size of the troop request.

Old, trusted friends like Senator Richard B. Russell, the Georgia Democrat who headed the Armed Services Committee, were complaining tartly about General Westmoreland. Influential men like Senator John Stennis, the Mississippi Democrat, were privately warning the President to go slow on mobilizing reserves.

As the task force persisted, Secretary Clifford himself was putting more pointed questions. "What is our military plan for victory?" he asked. "How will we end the war?" He was not satisfied.

Then the bombing campaign came under his scrutiny. Mr. Hoopes wrote him a memorandum urging a halt, arguing that the bombing was not having significant results and that, because of Soviet and Chinese Communist aid, North Vietnam had become "on balance a stronger military power today than before the bombing began."

Mr. Hoopes contended that it was "a military fiction" that American combat casualties would rise if the bombing were halted. American losses, he said, were primarily a result of the aggressive ground strategy in the South.

Under the impact of such arguments, Mr. Clifford's doubts became convictions. He supported the President's previous restrictions on the war—no invasion of North Vietnam, no expansion of the ground war into Laos or Cambodia, no mining of the Haiphong harbor—and he became convinced that within those restrictions there was no military answer. He began the search for a path to disengagement.

The debate, by now in the White House, seesawed through the middle of March. At this time Mr. Clifford began to state his case for a fundamental change in American policy: It was time to emphasize peace, not a larger war.

He now challenged the task-force recommendation for more troops. "This isn't the way to go at all," he told the President. "This is all wrong."

HIS WORDS CARRIED WEIGHT

With the nation bitterly divided over the war and in desperate need at home, he maintained, it would be immoral to consider enormous added investment in Vietnam—a "military sinkhole."

His outspoken challenge was deeply disturbing to President Johnson, who always preferred a consensus among his close advisers. Although he never turned his celebrated temper on Mr. Clifford, the argument chilled their personal relations and left the Defense Secretary, a friend for 30 years, feeling oddly frozen out of the White House at times.

Secretary Rusk apparently did not disagree with Mr. Clifford so sharply on troop numbers, but he was opposed to the long-run implications of Mr. Clifford's arguments—that in the end, the United States would have to settle for less. Mr. Rostow felt that the new Defense Secretary had fallen under the influence of "the professional pessimists" in the Defense Department.

At the Pentagon morale was rising among civilian advocates of a new policy. "We used to ask," a former Pentagon civilian said of the Secretary, "is he one of us? Well, there was 'one of us' at the White House." He was Harry McPherson, the President's speech drafter, who, unknown to the Pentagon or the State Department, was already at work on a major Vietnam speech. The final version was Mr. Johnson's address to the nation on Sunday, March 31.

FIRST A PLEA FOR A STIFFER STAND

The speech was originally conceived late in February on the basis of Mr. Rostow's analysis that the Tet offensive had not been a real setback and that the allies should pull up their socks and hang on until the enemy came to his senses. While the discussions of troop strength were proceeding, Mr. McPherson was developing his draft.

Initially, it included an opened-ended commitment to the war—a willingness to carry on at whatever the cost. But as the internal debate over troop figures raged on and the numbers dwindled down to 50,000 and the tone softened. But the President would not commit himself to any draft or any figure.

Then came a series of signal events: Senator Eugene J. McCarthy scored a stunning upset in the New Hampshire Democratic primary on March 1. American dead and wounded in Vietnam reached 139,801—exceeding over-all Korean-war losses. American and Western European bankers held an emergency meeting in Washington to stem the run of gold as the price soared. Senator Robert F. Kennedy announced on March 16 that he would seek the Democratic Presidential nomination.

All this formed the backdrop for the most delicate argument of all—that about the bombing.

On March 15, Arthur J. Goldberg, the American representative at the United Nations, sent an eight-page memo to the President urging him to halt the bombing to get nogotiations started.

Others in the Administration favored such a step—Mr. Katzenbach and Ambassador-at-Large W. Averell Harriman, among them—but it was Ambassador Goldberg, increasingly frustrated by his sense of powerlessness on the Vietnam issue, who dared brook the President's anger by raising the issue directly.

Few officials knew he had done so. He drafted the memo himself and sent it labeled "For the President's Eyes Only." Copies were given to Secretaries Rusk and Clifford, and Mr. Rostow, as the President's aide, saw it in due course, but Mr. Goldberg discussed it with none of them.

Still others, including Assistant Secretary of State Bundy, favored waiting for several weeks on the ground that another enemy offensive might be near.

A day after the Goldberg memo arrived, the subject came up in Mr. Johnson's inner circle. The President, his patience sorely tested, sat up in his chair and said:

"Let's get one thing clear! I'm telling you now I am not going to stop the bombing. Now I don't want to hear any more about it. Goldberg has written me about the whole thing, and I've heard every argument. I'm not going to stop it. Now is there anybody here who doesn't understand that?"

There was dead silence.

The bombing issue was dropped at that meeting, but it was not dead. Mr. Clifford, the lawyer, had noticed a loophole.

... He proposed that the bombing be restricted to the Panhandle region of North Vietnam south of the 20th Parallel.

* * *

... A cutback would not violate the President's insistence that there be no halt without matching restraint from Hanoi, he said. He added that it would not, as the military feared in the case of a halt, jeopardize American troops in outposts just south of the demilitarized zone—Khesanh, Camp Carroll, the Rockpile and others.

The region south of the 20th Parallel contains many of the "meatiest" targets. All North Vietnamese troops and most of the supplies heading into South Vietnam have to pass through this region.

The proposal was also thought to offer a diplomatic opening: If Hanoi and Washington were not able to walk directly to the negotiating table, Mr. Clifford suggested, perhaps they could begin to "crawl."

This was not a new idea. In the spring of 1967, Mr. Clifford's predecessor as Defense Secretary, Robert S. McNamara, had his aides draft a similar proposal for cutting back to the 19th or 20th Parallel as a means of starting the process of tacit de-escalation. For many months, too, Secretary of State Dean Rusk had been developing a variety of plans for cutbacks.

The theory was that if Washington made the first move, Hanoi might match it and, step by step, they could begin scaling down the war even without negotiations.

President Johnson refused to accept the plan after it ran into heavy opposition from the Joint Chiefs of Staff. There were reports at the time that some senior generals would have resigned if it had been carried out.

Nonetheless, gingerly and indirect soundings of Hanoi were made at the time through one diplomatic source called a "quasi-disavowable channel." The reaction from Hanoi, as read in Washington, was negative: Only a halt could produce talks. (The talks began in May, as it turned out, but the bombing did not come to a complete end until Nov. 1.)

Now, in March, 1968, the diplomatic experts thought that this was still a problem. Privately, the President had made no decision on the plan but publicly he was as stern as ever.

With Senator Robert F. Kennedy now in the race for the Democratic Presidential nomination and with the political tide apparently running against Mr. Johnson, he lashed back at his critics. In one of his pet phrases, he was "hunkering down like a Texas jackrabbit in a hailstorm."

PRESIDENT DERIDES CRITICS

On March 18 in Minneapolis, the President derided critics who would "tuck our tails and violate our commitments" in Vietnam. He raised the specter of appeasement in the Munich style. The Clifford camp took this as a counterattack aimed at them by the hawkish faction of the Administration led by Walt W. Rostow, the President's adviser on national security affairs.

President Johnson ridiculed proposals for shifting to a less ambitious ground strategy in Vietnam, as the doves wanted. "Those of you who think you can save lives by moving the battlefield in from the mountains to the cities where the people live have another think coming," he said acidly.

That remark in a speech and two more addresses in a similar tone discouraged the doves. Mr. Clifford, exhausted by his first two intensive weeks in office—during which he was directing the reappraisal of policy on the war—and suffering renewed complications from a case of hepatitis picked up in Vietnam the year before, felt that he had lost the argument.

The bombing cutback seemed to have been brushed aside. The only hopeful sign, Mr. Clifford thought, was the fact that Mr. Johnson had still not approved the troop reinforcements for Gen. . . . Westmoreland. . . .

It is clear in the middle of March that despite his public declarations, President Johnson was deeply uneasy and undecided.

Late in the afternoon of March 20 he met in his oval office with Arthur J. Goldberg, the United States representative at the United Nations. It was their first meeting since Ambassador Goldberg, in a secret memo to the President on March 15, had proposed a bombing halt.

GOLDBERG CALLS AT WHITE HOUSE

It was this proposal that had provoked the President's angry outburst at the White House meeting a day later. Mr. Goldberg had not been there and was unware of Mr. Johnson's reaction. Now the two men met alone, and the President seemed interested in Ambassador Goldberg's position. He asked him to go through his arguments again, listening carefully and putting questions now and then. There were no angry words.

Before they parted, Mr. Johnson invited the silver-haired envoy to take part in a secret council of "wise men" that was to meet in Washington March 25. "I hope you'll put these same views to them there," he said.

The next hint of the President's thinking—though its significance was denied at the time—came on March 22. He announced that he was making General Westmoreland Army Chief of Staff, effective in July. He insisted that this did not necessarily foreshadow a change in strategy.

The White House explanation was that the shift had been in the mill for weeks and that the President was rewarding the general with the best job he could give him.

President Johnson was upset over the immediate speculation that, as an aide put it, he was "sacking Westy because of Tet," the costly Lunar-New Year offensive the enemy had sprung in Vietnam on Jan. 30. To this day Mr. Johnson says privately as well as publicly that in his own heart that was not his motive. But some who know Lyndon Johnson extremely well believe that the shift came at this time—subconsciously, at least—as part of a gradual transition to a new policy.

Unknown to his political advisers, President Johnson was moving to settle the troop issue. He ordered General Wheeler to hold a secret rendezvous in the

Pacific with General Westmoreland to learn if massive reinforcements were still needed. On March 24 the generals met alone for 90 minutes in 13th Air Force headquarters at Clark Air Force Base, in the Philippines.

General Westmoreland reported that the battlefield situation had improved— the crisis around the isolated Marine garrison at Khesanh had eased, the enemy seemed to have run out of steam and the South Vietnamese military forces were rebuilding their depleted ranks and moving back into the countryside.

Considering this trend, General Westmoreland said he would be satisfied if he could keep the two 5,000-man brigades rushed to Saigon early in February, at the peak of the enemy offensive, and if he were also given about 13,500 support troops for them.

General Wheeler flew back to report to the President. General Westmoreland sent a follow-up summary of his needs on March 28, three days before the President was to address the nation. No one was informed of the Pacific meeting.

By March 22, the inner circle in Washington had been informed that the President was going to give a Vietnam speech and they gathered in the family dining room of the White House to discuss it.

Present were the men who had shared the agony of Vietnam decisions with President Johnson—Secretary of State Dean Rusk, Secretary Clifford, General Wheeler, Walt Rostow, George Christian, the press secretary, and Harry McPherson, a speech-writer.

SPEECH STILL HAWKISH IN TONE

The speech, conceived in the combative spirit after the Tet offensive, was still militant in tone. It deeply disturbed Mr. Clifford and others, who yearned to include some gesture of peace along with the scheduled reinforcements.

Once again Mr. Clifford urged the President to consider a bombing cutback on the ground that it would improve the Administration's position, internationally and domestically. Just two weeks before the crucial Democratic primary in Wisconsin, on April 2, most of the President's aides thought he needed a political shot in the arm. Vice President Humphrey believed that the bombing should be halted, not curtailed, if there was to be a change.

The discussion was exhaustive. How would a cutback affect Saigon? Would a bombing limitation to the 20th Parallel satisfy Hanoi? Were there other partial measures that made more sense?

After seven hours, Secretary Rusk gave a lucid summary. Mr. Rusk, who had himself raised the possibility of a bombing halt as early as March 3, said that there seemed to be a consensus that some step toward negotiations was desirable. But, according to one account, he cast doubt on whether a curtailment would satisfy the North Vietnamese.

"The feeling as we left," one participant recalled, "was that it would be nice if we could work it, but it wouldn't get anywhere."

The Administration doves had lost another round, but they did not relent.

The next morning Mr. McPherson, a bright, boyish-looking man, sent the President a memo that sought to strike a compromise between the general desire to make a peace gesture and the fear of rejection by Hanoi. The memo urged the President to stop the bombing north of the 20th Parallel and, simultaneously, to offer to stop the rest if Hanoi showed restraint at the demilitarized zone and left Saigon and other cities free from major attack.

The President sent the memo to Secretary Rusk, who later returned it with the comment that these were ideas that he had been working on and that they should be developed further. His reaction was favorable but, according to one account, he did not make any specific recommendation.

'WISE MEN' HAVE NEW THOUGHTS

Mr. Johnson also asked Mr. McPherson for another copy to send to Ambassador Ellsworth Bunker in Saigon. The answer that came back mentioned some of the problems Washington had anticipated but apparently did not raise any fundamental objections.

The time for decision was drawing near, but still the President hesitated.

"It was one of those periods when the President had everybody thinking he was about to make up his mind when actually he wasn't," a former White House official commented. "He has a facility for keeping his innermost thoughts to himself. He could keep everybody else lathered up the whole time. He just kept slipping back the deadlines for decision."

President Johnson, canvassing more opinion, was reaching outside the administration to summon to Washington the secret council of trusted advisers he mentioned to Ambassador Goldberg. They had a special and surprising impact on the President.

The previous fall, almost without exception and with Mr. Clifford a participant, they backed the President's policy. But in the wake of the Tet offensive several of these influential men had had a change of heart.

Mr. Clifford, in his new role as an advocate of change and looking for allies, encouraged the President to call them into council again in the hope that it would strengthen his argument.

They gathered at the State Department on Monday, March 25, with the President's address to the nation six days away. They constituted a "who's who" of the American foreign-policy establishment:

Dean Acheson, Secretary of State under President Truman; George W. Ball, Under Secretary of State in the Kennedy and Johnson Administrations; Gen. Omar N. Bradley, retired World War II commander; McGeorge Bundy, special assistant for national security affairs to Presidents Kennedy and Johnson; Arthur H. Dean, President Eisenhower's Korean war negotiator; Douglas Dillon, Secretary of the Treasury under President Kennedy.

Also Associate Justice Abe Fortas of the Supreme Court; Mr. Goldberg; Henry Cabot Lodge, twice Ambassador to Saigon; John J. McCloy, United States High

Commissioner in West Germany under President Truman; Robert D. Murphy, ranking diplomat in the Truman-Eisenhower era; Gen. Matthew B. Ridgway, retired Korean war commander; Gen. Maxwell D. Taylor, former chairman of the joint chiefs of staff and a constant Presidential adviser on Vietnam, and Cyrus R. Vance, former Deputy Defense Secretary and President Johnson's trouble-shooter.

SOME PESSIMISM IS VOICED

The wise men heard candid briefings, some of which bordered on pessimism, and then questioned Messrs. Rusk, Clifford and Rostow and others about the extent of the Tet disaster and the plans for the future. The discussion continued late that night and resumed the next morning at the White House.

For the first time President Johnson got the trend of their views. He was "deeply shaken," one aide said, by the change of temper of the wise men, who were deeply discouraged over the war after the exalted hopes of the previous fall.

The President was especially impressed by the fact that Mr. Acheson, McGeorge Bundy and to a lesser degree Mr. Vance had joined Mr. Ball and Mr. Goldberg in opposing further military commitments and advocating some way of getting out of the war. He was jolted when Mr. Bundy, one of the architects of intervention in the early sixties and of the bombing of North Vietnam in 1965, was now taking an opposite tack.

There was, to be sure, a faction that held firm in defense of the harder line—Justice Fortas, General Taylor and Mr. Murphy. Mr. Murphy wanted more bombing, not less.

Ambassador Lodge, now President Nixon's chief negotiator in Paris, left the other participants puzzled. Several found him hawkish, but at least one said he was "on all sides of the issue." Mr. McCloy leaned toward the hawkish group.

Mr. Dean, Mr. Dillon and Generals Bradley and Ridgway were now doubters. They were plainly war-weary if not yet ready to shift course dramatically. The waning public support of the war was a constant concern.

There was no consensus on the bombing issue. Mr. Goldberg and Mr. Ball advocated a halt as a way to negotiations. The others were uncertain but the impression left with Government sources was that the wise men as a group were saying: "We had better start looking for another way to get this war settled."

THE PRIMARY WAS SECONDARY

To the President and his senior advisers, one close observer said later, such shifts carried "more weight than something like the New Hampshire primary." Someone suggested that Mr. Johnson consider the impact of his Vietnam decisions on the coming election; he replied testily that the campaign was the least of his concerns.

Two days later, on March 28, Messrs. Rusk, Clifford, Rostow, McPherson and William Bundy met in Mr. Rusk's mahogany-paneled office on the seventh floor of the State Department to polish the President's speech.

It was still, in the words of one participant, a "teeth-clenched, see-it-through" speech, announcing that about 15,000 more troops would be sent to Vietnam. It made a pro-forma plea for peace at the negotiating table and said nothing about cutting back the bombing.

Secretary Clifford launched an impassioned plea against taking this approach.

"I can't do it—I can't go along with it," he said. "I can't be in the position of trying to polish a speech of this kind. This speech can't be polished. What's needed is a new speech. This one is irrevocably setting the President down the wrong road."

The others listened as he spoke for nearly an hour, using to enormous advantage his almost unique position of being able to speak for the views of many outside.

It would tear the country apart, the Defense Secretary argued, to hear a speech that promised only more war. What was needed, he said, was not a "war speech, but a peace speech—the issue is as sharp as the edge of an ax."

To Mr. Clifford's surprise, Mr. Rusk did not cut him short. The others chimed in. Mr. Rusk sent out for sandwiches. Mr. Clifford appealed for some compromise, and once again they debated the 20th Parallel idea.

By this time the military commanders were no longer raising strong objections. Some, like Adm. U.S. Grant Sharp, the Pacific Fleet commander, who had overall charge of the bombing, thought the cutback would fail. He fully expected that if it were tried, the President would order full bombing again in a month or so. Some officials thought this was Mr. Rostow's view also.

RUSK SWAYED BY THE DEBATE

Secretary Rusk, eager to find some way to the negotiating table, still did not think the cutback would satisfy Hanoi. The month's arguments had had a cumulative effect on him.

At the end of the day—the meeting lasted until 5 P.M.—Mr. Rusk had agreed with Mr. Clifford that Mr. McPherson should prepare "an alternate draft." That night, while the President was showing Senator Mike Mansfield, the Democratic majority leader, a draft of the original hawkish speech, Mr. McPherson began writing alternate draft No. 1. Working through the night, he had it ready by morning.

He sent the draft, the first one containing the proposal for a bombing cutback to the 20th Parallel, to Mr. Johnson withh a note saying that it seemed to reflect the sentiments of some of the President's leading advisers. He also offered to go back to the original version if that was Mr. Johnson's wish.

Later in the day the President called Mr. McPherson in to discuss changes in an item on "Page 3." He did not specify which draft, but it was clear that he was now working with the new speech. That was how he signaled a major break in the debate.

He had been deeply influenced by the shift in the public mood, as reflected in the wise men's meetings and his contacts on Capitol Hill. The country was in turmoil and the dollar was in danger.

He had been shaken by the change in his old friend, Mr. Clifford, and was finally persuaded to try a new tack by Mr. Clifford's sheer persistence. The mood of others had softened in the crucible of debate, too.

FIVE MORE DRAFTS OF SPEECH

From then until 9 P.M. on the 31st, the speech went through five more drafts. None changed the new essence, though there was one important tug-of-war over the wording on the bombing cutback.

Under Secretary of State Nicholas deB. Katzenbach, drawn into the top-level discussions since Secretary Rusk was leaving for a Pacific meeting with the Vietnam allies, opposed naming the 20th Parallel as the cutoff point.

Mr. Katzenbach had long favored a halt. Now he wanted the northern limit to be the 19th Parallel rather than the 20th, but the military insisted on the 20th so they could hit Thanhhoa, a railroad switching point, and Route 7, leading into Laos—both just south of the 20th Parallel.

The Under Secretary, who suggested that it not be stated so badly, was looking for a way to "winch" the limit further southward. And, like most Administration officials, he was operating under the mistaken assumption that one main purpose of the speech was to help President Johnson in the April 2 Democratic primary in Wisconsin.

Suggesting that the speech would have more public appeal if it emphasized that part of the bombing would be continued to protect American troops just south of the demilitarized zone, Mr. Katzenbach drafted a revision that said all bombing should stop "except in an area north of the demilitarized zone where the continuing enemy buildup directly threatens allied forward positions." His amendment specified that this would spare almost 90 per cent of North Vietnam's population.

ROSTOW PHONES KATZENBACH

The President liked that language and accepted it. On Saturday he asked Mr. Rostow to telephone Mr. Katzenbach, now Acting Secretary, to persuade him to accept the 20th Parallel as the northern limit.

Reluctantly Mr. Katzenbach agreed, but with a caveat: "Don't make the first big raid at 19 degrees 59 minutes. Make sure the orders are consistent with the speech." Mr. Rostow replied that this would be done.

But they had different interpretations of what they had agreed on. Mr. Katzenbach thought he had won agreement on a plan that would let the bombing "roll northward" gradually from the buffer area as battlefield conditions dictated. Mr. Rostow felt he had Mr. Katzenbach's approval for military orders saying simply that bombing north of the 20th Parallel was forbidden after March 31.

On the Saturday a small group worked with President Johnson, who was in good spirits going over the text line by line until about 9 P.M. The speech had become progressively more dovish until, one official said, "it ended up 180 degrees from where it started."

Late the previous day Mr. Clifford had been concerned that the peroration, left over from original drafts, was still too militant, so Mr. McPherson was to draft a substitute.

When the Saturday session ended Mr. Johnson asked for the revised peroration. Mr. McPherson said he had not had time to rewrite it but would do so promptly.

'I MAY HAVE ONE OF MY OWN'

The President, his shirt open and his tie down, muttered, "No need to—I may have one of my own." He winked at Mr. McPherson, who turned to Mr. Clifford and said: "My God? Do you think he is going to say sayonara?" Mr. Clifford responded with a strange and unbelieving grimace.

On Sunday the President had Horace Busby, another speech-writer, and Mr. Christian working on the withdrawal section. Mr. McPherson still officially in the dark on the President's political plans, assumed that he did not want his ending.

But Mr. Johnson kept sending word that he did indeed want Mr. McPherson's peroration, obviously intending to deliver both.

Initially, Mr. Johnson hesitated to make his withdrawal announcement with the policy declaration. But sometime near the end of March, as he became convinced of the need for a bombing cutback, he evidently concluded that it would be more effective if he made it clear that he was not just appealing for votes or pacifying domestic critics or serving some other personal interest.

The approach of the Wisconsin primary also served as a deadline for action, in the view of some of his political advisers. They thought his withdrawal would be more dignified and more effective if made before the primary rather than after the expected victory for Senator Eugene J. McCarthy of Minnesota.

By the eve of the speech the President's mind was made up.

He did not sleep particularly well that night, and he was up before dawn. In the afternoon, he began rehearsing the Vietnam portion of the speech. About 4 P.M. Mr. Busby gave him the revised ending on not seeking re-election. The President make a few final adjustments to insure that his motives would be understood.

At 8 P.M. the text was turned over to an Army Signal Corps man to put on Teleprompters, and the President told his aides to begin informing members of the Cabinet of his intentions. Secretary Rusk was informed while airborne in the Western Pacific.

Secretary Clifford and his wife were invited to the Executive Mansion half an hour before the President was to go on nationwide television. Mr. Clifford already knew of the Vietnam decision—the bombing cutback to the 20th Parallel, 13,500 more troops for General Westmoreland and more equipment for the South Vietnamese Army at a cost of $2.5-billion a year.

After the wrenching tensions of the policy debate and the chill that had crept into their personal relations, the secretary wanted to see him before delivering the speech. Upstairs in the family quarters, the Cliffords joined Mrs. Johnson and Jack Valenti, the President's former aide and an old Texas friend.

Mr. Johnson motioned Mr. Clifford into his bedroom and without a word handed him the last two paragraphs of the speech.

"With America's sons in the fields far away, with America's future under challenge right here at home, with our hopes and the world's hopes for peace in the balance every day," the President told the nation a few moments later, "I do not believe that I should devote an hour or a day of my time to any personal partisan causes or to any duties other than the awesome duties of this office—the Presidency of your country.

"Accordingly, I shall not seek, and I will not accept, the nomination of my party for another term as your President."

EPILOGUE

The President's speech brought Washington—and the nation—the relief it feels when a breezy summer day breaks a sweltering heat wave. The bitterness of months had been lanced in a stroke. There was a rare moment of harmony. But it was only an instant.

Within 36 hours, while the world awaited Hanoi's response, Navy jets struck Thanhhoa, 210 miles north of the demilitarized zone, the very kind of raid that Mr. Katzenbach had wanted to prevent.

The enormous relief evaporated. The heat wave was back. The politicians, not knowing that the Russians and Hanoi had been privately told that the northern limit of the bombing was the 20th Parallel, complained that the public had been misled. State Department officials privately accused the military commanders of trying to sabotage the President's peace initiative.

With a new political storm mounting, Mr. Clifford persuaded President Johnson to pull the bombing back to the 19th parallel on the pretext that some American planes might have strayed over the 20th Parallel. It was a decision that Mr. Rostow, General Wheeler, General Westmoreland and others tried many times to reverse.

And so it went—all summer, all fall—the two coalitions in the Administration battling for the President's favor: one insisting that an irrevocable turn toward disengagement had been made, the other denying it.

"It was like climbing the greasy pole," recalled an insider. "You wanted to continue climbing higher but you had to keep fighting to stay where you were."

In May, the Hawks were urging escalation after enemy forces had launched their mini-Tet offensive. Senior military commanders wanted to push the bombing back up to the 20th parallel to hit Thanhhoa to show Hanoi that America was impatient.

General Westmoreland also wanted approval to launch B-52 raids and small ground forays against enemy supply dumps and base camps in remote areas of Cambodia, when enemy forces pulled back to these sanctuaries from assaults on American outposts. But President Johnson rejected this plan firmly.

In June, when enemy rockets were falling on Saigon, Ambassador Ellsworth Bunker was privately urging that the United States retaliate by bombing Hanoi. One official said the United States was "within two days" of stepping up the bombing of North Vietnam when the attacks on Saigon stopped.

Next it was the doves. During the prolonged summer battlefield lull W. Averell Harriman and Cyrus R. Vance, the American negotiators in Paris, tried to talk the President into a total bombing halt.

They made their pitch at the end of July. It was strictly a ploy. They accepted the military estimate that the lull was not deliberate and that the enemy was merely regrouping and refitting his forces. But they suggested that President Johnson treat it as deliberate restraint anyway.

The proposal was to tell Hanoi that since it had de-escalated the war, the United States would end the bombing, but that to sustain this cessation, Hanoi would have to refrain from another offensive. The hope was to talk Hanoi into restraint.

Mr. Clifford and Vice President Humphrey promoted the idea. Mr. Katzenbach and Mr. Bundy were in Paris at this time, and simultaneously, *The New York Times* in a July 29 editorial advocated a similar tactic.

It was all too much for President Johnson. "He thought it was a conspiracy," said one high official. "There were so many coincidences that he thought it stank to high heaven." He rejected the plan out of hand.

The struggle for the President's mind persisted until the day he left office.

Nixon's Decision to Invade Cambodia[1]

HEDRICK SMITH

President Nixon's venture into Cambodia is ending with proclamations of unprecedented military gain, but it was launched for the broader purpose of rescuing Cambodia from sudden Communist domination and that purpose is still unrealized.

A reconstruction shows that the survival of an anti-Communist Government in Cambodia came to be seen by Mr. Nixon as essential for the defense of Vietnam and the American stake in Indochina. As pieced together by correspondents of *The New York Times* in Washington, Saigon and Pnompenh, Mr. Nixon's handling of his most serious crisis also involved the following main factors:

- The President, believing that Communist nations had long been trifling with him in Indochina, Korea and the Middle East, saw Cambodia as the first feasible opportunity to demonstrate that he could meet force with force.
- Mr. Nixon was haunted by intelligence reports that enemy commanders were moving against Cambodia, confident that American hands were tied by war-weariness at home.
- Before attacking, the Nixon Administration tried to signal circuitously to Hanoi that it would accept an accommodation—which the Cambodian Government was seeking—provided that Cambodia's principal port remained closed to Communist supply shipments. The overtures collapsed over the port issue.
- Once he felt himself militarily challenged by the enemy in Cambodia, Mr. Nixon pushed the pace of decision-making here—so much that one senior advisor cautioned him that the generals in Saigon might be giving the President only the advice they thought he wanted to hear.
- Repeated and forceful opposition to the use of American troops in Cambodia from Secretary of State William P. Rogers, stressing the risks of domestic discontent, caused Mr. Nixon to delay the operation 24 hours.

Once decided, Mr. Nixon also ordered four heavy bombing raids against North Vietnam, despite the year-and-a-half-old cessation of United States raids on the North—with the purpose, officials now acknowledge, of warning Hanoi against counterattacking across the demilitarized zone into South Vietnam. The four attacks appeared to be a violation of the private understandings with Hanoi prohibiting bombing of the North.

Formally, the Cambodian operations began with a Presidential announcement on April 30. But for Mr. Nixon, the beginning was well before that.

Like President Kennedy in the Cuban crisis and President Johnson in Vietnam, he felt Communist forces crowding and testing him. He had contained the frustration of not retaliating when the North Vietnamese shelled Saigon early in his term, when North Korea shot down an American intelligence plane, when the Paris peace talks bogged down. Now the Soviet Union was moving combat pilots into the United Arab Republic and Communist forces were threatening another nation in Indochina.

Of all these situations, Mr. Nixon felt, Cambodia offered the first opening for effective military reaction that would carry his larger political message. As the President confided to a senior adviser: This is a risk, but this is the kind of thing I have been waiting for.

Mr. Nixon's objectives in Cambodia centered on staying off Communist domination. Survival of Premier Lon Nol's Government, for a time, at least, appeared essential. It's survival was needed to assure the defense of South Vietnam and the process of American withdrawal, to spare Saigon the blow of seeing a neighbor collapse while the United States did nothing and to deny Hanoi a gain that would tempt it, in the words of one senior adviser, to "go for all the marbles" in Indochina and forever spurn negotiation.

An American attack from the rear, Mr. Nixon thought, would divert and disrupt the enemy forces threatening General Lon Nol and also give the Cambodian Premier a badly needed political lift. But it required no open commitment.

Despite his preference for orderly procedure, President Nixon, like his predecessors, reacted in crisis with rump-group meetings, late phone calls, an out-of-channel message to the field and other activities that bypassed planners at the State and Defense Departments.

The White House became so worried about security leaks that even members of the Joint Chiefs of Staff were late to learn of some critical discussions. State Department lawyers were not told to prepare the legal case for invasion until four days after it began.

The gestation process for Mr. Nixon's decision was much longer than Administration accounts suggested. It began almost immediately after General Lon Nol and others deposed Prince Norodom Sihanouk on March 18

For years, Cambodia was a twilight zone of the Vietnam war. Prince Sihanouk, balancing between the belligerents, had let the North Vietnamese create a dozen base areas to shelter 40,000 to 60,000 troops for use against South Vietnam.

American generals had periodically pressed the Johnson Administration for permission to attack these sanctuaries, but President Johnson had refused. The Nixon Administration grudgingly tolerated the situation. Its plans for a gradual troop withdrawal from Vietnam assumed that the enemy bases in Cambodia would remain intact.

Within the last year, however, even Prince Sihanouk began to worry about the expanding enemy activity on his soil. He allowed American B-52's to bomb the base areas. For a time, he curtailed the enemy supply shipments to the bases through the port then Sihanoukville, now Kompong Som.

Prince Sihanouk's ouster, described as a surprise in Washington, posed an opportunity. All foreign-policy agencies quickly drafted proposals for dealing with the new situation. In this process, Secretary of Defense Melvin R. Laird invited the generals in Saigon to submit contingency plans.

By April 1, Gen. Creighton W. Abrams, the United States commander in Vietnam had offered the Pentagon several options:

First, to let South Vietnamese troops harass the enemy across the border.

Second, to help the south mount larger attacks over a period of months to disrupt the enemy bases.

Or third, to let American forces join the South Vietnamese in a swift full-scale assault on the bases.

General Abrams did not formally recommend any course.

Washington was still looking for diplomatic ways to contain the Cambodian situation. Perhaps Hanoi, with its forces now less secure in Cambodia, would show interest in negotiation—if not on Vietnam alone then in the context of an international conference on all Indochina, which France proposed on April 1.

General Lon Nol tried to work out live-and-let-live arrangements with the North Vietnamese, first in direct talks and then through Chinese and other Communist intermediaries. He asked North Vietnam to reduce its military presence in Cambodia and its reliance on shipments through Sihanoukville. Hanoi refused.

Washington made no direct approach to Hanoi, but passed word to Asian intermediaries that it would respect any deal General Lon Nol made. It got no diplomatic reply.

One diplomat said the American approach was so feeble and casual that he was not sure the intermediaries understood that the messages were meant for Hanoi. American officials, moreover, were sure that Hanoi suspected the United States of having ousted Prince Sihanouk and could not, therefore, credit Washington with good faith.

South Vietnamese forces, meanwhile, were staging sporadic raids across the Cambodian border, against the advice of American officials in Saigon. The United States increased bombing raids against enemy concentrations in

Cambodia, but General Abrams's contingency plans, now sent by the Joint Chiefs of Staff to the White House, were in limbo. Secretary Laird, talking with President Nixon in the second week of April, opposed an American assault because he feared heavy casualties—as high as 400 to 800 dead in the first week alone—and a public outcry.

In mid-April the combat situation changed. Starting April 13, enemy forces were detected moving westward into Cambodia from the border areas, cutting roads, blowing up bridges, harassing military posts and towns. The White House interpreted the reports "leniently"—as reliable on the location of enemy actions, but not on their size, seriousness or intent.

In Saigon, however, General Abrams was particularly struck by the thinning out of enemy forces in the Fishhook, a Cambodian salient that juts into South Vietnam 75 miles northwest of Saigon, which was considered the most important enemy refuge area.

General Abrams and Ellsworth Bunker, the American Ambassador, met privately for several nights and about April 15, sent parallel recommendations to the Departments of State and Defense. They urged an American attack into the Fishhook and joint attacks with the South Vietnamese against other bases.

High military sources summed up General Abrams's arguments as follows:

One of the two American divisions standing guard against attacks from the enemy bases in Cambodia was going home soon under President Nixon's withdrawal program, shifting a major burden to Saigon's forces. With the rainy season approaching and the Lon Nol Government unlikely to survive until fall, the time was right. An attack would help the South Vietnamese and assure further American withdrawals. With a third of the enemy forces moved west, the risks of American casualties were reduced.

The general's argument envisioning benefits for the Vietnamization program, impressed Secretary Laird. The promise of lower casualties convinced him, and he endorsed the proposal.

But at the White House, the military possibilities were still offset by the fear of pushing the war deeper into Cambodia and the fear of spoiling the chances for negotiation.

The prospects for diplomacy had unexpectedly improved when the Soviet Union said that it, too, was interested in an Indochina conference. "Only a new Geneva conference could bring a new solution and relax tension," Yakov A. Malik, the Soviet representative at the United Nations, said on April 16. The Americans got private indications that this as a deliberate initiative and assumed that the Russians had cleared it with Hanoi.

Still, the pressures in Cambodia were building up. Premier Lon Nol pleaded with greater urgency each day. Mr. Nixon did not want another state in Southeast Asia, dependent on the United States but neither did he want to stand idly by. High officials felt the whole rationale for defending South Vietnam would collapse if they acquiesced in a Communist take-over of Laos and

Cambodia. Also, the President feared Prince Sihanouk, with Hanoi's aid, might be returned to power.

So Mr. Nixon set out to help Premier Lon Nol clandestinely. He let Saigon's forces increase the scope and frequency of their attacks into Cambodia. The purpose, one high official said later, was "to put pressure on the enemy forces so they wouldn't turn toward Pnompenh."

American advisers were told to help plan the enlarged raids, but not get into combat inside Cambodia.

By April 17, the President had also approved a secret shipment of 6,000 captured AK-47 rifles of Soviet design to the Cambodian Army. The United States first tried to use Indonesia as a cover for this aid, but for reasons of diplomacy, shifted to South Vietnam.

Plans were also made to assemble a force of 2,000 Khmer Krom troops to stiffen the Cambodian army. These mercenaries fighting in South Vietnam for the American Special Forces were later flown secretly to Pnompenh.

President Nixon evidently hoped that these measures would win time. He was, in any case, distracted by the battle over his Supreme Court nominees, the Apollo 13 astronauts and the need to announce another troop withdrawal.

Generals Abrams was pleading for a 60-day delay in withdrawals. Secretary Laird wanted a cutback of 50,000 by Aug. 15. With the issue unresolved, Mr. Nixon went to greet the returning astronauts in Honolulu.

He finally hit on a compromise, surprising even some senior advisers: to delay withdrawals for 60 days but to hide that fact in an announcement of a full year's pullouts—150,000 men by May, 1971. Mr. Nixon flew back to San Clemente, Calif., to make the announcement April 20—a long and, as it turned out, fateful day in his perception of the situation in Indochina.

The speech emphasized his terms for a political settlement in more flexible terms than ever before.

He did point with concern to "the enemy's escalation in Laos and Cambodia" and repeated warnings that if "increased enemy action jeopardizes our remaining forces in Vietnam, I shall not hesitate to take strong and effective measures to deal with that situation."

There was no real hint of the internal discussions about Cambodia.

Officials insist that Mr. Nixon's optimism did not disguise any secret calculations. Press dispatches had already reported the fall of Saang, a district capital 18 miles from Pnompenh, but official confirmation did not reach the traveling White House until late on April 20.

On that day, too—although it was probably unknown to Mr. Nixon as he spoke—Hanoi's spokesman in Peking indicated that Prince Sihanouk was joining a new united military front for the "liberation" of all Indochina; the Russians backed off their interest in a Geneva conference, and the Lon Nol regime submitted a request for more than $500-million in military aid.

Mr. Nixon was restless that night—"wound up," his wife said—and after his speech, abruptly flew back to Washington. One aide said afterward that the President might have sensed "something was up."

By morning, intelligence reports had built up a picture of steady deterioration in Cambodia, but the problem hit Mr. Nixon with sudden force.

From that day on, Mr. Nixon got daily briefings from Richard Helms, Director of Central Intelligence. Details were sketchy, but the Communists were attacking Saang, Takeo and Angtassom, south of Pnompenh and Snoul and Memot, to the north.

The State Department surmised that the enemy was using hit-and-run maneuvers to create an impression of civil war. The Pentagon view, more persuasive to the White House, was that the North Vietnamese had decided to overthrow Lon Nol by isolating his capital, or taking it.

Mr. Nixon summoned the National Security Council to meet on April 22, the group's first consideration of the contingency plans.[2] The talk centered largely on a proposed South Vietnamese offensive into the Parrot's Beak, an enemy position jutting into Vietnam 35 miles from Saigon. There was some discussion of an American attack into the Fishhook.

The next morning, the President seemed bent on some kind of action. He called for operational plans for the Parrot's Beak, forcing a crisis schedule upon the Washington Special Action Group—a body headed by Henry A. Kissinger, his special assistant for security affairs.

The group, which is called WASAG, was created in April, 1969, when North Korea shot down an American intelligence plane. It played a central role in the Cambodian venture from late March onward by assembling and refining all contingency plans, assessing their consequence, and managing the execution of Presidential orders.

At the peak of crisis, the group's members were Mr. Kissinger; David Packard, Deputy Secretary of Defense; U. Alexis Johnson, Under Secretary of State for Political Affairs; Mr. Helms; Gen. Earle G. Wheeler, then Chairman of the Joint Chiefs; Adm. Thomas H. Moorer, his successor, and Marshall Greene, Assistant Secreaty of State for East Asian Affairs.

The group met twice on April 23, again on April 24. In Saigon, the South Vietnamese generals were hesitant about a major strike without the Americans. General Abrams and Ambassador Bunker met with President Nguyen Van Thieu, after which Saigon finally geared for action, while General Abrams pressed Washington to use American advisers in the Parrot's Beak operation.

Mr. Nixon was now pushing the process of making decisions, irritated that the enemy appeared complacent. American intelligence confirmed anew that the enemy command was telling its troops to push west without fear of an American attack from the rear. The White House denounced the enemy moves as a "foreign invasion."

On Friday morning, April 24, the President called for operational plans for the Fishhook operation to be delivered from Saigon within 24 hours. He called a secret meeting of the National Security Council for Sunday, pointing toward a final decision Sunday night. This would give the generals the 72 hours they said they needed to attack on April 29, which would be dawn, April 30, Saigon time.[3]

The President flew to Camp David, Md., Friday afternoon. Mr. Kissinger brought the plans on Saturday and the two men studied them. In Washington that evening, they conferred with Secretary Laird and Attorney General John N. Mitchell aboard the Government yacht *Sequoia* on the Potomac. They then attended a private showing of "Patton," the film biography of the defiant general, which Mr.Nixon was eager to see for a second time.

Secretary of State Rogers returned from New York on Sunday morning and, with Secretary Laird, heard a Pentagon briefing on the Fishhook plans. Thus all participants in the afternoon meeting of the Security Council were prepared for the main topic of debate.

The two Secretaries joined the President, the Attorney General, General Wheeler, Mr. Helms and Mr. Kissinger at the Executive Office Building next to the White House. Two statutory members of the Council, Vice President Agnew and George A. Lincoln, director of the Office of Emergency Preparedness, were not present.

Mr. Nixon said that he had decided "to do something." The Parrot's Beak operation had his tentative approval, with American air support but not American ground advisers. The Fishhook was the problem at hand.

The Pentagon representatives argued that a full assault, with American troops, was essential. Military analysis showed the enemy seeking either to topple the Lon Nol regime or to clear a supply corridor to the sea in eastern Cambodia. Either prospect jeopardized the defense of South Vietnam and American withdrawal. The Parrot's Beak alone would serve only as a warning. Using the South Vietnamese in the Fishhook would require a major reshuffle of armies, and might prove too difficult for them. With the heavy rains due in a month, and Lon Nol unlikely to survive until fall, it was now or never.

Secretary Rogers carried the principal burden of opposition. The use of American troops in Cambodia meant widening the war. The risk was grave of becoming entrapped, as the Johnson Administration had been. The President won wide popular support for gradual withdrawal and should not risk losing it. The allies' military objectives could be achieved by South Vietnamese forces alone.

The debate lasted three hours, ranging over other enemy base areas. Mr. Nixon came away thinking he had a choice of doing nothing or involving American troops. An attack in the Parrot's Beak alone seemed unlikely to bring much military advantage. To use only South Vietnamese ground forces would be a pretense, for American air and logistical support was deemed essential. It was a line of thinking Mr. Kissinger appears to have shared. Besides, the President was determined to prove that he could meet force with force.

Mr. Nixon withdrew to his hideaway office and ordered a tray of dinner. On a pad of yellow legal paper he summarized the pros and cons. As disclosed by Stewart Alsop in *Newsweek* and later confirmed officially, the President's doodling showed how intimately the survival of the Lon Nol regime had become linked in his mind with American success in Vietnam.

In reviewing whether there should be some action in Cambodia, Mr. Nixon listed only arguments in favor: "Time running out" was followed by "military aid" to Lon Nol could be "only symbolic." Then came a scribble saying inaction might tempt Hanoi to install a puppet regime in Pnompenh and a final entry saying that inaction by both sides would leave an "ambiguous situation" with time favoring the Communists.

The President then listed the pros and cons for American action in the Fishhook and for a South Vietnamese attack alone in the Parrot's Beak. He recognized that the Fishhook move would bring a "deep division" of the American people. He feared that it might provoke a collapse of the Paris talks, an attack on Pnompenh or a major North Vietnamese attack across the DMZ.

Mr. Nixon seemed determined to attack, but the opposing arguments of Secretary Rogers evidently led him to break his own deadline. He called another meeting for Monday morning, April 27, with Mr. Rogers, Mr. Laird, Mr. Kissinger and H.R. Haldeman, his chief of staff, but without the military or intelligence chiefs.[4]

Someone—apparently still Mr. Rogers—suggested that the military might be telling the President only what it thought he wanted to hear. The suggestion haunted Mr. Nixon. Out of that meeting came his personal, out-of-channels message to General Abrams demanding "the unvarnished truth," man-to-man.

That afternoon, Mr. Rogers testified at a closed session of the Senate Foreign Relations Committee and ran into a storm of opposition to possible American involvement in Cambodia. Without directly disclosing the contemplated use of United States troops, he tried to hint at the imminence of a military decision. Mr. Rogers recounted the Senators' objections in a long telephone report to the President that evening.[5]

From Saigon, General Abrams replied that an American assault was necessary. With that message and new memos from other advisers, and after one more call to Mr. Laird, Mr. Nixon withdrew to make his decision. The next morning he conveyed it, first to Mr. Kissinger and then to Mr. Rogers, Mr. Laird and Mr. Mitchell, whose advice, always important, to the president is not known in this case.

Having decided to attack in the Fishhook, the President said that he was also sending American ground advisers into the Parrot's Beak and ordering consecutive attacks on a number of enemy base areas. As the operation unfolded, he also approved the four raids on North Vietnam.

352 CASE STUDIES: THE WAR IN VIETNAM

Ignoring some advice that he treat the event in a low key, the President prepared his own televsion address, working it through eight longhand drafts on Tuesday and Wednesday night, staying up till 5 A.M. Unlike President Kennedy and Johnson, he never submitted it for editing by his main cabinet advisers. All or Mr. Nixon's senior aides still wince at some of his rhetoric.

Some of Mr. Nixon's senior aides were troubled by the President's apocalyptic vision of the stakes. Others found some military points overdramatized.

The President's assertion that the enemy was massing in the sanctuaries to attack South Vietnam contradicted Secretary Laird's support of the American assault because of the enemy's movement the other way. It also contradicted the latest intelligence that the enemy forces had sensed what was coming and were dispersing faster than before with some of their arms caches.

The generals felt uneasy that Mr. Nixon, to give importance to his move, led the American public to expect the capture of top enemy commanders by announcing an attack on "the headquarters for the entire Communist military operation in South Vietnam." They knew the enemy command unit—the Central Office for South Vietnam, called COSVN—was always on the move and doubted they would catch its 200 men in Fishhook. Their troops were ordered to "neutralize the COSVN base area"—meaning arms caches, supply dumps and other facilities.

Notice of the President's speech reached Premier Lon Nol only after it was over, because the Pnompenh cable office was closed. Although he had agreed in mid-April to deeper raids by the South Vietnamese and more recently to the Parrot's Beak operation, his consent was not sought for the Fishhook. The White House believed if he said "no," it was in trouble; if he said "yes," he might be.

In the days following Mr. Nixon's speech, what the Congress and the public took to be limitations of time and scope on the invasion were only firm definitions of the Administration's private intentions: six to eight weeks and a limit to penetrations of about 20 miles. Some field commanders even found the time limit a welcome surprise; they had expected two to four weeks.[6]

But other rules of engagement had to be adjusted to the enemy's spreading attacks throughout Cambodia. To help Premier Lon Nol defend himself in the months ahead the Administration agreed to leave South Vietnamese troops behind after June 30 and tried to arrange Thai support as well.

American planes now fly tactical air support for the Cambodians under the guise of raids against enemy supply lines. American ships blockade Cambodia's coastline. And new military and economic aid is being prepared. Thus, the operation, now formally ended is, in fact, far from over.

NOTES

[1] This article was written in collaboration with Max Frankel and incorporates reports by William Beecher, Henry Giniger, Henry Kamut, Sydney H. Shanberg, Robert B. Semple Jr., Neil Sheehan, Terrence Smith, James P. Sterba, and Tad Szule.. Another valuable article on the President's Cambodian decision is David R. Maxey's "How Nixon Decided to Invade

Cambodia," *Look*, August 11, 1970, pp. 22-25. The additional information provided in the footnotes which follow comes from the Maxey article.

[2] Members of the National Security Council include the President, the Vice-President, the Secretaries of State and Defense, and the Director of the Office of Emergency Preparedness. Others may attend meetings of the NSC at the President's desire. In the Nixon administration, Attorney General John Mitchell and Special Assistant for National Security Affairs Henry Kissinger have met with the NSC. At this meeting, Admiral Thomas Moorer, Chief of Naval Operations and Chairman-designate of the Joint Chiefs of Staff, and CIA Chief Richard Helms were also present.

[3] On this day, Secretary of Defense Laird advised the President to probe congressional reaction to the proposed operation. As a result, Kissinger phoned Senator John Stennis, the Chairman of the Senate Armed Services Committee. At a subsequent meeting between the two, Stennis was generally approving of the plans described by Kissinger. That evening, Kissinger met with the five members of his own staff whom he thought would be most likely to be opposed to the Cambodian invasion. The result was a tempestuous discussion, which ended without any consensus. Several of the staffers later resigned when the President made public his decision.

[4] At this meeting, Maxey reports that one of the President's advisors told him: "Mr. President, I don't know much about domestic affairs, but if you do it, in my opinion the campuses will go up in flames." President Nixon's reply was: "I want to hear that now, but if I decide to do it, I don't want to hear of it again. If I decide to do it, it will be because I have decided to pay the price."

[5] On this day, Kissinger called Senator John J. Williams, the fifth-ranking Republican on the Senate Foreign Relations Committee, to check Williams' reaction to the course that the President was considering. Williams is reported to have viewed the incursions unfavorably.

[6] The extent of congressional involvement in this decision consisted of the consultations with Stennis and Williams. On April 29, Senate Republican Whip Robert Griffin called Kissinger to report that there were news wire stories coming in telling of a South Vietnamese attack into Cambodia. Griffin expressed concern that the White House had not briefed the Senate leadership on these operations. Shortly before his television speech to the nation, the President described his decision to leaders of Congress who had been assembled for briefing in the White House. He then left to give his television speech.